Nature Into Myth

NATURE INTO MYTH

MEDIEVAL AND RENAISSANCE
MORAL SYMBOLS

by

JOHN M. STEADMAN

DUQUESNE UNIVERSITY PRESS

PITTSBURGH

Copyright ©1979 by Duquesne University Press

Published by Duquesne University Press
600 Forbes Avenue
Pittsburgh, Pennsylvania 15219

Distributed by Humanities Press
Atlantic Highlands, New Jersey 07716

Library of Congress Cataloging in Publication Data

Steadman, John M.
Nature into Myth.

(Language and literature series; v. 1)
Includes bibliographical references.
1. English literature—History and criticism—Addresses,
essays, lectures. 2. Symbolism in literature—Addresses, essays,
lectures. I. Title. II. Series: Language and literature series
Pittsburgh); v. 1. III. Title: Medieval and renaissance moral
symbols.
PR161.s8   821'.009'15   77-25397
ISBN 0-391-00752-1

Manufactured in the United States of America

First Edition

"Omnis mundi creatura
Quasi liber et pictura
Nobis est et speculum. . . ."

— Alanus de Insulis

CONTENTS

ILLUSTRATIONS

Figure:

ACKNOWLEDGEMENTS

I am indebted to the editors and publishers of the following books and journals for permission to reprint (with revisions) material that I have previously published in their pages: "Iconography and Renaissance Drama: Ethical and Mythological Themes," *Research Opportunities in Renaissance Drama*, XIII-XIV (1970-71), ed. S. Schoenbaum (Northwestern University Press: Evanston, 1972), pp. 73-122; "Renaissance Dictionaries and Manuals as Instruments of Literary Scholarship: The Problem of Evidence," *New Aspects of Lexicography: Literary Criticism, Intellectual History and Social Change*, ed. Howard D. Weinbrot (Southern Illinois University Press: Carbondale and Edwardsville, London and Amsterdam, 1972), pp. 17-35, 173-176; "Chaucer's Eagle, A Contemplative Symbol," *PMLA*, LXXV (1960), pp. 153-159; "Chauntecleer and Medieval Natural History," *Isis*, L (1959), pp. 236-244; "Flattery and the *Moralitas* of the Nun's Priest's Tale," *Medium Aevum*, XXVIII (1959), pp. 172-179; "The Book-Burning Episode in the Wife of Bath's Prologue: Some Additional Analogues," *PMLA*, LXXIV (1959), pp. 521-525; "Old Age and *Contemptus Mundi* in *The Pardoner's Tale*," *Medium Aevum*, XXXIII (1964), pp. 121-130; "Falstaff as Actaeon: A Dramatic Emblem," *Shakespeare Quarterly*, XIV (1963), pp. 231-244; "Una and the Clergy: The Ass Symbol in *The Faerie Queene*," *Journal of the Warburg and Courtauld Institutes*, XXI (1958), pp. 134-137; "Spenser's House of Care: A Reinterpretation," *Studies in the Renaissance*, VII (1960), pp. 207-224; "The 'Inharmonious Blacksmith': Spenser and the Pythagoras Legend," *PMLA*, LXXIX (1964), pp. 664-665; "Spenser's *Errour* and the Renaissance Allegorical Tradition," *Neuphilologische Mitteilugen*, LXII (1961), pp. 22-38; "Sin and the Serpent of Genesis 3 (*PL*, II, 650-653), *MP*, LIV (1957), pp. 217-220; "Sin, Errour, Echidna, and the Viper's Brood," *MLR*, LVI

(1961), pp. 62-66; "Tradition and Innovation in Milton's 'Sin': The Problem of Literary Indebtedness," *PQ*, XXXIX (1960), pp. 93-103; "Busiris, the Exodus, and Renaissance Chronography," *Revue belge de philologie et d'historie*, XXXIX (1961), pp. 394-403; "The Devil and Pharaoh's Chivalry," MLN, LXXV (1960), pp. 197-201; " 'Memphian Chivalry': Milton's Busiris, Etymology and Chronography," *The University Review—Kansas City*, XXXVII (1971), pp. 215-231.

In revising these essays I have deleted many of the original footnotes or (more rarely) inserted others.

Illustrations are reproduced by permission of The Huntington Library, San Marino, California.

Introduction

THE THEME of this book is the conversion of natural detail into moral symbol in medieval and Renaissance narrative and dramatic poetry. Taking as points of departure several traditional motifs in the works of four major English poets, I shall explore the background of each, its conventional function as a vehicle for ethical commonplaces, and the poet's innovations in adapting it to the requirements of his theme and plot.

Like "convention and revolt," the terms "tradition and innovation" have a slightly archaic scent. (They are the literary chic of an earlier generation of critics, nostalgically redolent of lavendar and cedarwood.) Nevertheless they remain indispensable for the study of a literature equally committed to tradition and novelty, to veneration of antiquity and admiration of originality. They are a timely reminder that Renaissance literature, like modern physics, was conditioned by the principle of relativity, and that poetic communication depended in large part on the interaction of "disparates," or even the coincidence of contraries. To liken the Renaissance poet to a scribe instructed in the kingdom of heaven, bringing forth treasures both new and old, may seem excessive. At the very least, however, he merits comparison with a modern bride, eclectically arrayed in "something old, something new, something borrowed . . ."

The originality of a Renaissance orator usually appears in his treatment of rhetorical commonplaces; the novelty of a Renaissance poet, in his variations on conventional themes, images,

and principles of style and genre. In both cases our recognition of
tradition is essential not only for our appreciation of innovation but
(more significantly) for our discovery of meaning. The conventional
images form a common vocabulary, the traditional principles of
structure a common syntax; and, even when the poet radically
alters them, his meaning is fully intelligible only against the
background of the common system of conventions that he shared
with his intended audience.

Although the majority of the motifs I shall discuss belong to the
realm of nature, they are all essentially "bookish" symbols. Their
primary ancestry is literary: a genealogy of inherited erudition. For
the most part, they derive not so much from the poet's direct observation of nature as from a long, complex, and sometimes
rebarbative scholarly tradition. Shaped and reshaped by successive
generations of scholiasts before they underwent further transformations at the hands of Chaucer and Spenser, Shakespeare and
Milton, they acquired much of their meaning and authority from
the cumulative labors of classical, medieval, or Renaissance
exegetes. If they still strike the imagination of the twentieth-century
reader, they owe this power largely to the energizing skill of major
poets who succeeded in infusing the old symbols with new life and
meaning, adding Learning (no less than Reason) to Imagination.

This is not to discredit the powers of direct observation displayed
elsewhere by all four poets and by many of their contemporaries.Yet,
even so, their direct experience of nature frequently seems to have
been obscured by their efforts to assimilate it to literary tradition.
Descriptions of nature in medieval and Renaissance poetry, as well
as similes and metaphors derived from natural phenomena, often
become formulaic and conventional: "set pieces" on recognized
topoi and *loci communes*. Like the exemplars conveniently
provided in florilegia and treatises on rhetoric and poetics,
chronographias and topographias are often standardized, no less
stereotyped than the qualifying epithets applied to formulaic tree-
lists or to catalogues of flowers and streams. Noon and midnight,
dawn and evening, the procession of the seasons, tempests and
shipwrecks, mountains and forests and gardens and personifications
of Nature herself are depicted in terms that self-consciously evoke
an established literary tradition. Many of these descriptions (or

ecphrases) are recognizable variations on standard motifs: the *selva oscura,* the *locus amoenus,* the bower of Circe, the garden of Eden, the garden of Amor. Even when the poet is describing an actual locale, a specific setting (as in the locodescriptive poems of the seventeenth century) he may transform it by elevating its characteristic features into abstract types, by moralizing and generalizing the particular details of nature, or by subjecting them to classical or "metaphysical" idealization. Prone to discover sermons in stones and books in running brooks, he tends to translate the realm of nature into a realm of universals and separated essences, a realm of ideas. At times he seems to look through or beyond rather than directly at the visible world.

Nature thus becomes a kind of Aristotelian telescope (to adapt Tesauro's metaphor), where the poet contemplates the universal in the particular and the "concept" in the "percept." But telescopes may conform to more than one design; and the poet may select a Hermetic, a Neoplatonic, or even a Pauline model. In this case nature may serve, more obliquely, as a kind of giant reflector (like that of Palomar), mirroring transcendental realities in the dark glass of phenomena. In this "optics of the invisible" the true objects of contemplation are ideas; the concrete objects of nature serve primarily as figurative lenses for apprehending them. As images, examples, hieroglyphs, types these natural phenomena point to an intelligible order beyond that of sense, or a spiritual order beyond that of reason. For a poet trained in this mode of sensibility, the simple objects of nature are usually only the starting point, not the end, of contemplation. A yellow primrose will be more than a yellow primrose to him; he will read it as a hieroglyph or signature of some moral or metaphysical truth. In an oak or rock he will see more than a tree or stone; he will recognize an emblem of constancy.

Milton's image of the autumnal leaves and brooks of Vallombrosa may illustrate this point. Though his allusion probably derives from personal observation, he has "depersonalized" the image in adapting it to the requirements of heroic decorum and fictive situation. In the formal context of an epic simile his personal reminiscence of Tuscany has been definitively linked with an image derived not from personal experience but from books: the "scattered sedge" of the Red Sea. In this new context, moreover, the allusion has been further transformed by other, less explicit associations: the leaf-similes of Homer, Virgil, Dante, and other epic poets, and analogous imagery in Scripture. Deliberately assimilated to both sacred and secular literary tradition, the image of a Tuscan autumn has been obliquely "moralized" to suggest the spiritual death, no less than the immediate physical plight, of the fallen angels.

In several other instances, the original basis of a motif ultimately derived from nature has been obscured by accretions of classical myth, fabulous natural history, speculative etymology, the inventions of earlier poets or the subtleties of exegetes. In two of the motifs I shall examine, moreover, the primary images are derived from human industry and acquire a symbolic value as representative of human nature. The Pythagorean smithy in Spenser's House of Care, an emblem of discord rather than concord, symbolizes a dissonant *musica humana,* a spirit disordered by passion. The fate of Jankyn's anti-feminist compendium—like that of its earlier prototypes in Oriental tradition—may look like nature's revenge for an act of hybris, demonstrating the folly of attempting to understand the nature of women in the first place. But it is also nature's own lesson in human nature; the student of the fifth *veda* learns that the *natura muliebris* he seeks to comprehend is incomprehensible.

* * *

Originally published in different journals or anthologies, most of the essays in this book are nevertheless linked by common methodological assumptions. Each is concerned less with the problem of identifying specific sources than with the evolution and continuity of a tradition and with its potential value for interpreting a particular moral symbol in a specific literary context. Aside from the fact that seemingly definitive source studies often prove unreliable, encouraging an excessive or misdirected confidence, they generally obscure the complexity and diversity of the traditions accessible to a particular author and the variety of options available to him in selecting from a diverse and often contradictory tradition precisely those details and interpretations which could best meet the requirements of a specific literary context. The poet's relation to tradition was, on the whole, not passive but active, not rigid or submissive but flexible and eclectic. The tradition functioned, indeed, much like a collection of commonplaces; it offered him not only authorities and precedents but (more significantly) a wide range of variants, from which he might choose at will. Literary borrowing was an elective rather than a mechanical procedure; and even the selection of a particular model or authority or "source" usually demanded an active exercise of imagination and judgment. Like the invention, disposition, and expression of a rhetorical argument, the exploitation of a symbolic motif generally entailed a deliberate decision among conventional but various alternatives or an equally conscious fusion of details selected from several traditions.

In tracing these motifs I have been chiefly concerned with narrative, and less frequently with dramatic, contexts. Though most of them also appear in other genres, I have considered such instances less for their own sake than for their contribution to the traditions exploited by later narrative or dramatic poets. Both Spenser and Vaughan, for instance, allude to the *asinus portans mysteria,* but I have centered discussion of this tradition on an episode in *The Faerie Queene* rather than on the Silurist's poem "The Ass":

> Let me thy Ass be onely wise
> To carry, not search mysteries; . . .

Since many of these motifs recur in a wide variety of literary species and in pictorial tradition as well, I have necessarily followed an eclectic approach, utilizing on occasion natural histories, mythographies, lexicons, encyclopedias, iconographies, chronologies, commentaries on sacred or classical literature. The primary emphasis, however, falls on the poet's adaptation of a complex and manifold tradition. Insofar as the motif is traditional, it seems to demand an historical approach; insofar as the tradition itself is complex, it seems to require a multilateral approach, combining different modes and aspects of the historical method.

Finally, though the principal link between these essays is the moralization of certain conventional motifs ultimately derived from nature, there are other "constants" which have received almost equal emphasis: the diversity of the traditions associated with each motif, their rhetorical value as a sort of dispersed inventory of commonplaces, the variety of options each tradition offered the poet, the "aesthetic imperative" that conditioned not only his choice or modification of certain aspects of the tradition but also the role he assigned these aspects in the development of his plot and the moral interpretation that, implicitly or explicitly, he imposed upon them. The "variables," however, are equally numerous and no less significant. Most important are the nature and extent of the tradition familiar to a given author. In no instance, of course, was the entire tradition accessible to the poet — nor, for that matter, can modern scholarship hope to achieve an exhaustive survey of analogues. Chaucer could have known none of the Oriental sources and analogues — and few of the European versions — of the book of women's wiles and its incendiary fate; moreover, the immediate channels through which the tradition reached him still remain unidentified. In adapting this motif to the Wife of Bath's prologue, he displayed considerable freedom, transferring it to a different and more familiar European genre — the anti-feminist anthology — and heightening its effectiveness as anti-feminist commonplace by inserting it strategically into the ironic context of an outspoken feminist apologia.

Similarly, though many of Shakespeare's spectators would probably have encountered the major details of the Actaeon myth in a variety of sources — through Ovid, through contemporary poetic allusions, and possibly through mythographical handbooks or lexicons — they would have known few of the emblematic treatments of this myth other than Whitney's *Choice of Emblemes*. It was the influence of this book (apparently) which forged the essential link between the poet's text, the physical details of staging, and the imagination and memory of the audience — thereby converting the farcical climax of a bourgeois comedy into a parodic emblem of the mythical hunter who had outraged the goddess of chastity.

In other cases the poet's relation to tradition may be complicated both by his own learning and by his relation to his audience. Although familiar with a wide range of analogues, each capable of evoking a specific literary context, and each susceptible (perhaps) to more than one symbolic interpretation, he may prefer to allude, directly or obliquely, to a comparatively limited number of prototypes and to neglect the rest. He may deliberately stress certain classical or Biblical allusions — or possibly medieval and Renaissance analogues — in order to emphasize his indebtedness to or rivalry with an earlier author. Nevertheless such literary "quotations" and evocations may prove deceptive. They may undercut, parody, criticize, or radically revalue the very passages they profess to imitate. They may also obscure other patterns of indebtedness and channels of influence, thereby rendering a complex structure of allusion deceptively simple.

Chaucer's explicit references to the myth of Ganymede, for instance, and to Boethius' *Consolation of Philosophy* scarcely do justice to the tradition of contemplative flight in general or to the eagle as a symbol of revelation and contemplation; the majority of commentators appear to have recognized the danger of emphasizing explicit parallels, and have accordingly placed greater stress on unacknowledged analogues such as the eagle-imagery of Dante's *Commedia* and the eagle associated with Saint John the Evangelist. Similarly, though Milton explicitly evokes the image of Scylla's metamorphosis in his description of Sin, this acknowledged analogue is far less significant for the composition and significance of his portrait than other, unacknowledged parallels: the viper-women of Hesiod and Spenser, Fletcher's infernal portress, the serpent of Genesis 3. In this instance, even more than in Chaucer's case, the most significant analogues are, at best, obliquely hinted at by the poet; nevertheless the hints alone should have sufficed to inform his "fit audience though few."

* * *

Changing literary fashions and tastes and different attitudes towards the principles of genre, style, and decorum may further influence the poet's adaptation of these and related motifs. Most significant of all these variables, however — yet also the most elusive and most difficult to assess — are differences in the range and character of medieval and Renaissance learned tradition. The differences reside not only in the wider variety of classical authors accessible to Renaissance poets and their audience and in an educational program centered on close study and imitation of the classics. They extend to secondary texts and reference works— lexicons and encyclopedias, commonplace books, phrase books, mythographical or iconographical manuals, compendia of proverbs and emblems, and treatises on natural history.

Yet it would be profoundly misleading to emphasize these differences at the expense of the continuity between medieval and Renaissance tradition. This amounts to more than the survival of medieval textbooks, such as Cato's *Distichs,* into the curricula of Renaissance grammar schools, the continued popularity of Bartholomew's treatise on natural history, Boccaccio's *Genealogy of the Gods,* and Berchorius' *Ovidius moralizatus*; or the veneration bestowed by sixteenth-century Italian or English poets on four-teenth-century authors—Dante, Boccaccio, Chaucer—as founders of the vernacular tradition. The more important survivals are a moral and symbolic approach both to classical myth and to natural history, a typological approach both to the Book of Scripture and to the Book of Nature, and a tendency to perpetuate and exploit poetically the marvels of a fabulous natural history even when soberer critics were discrediting them as superstitious. No less significant is the tendency of the poets in both periods to base their images of "nature moralized" not only on classical or Biblical sources and on the poetry of their near-contemporaries but on convenient reference works, on encyclopedias and lexicons. The tropological approach to nature as well as to classical myth and Scripture survives intact, though altered, from the Middle Ages into the Renaissance, and the concept of a *mundus symbolicus* achieves a striking, often bizarre, efflorescence in the emblem literature and metaphysical poetry of the seventeenth century.

* * *

Though the major channels through which medieval and Renaissance poets inherited the multiple motifs of a "nature moralized" may appear to have shifted with alarming frequency, the continuity of tradition may be traced through other channels.

Zoological superstitions persist through a wide variety of media—
the natural histories of antiquity and their medieval or Renaissance
successors, hexameral treatises in verse or prose, moralized
bestiaries, Renaissance emblems and hieroglyphs. In describing the
works of the fifth and sixth days, late Renaissance hexaemerons like
Bartas's *La Sepmaine* and Tasso's *Il Mondo Creato*[1] follow the
hexaemerons of St. Basil and St. Ambrose in drawing moral or
theological inferences from the creatures of air, sea, and land. In
the *moralitas* of the *Phoenix*—one of several moralized animal
poems in the Exeter Book—C. S. Lewis[2] detects the combined
influence of St. Ambrose and Bede. Though Lewis notes the
absence of this kind of interpretation in the pseudo-zoology of
Isidore's encyclopedia, the method is fundamental to Theobald's
Physiologus, an eleventh-century work that would subsequently
influence Chaucer. The tropological approach to nature becomes
full blown, however, in the fourteenth century with Berchorius's
Reductorium morale, a moralized natural history based on Bartholomew's *De proprietatibus rerum.*[3] Berchorius follows a similar
approach, and includes much of the same material, in his
Repertorium morale,[4] an alphabetically arranged dictionary of
moral symbols. Both of these works remained current during the
Renaissance,[5] but to many of their readers they must have seemed
distinctly old-fashioned. For the symbolic interpretation of natural
history, men of the later Renaissance could find similar material
more conveniently at hand in the extensive and highly fashionable
collections of emblems and hieroglyphics.

Though Berchorius's *Repertorium* may seem to mark the end of
one tradition, and the rediscovery of Horapollo's *Hieroglyphica* (in
1419) the beginning of another, such an inference may be
deceptive; and it would be preferable, perhaps, to speak of a
reformation or reorientation of tradition. As in other cases, the
tropological approach to natural history, the preoccupation with
the marvels of pseudo-zoology,[6] and (in certain instances) the
encyclopedic range of subject matter continued well into the
Renaissance, albeit under a different guise and in a different kind
of book. The work of "Horapollo" (for the authorship and origins of
the *Hieroglyphica* are suspect) reveals embarrassing traces of the
fabulous natural history of classical antiquity; Endicott[7] detects the

influence of Aelian and Galen. Among numerous descendants of
this book one must reckon not only the *Hieroglyphics* of the sixteenth and seventeenth centuries but (more significantly) the
emblem books of Alciati (1531) and his numerous successors.[8]
Though these works often based their imagery on a wide variety of
sources—nature and art, history and myth, Scripture and classical
poetry—to illustrate an equally wide range of concepts, most of
them were concerned in varying degrees with the moral interpretation of natural history. Since the emblematic mode aimed
at brevity and allusive or enigmatic suggestion, deliberately
rejecting overt or expository statement, readers experienced an
understandable need for commentaries; the copious notes of expositors like Mignault and Solorzano tended to convert the emblem
book into a kind of illustrated encyclopedia. Even more comprehensive in scope was the *Hieroglyphica* of Valeriano (1556);
drawing extensively on natural history as well as on art and myth, it
could serve as an eclectic, but encyclopedic dictionary of symbols.

The popularity of this emblematic and hieroglyphic literature is
essentially a Renaissance phenomenon, though some of our
colleagues would prefer to associate it with mannerism or even with
baroque. On the whole, it coincides roughly with a revival of the
Hermetic tradition and with renewed veneration for the wisdom of
pre-classical antiquity cunningly disguised in fable and mystery. In
its later development, moreover, it parallels an increasing emphasis
(apparent both in rhetorical practice and in epistemological theory)
on things (*res*) rather than words (*verba*)—an emphasis that seemed
to heighten the value and significance of the hieroglyph—and a
conscious exploitation of visual media in striking the imagination,
aiding the memory, and thereby reaching the understanding, the
emotions, and the will. As a result, the tropological and anagogical
approaches to nature, so characteristic of the late Middle Ages, are
frequently transformed and assimilated to the emblematic or
hieroglyphic mode. In moralizing or spiritualizing the book of
nature, a seventeenth-century poet like Vaughan or an amateur
naturalist like Browne is likely to describe the objects of nature as
hieroglyphs, emblems, enigmas, signatures, mysteries, or (by
analogy with scriptural exegesis) as types. "The severe Schooles,"
asserts Browne,[9] "shall never laugh me out of the Philosophy of

Hermes, that this visible World is but a picture of the invisible, wherein, as in a pourtract, things are not truely, but in equivocall shapes, and as they counterfeit some more reall substance in that invisible fabrick." Nature is a "universall and publick Manuscript," and "surely the Heathens knew better how to joyne and reade these mysticall letters, than wee Christians, who cast a more carelesse eye on these common Hieroglyphics . . . ."[10] Browne is also sympathetic towards allegorical interpretations of the first chapters of Genesis; they are at least "probable," and perhaps they reflect "the mysticall method of *Moses* bred up in the Hieroglyphicall Schooles of the Egyptians."[11]

All the same, his attitude toward the allegorical interpretation of nature, the hieroglyphical tradition, and the fabulous natural history exploited by moralists and theologians remains ambivalent; and his own practice is often inconsistent. He recognizes their rhetorical and poetic efficacy and their ethical or religious value, but as a naturalist he is compelled to challenge them on scientific grounds. They perpetuate vulgar errors in natural history and substitute human inventions for the true works of God. In *Pseudodoxia Epidemica* Browne concludes his discussion of the loadstone with the reflection that other discourses might be made on this subject, "as Morall, Mysticall, Theologicall" — precisely the kind of approach that he himself follows elsewhere. Yet as a scientist and professed disciple of Bacon, he dismisses this kind of interpretation. Though "some have handsomly done" such discourses, "as Ambrose, Austine, Gulielmus Parisiensis, and many more," nevertheless "these fall under no rule, and are as boundless as mens inventions; and though honest mindes doe glorifie God hereby; yet doe they most powerfully magnifie him, and are to be looked on with another eye, who demonstratively set forth its Magnalities; who not from postulated or precarious inferences, entreat a courteous assent, but from experiment and undeniable effects enforce the wonder of its Maker."[12] Apposite though they are, such critical reflections did not deter the author from following an allegorical and symbolic approach to nature in *The Garden of Cyrus*; after considering the quincunxial lozenge "artificially" and "naturally," he explores its mystical significance.

In *Pseudodoxia Epidemica* he displays considerable knowledge of the emblematic and hieroglyphical literature of the Renaissance, but he is critical of the pseudo-zoological superstitions that it perpetuates. "Franciscus Sanctius in a laudable Comment upon Alciats Emblems, affirmeth and that from experience, a Nightingale hath no tongue . . . . Which if any man for a while shall beleeve upon his experience, he may at his leisure refute it by his own." Again, "what fool almost would beleeve, at least, what wise man would relye upon that Antidote delivered by Pierius in his Hieroglyphicks against the sting of a Scorpion? that is, to sit upon an Asse with ones face toward his taile; for so the pain leaveth the man, and passeth into the beast?"[13] What is "delivered as an Embleme of vigilancy, that the Hare and Lion doe sleepe with one eye open, doth not evince they are more awake then if they were both closed."[14] Though the pelican was a "Hieroglyphick of piety and pity among the Aegyptians," the tradition that she nourishes her young with her own blood must be taken symbolically rather than literally. In the testimonies of patristic and ecclesiastical authors "we may more safely conceive therein some Emblematicall then any reall Story"; and "under an Emblematicall intention, we accept it in coat-armour." The Egyptian hieroglyph was based on another consideration, the parental affection "manifested in the protection of her young ones, when her nest was set on fire. As for "letting out her bloud, it was not the assertion of the Egyptians, but seems translated unto the Pelecan from the Vulture, as Pierius hath most plainly delivered."[15]

The hieroglyphical doctrine of the Egyptians (possibly acquired from the Hebrews) has advanced "many popular conceits; for using an Alphabet of things, and not of words, through the Image and pictures thereof, they endeavoured to speak their hidden conceits, in the letters and language of nature." Although in pursuing this end they frequently conformed to "true and reall apprehensions," on occasion they "obliquely confirmed many falsities," either "framing the story" themselves, or "taking up the tradition, conduceable unto their intentions . . . ." These falsehoods subsequently passed "as authentick and conceded truths" to the Greeks, and from these to other nations, and are "still retained by symbolical writers, Emblematistes, Heraldes and others. Whereof some are strictly maintained for truths, as naturally making good their artificial representations; others symbollically intended are literally received, and swallowed in the first sense, without all gust of the second." Painters have similarly disseminated false opinions among the people. Moreover, "many holy Writers, Preachers, Moralists, Rhetoricians, Orators and Poets" have obliquely and unintentionally strengthened common errors; "for they depending upon invention, deduce their mediums from all things whatsoever; and playing much upon the simile, or illustrative argumentation, to induce their Enthymemes unto the people, they take up popular conceits, and from traditions unjustifiable or really false, illustrate matters of undeniable truth."

Thus "some Divines" have utilized the fables of the Phoenix, the Salamander, the Pelican, the Basilisk, "and divers relations of Pliny; deducing from thence most worthy morals, and even upon our Saviour." In his *Ethics* Aristotle "takes up the conceit of the Bever," and the "tradition of the Bear, the Viper, and divers others are frequent amongst Orators." Though these may convince the vulgar ("illiterate and undiscerning hearers"), a judicious audience can regard them as little more than "common Apologues" or fables; "which being of impossible falsities, do notwithstanding include wholesome moralities, and such as expiate the trespasse of their absurdities."

More culpable are the authors of fiction; " . . . Poets and Poeticall Writers have in this point exceeded others, leaving unto us the notions of Harpies, Centaurs, Gryphins, and many more." Browne concedes that the use of "fictions, Apologues and fables" is not unwarrantable, and that "the intent of these inventions might point at laudable ends . . . ." Nevertheless they are harmful to the young, "setling impressions in our tender memories, which our advanced judgements doe generally neglect to expunge." It would be better to educate a "pregnant wit . . . in ignorance hereof, receiving only impressions from realities . . . ."[16]

The tensions between Browne the Hermetic theologian and Browne the post-Baconian exorcist of popular (and learned) superstitions—between the hieroglyphist who perceived in music "an Hieroglyphicall and shadowed lesson of the whole world, and the Creatures of God,"[17] regarded the visible world as an equivocal image of the invisible, and recognized in its creatures stenographic and "short Characters" of divinity[18] and the critic who censured ancient and modern hieroglyphists alike for failing to discriminate between true and false natural history—are significant less of personal conflict or altered opinions than of different objects of concern, different angles of approach, and different modes of intentionality. The mystical expositor of quincunxes and the critic of moral, mystical, and theological interpretations of the loadstone are, on the whole, the same man writing in different capacities and for different ends. In *The Garden of Cyrus* the various kinds of approach reinforce rather than contradict one another; the detailed and comprehensive examination of the quincunx in art and nature provides the foundation for the mystical or symbolic interpretation. Though the tensions and apparent inconsistencies in Browne's thought are not altogether illusory, they have frequently been exaggerated; in many instances they result from complementary rather than contradictory approaches.

If I have dwelt on these tensions at disproportionate length, it is because Browne not only provides a sympathetic justification for the Renaissance emblematic mode but also foreshadows the kind of criticism that a later generation of authors and scientists would direct against it. The objections that he raises as a scientist against the spurious natural history of poets and orators are in some respects curiously reminiscent of the accusations that classical philosophers and Christian theologians had directed against poetic mythology; but the significant point is that these objections are advanced in the name of science and in the cause of experimentally verifiable fact. In preferring "solid Authors" to "Poeticall Writers" and in arguing that poets should base their images and examples, as well as their doctrines and ideas, on truth he not only reflects the views of contemporary exponents of the experimental philosophy but also anticipates the opinions of Sprat and other members of the Royal Society. This kind of criticism could have been lethal to the tradition we are examining; and, though it was only partially responsible for the latter's decline, it undoubtedly fostered a different approach (or approaches) to nature and natural history as sources of poetic imagery. In the following century poets would still endeavor to "moralize" the objects of nature, but they would reject much of the older natural history for other, more trustworthy sources of imagery. Dazzled by the achievements of Newton and the new science, many would base their arguments and their images alike on more modern, more rational conceptions of the natural order. Others would seek out the sublime or the picturesque, adopting the appropriate attitudes and cultivating the proper emotional responses. Though the symbolic and emblematic approach to nature (never altogether defunct) would revive with Romanticism, this was rather a metamorphosis than a literal resurrection. The assumptions, the orientation, the natural theology (if we may call it that) of the Romantics were different; and the nature they contemplated — an indefinable continuum in which they lived and moved and had their being, or (less imprecisely) a correlative object of the human soul — was no longer the nature of Basil or Tasso or Berchorius, or even the nature of Thomas Browne.

* * *

A salient feature of the traditions underlying most of the motifs under discussion is the interpenetration of natural history with mythography and with iconography. Closely interrelated since classical antiquity, these had been subjected, by medieval and Renaissance authors alike, to a process of deliberate moralization, which had converted the book of nature, the writings of ancient poets, and Holy Writ itself into repositories of ethical commonplaces and moral symbols. For Greek and Latin commentators, the same myth might be subjected to radically different interpretations; the same fable might illustrate historical fact or legend, moral or natural philosophy, or recondite metaphysical doctrines. With various mutations this polysemantic approach remained fashionable throughout the Renaissance. Interpretations tended to "snowball," and, for the sake of inclusiveness and scholarly thoroughness, the more exhaustive mythographies of the period usually supplied alternative explanations of the same myth, or reduced a variety of different myths to veiled expressions of the same doctrinal truth. Animal fables and parables, in turn, provided facile allegories or exempla of ethical or political doctrines.

This polysemantic or multilevel approach was also characteristic of medieval exegesis in its interpretation of sacred or profane authors. Even within the framework of the conventional fourfold method of interpretation, the same Biblical symbol often possessed multiple allegorical referents, alternatively signifying virtues or vices, angels or devils. In addition to historical, natural, or moral explanations, late medieval authors frequently imposed Christian interpretations on pagan myths.[19] Panofsky traces the conscious attempt to interpret Ovid's *Metamorphoses* as an allegorical statement of moral doctrine or Christian theology to the beginning of the eleventh century; and in the French *Ovide moralisé,* Ridewall's *Fulgentius metaphoralis,* Holcot's *Moralitates,* the *Gesta Romanorum,* and Berchorius's *Ovidius moralizatus,* he recognizes a further, more elaborate effort to interpret ancient myth not only in "a general moralistic way" but specifically in terms of the Christian faith.[20] Significantly, Berchorius endeavored to apply the same method of tropological exegesis to Ovidian myth, the iconography of the pagan gods, and natural history. Though their antecedents can be traced to earlier periods, the same tropological impulse underlies the *Bibles moralisés,* the *Ovides moralisés,* the moralized iconographies of pagan deities, and the moralized natural histories of the late Middle Ages.

In the mythographical and iconographical works of the Middle Ages and the Renaissance, efforts to rationalize the association of specific plants or animals with particular divinities also strengthen the tendency to seek allegorical significance in natural history. One encounters this approach not only in the mythographical works of fourteenth-century writers like Berchorius and Boccaccio and in the sixteenth-century manuals of Lilius Gyraldus, Conti, and Cartari but also in emblem literature. The late Renaissance *Iconologia* of Cesare Ripa derives imagery for its numerous personifications of abstract ideas alike from traditional natural history and classical mythology.

Like their ancient and medieval forerunners, Renaissance authors frequently tended to interweave natural history and myth and to subject both to moral or theological interpretation. In the body of classical myths Bacon perceived the veiled wisdom of the ancients, analyzed them as moral, political, or scientific allegories, and exploited them rhetorically in his philosophical works to

illustrate his own doctrines. Both "natural" and ethical interpretations were conveniently available in standard
mythographies; and the same myth was often read polysemously as
moral and natural philosophy. Conversely, the monsters of classical
myth occasionally reappear in Renaissance natural histories. A
further link between natural history and ancient myth was supplied
by natural theology.[21] According to a fashionable opinion, the
classical fables enshrined the *prisca theologia* of the Gentiles, "led
by nature's light." No less fashionable in the Renaissance, especially
among apologists for natural philosophy, was the medieval *topos* of
the two books fashioned by the same divine Word: the book of
nature and Holy Writ. The Deity could be contemplated in His
book of creatures, the invisible world of spirit cognized through the
visible, material universe. Taken as a veiled expression of natural
and moral philosophy rather than as the vestiges of an idolatrous
religion—as the joint production of human reason and poetic
imagination rather than as a rival faith—pagan mythology could be
safely appropriated by moralists, naturalists, and theologians,
utilized as a gloss on the book of nature, and thereby converted into
a handmaiden of revealed truth.

* * *

The first part of this study, centered on methodology, reconsiders
some of the dangers as well as the advantages of attempts to apply
the evidence of iconographical and lexicographical studies to the
interpretation of Renaissance literary symbols. Though this
discussion is primarily concerned with Renaissance literature, it
nevertheless has an indirect bearing on the interpretation of
medieval literature, which (like that of the Renaissance) was often
influenced by dictionaries, encyclopedias, and other compendia,
and by iconographical tradition. The second section, in turn, is
devoted to the problem of symbolic meaning in Chaucer's *House of
Fame* and in three of his Canterbury tales. The chapter on the eagle
considers the exegetical background behind both Dante and
Chaucer in their treatment of the eagle as a symbol of contemplation. The eagle appears as contemplative symbol in
mythography, natural history, poetic exegesis, Scriptural ex-

position, and in lexicons and etymologies. One of the salient
features of this complex background is the interpenetration of
secular and sacred exegesis, apparent in commentaries on the
Eclogue of Theodulus, Ovid's *Metamorphoses,* Dante's *Commedia,*
and Scripture itself. A similar exploitation of the sacred and
secular, along with the tendency to seek analogous meanings as well
as images in poetry, Scripture and natural history, appears in the
work of Berchorius.

One of the two chapters on the Nun's Priest's Tale reexamines the
moralitas of this fable against the background of implicit or explicit
warnings against flattery in classical and medieval versions of the
tale of fox and crow; the explicit statement of "moralitee" in this
tale is a typical convention of the beast-fable, though it is often
lacking in the beast epic. The other chapter on this tale reconsiders
the characterization of Chauntecleer in the context of various attributes ascribed to the barnyard cock in medieval natural history
and in terms of the principles of characterization set forth in
medieval poetics.

The chapter on Jankyn's "book of wikked wyves" relates this
episode to the "Studien über Weibertücke" in the legend of the
Seven Sages, or *Book of Sindibad.*

The final chapter in this section takes its point of departure from
the variety of meanings — literal or allegorical — that scholars have
attributed to the figure of the old man in this tale. The essay
reexamines the relationship of this figure to the *senex* and *senectus*
of Maximianus' elegies, to the messenger-of-death motif, to the
opposition between youth and old age, folly and wisdom in Ecclesiastes and Ecclesiasticus, and to the contrary themes of avarice
and *contemptus mundi.*

In the final section, three essays — centered respectively on
Shakespeare's adaptation of the Actaeon motif, Spenser's initial
portrait of Una mounted on a white ass and leading a white lamb,
and Milton's personification of feasting and Dionysiac revelry in the
sorcerer Comus — deal with the exploitation of emblematic and
other iconographical conventions in Renaissance poetry. A chapter
on Spenser's house of Care reexamines the figure of the blacksmith
and his six grooms in the light of musical theory, etymological
speculation, and medical literature concerning the lover's jealousy.

Two further chapters reconsider Spenser's monster Errour and Milton's personification of Sin against the background of viper-lore and traditional accounts of the *draconcopes* or woman-serpent in mythology and natural history. The essay on "The Devil and Pharaoh's Chivalry" reinterprets Milton's allusions to "scattered sedge" of the Red Sea and to the drowned Egyptian army against the background of Renaissance typology, chronography, and etymology.

PART ONE

A REAPPRAISAL OF METHODS

CHAPTER I

The Iconographical Approach*

IF PAINTING and poetry are sister arts, then literary history and art history are related disciplines, perhaps a little more than kin and less than kind. Sharing the same genes, they show strong family resemblances; and we are sometimes apt to mistake one for the other. They are the children of siblings; and the terms in which contemporary iconologists have described their own specialty bear a striking likeness to the aims of literary criticism. The student of

*This chapter has been adapted from a paper delivered at the seminar on Renaissance Drama and Iconographical Studies (Modern Language Association of America) in Denver, Colorado on December 29, 1969, under the chairmanship of Professor Cyrus Hoy of the University of Rochester. The three papers read on this occasion and the proceedings of the seminar have been published in *Research Opportunities in Renaissance Drama,* Vol. XIII-XIV (1970-71), edited by Professor Samuel Schoenbaum of Northwestern University. I am indebted to the Northwestern University Press for permission to reprint the revised version of this paper.

Renaissance poetry might indeed take them over virtually intact. For—like the iconographer—he is equally preoccupied with "subject matter or meaning" and the modes whereby this is communicated. He too must identify and decipher those "images, stories and allegories" which "ancient theorists of art called *invenzioni.*" With the iconologist, in turn, he must usually broaden his field to include historical conditions and "cultural symptoms,"[1] examining the "function of images in allegory and symbolism and their reference to . . . the 'invisible world of ideas.' "[2] Like the art historian, he must uncover the original meaning of a Renaissance artefact (a complicated, artificial "construct") by analyzing and resynthesizing its vocabulary of symbols and motifs, calling attention not only to the *language* of tradition but also (more significantly) to *innovations* on tradition. He too must play the challenging game of matching conventions and concepts, images and ideas. He too must unriddle enigmas and decode cryptograms.

Hence it is hardly surprising that literary critics have turned to the iconographers for support, and vice versa. Over the last quarter-century especially, literary historians have resurveyed their ancestral fields, and found them far too narrow. Like Mistress Anne Killigrew and other "young ambitious Souls," they have violated traditional frontiers and conducted sporadic forays into a more picturesque domain:

> Born to the Spacious Empire of the *Nine,* . . .
> To the next Realm [they] stretcht [their] Sway,
> For *Painture* neer adjoyning lay,
> A plenteous Province, and alluring Prey, . . .
> And the whole Fief, in right of Poetry [they] claim'd.
> The Country open lay without Defence:
> For Poets frequent In-rodes there had made . . .

Such incursions are not conducted without risk of reprisals, but these have usually proved rewarding to both sides—to painters as well as poets, to iconologists as well as literary critics. In the discussion which follows we shall consider a few of these rewards, noting some of the reasons why iconographical methods and materials may aid us in interpreting Renaissance literature.

Perhaps the most significant point is that Renaissance painters and poets had inherited the same ethical and mythological traditions. Though working in different media, they often selected the same subjects and endeavored to communicate the same "meanings." Moreover, neither pictorial nor poetic traditions could be rigidly separated. From classical antiquity onwards, poets and painters had borrowed extensively from one another. The result of their mutual borrowings had become "codified," so to speak, in iconological and mythological treatises consulted by painters and poets alike: Philostratus and Fulgentius, "Albricus" and Berchorius and Boccaccio, Horapollo and Valeriano, Lilio Giraldi and Natale Conti, Cartari and Ripa. Such manuals often fused iconographical and poetic materials, combining details derived from literature with those of the visual arts. Furthermore they usually transmitted not only symbols and motifs, but also moral and allegorical interpretations. If these may assist the modern iconographer to identify "images, stories and allegories," and to ascertain "meanings," they may prove equally useful to the literary scholar.

Secondly, in varying degrees, Renaissance poets and painters held certain basic aesthetic principles in common. (For better or worse, they had not yet heard of Lessing.) In theory, the final cause of both arts was the same — to teach, delight, and (as some would add) move or persuade. Under Horatian or Aristotelian influence, writers on painting introduced such "poetic" concepts as imitation of actions, manners, and passions; verisimilitude and decorum; the unities; distinctions in genre and levels of style. Conversely, writers on poetics and rhetoric urged the poet or orator to seek pictorial vividness — the quality of *enargeia*. The formal description or *ecphrasis* was conventional not only in classical, medieval, and Renaissance poetry, but also in iconographical manuals. (Indeed this term occurs in the very title of Callistratus's book.) Critics of both arts echoed Horace's dictum *ut pictura poesis* or Simonides's assertion that poetry is a "speaking picture" and painting a "silent poem." In the sixteenth and seventeenth centuries the parallel between the sister arts was still critical orthodoxy.

Thirdly, painting and poetry not only treated the same subjects and "meanings" but sometimes exploited the same technical devices (already conventional in classical rhetoric) for communicating them. Both utilized the *exemplum,* a form of inductive proof. Both on occasion employed personification and allegory, enigma and metaphor—or forms of wordplay such as *notatio* and paronomasia. Both might appeal to forensic, deliberative, or epideictic commonplaces—topics of justice or injustice, expediency or inexpediency, praise or blame. As the seventeenth century progressed, painters and poets alike exploited the conceit as an instrument of *maraviglia*.

Fourthly, in certain "synaesthetic"* art-forms fashionable in the Renaissance—its emblematic and hieroglyphic literature; its dramas and pageants, masques and processions—the parallel arts sometimes converged. Painting and poetry reinforced each other, developed the same image or allegory, embellished the same subject matter, illustrated the same meaning. In the emblem, for instance (which consisted normally of *sententia* or motto, verses, and picture, but sometimes of only one or two of these elements, and was often accompanied by expository glosses and commentaries)—in the emblem, speaking picture and silent poem were juxtaposed; they remained separate, though complementary, parts of a single whole. In the drama, on the other hand, they were frequently combined—but not invariably. The dumb-show was, like painting, essentially a silent poem. Through the influence of Vitruvius—and his Renaissance successors Serlio and Palladio—scenic design on the Continent became increasingly dependent on the specialized skills of architect and painter. In England, "the chiefe busynes of the office" of the Revels (according to an Elizabethan document) "resteth speciallye in three poyntes, in makinge of garmentes; in makinge of hedpeces, and in paynting. . . . The connynge of the office resteth in skill of devise, in understandinge of historyes, in iudgement of comedies, tragedyes, and shews, in sight of per-

---

* An infelicitous term — but the alternatives ("hybrid," "mixed," "double," etc.) possess specialized technical meanings which would make them inappropriate in this context. Critics of Renaissance literature have employed them to designate the combination of different genres (*e.g.*, tragedy and comedy) or of different mimetic modes (*e.g.*, narrative and dramatic). We are referring, however, specifically to the artist's more or less simultaneous appeal to different senses, hearing and sight; to his fusion of different channels of communication, verbal and visual; and to the combination of various arts — poetry and painting, architecture and music, sculpture and choreography.

spective and architecture, some smacke of geometrye and other
thynges."³ While seventeenth-century poets were busily transmuting
verses into "hieroglyphs" — altars and pillars and angel-wings —
court architects were sedulously reorganizing the masque-spectacle
in the light of the "arts of design." With the introduction of the
proscenium arch, the masque-stage would become, like a
Renaissance painting, essentially a *pariete di vetro*.

I

The title-page of Whitney's *Choice of Emblemes* (Leyden, 1586)
may appropriately illustrate some of these affinities between em-
blem-writer and dramatic poet — the combination of visual and
verbal method and the aim of uniting profit with delight. Whitney's
collection (we are informed) consists of emblems and "other Devises,
For the moste parte gathered out of sundrie Writers, Englished and
Moralized. . . ."⁴ It is "A worke adorned with varietie of matter,
both pleasant and profitable: wherein those that please, maye finde
to fit their fancies: Bicause herein, by the office of the eie, and the
eare, the minde may reape dooble delighte throughe holsome
preceptes, shadowed with pleasant devises: both fit for the vertuous, to their incoraging: and for the wicked, for their ad-
monishing and amendment." The term *emblem* (the author
continues, in his epistle to the reader) is derived from the Greek
emballesthai or *epemblesthai*, *"To set in, or to put in . . . ."* It
properly denotes "suche figures, or workes, as are wroughte in plate,
or in stones in the pavementes, or on the waules, or suche like, for
the adorning of the place: havinge some wittie devise expressed with
cunning woorkemanship, somethinge obscure to be perceived at the
first, whereby, when with further consideration it is understood, it
maie the greater delighte the beholuder." All emblems, for the most
part, may be reduced to three kinds — *"Historicall, Naturall, &*
Morall."

Heavily indebted to earlier emblem-writers, Whitney describes
his book as essentially a compilation — "gatheringes, and gleaninges
out of other mens harvestes . . . ." It is a compendium of "sondrie
inventions" of various "auctours . . . collected against such vices as

Pride, Envie, Concupiscence, Drunkennes, Covetousnes, Usurie, and such like. . . ." Like other works of its genre, it might serve as a sort of illustrated commonplace book, assimilating Biblical and classical material—myth and parable and proverb—to conventional moral *topoi.* Uniting verbal and visual appeal, it might function as an instrument of moral persuasion—for exhortation to virtue and dehortation from vice. Moreover, as a collection of topics of invention, an anthology of moralized pictures and adages and verses, it might also suggest themes and ideas, images and conceits, to painters and poets alike.

The 1492 edition of Franchino Gafuri's *Theorica Musicae*[5] contains a woodcut (Fig. I) that in certain details anticipates the forge-scene in Spenser's House of Care (*The Faerie Queene,* Book IV, Canto 5).[6] Spenser's icon of jealousy includes (as you recall) six blacksmiths standing about an anvil, wielding hammers that "like belles in greatnesse orderly succeed . . . ." Gafuri's picture portrays Jubal (the brother of Tubalcain and the legendary inventor of musical theory) watching the labors of six smiths whose hammers bear numbers indicating their relative weights. The following picture delineates Pythagoras's experiment with bells. Actually, both Jubal and Pythagoras were credited with discovering the principles of harmony at a blacksmith's forge; this illustration would not be unusual therefore, except for one detail, which is Gafuri's own innovation. To the four or five smiths conventional in the Pythagoras legend Gafuri has added a sixth blacksmith. This innovation first appeared in the 1480 edition of his treatise. Even though it is conceivable that later musicians or illustrators may have borrowed it, this detail places Gafuri's smiths in the direct ancestral line of Spenser's.

Nevertheless Spenser has radically altered what he borrowed. Gafuri's illustration is concerned with the principles of harmony, not with the torments of the jealous lover. For the ethical and psychological meaning—the central idea—underlying the forge of Care we must turn to other sources. The jealousy of Vulcan and Cain, the etymology of *zelotypia,* the idiomatic senses of *martello,* and perhaps the unillustrated emblem "*Ab Aetna*" in Bruno's *De gli eroici furori* could have suggested the correlation between image and idea in Spenser's allegory—the association between smithy and jealousy—but we cannot positively demonstrate whether or how far they did. In this allegory of Friendship, Gafuri's image of concord functions as an emblem of discord; the emphasis has shifted from musical theory to psychology, from instrumental music to *musica humana*.

Let us turn to another Spenserian crux. As the symbol of the True Faith or the True Church, Una first makes her appearance mounted on a white donkey, a "lowly asse" which at a later point in the fable (*The Faerie Queene,* Book I, Canto 6) a "salvage nation" superstitiously attempts to adore. A suggestive but ambiguous parallel occurs in a fable attributed to Babrius ("De Asino gestante simulacrum"), in which a donkey bearing the image of Isis (another traditional symbol of Truth) mistakes the adoration accorded the goddess as directed to himself. This episode provided the basis for emblems by Alciati and Whitney (Fig. II), and it recurs in an emblem-book by Gabriele Faerno of Cremona, a collection that illustrates selected fables drawn from various classical authors.[7] Like Babrius, Faerno applies this fable specifically to men invested with high authority. Claude Mignault retains this interpretation but extends it to ecclesiastical dignitaries—bishops and priests—as well. Whitney in turn applies the moral primarily to the preaching clergy. "The pastors good, that doe gladd tidings preache" are honored for messages they bear. "Yet, if throwghe pride they doe themselves forgett, / And make accompte that honor, to be theires," they should reflect on the fable of the ass, "Whoe thowghte the men to honor him, did kneele, / And staied therefore, till he the staffe did feele."

Like Whitney's visual emblem, Spenser's verbal emblem portrays a mounted woman who represents truth and religion. If the analogy between them is not fortuitous, one might logically infer that the lowly ass in *The Faerie Queene* symbolizes the preaching ministry— the vehicle of the orthodox doctrine and one of the signs or *notae* of the True Church. If so, the resemblances between these pictorial and poetic emblems appear less striking than their differences. If Spenser has indeed borrowed from Whitney, or from Alciati and Mignault, he has radically altered their material. In his version the credulity lies with the populace rather than with the ass. The worship accorded the donkey is real, not imaginary, and there is no indication that he deserves castigation for his pride.

In the emblems of Whitney and Faerno, moreover, the image of the goddess is *un*veiled. Una's veil thus marks another point of divergence between Spenser's icon and those of Whitney, Faerno, and late editions of Alciati. In this respect it is closer to traditional conceptions of Isis as veiled truth and to the 1531 edition of Alciati, which depicts her statue as veiled (Fig. III).

If the iconographical tradition behind the veiled (or unveiled) woman on the lowly ass appears complicated, the exegetical tradition associating the ass with the clergy seems still more complex. We shall resist the temptation to cite the encomia composed by Agrippa and Bruno in praise of the ass or to quote medieval commentaries on the "white asses" of Judges 5: 10 and the "jawbone of an ass" in Judges 15: 16. These might reinforce the interpretation of Una's steed as the vehicle of apostolic and evangelical doctrine, but they do not permit us to draw conclusive inferences as to the poet's immediate sources. Though there is a strong possibility that Spenser may have encountered the tradition of the *asinus portans mysteria* in iconographical works — the emblems of Whitney and Alciati — he could have met it elsewhere: in Babrius's fables, in Erasmus's *Adages,* in the encomia (or mock-encomia) of Bruno and Agrippa. In the light of these parallels (for they are no more than parallels) we can detect traditional Renaissance themes and images in Spenser's poetic icon, but the differences appear to be as striking as the points of resemblance. We can (legitimately, in my opinion) relate his verbal image to a Renaissance tradition that also finds expression in the visual images of some of his contemporaries and near-contemporaries; but we have as yet little valid evidence to determine his actual sources. The fact that he presents his image more or less "pictorially" does not, in and of itself, indicate that he derived it from a pictorial source.

II

From the verbal icons of non-dramatic poetry let us turn to the visual icons of the drama. Unlike the writer of epic and romance, the dramatist does not have to rely on exclusively verbal description to place a scene or a person or an action before the eyes of his audience. His method can be strongly emblematic even though it may not be clearly evident from the text alone. In Greene's *Friar Bacon and Friar Bungay* the formal contest between the intellectual champions of England and Germany centers upon a conventional symbol of heroic virtue. Friar Bungay conjures up an apparition of the golden fruit of the Hesperides and its dragon-warder. Vandermast in turn summons Hercules to break the branches, and Bungay is powerless to prevent him. Just as the honor of the British universities seems irretrievably lost and while Vandermast is arrogantly demanding the laurel crown of a conqueror, Friar Bacon appears, stays Alcides's hand, and bids him transport the Imperial champion back to Germany.

Not only was Hercules himself commonly regarded as the hero *par excellence,*[8] but the fruit of the Hesperides had itself been allegorized in terms of heroic virtue. Describing a bronze statue of Hercules in the Capitol at Rome, Valeriano (1556) explains the three apples he carries as the three outstanding virtues of a hero— moderation of anger, tempering of avarice, and noble contempt of pleasures. His slaying the dragon of the Hesperides represents his victory over concupiscence. His lionskin symbolizes magnanimity (strength of mind), and his club signifies reason and discipline. A similar interpretation of these motifs appears in Bocchi's emblem of Hercules (1555), which portrays the hero conventionally with club, lionskin, and apples of the Hesperides. The accompanying verses describe Alcides as the type of the wise and magnanimous man, the dragon as *dira cupido,* the club as a symbol of victory over the senses, and the golden apples as the conquest of three vices:

> Comprimitur furor irae, & habendi sacra libido
> Interit, & ventris desidiosus amor.

Two other writers—Cesare Ripa and Henry Peacham—reworked this material into emblems of heroic virtue. Both wrote too late, however, to have influenced Greene.[9]

The detailed ethical symbolism of Valeriano and Bocchi does not recur in Greene's text, and we have no real evidence to prove that he had read either the *Hieroglyphica* or *Symbolicarum Quaestionum.* The significant point is that, despite the combination of abstruse erudition and sheer horseplay, he has given additional force to the

intellectual duel between national champions—and stronger
emphasis to the triumph of his contemplative hero, Roger Bacon—
by centering the contest on a proverbial symbol of *virtus heroica*.
The hieroglyph of Valeriano, the symbol of Bocchi, and the later
emblems of Ripa and Peacham are significant for us not as sources
but merely as analogues—a few among many Renaissance
representations of Hercules's labors as emblems of heroic virtue.
When the iconographer or literary historian is confronted with
numerous instances of the same (or similar) commonplace, he must
usually eschew the search for immediate sources—whether among
the emblem-writers or the mythographers or the lexicographers.
Except in rare instances, the attempt to establish specific literary or
iconographical indebtedness can be misleading. In most cases the
parallels are valuable chiefly as parallels and nothing more; the
commonplaces as commonplaces, and precisely because they *are*
such; the tradition as tradition.

The metamorphoses of Falstaff under the influence of Eros are
scarcely more ludicrous than those of Jove, with whom the "unclean
knight" compares himself. In his own words, his concupiscence is "a
beastly fault," and behind the grotesque punishment it receives the
moralist may perhaps detect certain commonplaces of Renaissance
poetic theory—the interpretation of animal metamorphoses as the
disfigurement of the rational soul by passion, and the conception of
vice as a source of the ridiculous. In the episode of Herne the
Hunter we may recognize a dramatic emblem—a moral tableau
uniting verbal and visual presentation and (in Falstaff's own observations on his ordeal) including a moral commentary. Whether
or not this scene is actually a parody of the Actaeon myth and
whether or not it was influenced by Whitney's emblem[10] on this
theme cannot, in my opinion, be positively and "scientifically"
demonstrated; but there is at least a strong possibility. Like
Sprengius and several other emblem-writers, Whitney interprets
Actaeon's fate as a warning against "fancies fonde" and "affections
base." (Sprengius had allegorized the same fable in terms of *libido,
illicitus amor,* and *perniciosa voluptas.*) The stag's head on a
human body recurs in numerous Renaissance illustrations of Actaeon. Moreover, if Rowe's suggestion that Falstaff "lies down upon
his face" can be accepted, the analogy with the emblems of Sam-

bucus and Whitney would appear to be even more striking. One is tempted to see in this tableau a bourgeois parody of a myth which had already furnished images and themes for courtly panegyric. The role of the virgin-goddess Diana is transferred to two Windsor matrons. A throng of Windsor children and citizens, disguised as English (and even Welsh) fairies, substitute for Diana's train of nymphs. In this parody of Dianic imagery already thoroughly familiar at Windsor Castle, Falstaff—in Windsor Forest—usurps the role of Actaeon.

III

Sharing a common subject matter, literature and iconography were in a sense interchangeable. Art theory had not yet emancipated itself from poetic theory, and this (despite the influence of Aristotle's *Poetics*) was still strongly influenced by rhetorical or logical concepts. In the Renaissance as in the Middle Ages, the technical terms for the selection and arrangement of material—the "invention" and "disposition" of "arguments" or "themes"— belonged to the common vocabulary of the arts: to painting and poetics and music, as well as to logic or rhetoric. Even Bacon was unwilling or unable to discard this terminology. In his writings invention may refer to logical and rhetorical arguments, to scientific discoveries and technological inventions (such as guns and gunpowder, the mariner's compass, the printing press, optical lenses), or to the discovery of new arts and sciences.

Traditionally the invention and disposition of arguments belonged to both rhetoric and dialectic (or logic). Though the boundary between these arts was shifting (rhetoric was sometimes regarded as a branch of logic, but usually as a separate though related discipline; dialectic and logic were treated as virtually identical by certain authors, but differentiated by others), students of these disciplines were often guided by diverse criteria in selecting their arguments, and employed different instruments. The rhetorician employed the enthymeme instead of the syllogism, utilized ethical and affective as well as logical proofs, and was concerned (on the whole) rather with probabilities or apparent probabilities than with certainties. Peter Ramus eliminated much of this duplication, and simplified the problem of "finding" arguments, by assigning invention and disposition to dialectics (logic) alone, leaving to the rhetorician the problem of style and delivery. The Ramist orator, accordingly, must master logic as well as rhetoric (as well as the art of memory, which had been one of the traditional five parts of rhetoric). Although Ramus influenced theologians like Curcellaeus and men of letters like Gabriel Harvey and John Milton, the extent to which his methodological reforms conditioned the nature of late 16th and 17th century poetry or its methods of composition still remains undetermined.

Epistemological and aesthetic theories, speculations on the nature and modes of human knowledge and art, sometimes blurred the distinction between ear and eye or between formal aesthetic organization in time and space. Historical painters, like epic and tragic poets, depicted famous and often violent actions: battles and conflagrations and shipwrecks; assassinations and abductions; metamorphoses, apotheoses, and psychomachias. Conversely, poets (like painters) portrayed landscapes and edifices, men and women, personifications of virtues and vices. Still influenced by rhetorical conceptions, by Platonic and Aristotelian theories of imitation, or by the traditions of their predecessors, writers and artists frequently depicted the same subjects, taxing the resources of their respective modes. In portraying narrative or dramatic subjects, or in attempting to communicate strong emotions or states of character, painters often relied on a vocabulary of exaggerated expression and gesture, a sign-language (so to speak) for the passions of the soul. The art-treatises of the late Renaissance sometimes devoted considerable space to the techniques for expressing and differentiating the various passions. Partly conditioned by rhetorical discussions of pathetic proof, by neo-Aristotelian emphasis on imitation of the passions, and by seventeenth-century psychological theory, these conventions persisted in painting and theories of painting throughout the eighteenth century. As late as the nineteenth century, actors were still consulting manuals of gestures for the various emotions. If the historical tableaux of the late Renaissance sometimes strike us as melodramatic and theatrical, we should recall that, though the painter could not employ the verbal medium of the poet, he could at least exploit the sign-language of the stage.

Conversely, when the poet found himself on terrain that we would regard as the painter's territory, he too was constrained by the limitations of his own medium. Passages of pure description tended on occasion to become catalogs. Some of these were conventions of great antiquity. Spenser's forest with its detailed inventory of trees belongs to a tradition that includes Lydgate and Chaucer and classical poetry. A fashionable Renaissance formula for describing a woman's beauty—beginning at the top and proceeding systematically and anatomically from hair, brow, eyes, through limbs and torso and concluding with her feet—can be traced back to medieval treatises on poetics. Such formulas and the conventional imagery that usually adorned them invited travesty, and it was comparatively easy to ridicule them. A poet could invert the formula by reversing the usual order, beginning at the feet and ascending methodically to the head. He could retain the formula, but alter the conventional images and epithets, replacing golden hair with jet or silver, and teeth of ivory with ebony. In the latter instance the poet's wit would turn on the contrast between two rare and costly materials opposite in quality but bearing names very similar in sound. Ivory teeth occur frequently among medieval formulas for describing a woman's beauty; and in his *Ars Versificatoria* Matthieu de Vendôme utilizes this phrase (*dentes ebori* and *ebori dentes*) in two idealized descriptions of Helen of Troy.[11] The word-play (*eburneo-ebano*) would be fully intelligible in Renaissance Italian poetry; in Tasso's and Berni's allusions to ebony teeth,[12] the element of parody is probably heightened by punning. The poet might also "scramble" his images, as in Shakespeare's *Midsummer Night's Dream,* retaining the conventional epithets but deliberately misplacing them for comic effect: red eyes for rosy cheeks, cherry nose for ruby lips, cowslip cheeks for golden hair.[13] When the courtly rooster of the Nun's Priest's Tale extols Pertelote for the "scarlet-red" about her eyes, he is maintaining the decorum appropriate for a favorite hen while violating the conventions that would befit a man addressing his mistress under similar circumstances. The comic element in this scene is somewhat subtler than in the burlesque encomia of the Renaissance (with their comparatively simple substitution of red or black eyes for blue); in the context of Chaucer's courtly barnyard the praise of the hen's scarlet eye-lids appears to parody not only the conventions of the *encomium mulieris* but also the conventional parody of these conventions.

Again, in ridiculing these formulas of praise, the poet could protest against "false compare" (as in Shakespeare's sonnet "My mistress' eyes"), varying the conventions by substituting an unfashionable mode of beauty, ridiculing the tradition itself as artificial and false, yet simultaneously converting this ridicule to his mistress's praise. Or again (like Shakespeare's Olivia) he could mock the formal method of such conventions, deriding them less for their stale or insincere imagery than for their hackneyed procedure, ridiculing the conventional catalog of a mistress's beauty primarily on the grounds that it is, after all, little more than a catalogue and that its topics of praise are for the most part physical. The lover's eulogy had frequently been a mere catalogue of her anatomy, an "inventory" of beauty; and Olivia parodies its method by treating the same subject matter in the manner of another sort of catalogue—the formula for an "inventory" of property in legal documents:

> I will give out diverse schedules of my beauty. It shall be inventoried, and every particle and utensil labell'd to my will: — as, item, two lips, indifferent red; item, two gray eyes, with lids to them; item, one neck, one chin, and so forth.

The point of her "conceit" lies not only in her ability to turn Cesario's own argument and imagery against him, countering his argument that she should marry in order to leave the world some copy of her beauty, with the promise that she will provide such a copy in her will. Her wit also hinges on the substitution of one type of catalogue for another and on the implicit analogy between external beauty and external goods, the gifts of nature and of fortune.

Much of the charm of this scene results from the poet's ability to exploit a trite rhetorical device for a variety of dramatic ends and effects, simultaneously ridiculing the convention, emphasizing Olivia's physical beauty, and demonstrating her wit and character. She is clever enough and noble enough to see through both the rhetorical techniques of courtship and the physical insistence underlying the lover's *encomium mulieris*; and her insight enhances the comedy of the ironic situation that immediately ensues. For the intelligent and noble Olivia cannot and does not remain faithful to her own rational insights; she promptly falls in love with Cesario-Viola's outward form (which is an illusion) and with "his" rhetorical skill. In spite of her ridicule of the rhetoric of courtship and its catalogue of a lady's physical beauty, she herself is overcome by an appearance that is purely external and by the specious beauty of words.

Olivia unveils herself as though her face were a painting, and then proceeds to catalog it systematically, feature by feature. This may serve as an *exemplum,* if nothing else, of the different methods of the poet and the painter and of the peculiar difficulties that confronted them when, in treating a common subject matter, they found it necessary to trespass on the other's domain. Under such circumstances, where the painter must attempt to represent temporal events in terms of organized space, and the poet spatial patterns in terms of narrative organization, the nature of their own art-forms imposed inevitable limitations on their methods of rendering their subject. Once a satisfactory formula had been found, they continued to employ it until it became stereotyped or even trite. Indeed, the formulas themselves were sometimes indispensable in creating a common vocabulary to be shared by poets or painters and their audience. Without such conventions a spectator might be puzzled as to precisely what emotion was being registered in a particular painting, or whether the same gestures and expressions might not express "horror" for one artist and "surprise" for another. Similarly, the formal conventions of description in poetry could assist the reader in following the poet's intent. The conventional formulas might elicit a conventional response; and variations on these conventions might serve as signals for innovations in meaning and attitude—an aesthetic *nota bene.*

In the light of the aesthetic theories of the period it is hardly surprising that poets should be painterly and painters poetic, or that both should attempt on occasion to emulate the rhetorician: to persuade or dissuade; to teach, delight, and move; to confer praise or blame. If their choice of similar inventions sometimes involved distinctly different problems in composition in time or space, these were on the whole technical problems, and enabled poet or painter alike to demonstrate his virtuosity and skill in surmounting them.

The difficulties themselves were a stimulus to creative excellence, and even though the poet or artist might be compelled to rely on the conventional formulas, he could introduce his own variants and innovations, enlivening and embellishing the conventions, or in some instances radically transforming them. Paintings of violent action and violent emotion — battle scenes, the deluge, the last judgment — and poetic descriptions of enchanted gardens and forests may involve a confusion between the spheres of the verbal and visual arts; and this confusion may have prejudiced the achievement of lesser craftsmen. Major artists and poets, however, produced some of their finest "virtuoso-pieces" (if the term is not pejorative) in response to this challenge and on these very themes.

Poet and painter alike were expected to imitate abstract ideas through sensuous particulars, the forms of virtues and vices through individual examples, and to delineate actions and passions as well as moral character. Whereas the poet could express passion directly through words, the painter could only portray it indirectly through gestures and facial expressions. Whereas the former could depict inner psychological struggles and the process of moral decision, the latter must externalize the act of proairesis either through gesture or through the introduction of personified abstractions and allegorical figures, as in the Choice of Hercules and the Judgment of Paris. Whereas the poet could narrate a continuous action, relating its beginning, middle, and end, the artist must restrict his vision to a single moment in time; instead of the development and unravelling of a plot — a complete and entire dramatic action — he must reduce the narrative to a tableau in a peep-show, an image in a camera oscura.

IV

From the relevance of iconographical materials to literary studies, let us turn to the more embarrassing problem of evidence. Unlike the student of emblems and hieroglyphs, the literary scholar often has little visual evidence to guide him. The tragedy may have been a dramatic emblem, the masque a moving and speaking hieroglyph; but as a rule the visual image — the icon — lived only in and during the performance. We are compelled therefore to reconstruct it ourselves, painfully, from the poet's text, from his own notes or the testimony of his spectators, from whatever hints he may have given us as to his sources, from property-records, or from the drawings of the costume- or scene-designer. Finally, with varying degrees of plausibility, we may seek guidance from contemporary pictures. Thus, during the century that has intervened between Henry Green's pioneer researches and Schoene's recent book on *Emblematik und Drama im Zeitalter des Barock,* an increasing number of scholars have sought guidance from emblem-books and iconographical manuals. In several cases — the dramas of Gryphius, certain of Jonson's masques, heraldic devices in Shakespeare's *Pericles* — this approach has been eminently successful. In other instances it has produced suggestive, though hardly conclusive, results. In seeking to recover the emblematic and iconic element in Renaissance drama, one is naturally tempted to look for it in contemporary emblems and iconologies. Only rarely, however, can these provide us with demonstrable sources. They are significant primarily as compendia of Renaissance motifs and ethical commonplaces — as testimony to, and links in, a symbolic tradition that is not only complex but often ambiguous and equivocal.

For the student of drama the problem of ascertaining iconographical sources may, if anything, be greater than for the specialist in non-dramatic literature. Lacking the visual mode available to the dramatist, the epic or lyric poet was compelled to rely on descriptive detail, to impress his image on the eye of the imagination instead of the physical retina. In some cases these pictorial details enable us to identify a particular emblem as his probable source. As a rule, however, he has so altered his borrowing — by adapting it to the larger context of his poem, by transferring it to a purely verbal medium, and assimilating it to the narrative mode, or by fusing it with details derived from other sources — that its immediate origin is obscured.

The problem of identifying sources is further complicated by the constant interaction between verbal and visual traditions. In the first place, emblematic and iconological literature is not consistently pictorial. Philostratus's *Images* was sometimes printed with illustrations, but sometimes without a single picture. Few of

Valeriano's hieroglyphics were illustrated. Many of the emblems and *imprese* published during the Renaissance consisted only of mottoes or verses. In others, the actual illustrations varied in different editions.

Secondly, almost any proverb or descriptive passage of prose or poetry could be — and often was — converted into an emblem. Non-pictorial works — epics, romances, theological treatises — could be rendered emblematic through illustrated title-pages or through pictures portraying the arguments of specific books or cantos and the contents of particular episodes. Alciati ransacked the Greek Anthology for emblematic materials. Other editors devoted entire volumes to emblems drawn from the poems of Homer, Ovid, and Horace.

Thirdly, just as a writer might draw on non-pictorial sources for a strongly emblematic scene in epic or drama, he might (conversely) divest an actual emblem of all its visual associations and reduce it simply to its doctrinal content. Thus Burton made extensive use of the emblem-books as sources for fables, adages, and ethical or psychological *topoi,* but showed little interest in their iconographical details. If he had not conveniently documented his sources, we would have had little valid evidence for ascertaining them.

We must resist, therefore, the temptation to oversimplify the impact of iconography on poetry. To take the presence or absence of the "pictorial" element as an index of the poet's indebtedness or non-indebtedness to iconographical materials is dangerous. In some of the rare cases where we *can* trace a pattern of indebtedness he alters his borrowings almost beyond recognition. In some instances only the motto remains; in others, only the *exemplum.* On other occasions he retains the image but varies much of the concrete detail, investing it with a different meaning. The emblematic and pictorial element in dramatic and non-dramatic poetry alike is, in many cases, rather a reflection of aesthetic ideals traditionally held in common with painting than evidence of direct indebtedness to pictorial sources.

Despite the real and highly important impact of iconography on poetry, it is difficult to trace such influence with precision. The degree of pictorial vividness in a given poem may not help much;

indeed it may mislead us. For there is no clearly definable or inevitable relationship between visual and verbal icons. If a narrative or dramatic poet develops an image or idea "pictorially," this does not necessarily indicate that he derived it from a particular picture. Painters were constantly borrowing details from poets and vice versa; iconographers were constantly drawing on both visual and verbal authorities. Emblem-writers were constantly pillaging classical and Biblical literature and ransacking Erasmus's *Adages* for "sentences." Visual materials were constantly being transformed into verbal, and back again. In the complex mythographical tradition of the Renaissance it is almost impossible to draw a sharp line between painting and poetry, iconography and literature. Both of the sister arts served as channels for transmitting and elaborating the same concepts and symbols, the same images and ideas. As Mistress Anne Killigrew correctly recognized, the two provinces were, after all, one.

Mistress Killigrew, however, was admittedly "young" and "ambitious." Those of us who follow her are neither, and we may be understandably reluctant to emulate her enterprise. For us, it is enough to acknowledge the interdependence of painting and poetry without attempting to annex the adjacent domain. Although the sister arts may form a united realm, they have retained their separate identity notwithstanding — like England and Scotland, or New York and New Jersey. Though the customs barriers are down and the frontiers no longer patrolled, art history and literary history remain separate; they are related, not identical disciplines. Literary criticism is as distinct from iconography as Trenton from Albany or an Englishman from a Scot. The two disciplines require different skills and diverse techniques; and if the literary scholar *must* encroach on the iconographer's province he must do so with caution — combining the wariness of the poacher with the humility of the amateur.

For, unlike the trained iconographer, the literary critic is not on his own ground. As a rule he has received little formal instruction in the techniques of art history. His firsthand acquaintance with pictorial materials is sometimes limited, arbitrary, and sporadic. Neither erudition nor critical skill can altogether safeguard him against the danger of misreading iconographical evidence. Some of

his errors, moreover, may indeed be "pre-iconographical"—
resulting from misinterpreting "artistic motifs" and "factual" or
"expressional" subject-matter.[14] By mistaking a fairly conventional
countryman for a woman and a hilltop town for a riverside palace,
he may convert a typical woodcutter into an atypical portrait of a
queen. By confusing blood-drops with tears, he may transform a
bleeding into a weeping heart, or vice versa. By associating turbans
(fashionable in Renaissance Europe) specifically with Orientals, he
may bestow an exotic Levantine setting on an allegorical banquet
scene. By misreading gestures and facial expressions (one of the
most difficult and ambiguous aspects of painting, as Renaissance
theorists themselves acknowledged), he may misinterpret the
character and emotions—the attitudes and perhaps the identity—of
the persons represented. Occasionally he may even "invent" his own
interpretation of the scene—a commendable exercise of the
mythopoeic imagination, but with little relevance to Renaissance
mythography or to iconographical conventions.

The emblematic tradition, as we now recognize, was far more
than the mere "bypath" an earlier generation of scholars believed it
to be, and iconography has become in recent years a well-travelled
road. If some of its lanes still seem unexplored—green, fresh, and
relatively untrodden—the reason may be that it is, after all, another
Renaissance maze, in which more than a few literary trespassers
have lost their way. Before penetrating more deeply into that
Wandering Wood, let us be fairly certain that we can distinguish
the true path from the blind alleys. Perhaps our best hope of finding
our way safely through that "leavy labyrinth" is to hold fast to the
clue that the professional iconographers have conveniently left us.

Fig. I.   *Theorica Musice Franchini Gafuri* (Milan, 1492), sig. Bvi, HEH 87539. *Reproduced by permission of The Huntington Library, San Marino, California.*

Non tibi , sed Religioni.

Fig. II.   Geoffrey Whitney, *A Choice of Emblemes* (Leyden, 1586),
                p. 8, HEH 79714. *Reproduced by permission of The Hunt-
                ington Library, San Marino, California.*

NON TIBI SED RELIGIONI

Fig. III. Andrea Alciati, *Emblematum liber* (1531), p. [B7]; reproduced in *Fountains of Alciat,* ed. Henry Green, Holbein Society (London, 1870).

CHAPTER II

The Lexicographical
Approach

IN A SATIRE written near the close of the sixteenth century, John
Marston pilloried a rival satirist for obscurity. Precisely whom he
was satirizing and whether or not the charge was really justified
need not concern us here. The significant point is that Marston
pretended to seek enlightenment from popular reference books.

> I'le leaue the white roabe, and the biting times
> Vnto our moderne Satyres sharpest lines;
> Whose hungry fangs snarle at some secret sinne.
> And in such pitchy clouds enwrapped beene
> His *Sphinxian* ridles, that old *Oedipus*
> Would be amaz'd and take it in foule snufs
> That such *Cymerian* darkness should inuolue
> A quaint conceit, that he could not resolue.
> O darknes palpable! Egipts black night!
> My wit is stricken blind, hath lost his sight.
> My shins are broke, with groping for some sence
> To know to what his words haue reference.

Certes (*sunt*) but (*non videntur*) that I know.
Reach me some Poets Index that will show.
Imagines Deorum, Booke of Epithites,
Natales Comes, thou I know recites,
And mak'st Anatomie of Poesie.
Helpe to vnmaske the Satyres secresie.
Delphick *Apollo,* ayde me to vnrip,
These intricate deepe Oracles of wit.
These darke Enigmaes, and strange ridling sence
Which passe my dullard braines intelligence.[1]

This passage has been frequently quoted in recent years (sometimes quite out of context) by students of Renaissance mythography.[2] In their opinion it throws indubitable light on contemporary methods of literary composition and interpretation. It provides definitive evidence as to how Renaissance poetry was originally written and how it was originally read. It offers an authoritative commentary on the nature, sources, and techniques of poetic and iconographic allusion. And (perhaps most important of all) it illuminates the relationship between the poet and his audience. The Renaissance poet might speak in cryptograms, but with a modicum of patience and a good library his readers might decipher them. With a little labor and intent study they could break his code. For in actuality the same systems of allusive shorthand, the same cryptographic codes were available to the poet and his audience. Within convenient reach—on the library shelf—lay the indispensable tools: the manuals of mythography, the handbooks of epithets, the dictionaries and lexicons. Between the enigmatic poet and an audience that delighted in enigmas stood that useful intermediary, the lexicographer.

The Renaissance poet (as these scholars view him) was no congenital horseman. He did not mount Pegasus at one bound and soar instinctively toward whatever altitudes his talents merited—Olympus, the Empyrean, the Paradisus Stultorum. Far from it. Instead of vaulting boldly onto his feathered steed, he climbed his way painfully into the saddle, teetering precariously on a stack of accumulated handbooks. He wrote with ears attuned to the Muse, eyes focused on reference manuals.

If his readers desired to follow him, they too must mount by the same humble but indispensable footstool. It was from the lexicographers that they must learn the difficult techniques of equitation — the art of mounting among the "feathers of imagination" and (once mounted) managing to stay safely on. Shod *in Musarum incude* at second or third heat, the Renaissance Pegasus reeked (it would seem) not so much of the stable as of the oil lamp and the forge.

In recent years sweeping claims have been made for the direct influence of dictionaries and similar reference books on Renaissance literature and art. Such an influence undoubtedly did exist, and it can hardly have been negligible. In certain instances it has been established with reasonable certitude. In others, it remains a strong probability, if not a historical fact. In many cases, however, it is little more than a remote, though tempting, possibility. Before accepting at face value the recent claims made for these lexicons and manuals, we must first evaluate the evidence on which such claims have been based. In some instances this seems very tenuous indeed; the quotation with which we began is a case in point.

Marston's lines may conveniently serve as an introduction, if not an epigraph, to this discussion of the use and abuse of lexicography for they provide a clearcut example of the misuse of evidence. Though they are really concerned with the abuse of poetry, recent scholarship has sometimes detached them from their satiric context and applied them literally to the use of dictionaries and handbooks. Here, for example, is Jean Seznec's comment. The writings of Conti, Cartari, and perhaps Ravisius Textor are, in his opinion, "the works which Marston call[ed] upon spontaneously to help him resolve the enigmas posed by contemporary poets." "It would seem," Mr. Seznec adds, "that Marston had all these works conveniently at hand ('reach me') on his library shelves — proof that they were currently consulted at the time, and that they served as indices not only for poets, but for their readers as well."[3]

Even the most conscientious scholar may occasionally stretch his evidence beyond the breaking point. If one is not altogether convinced by Mr. Seznec's "proof," it is because — like several other commentators before or after him — he has mistaken an artificial dramatic situation for literary history. Marston was, of course, writing a satire, not a library catalogue. Seznec's argument hinges apparently on the phrase "reach me"; these words refer, however, only to the fictional situation deliberately created by the satirist, not (surely) to bibliographical detail or to autobiographical fact. They do not indicate that Marston himself really possessed these books or that he himself normally made a practice of consulting them. He is, after all, speaking in the *persona* of the satirist, not *in propria persona.* The phrase "poets index," in turn, can conceivably be interpreted literally, but it may well be simply a trope, intended to heighten the satire against the abuse of poetry. It would conform, therefore, to the principles of ironic, not bibliographical description. The notion that these manuals served as "indices for poets" is admittedly explicit in the text, but it must be appraised through yellow spectacles; for it reflects the characteristic colors, the jaundiced vision, of the satirist. On this point we should accord Marston the charity of poetic faith, not the strict justice of historical assent.

Similar protests against obscurity in literature are (as we well know) fairly common today. Having grown thoroughly accustomed to them, we are usually cautious about accepting them at face value. A critic might well complain that he required a copy of the *Summa Theologiae,* several annotated anthologies of Irish ballads, and a street map of Dublin in order to make the most of *Finnegan's Wake*; yet we should hardly take him at his word. Still less should we interpret his remarks (as Seznec does Marston's) as proof positive that these were common "indices" for poets and readers.

For Seznec unfortunately insists on this point. Marston's satire does (he argues) provide demonstrable "proof" for the formative influence of mythographical manuals on the Renaissance poetic imagination. Yet in fact these lines offer no solid evidence for the major generalizations he extracts from them. We may agree with him that they constitute "evidence of the highest interest concerning the popularity of Cartari and Conti in the late sixteenth century," but that is all. In and of themselves they throw very little light on how poets or readers actually utilized these manuals.

Finally, there is considerable room for doubt as to how relevant these particular authors are to the problem that Marston describes. The charge of obscurity had frequently been leveled against Roman satirists—especially Persius and to a lesser extent Juvenal and even

Horace. It is scarcely appropriate, however, to Joseph Hall's *Virgidemiae,* commonly regarded as the target of Marston's invective. Although Marston presses the same charge against his opponent in other satires,[4] Hall himself complains that he has been accused not of being too obscure but of being too plain and outspoken:

> Some say my Satyrs ouer-loosely flow,
> Nor hide their gall inough from open show:
> Not ridle-like obscuring their intent:
> But packe-staffe plaine vttring what thing they ment:
> Contrarie to the Roman ancients,
> Whose wordes were short, & darkesome was their sense.[5]

To a modern reader Hall's assertion that his satires are more "open" than those of "blindfold" Juvenal, "darke" Horace, and "roughhew'ne" Scaliger seems justified.[6] Marston has boldly given his opponent the lie by flatly denying Hall's insistence on his clarity. This disingenuous rhetorical maneuver may be effective as satire, but it tends to undermine Marston's value as literary evidence. The reference works to which he appeals (ironically) for aid would, moreover, have been of negligible value in enabling him to decipher Hall's meaning. As Hall makes little use of classical mythology in his satires, these manuals would have thrown scant light on his "ridling sence." They would have been highly appropriate, on the other hand, had Marston directed his satire against Chapman; the latter did in fact draw heavily from Conti and perhaps Cartari.

In pressing the charge of obscurity, Marston made use of a variety of convenient commonplaces — the proverbial ambiguity of several Latin satirists, the abstruse allegories of contemporary mythological poets, and possibly the riddling enigmas of Renaissance emblem-literature. ("Egipts black night" might well serve as a label for some of the fashionable hieroglyphics of the period.) None of these references was strictly relevant to Hall's *Virgidemiae,* but they could effectively remind the reader of notorious forms of ambiguity he had encountered elsewhere, either in art or in poetry. As critics we may admire Marston's tactical audacity. As scholars we must question the authority that Seznec and other commentators attribute to him. His lines belong rather to the history of satire than to the history of manuals and dictionaries. They demonstrate rather the type of abuse Renaissance satirists heaped on one another than the use they actually made of the manuals.

Finally, in two of the three references Marston gives us we have no real evidence that he had any specific work in mind. As Seznec himself points out, "many other manuals" of epithets existed beside Textor's.[7] *Imagines deorum* were likewise fairly numerous. Du Verdier's Latin translation of Cartari's book was known by this title, but so was Philostratus' *Icones*. Several Renaissance authors cite du Choul's unpublished *De Imaginibus deorum;* nor should we forget the two medieval works that circulated under this title—the *Liber imaginum deorum* and the *De deorum imaginibus libellus*.[8] Though it is unlikely that Marston had the latter works in mind, we should not rule out the possibility that he may be referring to Philostratus instead of Cartari—to a classical manual rather than a Renaissance work. (Burton, for instance, refers to the work of both authors as *Imagines deorum*.)[9]

The same tendency to inflate the limited evidence concerning the mythographers and their general influence appears in recent discussions of other sixteenth- or seventeenth-century writers. Though Chapman and Jonson allude to the manuals—and are in fact even more deeply indebted to them than they acknowledge—they are not altogether representative of their period. Jonson was one of the most learned poets of his day, Chapman one of the most obscure; both achieved—and perhaps literally enjoyed—a contemporary notoriety for pedantry. Nor is the influence of the manuals apparent in their works as a whole. In both cases it is limited by generic considerations—the allegorical and iconographical demands of the Jonsonian masque, the Orphic darkness of Chapman's esoteric hymns. This is hardly sufficient evidence to establish the general influence of the manuals on Renaissance poetry.

Burton's allusions to the mythographers have similarly been cited as evidence for their widespread diffusion. He does indeed refer on occasion to Boccaccio, Conti, Giraldi, and Cartari, but he also alludes to older mythographers and iconographers, such as Philostratus and Phornutus [Cornutus], or lists them alongside authorities of a very different nature: Guicciardini, Ficino, Pomponazzi, Delrio, Weyer, and Cornelius Agrippa.[10] Burton was too omnivorous a reader, and too generous an annotator, for us to attach much weight to his passing references to the mythographers. Though his footnotes demonstrate that he had read the manuals, they do not permit us to draw any major conclusions about their general influence.

At this point one would like to add a word of warning. One is not contesting either the general or the specific influence of the manuals, but rather the type of evidence that has all too frequently been adduced in order to demonstrate or prove such influence. Scholars have tended, all too often, to interpret dubious or unrepresentative cases of specific influence as valid proof of general influence, or (conversely) to argue from general to specific indebtedness. Both types of influence can (one feels) be taken for granted; yet both are hard to demonstrate, and the evidence adduced for them is sometimes profoundly disturbing.

Thus far one has refrained, moreover, from drawing a sharp distinction between dictionaries and other types of compendia— mythographical manuals, emblem-books, iconologies, and the like. Though this distinction may be highly significant in other contexts. it can become misleading when applied to the Renaissance mythographical tradition. The boundary line between the dictionary and other forms of reference works has been fluid, not fixed; it has shifted constantly, and one does not wish to take up the complex question of riparian rights. The chief reason for avoiding a clearcut distinction, however, is that the same claims have been advanced for both genres. They share, not infrequently, the same subject matter; and they have been credited with the same type of influence on the same authors. Scholars have sometimes blurred the distinction between dictionaries and manuals in examining Renaissance mythological poetry, or else treated these categories more or less on a par, as rivals. So far as the transmission of classical myth is concerned, a sharp dichotomy between lexicographical and mythographical works would not be a functional distinction. We might well bear in mind, therefore, that convenient, though equivocal, category (still preserved in library catalogues)— Dictionaries and Encyclopaedias.

Recent scholarship on these references works has stressed their importance as intermediaries between classical mythology and

Renaissance poetry and painting. Controversy has centered largely on channels of transmission, on the secondary sources, medieval or Renaissance, that conditioned a writer's interpretation of his primary sources (the classics themselves) and sometimes served as a convenient substitute for them. For well over a half-century, scholars have demonstrated an increasing awareness of the specifically Renaissance context of the mythological themes so prominent in the literature and art of the period. Since Henry Green's pioneer researches into the influence of emblem-books on drama (nearly a century ago) both iconographers and literary scholars have achieved clearer insights into the complex nature of the "Renaissance Tradition" underlying the presentation and interpretation of classical mythology. The problem of Milton's, or Spenser's or Jonson's, indebtedness to the ancients is not, as we now realize, quite so simple as eighteenth- and nineteenth-century critics often believed. We owe, therefore, an incalculable debt to twentieth-century researches on Renaissance iconography and mythography.[11] Though this is not the place fully to assess their contribution, I should like to emphasize two points in particular that we owe especially to them: first the value of these manuals and lexicons for the reevaluation of earlier source studies; secondly, their usefulness as glosses on obscure or difficult passages in Renaissance poetry or art. As materials for source studies they have provided a significant, though limited, basis for "revisionist" views. Except in a few notable instances — such as Chapman's hymns and Jonson's masques — these manuals and dictionaries are chiefly useful to us as negative evidence, for refutation rather than confirmation, and for denial rather than assertion. By emphasizing specifically Renaissance channels of transmission, they may make us more skeptical of earlier studies which stressed classical sources at the expense of Renaissance contexts. They effectively challenge the methods and conclusions of nineteenth-century source-hunters, but (again with a few notable exceptions) they rarely enable us to ascertain specific indebtedness to specific sources. There is a world of difference between considering these reference works as possible sources and accepting them as actual sources. It is the difference between the skeptical and the gullible mythographer.

In the present state of source studies (which is far more complex than a half-century ago) the second approach would appear to be the more profitable of the two. The parallels we encounter in these reference books are primarily significant as analogues rather than as immediate sources. They represent a tradition that they themselves helped to diffuse and popularize. In emphasizing a poet's or painter's general indebtedness to a tradition we are on relatively safe ground. When we argue for his specific indebtedness to a particular passage in a particular work, on the other hand, we venture on more treacherous terrain.

A principal merit as well as a major danger of recent studies of the manuals and lexicons lies (it would seem) in their bearing on source studies. Nineteenth-century criticism often tended to stress primary sources at the expense of secondary materials; in investigating Milton's or Spenser's, Mantegna's or Correggio's indebtedness to the ancients it seemed sufficient to cite analogues in classical texts, without considering secondary channels of transmission or the various ways in which classical motifs had been sifted and combined, allegorized and moralized, transformed and perhaps deformed by medieval and Renaissance accretions. Despite its obvious limitations, however, this approach produced results that (with proper qualifications) are still valid today. Nor was its method quite so anachronistic as it may seem; its own classical bias tended to coincide with that of the Renaissance. In stressing primary sources rather than more recent channels of transmission, it fostered perhaps the very impression a Renaissance poet or painter would have liked to make. Finally, it is still a fairly reliable method as long as one recognizes its limitations. In many cases it is extremely difficult to identify immediate secondary sources with precision; to identify primary sources is sometimes less hazardous, provided one does not mistake these for immediate sources.

To this approach the recent emphasis on specifically Renaissance sources has been a healthy restorative, though not an infallible cure. To its credit, it succeeded in viewing Renaissance classicism in a distinctively Renaissance context. Cinquecento and seicento mythography (as it justly observed) was an eclectic and synthetic tradition, sometimes less faithful to the classics themselves than to the encyclopedic preoccupations of more barbarous ages. Collecting, organizing, and diffusing classical allusions and motifs, imposing upon pagan superstitions the categories of classical and Christian ethics or medieval science, Renaissance mythographers made these motifs readily available to poets, artists, and laymen in an intelligible and readily comprehensible form.

The importance of these manuals and lexicons, in the eyes of recent critics, can be summarized briefly as follows. First, they constitute possible sources for classical allusions or quotations that Renaissance authors conceivably encountered in the classics themselves but which they might, with equal or greater probability, have encountered in contemporary reference works. Secondly, in selecting and combining classical allusions on particular themes, these reference books encroached on the poet's own domain. They usurped, to a degree, the eclectic and synthetic prerogatives of the poetic imagination. (In some instances, Renaissance poets have been praised for achieving a synthesis that they probably owed to mythographers or lexicographers.) Thirdly, by moralizing and allegorizing classical motifs, these works further aided the poet or artist by suggesting the interpretation or application he might appropriately give them; here again they provided the spadework for the creative imagination. Finally, these reference works helped to create or diffuse a common stock of ideas and symbols that the poet or painter might share with his audience.

Though we are indebted to recent scholarship for emphasizing these functions, we must be cautious in applying them in specific instances. While there is no doubt of the important general influence of these reference books, it is still hard to demonstrate their particular influence on particular authors. Indeed several major scholars who have attempted this task acknowledge its difficulties, if not its dangers. "When we attempt to specify the precise role and influence of the manuals," Seznec observes, "it is difficult to find evidence. The books that everyone consults and keeps constantly at his elbow are never, or hardly ever, mentioned; by reason of their popularity, they soon become anonymous handbooks; no one quotes a dictionary." Starnes and Talbert similarly find it "extremely difficult" to demonstrate "indebtedness to the lexicons on the part of a writer who was continually reading the classics."[12]

A further reason has also been advanced for the apparent dearth of evidence. In an age that prized erudition in poetry and painting alike, perhaps the artist consciously concealed his dependence on secondary sources? "A writer or artist who wishes to display his erudition is not particularly eager," Seznec suggests, "to reveal the source of the learning that he has acquired with so little expenditure of time or energy: those who owe the most to Giraldi, Cartari, and Conti are *usually careful not to acknowledge* their indebtedness" (italics mine). Starnes and Talbert make similar charges in discussing E. K.'s gloss on Flora in Spenser's March Aeglogue: "Flora, the Goddesse of flowres, but indede (as saith Tacitus) a famous harlot . . . whom the Romans called not Andronica, but Flora."

On the basis of certain verbal parallels in this passage, Starnes and Talbert argue that E.K.'s "immediate source" was Cooper's *Thesaurus*. On this point they may well be correct. They are less convincing, however, when they attempt to explain away apparent discrepancies between Cooper's and E. K.'s accounts: "E. K.'s insertion of the parenthesis, 'as saith Tacitus,' and the name 'Andronica,' may [they declare] be designed to mislead, since there is no such comment in Tacitus and no Andronica notorious as a harlot."[13] Like Seznec, these critics resort to ethical rather than logical proof in order to explain away the paucity of reliable data. Like Seznec, they accuse the Renaissance author of consciously concealing his debt. If the evidence for his immediate sources seems insufficient, it is (they suggest) because the artist or writer has deliberately suppressed it.

Admittedly the Renaissance was the age of Machiavelli, but perhaps we have exaggerated Machiavelism in the arts. The Renaissance poet or painter was certainly capable of disingenuousness; but one suspects that this is not really the principal issue here. If we approach the problem of evidence in terms of its Renaissance context, the point at issue is actually the question of authority rather than the question of immediate sources. On questions of mythology, the highest authority clearly belonged to the ancients themselves; after all, they had made, transmitted, and "in part believed" the archaic myths. Whatever authority the moderns might possess in this field was clearly secondary to that of the ancients themselves. It is hardly surprising, therefore, that the Renaissance writer should have preferred to cite primary rather than secondary sources; the former were, in his opinion, the real and ultimate authority. In stating his authority for a Virgilian or an Ovidian detail he had encountered in some reliable manual or dictionary, he was surely justified in adding *"dixit Virgilius"* or *"legitur in Ovidio"* instead of *"apud Stephanum"* or *"dixit Comes."* One finds, in fact, little evidence that he deliberately concealed his debt to other moderns. When he does actually cite them, moreover, it is usually as authorities rather than as sources. Desiring to refer his reader to an extended and systematic discussion of a particular myth, to a detailed allegorical interpretation, or to a definitive iconological description, he may allude explicitly to Cartari or Conti or Ripa. In such cases he is not as a rule confessing a debt; he is adducing support for his own statements, and perhaps saving space by citing a standard reference work instead of printing an extended footnote. Where the authority of the ancients will not stretch, he appeals to modern authorities.

Our own approach, we should remember, is in large part anachronistic and, unless we bear this fact in mind, we are apt to misconstrue the intent and methods of Renaissance poets and their early commentators. In examining their use of mythological themes, we look for sources; they were, on the whole, concerned with authorities. For us, the significant question concerning a borrowed detail is its channel of transmission, its immediate derivation. For them, the significant point was its original provenance, its antiquity, its classical sanction.

In tending to think in terms of sources and influences rather than authorities and precedents, we are apt to create an artificial tension between the Renaissance reference books and the classical materials to which they refer. In mythography at least there is no real "quarrel of ancients and moderns." These Renaissance manuals and dictionaries were, after all, tools of classical scholarship; not surrogates for the classics, but guides to them. Bringing together in systematic form themes and motifs, fables and quotations that lay scattered and dispersed throughout the corpus of classical literature, they subjected these allusions to rational order and discipline. The manuals were, in short, mythology methodized. Far from being substitutes for direct knowledge of the classics, they were convenient instruments for the rhetorical or iconographic exploitation of classical learning. Like the topics of invention, the collections of *exempla*, the mnemonic tables and commonplace-books so dear to humanist educators, they served a practical end. They enabled orator, poet, and painter to draw at will on an organized, comprehensive body of classical learning — aiding invention, assisting memory, embellishing style. They did not represent learning for learning's sake so much as learning for the sake of communication. Ancillary to the spoken rhetoric of poetic discourse and the silent rhetoric of painting, they served the ends of verbal and visual persuasion. If we view these manuals primarily against the background of the Renaissance rhetorical tradition — as handbooks designed to assist composition and description; as guides for making the most effective practical use of classical materials rather than as rival or alternative sources — we shall not, in my opinion, be far wrong.

The Renaissance ideal of imitation, as Bolgar has justly observed, entailed not only close "analytical" study of classical texts, but also the preparation of rhetorical aids for composing in the classical manner: lists of idioms, proverbs, or *exempla* compiled under convenient headings or *topoi*. The "notebook and heading method" was advocated by numerous Continental educators — Guarino of Verona, Agricola, Vives, Erasmus — and later by British School-masters Brinsley and Hoole. Many of the standard reference works — florilegia, compendia of proverbs and epithets, and dictionaries — were in fact to serve essentially the same functions as the more primitive phrase-lists and commonplace-books kept by schoolboys. Erasmus's *Copia verborum* and *Copia rerum* were a direct outgrowth of the "methodical" and "historical" notebooks of Guarino's school. [14]

As an instrument of persuasion, mythology too might serve rhetorical ends. Cartari's work was expressly designed to provide "inventions" — arguments, topics, and themes — for artists and poets. Allegorized myths could easily serve as *exempla* of virtues and vices; they could be readily adapted to deliberative or demonstrative rhetoric, to exhortation or dehortation, encomium or diatribe. Iconographic details, meticulously moralized, were in themselves rhetorical arguments. Extensive quotations from the classics in many of the manuals assisted "imitation" in diction as well as in imagery and in allegorical symbolism.

The statements of Renaissance schoolmasters concerning the value of these reference manuals in training the student to imitate the ancients offer, it would seem, little warrant for the current tendency to treat the Renaissance compilations as rivals of the classics themselves and to weigh the relative claims of lexicons and manuals as alternative sources. The student was generally expected to use these works more or less simultaneously, reading the classical texts with the aid of commentaries, lexicons, and mythographies and drawing therefrom examples and topics, images and idioms to be exploited in his own Latin prose or verse. Hoole directs the student to a variety of sources: aids to versifying (Textor, Buchler, Henrich Smet); mythographical manuals or annotations (Conti, Cartari, Ross, Bacon, and Sandy's translation and commentary on Ovid); and of course the classics themselves ("the best means of arriving at excellence in poetry").[15]

While recent scholarship has effectively cast doubt on some of the older types of source study, it has not, on the whole, succeeded in displacing them. If eighteenth- and nineteenth-century critics sometimes exaggerated a poet's direct debt to the classics, recent scholars frequently show an equal tendency to underestimate his knowledge of, and reliance on, classical authors. Brandishing Ockham's razor with the zeal of a Demon Barber, several of the new mythographers boldly excise the primary sources, or many of them, as "unnecessary principles." Since so much that Milton allegedly derived from Virgil and Horace and Seneca was already conveniently at hand in Conti, the law of parsimony would, they suggest, designate the *Mythologia* as his immediate source. That this sort of argument has been turned against its advocates is merely poetic justice. For Starnes and Talbert, as we have seen, the manuals themselves would appear to be, in certain notable cases, unnecessary principles. Instead of consulting the chief Italian mythographers—Conti, Cartari, Giraldi—English poets could have found the material they needed much closer at hand in their own language, in the lexicons of Elyot and Cooper and Thomas.

To establish a probable case for the general influence of the manuals has not been difficult; in spite of the shaky evidence sometimes adduced for such influence, bibliographical evidence alone indicates their widespread diffusion on the Continent and in England. To prove their specific influence, on the other hand, has been much more difficult, except in the cases of writers like Chapman and Jonson, who sometimes acknowledged their debt. The new mythography has successfully challenged earlier efforts to trace specific debts to the ancients, but it has not, on the whole, succeeded in demonstrating specific debts to the moderns.[16] In some instances it has resorted to circular arguments. (The specific influence of the manuals in the case of Jonson and Chapman demonstrates their general influence; their general influence, in turn, is a cogent argument for their specific influence on other writers.) All too frequently, moreover, scholars have weakened their case by mixing solid and dubious evidence, piling doubtful examples on sound ones, like Pelion on Ossa, and overwhelming the "skeptical reader" by sheer volume and quantity of parallels.

The problem of sources has, in fact, become far more complex during the last half-century. Examination of the manuals forced reappraisal of previous source studies oriented primarily towards the classics. Scholarship on the lexicons and dictionaries, in turn, led to reevaluation of the role of the manuals. And perhaps more intensive study of other types of reference works—emblem-books, florilegia, hieroglyphics, and natural histories—may compel us to reappraise the role of the dictionaries themselves.

Patterns of influence are clearest, perhaps, among works of the same genre. The scholar can demonstrate with reasonable certitude Giraldi's influence on Conti, Valeriano's impact on Cartari, Stephanus's debt to Calepine and Torrentinus or his influence on English lexicographers. Arguments for the influence of one dictionary on another are usually far more successful than attempts to identify lexicographical elements in Renaissance literature. While Professor Starnes's brilliant studies of the English lexicographical tradition have placed us permanently in his debt, attempts to treat the dictionaries as sources of particular passages or motifs in literary works are far less convincing.[17] One is reluctant to attach much weight to parallels like Spenser's "Lybicke ocean" and Stephanus's "mari Libyco" or to such familiar commonplaces as the twinship of Castor and Pollux, the pride of Tarquinius Superbus, the Minotaur's association with the Cretan Labyrinth, or "the voluptuousness or lustfulness of the sirens." Nor is one able to find the analogy between Shakespeare's poem and Cooper's reference to "the noble and chaste matron Lucrece [quite] so significant" as recent scholars regard it. "Cooper's concise summary," they suggest, "could indeed have served as an outline, which the poet filled in with suggestions from various other sources and with his own invention." For "in the first sentence of the dictionary account Cooper presents Lucrece as a model of Chastity; so in the first stanza of his poem Shakespeare refers to 'Lucrece the chaste.' . . . Chastity indeed, as emphasized in the preliminary argument and as the leitmotif of the whole poem, may well have been inspired by the initial statement of the Lucretia sketch."[18]

This type of source-hunting—utilizing commonplaces as evidence of direct borrowing, and alleged borrowing as evidence for a poet's method of composition—constitutes, one feels, a grave danger in the lexicographical approach to literary studies. The authors achieve less sensational, but more significant results when they stress "the value of the dictionaries and other current reference works in an explanatory and illustrative capacity," utilizing them less as probable sources than as representative glosses for annotating "important passages" in sixteenth and seventeenth-century poetry.[19]

If patterns of indebtedness are clearer within the strictly lexicographical tradition than within the broader literary tradition, they are also, on the whole, easier to trace in prose than in verse. The poet does not necessarily attempt to achieve literary fidelity to his sources; selecting and altering his material, he paraphrases it in accordance with narrative or metrical demands. He amplifies or diminishes his borrowings, with the license rhetoric has traditionally afforded him, altering and embellishing them with schemes and tropes. One cannot always rely on verbal parallels, therefore, to establish a poet's sources or the extent of his indebtedness to them.

Indeed, in tracing the influence of the manuals and lexicons on Renaissance poetry, modern scholars have been compelled to draw much of their more reliable evidence not from the poetry itself but from marginal glosses and commentaries. In Muret's commentary on Ronsard, Goulart's commentary on DuBartas's *Sepmaine,* Chapman's notes on his own nocturnal hymns, and Jonson's annotations to his own masques, the influence of the manuals is more easily demonstrated than in the poetry itself. Even in these cases, however, the source-hunter is sometimes largely dependent on the charity of the early commentators. Without the lead they had given him, by occasionally identifying one or more of their sources, his task would have been far more difficult.

The evidence concerning the influence of the manuals sometimes raises far more questions than it answers. What are we to make, for instance, of the striking parallels between Vasari's and Cartari's descriptions of the goddess Ops? Iconologists have noted their point-by-point resemblances both in iconographical details and in allegorical interpretations. "Even if we did not have [Vasari's] *Ragionamenti,*" Seznec comments, "Cartari's text would apply perfectly to [Vasari's] Palazzo Vecchio goddess, and would account for her slightest attribute." Nevertheless, as Seznec himself observes, this parallel presents certain difficulties. Though Cartari's *Imagini* was published in 1556 — two years before the completion of Vasari's frescoes — the "painting of the Camera di Opi was begun before the first publication of the book."[20] As Seznec justly observes, "no final conclusions as to the influence of the *Imagini* can be drawn from this parallel." Instead we are confronted with a confusing multiplicity of hypothetical alternatives. Had Vasari seen part of the *Imagini* in manuscript? Had he and Cartari consulted a common source or enlisted the aid of the same humanistic authorities? (Other authors sought iconographical information from contemporary scholars, and we know that Vasari relied heavily on letters from Cosimo Bartoli.) Or did Vasari rely on other sources for his painting of Ops and afterwards turn to Cartari for aid in compiling his commentary? If the last alternative seems at all probable, one wonders how many other Renaissance poets or painters may have followed a similar procedure — relying on the mythographers more heavily in writing the commentary than in composing the actual poem or picture. We cannot always accept an allusion in a footnote as the actual source of the poet's verses; and we should be especially cautious when the commentary has been written by another author, eager to display the poet's erudition — and his own.

To conclude, the chief weaknesses of recent scholarship in this area are (it would seem) threefold. First, an overemphasis on sources. These are usually hard to establish, since the parallels adduced frequently involve commonplaces. Secondly, the tendency to create an artificial dichotomy between primary and secondary materials, classical and Renaissance works. These were, on the whole, interdependent and were, in fact, usually studied together. Thirdly, the tendency, apparent in at least one standard work on this subject, to draw an arbitrary distinction between the lexicons and dictionaries, on the one hand, and the mythographical manuals and related types of reference works, on the other. It would be wiser and more fruitful, one feels, to avoid such sharp distinctions between lexicographical and mythographical works or between classical and Renaissance materials, and to subordinate the quest for specific sources, whether primary or secondary, to the elucidation of contemporary commonplaces. Rightly handled, the dictionaries and manuals can be useful aids for the literary scholar. But they are not precision tools, and to employ them effectively he must be aware of their limitations. In the hands of the source-hunter they are especially dangerous and, like other hunters, he is apt to be injured by his own weapons.

But surely the open season on sources is long past. The bounties are negligible, and the trophies themselves sometimes a greater tribute to the taxidermist's art — his skill in stuffing and padding — than to the hunter's expertise.

Paradoxically, the very factors that make these reference works dangerous tools for the source-hunter can make them useful instruments for the explicator. As collections of commonplaces (and I use the term in its rhetorical sense) they assisted the Renaissance poet and artist; perhaps it is in this respect, moreover, that they may prove most helpful to the modern scholar. Though we should not deny their potential yet limited value for source studies, they are primarily useful to us as representative statements of a tradition. Men of the Renaissance employed them as sources of "inventions": we may employ them as glosses.

PART TWO

CHAUCER AND MEDIEVAL TRADITION

CHAPTER III

"The House of Fame:" The Eagle as Contemplative Symbol

THE SIGNIFICANCE and literary antecedents of the garrulous bird which seizes Chaucer "at a swappe" and bears him aloft "to a place, Which that hight THE. HOUS OF FAME" have long been subjects of controversy. Garrett identified him with "the eagle of folk-tales who carries the hero to a high mountain."[1] Rambeau regarded him as "ein symbol der philosophie, aber einer sehr humoristischen art von philosophie, die ihn tröstet und mit seinem loos versöhnt."[2] In Sypherd's opinion, the eagle combined "three functions — 1. the messenger of a divinity; 2. the guide to a hero on his journey; 3. the helpful animal" (p. 86). Whereas Lounsbury[3] stressed the influence of Ovid's account of Ganymede, both Rambeau and Chiarini[4] emphasized Chaucer's indebtedness to the eagle of Dante's *Commedia*.

Both Chaucer and Dante explicitly allude to the Ganymede myth, which had been subjected to extensive allegorical analysis by medieval exegetes. In commentaries on Ovid's *Metamorphoses* and on the *Eclogue of Theodulus,* Chaucer could have encountered the widespread medieval tradition which conceived the eagle as a symbol for contemplation. Though primarily based on the writings of Saint Gregory the Great, this interpretation also found expression in early commentaries on Dante's *Commedia.* It could have reached Chaucer, accordingly, through a variety of sources — mythography, natural history, poetic exegesis, and Scriptural exposition. Despite their diverse contexts, these commentaries often exhibit cross-influences and advance similar interpretations. They are, on the whole, different strands in a unified exegetical tradition.

I

As *The House of Fame* belongs to "the literary type which describes an intellectual or mental flight,"[5] it may be helpful to re-examine Chaucer's aerial guide in the light of medieval expositions of the soaring eagle as an image of the flight of thought. The tradition emphasized two primary characteristics of the species — its keen vision and the altitude of its flight. Like Isidore of Seville, many medieval commentators derived the name *aquila* from the eagle's acute sight,[6] and repeated three widespread legends[7] about its remarkable powers of vision: 1) that, soaring beyond the range of human sight, it could nevertheless distinguish fishes swimming in the sea; 2) that it could gaze on the sun without blinking; and 3) that it tested its offspring by exposing them to the rays of the sun:

> Aquila ab acumine oculorum vocata. Tanti enim contuitus esse dicitur, ut cum super maria inmobili pinna feratur nec humanis pateat obtutibus, de tanta sublimitate pisciculos natare videat, ac tormenti instar descendens raptam praedam pinnis ad litus per-trahat. Nam et contra radium solis fertur obtutum non flectere; unde et pullos suos ungue suspensos radiis solis obicit, et quos viderit inmobilem tenere aciem, ut dignos genere conservat; si quos vero inflectere obtutum, quasi degeneres abicit.[8]

All three of these traits were frequently allegorized in terms of contemplation.

The most significant influence on the tradition of the eagle as an intellectual symbol was Gregory's exegesis of several Biblical texts — Job ix.26 ("sicut aquila volans ad escam"); Job xxxix. 27-29

("Numquid ad praeceptum tuum elevabitur aquila, et in arduis ponet nidum suum? . . . Inde contemplatur escam, et de longe oculi ejus prospiciunt"); Isaiah xl.31 ("assument pennas sicut aquilae"); Ezekiel i.10 ("et facies aquilae desuper ipsorum quatuor"); Apocalypse iv.7 ("et quartum animal simile aquilae volanti"). Like the eagle of Job ix.26, the ancient fathers had raised their thoughts to the contemplation of the Creator's light, but had lowered their eyes to the earth to contemplate His future incarnation. Similarly the righteous man elevates his mind to contemplate the divinity of Christ but descends like the eagle to consider the grace of dispensation through his flesh.

> Moris quippe est aquila ut irreverberata acie radios solis aspiciat; sed cum refectionis indigentia urgetur, eamdem oculorum aciem, quam radiis solis infixerat, ad respectum cadaveris inclinat; et quamvis ad alta evolet, pro sumendis tamen carnibus terram petit. Sic videlicet, sic antiqui patres fuerunt, qui in quantum humanitatis infirmitas admittebat, Creatoris lucem erecta mente contemplati sunt; sed incarnandum hunc in mundi fine praescientes, quasi a solis radiis ad terram oculos deflexerunt . . . Sublevata ergo in divinitatem mens justi, cum dispensationis gratiam ex ejus carne considerat, quasi a summis repente, ut aquila ad escam volat.[9]

Again, the eagle's flight resembled the "height of reason" in mankind before the Fall: "Sic sic humanum genus in parente primo ad ima de sublimibus corruit, quod nimirum conditionis suae dignitas in rationis celsitudine quasi in aeris libertate suspenderat. . . ."[10]

Interpreting Isaiah xl.31 as a reference to the constancy of the righteous ("justorum constantiam"), Gregory explained the promise that the just should "mount up with wings as eagles" specifically in terms of a contemplative flight: "Assumunt autem pennas ut aquilae, quia contemplando volant."[11] In Job xxxix.27 the eagle represented "the subtle understanding of the Saints" and their lofty contemplation. As the eagle "mounts up" at God's command, the life of the faithful conforms to the divine precepts and is consecrated to heavenly things. As the eagle builds its nest on high, they despise earthly desires and draw their nourishment from hope of celestial rewards instead of building the habitation of their minds in low and abject conversation. Thus Ezekiel had employed the eagle-symbol to designate John the Evangelist, "who left the earth in his flight, because, through his subtle understanding, he penetrated, by beholding the Word, inward mysteries": [12]

> Aquilae vocabulo . . . subtilis sanctorum intelligentia . . . exprimitur. Unde . . . quartum procul dubio animal Joannem per aquilam designans, qui volando terram deseruit, quia per subtilem intelligentiam interna mysteria Verbum videndo penetravit.

> Sed hoc loco aquilae nomine subtilis sanctorum intelligentia et sublimis eorum contemplatio figuratur. Cunctarum quippe avium visum acies aquilae superat, ita ut solis radius fixos in se ejus oculos nulla lucis suae coruscatione reverberans claudat. Ad praeceptum ergo Dei elevatur aquila, dum jussionibus divinis obtemperans, in supernis suspenditur fidelium vita. Quae et in arduis nidum ponere dicitur, quia desideria terrena despiciens, spe jam de coelestibus nutritur. In arduis nidum ponit, quia habitationem mentis suae in abjecta et infima conversatione non construit. [13]

Gregory's comparison of the eagle's flight to the act of contemplation reappeared in numerous subsequent writers. According to Isidore of Seville, the saints sometimes turn from contemplation to the active life just as the eagle diverts its gaze from the sun in search of food: "Sicut aquilae moris est semper oculum in radium solis infigere, nec deflectere, nisi escae solius obtentu, ita et sancti a contemplatione ad actualem vitam interdum reflectuuntur. . . . "[14] Rabanus Maurus compared the eagle to the human soul exalted through contemplation; as the eagle builds its nest on high, the soul is elevated by contemplation and fixes its desire in the heavens: "*Aquila* animam significat, ut in Job: 'Elevabitur aquila, et ponet in arduis nidum suum,' [Job xxxix.30] quod per contemplationem exaltatur anima, et in coelis defigit desiderium suum."[15] Hugh of St. Victor presented this symbol in a pejorative, as well as in a favorable, light. On the one hand, it referred to those who forsake the earthly and seek the celestial through contemplation ("qui haec terrena mente deserunt, velut aquila cum Joanne per contemplationem coelestia quaerunt"). [16] On the other hand, Obadiah i.4 ("Si exaltatus fueris ut aquila, et si inter sidera posueris nidum tuum") could be applied to sophists and philosophers; after fixing their gaze on the ray of truth, they revert to the darkness of error: "ALLEG. Sophistae vero, et philosophi ut aquila. Aquilae nempe juxta aliquid visi sunt philosophi et sophisti, dum cordis oculos ad solem justitiae erigunt, dum aciem mentis in ipsum veritatis radium irreverberate figunt. Sed aquila inde statim retrahitur; quia post acceptam veritatis insitam notitiam, elationis merito philosophus et sophista ad errorum caliginem revertuntur."[17]

Alexander Neckam, comparing "aquila . . . alta petens" to "nos arcanas rerum sublimitates perscrutantes," declared that in exposing its young to the rays of the sun the eagle resembles "viros contemplativos in lucis aeternae gloriam oculos considerationis et devotionis figentes." Particularly interesting, however, in view of recent interpretations of Chaucer's bird as "ein Symbol der Philosophie," is Neckam's statement that the eagle may signify Philosophy because of its keen sight. Like the eagle, Philosophy despises those who refuse to turn their minds towards lofty subtleties, but acknowledges as her own those who penetrate the secrets of reality by contemplation: "Philosophia etiam, quae aquilae nomine designari potest, tam propter aciem luminum, quam propter multas sui proprietates commendatione dignas, eos reputat contemptibiles, qui in arduas rerum subtilitates mentis oculos dirigere nequeunt. Illos vero suos esse gloriatur, qui rerum arcana subtili penetrant intuitu."[18]

Berchorius' *Reductorium Morale super Totam Bibliam* explained the "facies aquilae" of Ezekiel's vision of the four cherubim (Ezekiel i.10) as prudence: "Aquila vero qui visum habet clarissimum, significat prudentiam."[19] Similarly, his chapter *"De Aquila"* in the *Reductorium Morale* allegorized the eagle's sharp vision as intellectual acumen. Just as the sea-eagle possesses such clear sight that even in its loftiest flight it can discern fishes in the sea, so the prelate should be able to remain on the height of contemplation and yet behold with the clear sight of discretion whatever exists in the sea of this world. Again, just as the eagle perceives its prey from on high and immediately returns to the skies after seizing it, so the prelate needs clear discretion and knowledge in order to discern from afar whatever occurs among his subordinates. If necessary affairs compel him to descend to earthly matters, he should return immediately to the height of contemplation:

> Item est quaedam species aquilae, quae quando altissime volat, talem tamen & tam lympidum habet visum quod in mari videt pisciculos natare . . . secundum Plinium libro .10. ubi istam

aquilam vocat halietum, quam dicit esse quandam specie aquilarum. Sic vere licet praelatus & in altitudinem contemplationis commoretur, tamen lympitudine visus discretionis debet videre & considerare quid sit in mari mundi . . . unde de aquila dicitur Job.39. De longe contemplatur escam.

Item secundum Gregorium in moralibus. Aquila necessario indiget aculo [sic] visu, ut praedam suam a longe videat, quia scilicet super remanet in locis altissimis, & tutissimis, & si pro praedam ad terram descenderit, parum ibi remanet, imo superius cito se extollit, secundum Gregor. Sic vere praelatus indiget discretione & scientia lympida & discreta, ut a longe videat & cognoscat quicquid sit inter subditos faciendum [.] Esai.33. Oculi eius cernent terram de longe. Et semper debet in virtutum vel contemplationis celsitudine conversari, & si pro necessarijs negotijs ad terrena descenderit, debet statim sursum ad contemplationis apicem elevari. Job.39. Elevabitur aquila, & in arduis ponet nidum suum.[20]

According to the *Repertorium Morale,* the perfect man should imitate the eagle's high flight and clear vision—soaring through contemplation, persevering without weariness, and seeing clearly through discretion: "Volat nam sine fatigatione diutissime, videt sine obscuritate clarissime . . . . Sic . . . nos debemus . . . alte volare per contemplationem, & hoc infatigabiliter per perseverantiae durationem, clare videre per discretionem . . . ."[21]

Both Chaucer and Dante could draw on a well-established tradition which conceived the eagle as a symbol of contemplation.[22]

II

Despite the controversy over the extent of Dantesque influence in *The Hous of Fame,* comparatively little attention has been devoted to the earlier commentaries on the *Commedia.* These have, however, a significant bearing on the problem, both because they may have contributed to Chaucer's understanding of the *Commedia* and because they represent a further development of the conception of the eagle as a contemplative symbol.

In Canto ix of the *Purgatorio* Dante expressed the same spiritual event through two different allegories—his flight with the golden eagle and his ascent with Lucia. The poet dreams that an eagle with feathers of gold swoops down from the skies, seizes him in its talons, and bears him upwards to the sphere of fire:

> in sogno me parea veder sospesa
> un' aquila nel ciel con penne d' oro
> con l' ali aperte, ed a calare intesa.

> Ed esser mi parea là dove foro
> abbandonati i suoi da Ganimede,
> quando fu ratto al summo consistoro . . .

> Poi mi parea che, roteata un poco,
> terribil come folgor discendesse,
> e me rapisse suso infino al foco.

Upon waking, he learns that a lady called Lucia has carried him to the entrance of Purgatory in his sleep. According to Jacopo della Lana, both Lucia and the eagle represented the intellect:

> Qui l'autore vide un' aquila condizionata come appare nel testo per la quale elli figura il suo intelletto esser abile e disposto ad ascendere; la quale aquila, sicome elli recita nel processo del presente capitolo, elli pone essere quella Lucìa, di che fu fatto menzione nel secondo capitolo dello Inferno.[23]

> . . . elli ascese suso per lo monte alla porta del Purgatorio per essere portato da Lucìa, cioè dal suo intelletto chiaro e nobile, la qual possenza elli nella presente Comedia appellava Lucia. (Ibid., p. 98)

Pietro Alighieri likewise recognized that the two symbols have the same allegorical referent. In his opinion, both represented the science of mathematics, which (comprising geometry, arithmetic, music, and astronomy) was called Lucia "propter lucem siderum et coelorum, de quibus tractat."[24]

> Modo ad figuram hujus aquilae et Luciae veniamus. Et dupliciter potest figura colligi . . . ut figuraret partem illam philosophiae, quae dicitur mathematica, pro ista Lucia, ut aquila, quae habet nos elevare ad ea quae in imaginatione sunt, ut sic nunc auctor elevaretur per eam ad ingressum Purgatorii, idest ad principium actonis virtuosae et moralitatis. (pp. 357-358)

Although, unlike Chaucer's fowl, the golden eagle of the *Purgatorio* remains silent, a parallel to the loquacious bird of *The Hous of Fame* has been noted in *Paradiso,* Canto xix.[25] Moreover,

comparison of the two passages reveals a certain similarity between
Chaucer's method and Dante's. The poet is not only confronted, in
either instance, with a speaking eagle. In both cases he gives expression to an intellectual doubt, which the bird immediately
answers with considerable erudition and detail. In its summary of
Canto xix, *L'Ottimo Commento* calls attention to Dante's method
in words which could apply almost as well to the dialogue of Book II
of *The Hous of Fame:* " . . . nella prima parte introduce a parlare
la detta aquila . . . nella seconda propone uno dubbio senza
palesarlo; nella terza il solve. . . . "[26] The problems, however, are
distinctly different. In Dante's case the issue is "se senza battesimo e
fede cristiana si puo salvare."[27] In Chaucer's instance, the difficulty
is simply the apparent impossibility that Fame "shulde here al this."

Medieval interpretations of the myth of Ganymede also treated
the eagle as a contemplative symbol. Berchorius' *Ovidius
Moralizatus* explained it as the subtlety and clarity of intellect which
enabled John the Evangelist to speak of heavenly matters:
"Ganimedes phrygius . . . intantum a Jove dilectus fuit quod ab
ipso mutato in aquilam fuit raptus. . . . Ista aquila significat
limpitudinem sicut ganimedes significat Joannem evangelistam
iuvenem & gratiosum: quia scilicet aquila .i. subtilitas & claritas
sicut ipsum rapuit in celum in quantum ipsum loqui de celestibus
alte fecit."[28] The mythological commentary preceding Berchorius'
exposition of Ovid allegorized Jove's eagle as the prudent councillors
whose instruction elevates the simple to the contemplation of
celestial things: "Aquile que clare vident .i. viri discreti prudentes
& astuti debent talibus assistere qui scientia & doctrina pueros .i.
simplices ad amorem .i. ad contemplationem celestium elevant.
Prelatos enim et principes decet tales consiliarios habere et
familiares qui more aquile possunt pueros .i. simplices sursum
rapere & a carnalibus verbo et exemplo ad celestia elevare. Job.
xxxix. Nunquid ad preceptum tuum elevabitur aquila?"[29]

Chaucer's near-contemporary, Odo of Picardy,[30] explained this
myth in practically identical terms. Eagles should be interpreted as
prudent men, who ought to raise their simple subordinates through
contemplation from the depth of vice to the height of virtue. The
eagle also represents the clarity of wisdom (*limpitudinem sapientiae*), and Ganymede symbolizes John the Evangelist; an aquiline
contemplation raised him to heaven, inasmuch as he spoke
profoundly of celestial matters:

. . . per aliquilas [sic] intelliguntur viri prudentes, discreti, clari et viventes per prudentiam qui debent pueros .i. simplices subditos sursum erigere per contemplationem exeundo a profundo vitiorum ad altitudinem virtutum.[31]

Preter ista dicitur aliter quod aquila significat impetudinem[32] [sic] sapientie. ganimedes significat evangelistam iohannem . . . graciosum. quia aquilina sublimitas, claritas vel contemplatio ipsum in celum rapuit. inquantum locutus est profunde de celestibus.[33]

III

Thus interpretations of the eagle as a contemplative symbol had ranged from the spiritual to the secular. Originally allegorized as the "subtle understanding of the Saints," it had also been explained as the intellect, as Philosophy in general, or (more narrowly) as a single branch of philosophy—mathematics.[34] Chaucer's vehicle on his astral journey was a conventional symbol for the flight of thought.

The character of Chaucer's eagle is thoroughly in keeping with its traditional significance. A symbol of celestial contemplation, it speaks with authority on heavenly phenomena. Allegorized as Philosophy and Mathematics, it displays an appropriate knowledge of physics (natural philosophy) and its subdivision, astronomy. In allocating to an eagle's beak discourses on the stars and on the nature of sound, Chaucer aptly employed a conventional symbol of philosophy as his mouthpiece for philosophical material. Moreover, in discussing both of these subjects, the learned bird appeals to the authority of classical philosophers. After demonstrating that "every thing . . . Hath his propre mansioun, To which hit seketh to repaire," it cites the opinion of Aristotle and Plato:

> Lo, this sentence is knowen couthe
> Of every philosophres mouthe,
> As Aristotle and dan Platon,
> And other clerkes many oon . . .

Again, in pointing out "the eyrish bestes" it observes that

> . . . in this regioun, certein,
> Dwelleth many a citezein,
> Of which that speketh dan Plato.

Not only the eagle's role, but Chaucer's part as well had been anticipated by these medieval expositions of the eagle's flight. The poet depicts himself as a "lewed man"[35]—one of the "simplices" described by Berchorius—elevated by "scientia & doctrina . . . ad contemplationem celestium."

Though the significance of Chaucer's guide should have been apparent to those of his contemporaries who were familiar with the Gregorian interpretation of the eagle or with commentaries on Ovid, the *Ecloga Theoduli,* or (less probably) Dante's *Purgatorio,* the text provides an additional indication of its meaning through the quotation from Boethius:

> And tho thoughte I upon Boëce,
> That writ, "a thought may flee so hyë,
> With fethers of Philosophye,
> To passen everich element . . ."

Though identification of the eagle with Philosophy in this passage is implicit rather than explicit, such an inference is virtually unavoidable, for the poet explicitly compares his situation with that of the philosopher in *De Consolatione Philosophiae.* Looking "under me," Chaucer beholds "the eyrish bestes, Cloudes, mistes," etc., just as Boethius' philosopher sees "behind his bak, Cloud, and al that I of spak." This identification is further strengthened by the analogy between the "fetheres of Philosophye" and "the egles fetheres brighte" that shone "as of gold."

As Chaucer is alluding to the first Prose and Metre of Book IV of the *Consolation,*[36] it is instructive to examine other medieval interpretations of this passage. According to a ninth-century commentator, the feathers of philosophy are the subtle thoughts whereby man contemplates the heavens:

> Id est PENNAS. id est subtilissimas intelligentias vel alias contemplatione, TVAE MENTI AFFIGAM et apponam. . . .

> SUNT ETENIM PENNAE . . . Considerandum est quod gradatim dicit mentem cuncta prospicere: primum terras aerem nubes deinde aetherem planetas omnemque astronomiam postremo caelestia ipsiusque divinae maiestatis potentiam secundum aliquid contemplari dicit. PENNAE. id est alae . . . Philosophiae PENNAS. id est sensus acutissimos intelligentias subtiles, accipe quibus caelum scanditur. Dum divinam naturam rimatur philosophia caelum

conscendit. Bene dicit VELOX: nihil enim mente velocius (est) ad cogitanda profunda, quia citissime ad cogitationes diversae fertur.[37]

This conception of philosophy's feathers as "subtilissimas intelligentias" recalls Gregory's explanation of the eagle as "subtilis . . . intelligentia."

Chaucer's echo of Boethius' *Consolation* thus serves to underline the speculative significance of his eagle. Fusing two familiar symbols of contemplation—Boethius' *pennae* and the *aquila* of medieval tradition—he emphasizes the purely intellectual character of his journey, the fact that his aerial visit is essentially a flight of thought. It is fitting that this "Symbol der Philosophie" should wear the "fetheres of Philosophye."

CHAPTER IV

"The Nun's Priest's Tale": Flattery and the Moralitas of the Beast

LIKE ITS remote ancestor—the tale of fox and crow—the mediaeval story of cock and fox hinges almost entirely on flattery. In the classical fable the crow drops its morsel of food to the fox, who has declared that it would be "the first among birds if only it could sing." The Nonne Preestes Tale contains a "framework of two similar tricks: (i) The Fox flatters the Cock into singing with eyes shut, so that he is caught; and (ii) the Cock flatters his captor into shouting back at the pursuers, and escapes as the Fox opens his mouth."[1]

Though flattery is an underlying motif in practically all versions of the latter story, it is usually implicit rather than explicit. Rarely does the narrator issue a direct warning against the peril of trusting the flatterer. Instead, the two principal characters comment separately on the folly of speaking when one should remain silent and the foolishness of closing one's eyes when one should remain on guard.[2]

Chaucer's story differs from most versions of this tale in its explicit, reiterated warning against flattery. At the crucial moment when Chauntecleer is "ravisshed" with the fox's "flaterye," the priest interrupts the narrative to emphasize the appropriate moral—to warn his audience against the "fals flatour" and "losengeour" and to introduce a reference to "Ecclesiaste of flaterye."

Again, after narrowly escaping the penalty of his gullibility, the cock himself draws the correct inference from his experience:

> Thou shalt na-more, thurgh thy flaterye,
> Do me to singe and winke with myn yë.

Finally, the narrator himself points out the twofold "moralitee":

> Lo, swich it is for to be recchelees,
> And necligent, and truste on flaterye.

Though these explicit admonitions against flattery set the tale apart from most other versions of the fable of cock and fox, they can be paralleled to some extent in the fable of fox and crow. The opening lines of Phaedrus' "Vulpes et corvus" point out the danger of believing fraudulent praise:

> Qui se laudari gaudet verbis subdolis,
> Fere dat poenas turpi pænitentia.[3]

This warning recurs frequently in later versions of the fable—in the first or final lines or even in the title. In *Phaedrianae fabulae* the story is entitled "De his qui se laudari gaudent" and begins:

> Qui se laudare [sic] gaudet, sit sollicitus ad verba subtilia, ne postea peniteat.[4]

Romuli vulgaris fabulae gives it the heading "Qui se laudari gaudent verbis subdolis, decepti penitent; de quibus similis est fabula."[5] In Vincent of Beauvais' *Speculum Historiale* it opens with the same moral:

> Item contra illos qui laudati verbis subdolis gaudent et postea penitent, hanc fabulam fingit . . .[6]

The *Monachii Romuleae et extravagantes fabulae* gives it a similar beginning;[7] and in *Romuli Florentini fabulae* it bears the heading "Qui se laudari gaudent verbis subdolis, decepti penitent. De quibus similis est fabula."[8] *Romuli Vindobonensis fabulae* simply entitles it "Qui dolose laudatur decipitur."[9]

Several versions placed primary emphasis on vainglory. In

Gaulteri Anglici fabulae the *moralitas* of the fable warns against vainglory and false honour:

> Fellitum patitur risum, quem mellit inanis
> Gloria: vera parit tedia falsus honor.[10]

In *Gualteri Anglici fabularum subditiciae moralitates* it concludes with an additional admonition:

> Hoc faciunt stulti quos gloria vexat inanis:
> Insanire malos gloria magna facit.
> Qui nimis apparens cupit est inglorius ipse;
> Vertitur in storiam gloria dicta frequens.[11]

Vincent's *Speculum Historiale* includes it among "fabulis . . . moraliter fictis contra vane gloriosos, superbos, presumptuosos, contemptores."[12] Odo of Cheriton allegorizes it in terms of the devil's incitement to vainglory.[13] *Johannis de Schepeya fabulae* entitles it "De vana gloria."[14]

Other versions stress the deceitfulness of the *adulator*. *Romuli Anglici nonnullis exortae fabulae* links this theme of flattery with that of vainglory:

> Sic evenit frequenter glorie inanis cupidis, qui bona sua imprudenter dilapidant et amittunt, fictis adulancium laudibus delectati.[15]

In *Romuli Nilantii Fabulae* the story begins:

> Testatur subsequens fabula, quod multi in fine penitent qui falsis adulationibus facile assenciunt.[16]

In *De Naturis Rerum,* Neckam points out a double moral in the story—the folly of talking out of turn[17] and the danger of flattery. Adulation so blinds the mind that man forgets his own weakness.[18]

Admonitions against flattery and vainglory are also fairly common in French versions of the fable. In *Isopet II de Paris* the story ends with a warning against "faus losengiers":

> Qui croit quan que il ot,
> Il est musart et sot,
> Il est souvent dolant:
> Trop est de mençongiers
> Et de faus losengiers
> Pour decoivre la gent.[19]

The *Isopet de Lyon* warns against vainglory and false honour:

> Qu'en vainne gloire se delite,
> Essez trueve qui lo despite.
> Sovantes foiz lo cuer li lime.
> Faus ris cui malice envenime.
> Cil pert honour hontousemant,
> Qui la vuet avoir fausemant. [20]

Marie de France also interprets it as an example of pride's vulnerability to flattery:

> C'est essamples des orguillus
> Ki de grant pris sunt desirus:
> Par losengier e par mentir
> Les puet hum bien a gre servir;
> Le lur despendent folement
> Pur false losenge de gent. [21]

Thus, in mediaeval versions of the tale of fox and crow, the narrator commonly interprets the fable as an example of the vulnerability of the vainglorious man to fraudulent praise. [22] The conventional *moralitas* of this story—like that of The Nonne Preestes Tale—is a warning against trusting the flatterer.

In the fable of cock and fox, on the other hand, the narrator's *moralitas* is often little more than a restatement of the moral observations already made by the two principal characters. Adhemar's fable of fox and partridge concludes with the appropriate comment:

Qui, ubi eis necessarium non est, loquuntur, et ubi eos vigilare oportet, dormiunt. [23]

In the *Monachii Romuleae et extravagantes fabulae* the emphasis falls entirely on the fox's loquacity. The fable begins by stating this moral:

> Sunt homines multi, qui, non previdentes sua dicta, frequenter talia dicunt, unde postea docuntur in penitentiam et accipiunt dampna. Unde audi fabulam.

and ends with a similar warning:

> Sic multi homines, cum multa locuntur, dampnum non effugiunt. [24]

Significantly, in this version it is only the fox who acknowledges his own folly; the cock merely taunts his captor for allowing him to escape.

In the *Bernæ Romuleæ et diversæ fabulæ* the moral is the same
(*Docet non multum loqui*);[25] again, the fox alone admits his
mistake. In *Romuli Anglici cunctis exortæ fabulæ* both characters
blame their own heedlessness, but the *moralitas* is entirely
concerned with the fox's error of talking too much:

> *Moralitas.* Non est exigua res suo tempore loqui, et suo tempore
> reticere; mors enim et vita in manibus lingue sunt.[26]

In *Baldinis fabulæ* the story concludes with an admonition against
idle talk:

> Sic, deluduntur multi, dum vana loquuntur,
> Iure, satis culpis, patiendo simillima vulpis:
> Sepe volet tales deludere provides ales.[27]

In Marie de France's fable both animals moralize on their folly, but
the final lines simply condemn loquacity:

> Ceo funt li fol: tuit li plusur
> Parolent quant deivent cesser,
> Taisent, quant devreient parler.[28]

In *Le Roman de Renart* and *Reinhart Fuchs* the only moral comment on the episode occurs in the conventional remarks by cock and
fox on the folly of their own behaviour.[29]

On the other hand, the author of the Latin poem *Gallus et vulpes*
explicitly warns his audience against vainglory. Allegorizing the
cock as *doctores* of the church and the fox as the devil,[30] he compares the sinful clergyman to salt which has lost its flavour and
fallen *per inanem gloriam* into the jaws of Leviathan:

> Valemus hinc perpendere,
> Hos posse fatuescere,
> Ut per inanem gloriam
> In os ruant Leviathan.[31]

With its explicit, reiterated admonition against trusting in
flattery, the "moralitee" of The Nonne Preestes Tale reflects the
moralitas of the fable of fox and crow rather than the conventional
moral of the tale of fox and cock.[32] Deriving his story from the latter
tradition, Chaucer appears to have transferred to it the usual interpretation of the former. Since in both instances the trick hinges
on flattery, this cross-grafting does not affect the validity or
propriety of his moral; it is as appropriate to its foster-trunk as to its
parent stock. Similarly, the narrator's warning against recklessness

and negligence can also be paralleled in several analogues which emphasize the crow's imprudence and lack of foresight.[33]

In concluding his story with an explicit statement of its "moralitee" the Nun's Priest was observing a convention characteristic of the beast-fable, but usually lacking in the beast-epic. Normally the fable ended — or, less frequently, began — with a brief summary of its moral;[34] and in numerous instances this interpretation was expressed in a single couplet.[35] Several mediaeval fable-cycles,[36] furthermore, labelled this final section *Moralitas* or *La moralité*. The Nun's Priest's moral conforms to this pattern in its brevity (like several mediaeval fabulists he states his point in a single couplet), in its position at the end of the narrative, and in the narrator's explicit reference to "the moralitee."

The two lines in which Chaucer unhusks the "fruyt" of his story

Lo, swich it is for to be recchelees
And necligent, and truste on flaterye

represent essentially an indebtedness to the tradition of the beast-fable rather than (as Donovan suggested)[37] a reaffirmation of "the intent of the poem as a sermon."

***

Is the priest's allusion to "Ecclesiaste of flaterye" also a legacy of the beast-fable? In four fables, linked by the common theme of the danger of believing an enemy,[38] John de Sheppey had emphasized his moral by quoting an apposite text from Ecclesiasticus.

In Fable No. 65 ("Leo et unicornis") a lion persuades a unicorn to lend him his horn, but repays the gift by wounding the giver with his own weapon:

Unde, cum dicitur Ecclesiastico, xii [12, 10]: Non credas inimico in eternum. Semper, etsi humiliatus vadat et curvus, custodi te ab illo; quod satis hoc patet.

The same text is cited in Fable No. 69 ("Lupus, sus et porcelli"). In this tale, a sow persuades a hungry wolf to hear mass before devouring one of her litter. On the pretext of summoning a priest, she assembles all the hogs in the forest to harass her enemy:

Inde est quod dicitur Ecclesiastic, xii: Non credas inimico tuo in eternum. Et Joannes, iv: Nolite omni spiritui credere; sed probate spiritus, etc.

In Fable No. 67 ("Vulpes et gallus")[39] a fox persuades a reluctant cock to act as his confessor, then strangles him and carries him off to the forest:

> Ideo competenter dicitur Ecclesiastic., xi [11, 31]: Non omnem hominem inducas in domum tuam; multe enim sunt insidie dolosi.

The triumph of guile over gullibility also recurs in Fable No. 68 ("Oves et lupi"), where a pack of wolves, after persuading certain shepherds to surrender their dogs, proceeds to devour the flock:

> Et ideo dicitur Ecclesiastic., xxx [19,4]: Qui cito credit, levis est corde et minorabitur; quod hic patet.

In each of these tales, as in The Nonne Preestes Tale, there is a basic pattern of treacherous persuasion on the one hand and disastrous credulity on the other. The three texts from Ecclesiasticus, which indicate the moral of these fables, are equally applicable to Chauntecleer's predicament. Believing all too readily (*cito credit*) the persuasions of his natural enemy (*his contrarie*), he falls a victim to "insidiae dolosi".

Though attempts have been made to pinpoint Chaucer's reference — narrowing it to Ecclus. 12, 10; 11, 16; [40] to Ecclus, 27, 26; or to Prov. 29, 5[41] — in all likelihood he was alluding not to a single passage, but to a theme expressed in various texts cited above. Like John de Sheppey, he probably had Ecclus. 12, 10 in mind, but his allusion to the "trecherye" of the false flatterer "in your courtes" may echo the warning (Ecclus. 31) against the plots of the deceiver "in domum tuam." Moreover, it is quite conceivable that the allusion to "Ecclesiaste" was also intended to comprehend Ecclesiastes and Proverbs.[42] Though the texts usually cited by Chaucerians from Ecclesiasticus warn against deceit, none of them (with the possible exception of 27, 26) specifically concerns flattery. Admonitions against the flatterer are, however, relatively numerous in Proverbs — not only in 29, 5, but also in 6, 24; 7, 13; 7, 21; and 28, 23 ("ille qui per linguae blandimenta decipit"). Eccles. 7, 6 also refers explicitly to flattery ("Melius est a sapiente corripi, quam stultorum adulatione decipi").[43]

If the primary object of Chaucer's allusion was a group of texts in Ecclesiasticus, it may lend support to Donovan's conception of "Daun Russell as heretic."[44] Both the *Glossa Ordinaria* and Rabanus' *Commentaria in Ecclesiasticum,* to which "Strabus" was heavily indebted, explained several of the relevant texts on two levels. In one sense they referred to the dissimulating enemy, the false friend, or the traitor. Allegorically, however, they denoted the heretic. Thus Rabanus interpreted Ecclesiasticus 11, 31 as a warning against (1) the "simulata species" of "ignotos et alienos" and (2) the heretic—a wolf in sheep's clothing.[45] The same dual significance could be found in Ecclus. 12, 10,

> Praesens ergo capitulum licet juxta historiam de falsis amicis, hoc est, dolosis inimicis possit intelligi, qui nequaquam firmi sunt in fide et dilectïone, quibus utique non debet facile credi, sed magis a talibus convenit caveri; tamen altiori sensu denotat haereticos, quos et superius vituperavit. Illi enim veri inimici sunt, quorum doctrina plena est rubigine erroris et nequitiae. "Sermo enim illorum ut cancer serpit," et ideo non debet eis credi in aeternum, etiam si se humiliantes fingant esse fideles et catholicos: quibus in nulla parte debemus consentire, nec potestatem in nobis tribuere, quam significat dextera, ne forte nos a loco nostro, hoc est, a statu rectae fidei amoveant. Inquirunt enim cathedram nostram, hoc est doctrinam sua malitia student subvertere. Quibus quicunque consentit, aeterno dolore in gehenna ignis cruciabitur.[46]

CHAPTER V

"The Nun's Priest's Tale": Chauntecleer and Medieval Natural History

LIKE VIRGIL's "Culex," Chaucer's "Nonne Preestes Tale" secures its special effect—the mock-heroic—through deliberately exaggerating the disparity between content and style. For so commonplace an incident as a fox's raid on a hen-coop, so humble a setting as a barnyard, *personae* so insignificant as a cock and a hen, medieval poetic theory demanded an answerable style. Instead of the *stylus humilis,* however, Chaucer amplifies his base material with all the resources of the *stylus altus* or *gravis.*[1] Though he begins with the low style appropriate for his subject and returns to it briefly at a crucial moment to describe the pursuit of the fox, he usually employs the loftier style[2] suitable for persons of the courtly sphere and the subject matter of tragedy. It is this conscious disproportion between matter and manner, between the objects and the idiom of his description, which makes his tale "of a cok and hen" a comic masterpiece. His barnyard fowl—the lowest of *rurales*—speak, feel, and act like *curiales.*[3] They display the sentiments of courtly lovers, the erudition of prelates, the pride of kings.

Nevertheless, for all their "chere of court," Chauntecleer and Pertelote remain merely "a cok and hen" writ large. However "estatlich of manere" and "digne of reverence" they may appear, they represent a thoroughly conventional conception of domestic poultry. Though Chaucer exaggerates these attributes to the point of absurdity, they are nonetheless firmly grounded in medieval natural history. Chauntecleer's uxoriousness, regal pride, and choleric temperament are characteristic traits of *gallus domesticus*. Beneath Chaucer's ludicrously inflated portraits of the cock and his paramours there is a firm core of orthodox scientific doctrine. [4]

I

"Ye been ful colerik of compleccioun," [5] declares Pertelote, and advises her husband to purge himself "bothe of colere and of malencolye." Though her diagnosis—that the cause of his dream was "the grete superfluitee Of youre rede *colera*"—proves false, it nevertheless reflects the contemporary belief that the cock was by nature a choleric animal, hot and dry in complexion. According to Bartholomeus Anglicus, this was responsible for his belligerence: "Also the cocke is hotte and drye of complection. And therefore he is full bolde and hardy, and so fyghteth boldly for his wyves agaynste his adversaryes / and assayleth and reeseth on them, and teareth and woundeth theym with is *[sic]* byl & with his spores." [6]

St. Albertus found in the cock's choleric temperament an explanation for his regularity in crowing. According to medical theory (he explained) the movements of choler occur at intervals of three— at every third year, every third month, every third day, or every third hour. As a choleric animal, the cock is subject to the movements of choler at every third hour. At this time he sings most, because choler is produced in the gall-bladder and transmitted to the heart. [7]

In attributing Chauntecleer's dream to "fume" and "compleeciouns, Whan humours been to habundant in a wight," Pertelote demonstrates her familiarity not only with the theory of dreams but also with the physiology of *gallus domesticus*. In St.

Albertus' opinion, such "fumositates cholericae" were the reason
why the cock usually flapped his wings before crowing.[8] Moreover,
according to the same scholar, the hen is less choleric than her
mate, and this difference in complexion makes the voice of the male
more shrill than that of the female.[9]

Both the timbre of Chauntecleer's voice and the regularity of his
crowing depended largely on his choleric temperatment. It is,
therefore, quite understandable that he should resent Pertelote's
suggestion that he purge himself of excess choler by taking laxatives.
Aside from a natural dislike of unpleasant medicines—and a
natural resentment at being flatly contradicted and finding his
dignity as the special object of providential solicitude and prophetic
warning impugned—Chauntecleer runs the risk of marring both his
song and his valor. Moreover, as Pertelote herself was less hot and
dry in temperament than her husband, she might easily exaggerate
the extent of his "superfluitee" of choler. Even his normal state
might appear to her excessively choleric.

II

Chauntecleer's role as Venus' servant and courtly lover is also
distinctly in character. Aristotle[10] had described "the barn-door
cock" as "peculiarly salacious," and Bartholomeus emphasized his
generosity and devotion to his wives ("uxores suas"):[11]

> And he loveth iolousely [sic] his wives. And whan he findeth meate /
> he calleth his wyves to gether with a certaine voyce / & spareth his
> own meate to fede therwith his wives. And he setteth nexte to hym on
> the royste the henne that is mooste fatte and tender, and loveth her
> best, and desyreth mooste to have her presence. In the morowe tide,
> whan he fleeth to get his meate, fyrste he layeth his syde to her syde:
> and by certayne tokens & beckes, as hit were love tatches, he woweth
> & praieth her to tredynge. And he fyghteth for her specially, as
> thoughe he were Jelouse. And with bylle and spores he chaceth and
> dryveth away from hym other cockes, that come nyghe his wyves.
> The cocke he secheth his meate with his bylle and fete, and scrapeth
> and over torneth strawe and duste: And when he fyndeth a greyne /
> he calleth and cryeth to hym his hennes.

According to Vincent of Beauvais[12] and Conrad of Megenberg,[13]
the grief-stricken rooster refrains from song after the death of his

hens. Both of these writers called attention to the "gentle murmur" with which he invites his wives to partake of a grain of corn. Neckam[14] elevated the same behavior into an example of munificence, describing the cock himself as "munificent" and the grain of corn as a "noble grain."

The conventional barnyard cock of these accounts behaves, in fact, very much like the conventional courtly lover. He sues for his lady's favors, fights jealously for her, displays generous and considerate table manners, and mourns for her death. His jealousy in particular tends to invest him with the traditional character and passion of the lover. This was a conventional attribute of the *amant* in medieval and Renaissance literature and a characteristic feature of the lover's malady of *Hereos* as diagnosed by medieval and Renaissance physicians. It would subsequently drive Ariosto's hero mad, and subject Spenser's archetypal lover to the tortures of jealous solicitude in the house of Care. The domestic cock was (it would seem) no less a gallant and a cavalier than the featherless bipeds of a higher species. It is not surprising, therefore, that several details in Chaucer's description of Chauntecleer as a mock-chivalric or mock-heroic lover should bear so close a resemblance to Bartholomeus' description of the cock. Chauntecleer too "loveth iolousely [*sic*] his wives." He too singles out the most attractive of the hens as his special favorite, sets her beside him on his perch at night, and in the morning avows his love to her. Whether Dame Pertelote is the "mooste fatte and tender" of Chauntecleer's "paramours" Chaucer does not say; nevertheless she definitely excells the others in beauty ("the faireste hewed on hir throte"), and this gives her a special claim on her lord's affections:

> That trewely she hath the herte in hold
> Of Chauntecleer loken in every lith;
> He loved hir so, that wel was him therwith.

When the tale begins, she is appropriately seated beside Chauntecleer on his perch:

> As Chauntecleer among his wyves alle
> Sat on his perche, that was in the halle,
> And next him sat this faire Pertelote . . .

And when Chaucer's fowl declares to his favorite the "joye" and "solas" he experiences "whan I fele a-night your softe syde," he seems to be echoing Bartholomeus' account of *gallus domesticus* and his favorite hen ("fyrste he layeth his syde to her syde," etc.).

Again, Chauntecleer displays the cock's conventional generosity in sparing "his own meate to fede therewith his wives":

> And with a chuk he gan hem for to calle.
> For he had founde a corn, lay in the yerd.
> He chukketh, whan he hath a corn y-founde,
> And to him rennen thanne his wyves alle.

The barnyard cock, as Bartholomeus described him, is so close to the medieval conception of the courtly lover that Pertelote's dismay at Chauntecleer's confession of fear is hardly surprising. A cock emboldened by love and jealousy to "fyght for her specially" would have measured up to her ideal of the chivalric lover, but a paramour "aghast of swevenis" violates not only the essential principles of *l'amour courtois,* but also the basic traits of *gallus domesticus.* Chauntecleer's lapse from the courtly ideal proves, however, to be merely temporary; his love for his mistress dispells his dread, and he behaves like the "gentil cok" Bartholomeus had portrayed, devoted to his wives and proving himself "free . . . and no nigard" by reserving the "corn" he finds for the ladies.

III

"Thus royal, as a prince is in his halle," Chauntecleer "deyned not to sette his foot to grounde." This regal pride is likewise characteristic of his species. According to Pliny, the vanity of *gallus domesticus* nearly equalled that of the peacock. The foremost (*princeps*) exercised royal dominion over his companions, and even the common herd (*plebs*) flaunted its pride:

> Nearly equally proud and self-conscious are also our Roman night-watchmen, a breed designed by nature for the purpose of awakening mortals for their labours and interrupting sleep . . . They lord it over their own race, and exercise royal sway in whatever household they live. This sovereignty they win by duelling with one another, seeming to understand that weapons grow upon their legs for this purpose, and often the fight only ends when they die together. If they win the palm, they at once sing a song of victory and proclaim themselves the

champions . . . Yet even the common herd struts no less proudly, with uplifted neck and combs held high, and alone of birds casts frequent glances at the sky, also rearing its curved tail aloft. Consequently even the lion, the noblest of wild animals, is afraid of the cock.[15]

Berchorius likewise stressed its regal and warlike characteristics, comparing its crest to a crown[16] and developing in detail the analogy between the haughty barnyard cock and the arrogant soldier. Its spurs could be likened to the warrior's weapons, its comb to a helmet, its tail to a banner, its song to a military watch, and a cock-fight to a pitched battle.[17]

Moreover, certain fighting-cocks had, according to Pliny, won high honors for their countries:

> . . . some cocks are born solely for constant wars and battles — by which they have even conferred fame on their native places, Rhodes or Tanagra; the fighting cocks of Melos and Chalcidice have been awarded second honours — so that the Roman purple confers its high honour on a bird fully worthy of it.[18]

Bartholomeus had depicted the cock as fighting "boldly for his wyves agaynste his adversaryes," and Alexander Neckam[19] had described a cock-fight in terms appropriate for loftier conflicts, speaking of "dire battles," "Parthian tactics," and the "palm" of victory.

Gallus domesticus was, then, both king and soldier.[20] His royal eminence, his military valor, and his pride made him, in several respects, a barnyard epitome of the typical hero of epic and romance.[21] That such a conception should lend itself readily to caricature is hardly surprising. Pagan and Christian[22] had vied in eulogizing his voice and prowess, and the line of demarcation between Neckam's stilted diction and the burlesque exaltation of the cock is narrow indeed. Chaucer's mock-heroic treatment of Chauntecleer and his household was rooted not merely in the tradition of the beast-epic, but also in a conventional picture of the domestic cock as prince and warrior. It is this background which confers meaning on Pertelote's dismay at her lover's exhibition of fear ("I can nat love a coward, by my feith") and on the petty kingdom where Chauntecleer exercises royal "governaunce" over his hens: "Regimini plurium sufficit iste gallinarum. . . ."[23]

IV

In stressing Chauntecleer's choleric temperament, his royal jurisdiction and pride, and his uxorious disposition and fidelity to the principles of courtly love, Chaucer went beyond the narrow limits of the usual beast-fable and exploited the fresh source of humor afforded by medieval natural history. To the same tradition belongs Chauntecleer's instinctive knowledge of astronomy and his punctuality in announcing the hours.

The common belief in the regularity of the cock's crowing fostered the idea of his instinctive knowledge of astronomy: "They are skilled astronomers," declared Pliny,[24] "and they mark every three-hour period in the daytime with song . . . ." Neckam[25] likewise believed that the cock distinguished the hours by instinct. The usual explanation medieval scientists gave of this phenomenon was that his song was prompted by the regular movements of certain humors. Besides St. Albertus,[26] Vincent of Beauvais[27] and Alexander Neckam[28] also held this opinion.

Knowing by nature — "by kynde, and by noon other lore" — "ech ascencioun Of equinoxial in thilke toun," Chauntecleer displays a familiar aptitude of the barnyard cock, exaggerated to the point of absurdity. Parodying medieval scientific doctrine, Chaucer elevates Chauntecleer's conventional ability to sound the hours[29] into a technical knowledge of astronomy:

> "The sonne," he sayde, "is clomben up on hevene
> Fourty degrees and oon, and more, y-wis."

In comparing the cock's "crowing in his logge" to "a clokke, or an abbey orlogge," the poet may have had in mind St. Albertus' statement that this fowl sings at certain hours "quasi horologium."

Several other details in "The Nonne Preestes Tale" may also reflect the influence of medieval natural history. The deliberate anthropomorphism of Pertelote's query "Have ye no mannes herte, and han a berd?" derives its point from the fact that the cock's wattles or gills were commonly known as "beards" (*barbae*).[30] Again, her condemnation of his apparent cowardice ("I can nat love a coward, by my feith") seems all the more appropriate inasmuch as Bartholomeus had alluded to the possibility of occasional cowardice in this species: "The cocke beareth a red combe . . . : whiche beinge loste / he leseth his hardynes, and is more slowe & cowarde to assayl his adversary."

Chauntecleer's impressive display of erudition could be supported by divine authority, which credited the cock with intelligence ("vel quis dedit gallo intelligentiam?").[31] Moreover, Neckam had explained the cock allegorically as "doctor ecclesiae."[32]

The cock's keen eyesight was likewise conventional. According to Bartholomeus,

> . . . the cocke is ryghte sharpe of syghte, and therfore he loketh downwarde with the one eye to seche his meat, and upward in to the ayre with the other eye / to be waare of commynge of the egle and of the gossehauke. And if he see one of them come aferre / anone he cryeth to the hennes, and fleeth away / and hydeth him selfe in houses amonge stones or in hedges . . . [33]

In "The Nonne Preestes Tale" it is, significantly, Chauntecleer who first detects the fox, while he is seeking food:

> And so bifel that, as he caste his yë,
> Among the wortes, on a boterflye,
> He was war of this fox that lay ful lowe.

In several analogues, on the other hand, the cock remains blind to his danger; the hens first make the discovery, and in *Le Roman de Renart,* Renart surprises Chauntecleer in his sleep.[34] As Chaucer's version is obviously closer to Bartholomeus' idea of the *natura galli,* it seems probable that he altered the beast-fable to reflect the orthodox conception of the cock's proverbial vigilance.

V

Like the digression on the nature and significance of dreams, Chaucer's portrait of the choleric, uxorious monarch of the barnyard is indebted to medieval scientific doctrine. The mock-heroic technique, which lifts Chauntecleer and Pertelote virtually into the sphere of *curiales,* and the parody of the conventions of courtly love are really a *reductio ad absurdum* of several characteristic attributes of the species—attributes on which natural historians had already lavished extravagant praise. Though Chaucer burlesques them, these traits reflect current scientific belief.

Chaucer's fidelity to the *natura galli* may have been partly conditioned by medieval poetic theory. Matthieu de Vendôme's *Ars Versificatoria* placed considerable emphasis on Cicero's *attributa personae*.[35] Among the most important was *natura*, which involved not only such factors as age, sex, natural advantages or disadvantages in mind or body—"quae a natura dantur animo et corpori"—but also whether the character was a beast or a human being.[36] If Chaucer's *argumentum a natura* (i.e., "per naturales proprietates de persona aliquid probare vel improbare, personam propriare vel impropriare")[37] were to have any valid basis, it must be founded on an orthodox conception of the *natura galli*, the nature of the barnyard cock.

As Chauntecleer bears a marked similarity to the conception of the domestic cock as set forth in Bartholomeus' chapter "De Gallo," it seems probable that Chaucer was indebted for several details to the *De Proprietatibus Rerum*, one of the most popular encyclopedias of the thirteenth and fourteenth centuries.[38] He could have derived them directly from this work, or else indirectly through Berchorius' *Reductorium Morale*, which had been strongly influenced by Bartholomeus' encyclopedia.[39]

CHAPTER VI

The Wife of Bath's Prologue: Book-Burning and the Veda of Women's Wiles

THOUGH SCHOLARS have long recognized the influence of the antifeminist tradition[1] on the Wife of Bath's Prologue, they have
overlooked its possible impact on the fate of Jankyn's "book of
wikked wyves."[2] Fansler[3] noted "a rather curious literary precedent"
in Marie de France's "Li Lais de Gugemar," which described a
painting of Venus committing Ovid's *Remedia Amoris* to the
flames. A closer parallel to the scene in which Dame Alisoun "made
him brenne his book anon right tho" exists, however, in several of
the "Eastern" versions of the legend of the Seven Sages, or Books of
Sindibad.[4]

In its usual form, the story known as "Studien über Weibertücke"[5] or "The Man Who Understood Female Wiles"[6] exposes the
naïveté of a young man who has compiled a supposedly complete
collection of women's wiles, only to be tricked by a woman on his
homeward journey. Realizing that he has attempted the impossible
and that his collection is valueless, he burns his manuscript in
disgust and goes home to marry.[7]

I

Syntipas, "a Greek text translated from the Syriac by Michael Andreopulos, during the last years of the eleventh century,"[8] gives the following version of the incident: [9]

> Il y avait un homme qui s'était juré à lui-même de ne se fixer nulle part, de ne flâner en aucune promenade, comme fait tout jeune homme, et de ne pas prendre femme, avant d'avoir appris à connaître toutes les méchancetés et les ruses des méchantes femmes. Ayant pris cette résolution, il sortit de sa propre patrie et voyagea par les villes et les campagnes, s'efforçant d'apprendre ce qu'il voulait savoir. Or un autre homme l'ayant rencontré dans ses voyages, le questionna et ayant appris de lui que le but de son voyage était d'arriver à connaître la méchanceté et la perversité des femmes, il lui dit, "ô homme, tu te fatigues inutilement. Car tu ne pourras découvrir ni apprendre les pensées secrètes et les méchancetés des femmes. Si tu veux en connaître quelque peu . . . cherche un endroit solitaire, amasses-y beaucoup de fine poussière de la terre, et assieds-toi sur ce monceau quarante jours et autant de nuits, mangeant peu et buvant peu. Alors tu pourras découvrir les ruses des femmes."[10]

Obeying these instructions, the youth devoted forty days and nights to writing down the ruses of women. Then, "pensant, qu'il n'avait omis aucune méchanceté des femmes sans en prendre note, il prit les livres où il les avait toutes inscrites et se mit en route pour retourner chez lui." Offered hospitality by a stranger, he informed his host of his exploit. "Car j'ai quitté ma patrie pour apprendre la prudence et m'instruire sur les méchantes actions des méchantes femmes." The host then instructed his wife to prepare a separate table for the guest, informing her that "il a appris, et consigné par écrit toutes les méchancetés des femmes."

Serving the young man in an inner chamber, his hostess inquired about his books:

> "Qu'as-tu fait, ô homme? As-tu écrit toutes les méchancetés des femmes?" — "Oui, dit'il, je n'ai omis aucune méchanceté, ni artifice, ni perfidie des femmes." En entendant cela, la femme comprit qu'il était un ignorant et un sot, et lui dit ironiquement: "Puisque, comme tu le dis, ô étranger, tu as inscrit toutes les méchantes actions, il est impossible, qu'une femme — et j'en suis une — puisse tramer contre toi quelque méchanceté, soit en paroles, soit en action. Cependant, que je te dise ce que fit une femme, et vois si tu l'as inscrit." (Macler, p. 63)

After recounting an anecdote about a wife who left fish in her husband's field and accused him of insanity when he declared he had found them there, the hostess encouraged the youth to make love to her. Suddenly she screamed for help. When the neighbors rushed in, she explained that her guest had choked on a morsel of food and she had feared for his life. Upon their departure, she explained to the terrified man the point of this demonstration — it is impossible to know all the ruses of women:

> Cette femme s'approchant de l'hôte lui dit: "Ainsi, tout ce que je viens de faire, tu l'as inscrit dans ton livre?" L'étranger répondit: "Point du tout," Elle lui dit: "C'est donc en vain, ô homme, que tu as pris tant de peine et fait tant de voyages. Tu t'es donné beaucoup de peine pour rien, et tu n'as pas encore observé toutes les ruses des femmes." Et lui, se levant à cette parole de la femme, et ayant pris toutes les notes qu'il avait écrites sur les ruses des femmes, les jeta au feu, et rempli d'admiration, dit: "Aucun homme ne peut connaître les ruses des femmes!"[11] Après cela, ne sachant quel parti prendre, ni que faire, il ne continua pas à chercher davantage les méchancetés des femmes. Il retourna dans sa patrie et se maria tout simplement. (Macler, p. 68)

II

The Castilian *Libro de los engaños e los asayamientos de las mugeres*,[12] translated from an Arabic text in 1253 at the order of Prince Fadrique, contains much the same tale[13] under the title "Enxemplo del Mançebo que non queria casar fasta que sopiese las maldades de las mugeres":

> E, señor, dixieronme que un omme que non queria casar fasta que sopiese e aprendiese las maldades de las mugeres e los sus engaños; e anduvo tanto fasta que llego a un aldea, e dixieronle que avie buenos sabios del engaño de las mugeres, e costole mucho aprender las artes. Dixole aquel que era mas sabidor: — "Quieres que te diga? jamas nunca sabras nin aprenderas acabadamente los engaños de las mugeres, fasta que te asientes tres dias sobre la çenisa, e non comas sinon un poco de pan de ordio e sal, e aprenderas." E el le dixo que le plasia, e fisolo asi. Entonçes posose sobre la çenisa, e fiso muchos libros de las artes de las mugeres; e despues que esto ovo fecho, dixo que se queria tornar para su tierra, e poso en casa de un ome bueno; e el huesped le pregunto de todo aquello que levava, e el le dixo donde era, e como se avia asentado sobre la çenisa de mientra

trasladara aquellos libros, e como comiera el pan de ordio, e como
pasara mucha cueyta e mucha laseria, e traslado aquellas artes; e
despues questo le ovo contado, tomolo el huesped por la mano, e
levolo a su muger e dixole: — "Un omme bueno e fallado, que viene
cansado de su camino." E contole toda su fasienda, e rrogole que le
fisiese algo fasta que se fuese esforçndo, [ca] estonçes era flaco. E
despues questo ovo dicho, fuese a su mandado, e la muger fiso bien lo
que le castigara. Estonçes commenço ella de preguntalle, que omme
era o commo andava, e el contogelo todo; e ella, quando lo vio,
tovolo por omme de poco seso e de poco rrecabdo, porque entendio
que nunca podia acabar aquello que commençra, e dixo: — "Bien
creo verdaderamente que hunca muger del mundo te peuda
engañar, e mas con aquestos libros que as adobado." E dixo ella en su
coraçon: "Sea agora quam sabidor quesiere, que yo le fare conosçer
el su poco seso, en que anda engañado; yo so aquella que lo sabre
faser!" (Gonzalez Palencia, pp. 46-47)

As in *Syntipas,* after tricking the youth and her neighbors, the
hostess pointed out the futility of such a collection:

"Amigo, en tus libros ay alguna tal arte como esta?" E dixo el: — "En
buena fe nunca la vi, nin la falle tal commo esta!" E dixo ella: — "Tu
gastaste tu tiempo y pasaste mucha fatiga y malos [dias, e non]
esperes nunca [ende al]; que esto que tu demandas nunca lo
acabaras tu nin ome de quantos son nascidos." E el, quando esto vio,
tomo todos sus libros e metiolos en el fuego, e dixo que de mas avia
despendido sus dias."[14]

III

The Persian poet Nachschebi (d. 1329) inserted a similar story in
the Eighth Night of his *Tuti-nameh (Tales of a Parrot):*

Ein junger Mann fasst den Plan, Alles niederzuschreiben, was er über
die Listen und Tücken der Weiber erfahren kann, um sich so selbst
gegen ihre Ränke sicherzustellen. Nach kurzer Zeit hat er schon
einen ganzen Korb voll Papiere. Eines Tages begegnet ihm ein
Mann, der ihn in sein Haus führt, ihn dort der gastlichen Pflege
seiner Frau überlässt, und dann seinen Geschäften nachgeht. Die
Frau fragt den Jüngling: "Was hast du da im Korbe?" "Es sind
Papiere." "Und was steht auf den Papieren?" "Die Listen und Ränke
der Frauen." "Man kann also jede List, welche die Frauen jemals
begehen könnten, hier bereits aufgezeichnet finden?" "Ja, sicher."

> Nach dieser Unterhaltung fasst die Frau den Jüngling bei der Hand
> und führt ihn lüstern in ein Zimmer. Plötzlich erhebt sie ein
> Geschrei: "Hülfe ihr Nachbarn, Hülfe!" (Brockhaus, No. 243)

As in *Syntipas* and the *Libro de los Engaños,* she explained that
her guest had choked on a morsel he had eaten:

> Als die Leute fort sind, fragt der Jüngling, warum sie so gehandelt,
> wodruch sie ihn dem Untergang so nahe gebracht. Die Frau ant-
> wortet: "Es war nur eine Probe meiner List. Doch ich habe eine
> Schwester im Serail des Königs, deren Listen die meinigen weit über-
> treffen." (Brockhaus, No. 243)

Sending the youth to the palace, she also despatched a message to
her sister, informing her that "dieser Jüngling schreibe alle Listen
der Frauen auf; sie möge daher eine solche List ersinnen, dass er alle
seine Papiere vor Verdruss verbrennen werde."

While the Sultana was entertaining her guest, the Sultan himself
returned. Hiding the young man in a chest, she adroitly escaped
detection by telling her husband the truth, but ridiculing his
credulity when he believed her. When the Sultan had departed,
leaving the chest unopened, she returned her paramour safely to her
sister:

> Die Frau fragt ihn: "Steht die List meiner Schwester schon in deinen
> Büchern oder nicht?" Der junge Mann nimmt seine Papiere, wirft sie
> ins Feuer und verlässt das Haus.[15]

IV

A brief allusion to the book of woman's wiles and its destruction
occurs in *Castigabricon,* or *Proverbia quae dicunter super natura
feminarum*—an Italian poem usually assigned to the twelfth[16] or
thirteenth[17] centuries. Among numerous examples—classical,
Biblical, and medieval—of perfidious women, the author describes
the case of a Roman who had devoted seven years to compiling a collection of female ruses. In the end he was tricked by a woman, who
made him burn his books:[18]

> Et un Roman set ani cercando andá li regni,
> Scrivendo de le femene le art e li ençegni;
> Et poi una vilana lo scerní com ençegni,
> C'arder li fe li libri en gran fogo de legni.

All four of these analogues involved the same essential irony—the expert on female ruses himself falls victim to a woman's trick. In all four versions his defeat culminates in the destruction of his collection.

What is the relation of this tale to Jankyn's predicament? Let us briefly examine some of the similarities and differences between Chaucer's version of the book-burning episode and the story as it appears in the Sindibad tradition.

The most significant points of resemblance can be summarized as follows:

1) A relatively inexperienced youth shows an inordinate regard for a "book of wikked wyves" in his possession.

2) An experienced woman outwits him and causes him to destroy his anti-feminist compilation.

3) Jankyn resembles the young man of the Sindibad story both in his youth[19] and in his scholarly background.[20] He is, significantly, the only one of Dame Alisoun's five husbands to whom these qualities are specifically ascribed.

4) The young man's antifeminist lore fails him in a moment of crisis. In spite of his erudition, the woman scores a clear-cut victory over him.

5) The episode involves, in a varying degree, the related themes of *maistrie* and matrimonial felicity. In both instances the man abandons the attempt to achieve effective control over his wife. Jankyn bids his bride to "do as thee lust the terme of al thy lyf," and his counterpart in the Sindibad cycle recognizes the futility of attempting to anticipate his wife's stratagems. In both cases the destruction of the antifeminist collection has a direct bearing on his marital happiness. The Oriental youth burns his manuscript, returns home and marries. Jankyn surrenders the *soveranyetee* to Dame Alisoun and commits his book to the flames; "after that day we hadden never debaat."

Nevertheless Chaucer's version diverges significantly from the Sindibad tradition in several important details—the composition of the "book of wikked wyves," the motives for burning it, and the relationship between the two principal characters.

1) In the Sindibad cycle only the general nature of the antifeminist collection is described. The narrator identifies it merely as an extensive but incomplete compilation of *Weibertücke* and

does not attempt to provide concrete examples of its contents. The only ruses he describes in detail are those which had been *omitted* from the collection.

Chaucer's approach, on the other hand, is detailed and particular. He identifies many of the specific authors and works represented in Jankyn's volume and repeats several *exempla* characteristic of its contents. Where the Sindibad story is abstract, he is concrete. After stating the general nature of Jankyn's collection ("this book of wikked wyves"), he proceeds to such individual instances as Adam and Eve, Samson and Dalilah, Hercules and "his Dianyre."

2) Unlike its Oriental counterparts, Jankyn's book is essentially and distinctively European in its contents. Its authors belong unmistakably to Western classical and Christian traditions.[21] It is also far more formidable in its array of scholarship and "auctoritee."[22] Such authorities as Ovid, Jerome, Tertullian, Theophrastus, and Walter Map render it much more impressive than the book of female ruses in the Sindibad cycle; and, unlike its analogues, it can hardly be dismissed as ridiculous. In the Oriental tale the antifeminist compilation merely invites the woman's scorn; in Chaucer's version it arouses her passionate indignation.

3) Jankyn's book is more comprehensive in scope than its analogues in the Sindibad legend. It is not limited specifically to women's ruses.

4) In the Sindibad tradition the youth achieves his compilation through travel and fasting.[23] Both of these motifs are missing from Chaucer's narrative. Jankyn's book is not the product of his own researches.

5) In the Oriental tale the young man refuses to marry until he possesses a complete collection of female wiles. This motif does not occur in Chaucer's tale. Jankyn is already a married man when we first encounter his book.

6) In the Sindibad cycle the youth destroys his book only because the new ruses practiced against him—the coffer trick or the table-incident or both—convince him that he has attempted the impossible and that his collection is therefore worthless ("Aucun homme ne peut connaître les ruses des femmes!"). Chaucer and *Castigabricon,* on the other hand, allude to neither of these tricks. Jankyn burns his book at his wife's command. Its destruction is the

direct result of his capitulation to female *soveraynetee,* a tacit acknowledgement of his wife's *maistrye.* Neither Jankyn nor the Wife of Bath suggests that his book is valueless.

7) The woman's motivation varies in different versions of the story. Both Chaucer and *Castigabricon* declare that she "made him brenne his book" ("arder li fe li libri"), and in Nachschebi's account she explicitly declares her intent to make the youth commit his papers to the flames. Neither *Syntipas* nor the *Libro de los Engaños,* however, mentions such a purpose; in these versions her paramount aim is, ostensibly, to teach him a lesson—to punish him for his folly and conceit.

8) In the Sindibad tradition the two principal characters of the book-burning episode are comparative strangers, hostess and guest. In the Wife of Bath's Prologue they are man and wife. *Castigabricon* leaves their relationship ambiguous; the man is simply "un Roman"[24] and the woman "una vilana."

These divergences reflect a difference of emphasis which resulted in part from differences in the narrative context of the episode. In the Seven Sages the narrator of this tale is one of seven councillors attempting to dissuade their king from believing his wife's perjuries by recounting instances of female perfidy. In his account the primary stress falls appropriately on the hostess' ruses rather than on the specific contents of the young man's book or the fact of its destruction. In Chaucer's version, however, the speaker is a woman arguing the merits of female sovereignty, a widow with wide experience of "wo that is in mariage"; and her account of the book emphasizes its relation to both of these themes. As she describes it, Jankyn's collection is not only a bone of contention—a cause of domestic strife—but also a focal point for the controversy over *maistrie.* It is a test case for the issue of woman's sovereignty.

In what form could Chaucer have encountered the book-burning episode? While we must rule out any *direct* influence of the Greek, Syriac, Persian, Arabic, or Hebrew[25] versions, it is conceivable that he may have known the version in the *Libro de los Engaños* or the briefer account in *Castigabricon.* We have, however, no conclusive evidence that he was familiar with either of these works.

Oral transmission from the *Libro de los Engaños* or some other member of the "Eastern" branch of the Seven Sages cycle seems not improbable. This alternative seems especially attractive since the factor of oral transmission may have been responsible for some of the major differences between the "Eastern" and "Western" groups of the Sindibad story (Campbell, p. 13).

CHAPTER VII

"The Pardoner's Tale": Old Age
and Contemptus Mundi.

IN THE OLD man of *The Pardoner's Tale,* scholars have detected
an embarrassing profusion of meanings. Bushnell stressed his affinities with the Wandering Jew. In Robinson's opinion, he was "a
symbol of Death itself, or possibly of Old Age, conceived as Death's
messenger." Mrs. Hamilton argued that "if Chaucer's character was
meant to be anything more than a pathetic old man who has
outlived all zest for living, he must stand for Old Age as the Harbinger of Death . . ." Miss Strang has maintained that, since "the
Old Man's speech . . . introduces a great deal of information to
which no literal meaning can be assigned," it ought, accordingly, to
be interpreted allegorically. On the other hand, Owen rejected the
allegorical approach entirely. Chaucer was simply describing a
"notion of aged humanity" he "could have found already well
developed" in Maximianus, and "the old man is merely an old
man."

We are confronted, then, by two related, but unresolved

problems—whether Chaucer's old man should be interpreted allegorically, and if so, which of several alternative interpretations is the most pertinent and the most probable.

I

Before attempting to answer either of these questions directly, let us examine some of the arguments on which these various interpretations have been based. A chain is only as strong as its weakest link, and there appear to be several flaws in the current arguments for and against allegorical interpretation.

In Owen's opinion, it was "contrary to the logic of allegory that Old Age as the messenger of Death should appear to a company of young men." Though this may indeed seem to violate logic, it *does,* nevertheless, occur in allegory. *Piers Plowman,* in fact, provides striking evidence against Owen's assumption. In Passus XI, Elde admonishes the dreamer while he is still "yonge and yepe," with "Yeres ynowe, Foreto lyve longe and ladyes to lovye":

Thanne was there one that highte elde that hevy was of chere, "Man," quod he, if I mete with the, bi Marie of hevene, Thow shalt fynde fortune the faille at thi moste nede, And *concupiscencia-carnis* clene the forsake. Bitterliche shaltow banne thanne bothe dayes and nightes Coveytise-of-eyghe that ever thow hir knewe, And pryde-of-parfyt-lyvynge to moche peril the brynge."

(B XI 26-32)

Like the three rioters, however, the dreamer disregards this warning and plunges into a life of dissipation, while Old Age and Holiness lament his lapse:

"Allas, eye!" quod elde and holynesse bothe,
"That witte shal torne to wrecchedness for wille to have his lykynge!"

In the final passus Elde returns, fights with Life, and afflicts the dreamer. Oppressed by old age, the latter—much like Chaucer's old man—beseeches Nature ("kynde") for release (XX 200).

In view of the marked affinities between Chaucer's old man and the *senex* of Maximianus' First Elegy, it seems difficult to accept Miss Strang's argument that no ordinary old man is "rejected by Death (C727); nor is the ground the gate of any ordinary man's mother (C729), at which he knocks invoking his mother within (C 737-38)." Maximianus had, in fact, employed these very details in his characteristic portrait of the miseries of old age.[2] Though his manner of expression is obviously figurative and dramatic, the details themselves are clearly intended to be typical of the "ordinary old man." Like Chaucer's old man, Maximianus' *senex* is more eloquent than the average old man, but the content of his lament is the common fate of all old men, the *miseria senectutis.*

The analogy with Maximianus does not, however, provide absolutely firm support for Owen's conclusion that Chaucer's old man is merely "an old man and nothing more." In the very passage which apparently inspired Chaucer's picture of the aged man knocking at the ground for admittance, Maximianus chose the feminine abstract noun *senectus* (sometimes capitalized, as though it were a personification, like Virgil's *tristis Senectus, Aen.* VI 275), instead of *senex* or the masculine adjective *senectus:*

> Nec cælum spectare licet, sed prona senectus
> Terram, qua genita est et reditura, videt . . .

> Hinc est quod bacula incumbens ruitura senectus
> Assiduo pigram verbere pulsat humum . . .[3]

Is Chaucer's old man a personification of old age, or is he merely a typical example of "aged humanity"? Though the analogy with Maximianus' elegy lends a measure of support to either view, it gives stronger probability to the latter interpretation. In the passages quoted above *senectus* can mean either "old age" or "old men." Elsewhere in the elegy Maximianus tends to use the terms *senex* and *senectus* virtually interchangeably. The speaker—the *persona*—in the Latin poem is, moreover, not Old Age, but an old man, lamenting the miseries of old age. This is obvious from the first lines of the elegy, where the aged speaker (the *senex*) apostrophizes Old Age (*senectus*):

> Æmula quid cessas finem properare senectus?
>   Cur et in hoc fesso corpore tarda venis?
> Solve precor miseram tali de carcere vitam:
>   Mors est iam requies, vivere poena mihi.
> Non sum qui fueram: periit pars maxima nostri;
>   Hoc quoque quod superest languor et horror habent.[5]

The speaker here is clearly the typical *senex,* describing the characteristic *incommoda senectutis.* The same may be said of Chaucer's figure.

Though the aged stranger of *The Pardoner's Tale* is not Old Age, he is not simply "an old man and nothing more." Owen has failed to distinguish between "an old man" and a "notion of aged humanity." The very details Chaucer apparently borrowed from Maximianus indicate his concern for the general idea rather than the individual example, for the universal rather than the particular. The aged man whom the rioters encounter is important primarily as a type rather than as an individual. He is the *senex* par excellence — not merely *an* old man, but *the* old man. In conveying this abstract concept of the miseries of senility through a concrete example, Chaucer has presented the *universale in re.* His attempt to delineate the general through the particular brings him close to the frontiers of allegory, but he does not actually cross.

The old man's relation to the Messenger-of-Death motif also requires re-examination. Does the text really offer us sufficient foundation for the view that he is harbinger of Death? To be sure, Sackville combines the Messenger-of-Death motif with details reminiscent of Maximianus' *senex.* But he also gives us an explicit personification of Old Age[6] — which Chaucer does not do. It is significant that, despite the highly figurative language Chaucer employs in this scene, he makes no overt use of the Messenger-of-Death metaphor. The Pardoner does indeed introduce into his sermon representative instances of sickness, disaster, and old age — the lethal triad of the Messenger poems — but he does not represent them figuratively in terms of the messenger-symbol. Neither sickness nor disaster is personified. Though the tale includes examples of death by pestilence and *aventure,* none of the characters die of old age. Nor is the old man's role that of a messenger. He does indeed inform the rioters where they may find Death, but this is not the office of a messenger, but rather the function of a guide. Though the "other hasardour" accuses the ancient stranger of being Death's "aspye" and "oon of his assent, To sleen us yonge folk," a spy and a messenger are by no means identical, and in fact all three rioters perish by *aventure,* not by old age. If Chaucer had really intended to represent this character as a *nuntius mortis,* he would surely have made a more clear-cut and emphatic use of the Messenger-of-Death symbolism.

In rejecting this interpretation, however, we are not forced to accept the alternative Mrs. Hamilton has offered us—that the aged stranger must be nothing "more than a pathetic old man who has outlived all zest for living." He is, on the contrary, not simply an individual old man, but a *type*—a representative portrait of the ideal *senex* and the miseries of old age. In the last stage of human life (*senium*) as it approaches death (*ad mortis terminum pervenit*),[7] his predicament is essentially that of the dreamer in the final passage of *Piers Plowman*. Oppressed by old age, both long for death as a release. Chaucer's old man is not "Death's messenger," but he is still a *memento mori*.

II

To concur with Owen's preference for a literal, rather than an allegorical, interpretation of Chaucer's old man, is to be faced with another problem. Why does Chaucer deliberately stress the "greet age" of the old man? The poet's emphasis on the character of the *senex* represents a distinct variation on traditional versions of the treasure-story, and the old man's search for death "is a feature not paralleled in any known analogues of the tale."[8] What is the literary function of this innovation? What bearing does it have on the tale as a whole and on the Pardoner's central theme of avarice?

One of the most obvious features of Chaucer's characterization of the old man is his ethical contrast with the three rioters. The encounter between them juxtaposes youth and age, pride and humility, impatience and patience, blasphemy and piety, "vileinye" and "curteisye," folly and wisdom, avarice and *contemptus mundi*. Though these moral opposites seem self-evident, it seems advisable to discuss them in detail, especially as the old man has been interpreted so frequently in a pejorative or sinister light.

The opening lines of the tale call attention to the youth of the rioters ("a companye of yonge folk"). The opposition between youth and age is given explicit expression by the old man (who can find no one willing to "chaunge his youthe for myn age") and also by "this other hasardour" (who regards the stranger as one of Death's "assent, To sleen us yonge folk"). The antithesis of youth and age is also apparent in Maximianus' First Elegy, *Horrent me pueri, nequeo velut ante videri.*[9]

The concept of old age receives even stronger emphasis in *The Pardoner's Tale* than the idea of youth. Mrs. Hamilton observed that the term "old man" is applied to [the aged stranger] seven times, "old churl" once, and "age" meaning old age four times. The first remarks the rioters address to him concern his "greet age," and the concept acquires further emphasis through his own elegiac complaint concerning the miseries of *senectus* and through his quotation from Leviticus xix. 32. Moreover, his warning ("Ne dooth un-to an old man noon harm now, Na-more than ye wolde men dide to yow In age, if that ye so longe abyde") bears a striking resemblance to the admonition in Innocent III's chapter *De incommodis senectutis:*

> Porro nec senes contra juvenem glorientur, nec insolescant juvenes contra senem, quia quod sumus iste fuit, erimus quandoque quod hic est.[10]

The implications of the old man's rebuke are obvious. Old age is part of the inevitable misery of man's lot — *la condition humaine* — and the same fate awaits the young revellers if they live long enough. Like all other young men, they are unwilling to "chaunge [their] youthe for . . . age," but they must.

The contrast between youth and age underlies the significant difference between the old man and the rioters in their attitudes toward death. The *senex* desires death because he suffers from the infirmities of old age. The *juvenes* attempt to overcome death because they are young and wish to perpetuate their life of riotous pleasures. For one, death is a release; for the others, a deadly enemy. We should recall the similar antithesis expressed in Ecclesiasticus xli. 1-4,

> O' mors, quam amara est memoria tua homini pacem habenti in substantiis suis . . . et adhuc valenti accipere cibum! O mors, bonum est judicium tuum homini indigenti, et qui minoratur viribus, Defecto aetate, et cui de omnibus cura est . . .!

The antithesis between youth and age also has a significant bearing on the theme of repentance. The encounter with the old man should have induced the rioters to "remember [their] Creator in the days of [their] youth," but they fail to heed the implicit warning in the spectacle of the *tempus afflictionis*. Characteristically they had already grossly misconstrued two previous exhortations to repent in time (ll. 680-691). In their failure to perceive that "adolescentia . . . et voluptas vana sint," they are like the *juvenis* of Ecclesiastes xi. 9-xii. 1-7 (*Lætare ergo, juvenis, etc.*).

The very lines which stress the youth of the rioters also declare that they "haunteden folye, As ryot, hasard, stewes, and tavernes." Their subsequent behaviour is in keeping with this characterization. They flagrantly misinterpret the advice to prepare for death ("Beth redy for to mete him evermore"and "To been avysed greet wisdom it were"), and rashly assay the impossible—to "sleen this false traytour Death." Their very words after finding the treasure ("Now let us sitte and drinke, and make us merie") are patently reminiscent of the remarks of the rich *stultus* in Luke xii. 19, *requiesce, comede, bibe, epulare.* In their sensual folly they ignore the fatal results of avarice and forget Death in their enjoyment of the treasure.

The old man's wisdom stands in clearer relief by contrast with their folly. He warns them of the approach of old age in words very similar to those of Pope Innocent III. Like his counterparts in analogues of this story, he equates the treasure with death and thus displays a moral insight unsurpassed by any other character in the tale. He is, in fact, the only person in *The Pardoner's Tale* who gives expression—however oblique and figurative—to the central theme, *Radix malorum est cupiditas.* The fact that he expresses it in a veiled metaphor rather than through a bald and overt statement does not discredit his insight. It simply lends greater intensity and power to the ethical truth he is describing.

Chaucer's old man appears, then, to be an example of that "honorable old age" whose essence is "understanding" and "an unspotted life" (Wisdom iv. 8-9).[11] Like his counterparts in the analogues, he is a wise man, and in emphasizing his "greet age" Chaucer is exploiting the conventional link between wisdom and old age. The quotation from Leviticus reinforces this interpretation. According to Rabanus and "Strabus," the *senex* represents the *sapiens,* and both Old and New Testaments command that he be honoured for his wisdom:

"Coram cano capite surge," id est sapientem honora: cani enim sunt sensus hominis. De quibus senioribus, id est sapientibus, Paulus dicit: "Presbyteri duplici honore digni habeantur, maxime qui laborant in verbo et doctrina" (I *Tim.* v). Et Dominus ad Moysen: "Elige septuaginta viros, quos tu nosti, quod seniores sunt populi" (*Exod.* xxiv).[12]

Coram cano capite consurge, et honora personam senis, et time
Dominum Deum tuum . . . Bonum est quidem et eum, qui jam ad
canitiem pervenit, honorare. Habet enim tempus aliquid amplius
procul dubio ad prudentiam, sed et honorem quem provectioribus
impendimus, nos quoque a minoribus meremibur, atque ex hoc ordo
bonus vitam nostram in honestate custodiens nobis profligatur.
Canum autem vere senem, id est, eum qui sapientia, profectus est,
intelliget, de quo ait *seniores tuos, et dicent tibi* (*Deut.* xxxii). Sed et
Paulus: *Presbyteri duplici honore digni habeantur, maxime qui*
laborant in verbo et doctrina. [13]

In contrasting the old man's wisdom with the rioters' folly,
Chaucer is closer to the literary tradition behind *The Pardoner's*
Tale than recent scholarship has recognized. In the analogues, the
old man's counterparts are usually wise and holy men—Christ and
his disciples, St. Anthony, holy hermits, a moral philosopher.[14] To
credit the pejorative interpretations scholars have frequently at-
tached to Chaucer's figure, one must assume a radical departure
from the conventional conception of his character. But this
assumption is neither necessary nor probable. The chief differences
between the old man and these literary counterparts lie in the
emphasis on his old age and his desire for death, and these are by no
means incompatible with the character of the *sapiens.*

As a result of these antithetical attributes—youth and old age,
folly and wisdom—Chaucer's characters exhibit sharply contrasted
attitudes towards the treasure. For several reasons Owen's view that
"there is nothing in Chaucer to suggest that the old man has seen
the gold"—that "he does not know . . . what the revellers will find
under the tree"—does not seem altogether probable. In the first
place, it is at variance with the tradition behind the tale. In the
analogues the wise men who discover the treasure shun it because
they are aware of the fatal consequences of avarice; there is nothing
in Chaucer's story to suggest that the old man has not passed it by
for similar reasons. Secondly, the stranger could hardly have given
such precise directions to the rioters unless he had actually seen—or
heard of—the gold. Owen's suggestion that these detailed instructions are simply an improvised ruse devised by "senile cunning"
defies all laws of probability, and there is certainly "nothing in
Chaucer to suggest" that they are just an improvisation. Surely, the
most obvious—indeed, the only feasible—inference we can draw
from ll. 760-765 is that, like the holy men of the analogues, the old

man has discovered the gold and deliberately shunned it because he knows the causal relation between cupidity and death. The passage points distinctly to his moral insight rather than to his ignorance. Thirdly, Owen's assumption that, if the old man *had* known what the revellers would find under the tree, "he ought, according to his earlier speech, to have remained with the gold, seeking his death in it" proposes an alternative which would have been flagrantly out of character. Though the old man wishes to die, he does not attempt to shorten his life through his own agency. He is, instead, resigned to "han myn age stille, As longe time as it is goddes wille."

Thus, despite his indigence, the "povre" stranger contemns the riches which ensnare the youthful rioters. The ethical contrast between them is deepened by a further antithesis — the opposition between avarice and *contemptus mundi.* According to a *Precatio* formerly attributed to St. Ambrose, these are logical contraries; and the author concludes a denunciation of avarice with the prayer,

> . . . semper illius sententiae meminerim, qua dicitur: *Nudus egressus sum de utero matris meae, nudus revertar illuc (Job* 1, 21). Atque illius: *Nihil intulimus in hunc mundum, sed nec auferre quid possumus* (1 *Tim.*vi, 7). Quae nimirum dum pie considerantur, mundi contemptum auferre videntur, qui avaritiae contrarius est.[15]

Significantly, Innocent makes use of the same concepts as an argument against avarice; in his *De Contemptu Mundi sive de Miseria Conditionis Humanæ,* he declares that

> Omnis cupidus et avarus contra naturam nititur et molitur. Natura enim pauperem adducit in mundum, natura pauperem reducit a mundo: nudum namque eum terra suscepit, nudum etiam suscipiet: cupidus autem cupit et curat fieri dives in mundo.[16]

Old and poor, Chaucer's *senex* is representative of the misery of man's condition. In his readiness to return to the earth his mother, stripped of all possessions except a "heyre clout,"[17] he demonstrates not only his misery, but also his awareness of *la condition humaine.* His poverty itself is emblematic; he can take nothing with him to the grave except his shroud.

Both Maximianus and Job employ the earth-mother metaphor, and Chaucer appears to have combined details reminiscent of both. In their new context they serve not only to express the miseries of old age, but also to convey the antithesis between *contemptus mundi* and *cupiditas.*

In contrast to the old man's *contemptus mundi,* the rioters are lovers of the world, *mundi dilectores.* Unlike the stranger, they ignore the true condition of man, and their quest to slay Death is (like avarice itself) *contra naturam.* Where the old man exhibits the truth of I John ii. 17, that *mundus transit, et concupiscentia ejus,* the revellers manifest the three worldly vices—"the lust of the flesh, and the lust of the eyes, and the pride of life." According to Innocent, *Concupiscentia carnis ad voluptates, concupiscentia oculorum ad opes, superbia vita pertinet ad honores. Opes generant cupiditates et avaritiam: voluptates pariunt gulam et luxuriam: honores nutriunt superbiam et jactantiam.*[18] *Concupiscentia carnis* is evident in the rioters' addiction to the delights of the tavern— gluttony, lechery and the like. *Superbia vitæ* is apparent in the insolent behaviour of the "proudest of thise ryotoures" towards the old man. *Concupiscentia oculorum* is manifested in the fascination of the treasure, and it is significant that Chaucer stresses its visual appeal:

> But ech of hem so glad was of that sighte,
> For that the florins been so faire and brighte . . .
> Ful ofte in herte he rolleth up and doun
> The beautee of thise florins newe and brighte.

The rioters' "hasardrye" is closely related to the Pardoner's theme, for *The Parson's Tale* discusses this vice under the heading of *Avaricia.*

There is a further contrast between the old man's meekness and the rioter's pride[19] when they first meet. He greets them "ful mekely" as "lordes" and "sirs" or with blessings ("god you see!" "And god be with yow, wher ye go or ryde," "God save yow, that boghte agayn mankinde, And yow amende!"). The rioters, on the other hand, heap upon him such opprobrious epithets as "carl," "olde cherl,"[20] and "false theef." In contrast to their grisly oaths ("And Cristes blessed body they to-rente"), the old man does not swear, but replies to their taunts with a quotation from Scripture. His piety, "curteisye," and humility are sharply distinguished from their blasphemy, "vileinye," and pride. He meets their threats of violence with "Debonairetee" and "Pacience or Suffrance."[21]

Finally, the old man's patient acceptance of the miseries of man's condition and his resignation to the divine will provide a striking contrast to the rioters' violent opposition to *la condition humaine* and their rash and impatient quest to slay death. Despite the old man's desire to die, he does not actually "seek" death.[22] The rioters, on the other hand, *are* engaged on a quest for death, and they "seek" him precisely because they do *not* wish to die.

III

To conclude, Chaucer's *senex* is quite intelligible on the literal level without resort to allegorical explanations. His chief significance is to be found in the ethical contrast he provides to Chaucer's characterization of the rioters. The encounter between them serves to emphasize such antithetical concepts as youth and age, folly and wisdom, avarice and *contemptus mundi*. As the moral opposite of the revellers, the old man lends additional proof to the Pardoner's theme.

He also serves a more practical end. Presumably the "lewd peple" who hear the Pardoner's sermon include both young and old. It is worth reminding them that death comes to all and by various means. Hence he includes an additional detail in his *exemplum* of the young men who perish by *aventure*—an old man *ad mortis terminum*. He has no desire for the treasure or the "cheste" in his chamber. He can carry nothing to the grave except a "heyre clout." This demonstration of the uselessness of worldly possessions in "greet age" and in the face of death is calculated to serve the principal "entente" of the Pardoner's sermon — "for to make hem free To yeve her pens, and namely un-to me."

PART THREE

THE RENAISSANCE TRADITION:
SHAKESPEARE, SPENSER, MILTON

CHAPTER VIII

"The Merry Wives of Windsor:" Falstaff as Actaeon. A Dramatic Emblem.

IN THE FINAL act of *The Merry Wives of Windsor,* Shakespeare confronts his audience with an obvious burlesque of the Actaeon myth. In impersonating Herne the Hunter, Sir John becomes a comic counterpart of the legendary hunter from Thebes. As Geoffrey Bullough has observed, there is a certain "poetic justice" in Shakespeare's exploitation of this parallel. "Actaeon had become a cant-name for a cuckold", and when Falstaff "dons the horns which he would have placed on Ford's brows he suffers the poetic justice of a failed Don Juan."[1] Professor Bullough has likewise emphasized the dramatist's indebtedness to Golding's translation of the *Metamorphoses:* "That Shakespeare had Ovid in mind when Falstaff assumed the disguise is proved by the latter's allusions at V.v.2-17 to the amorous metamorphoses of Jove. . . . Actaeon was bitten by his own dogs, of whom Ovid names thirty-five and Golding calls one 'Ringwood' (a common name). Shakespeare substitutes the fairies who burn and pinch the fat knight; and for this part of the scene he takes hints from Lyly's *Endimion*" (p. 18).

Shakespeare's treatment of the Falstaff-Actaeon parallel also displays several marked affinities with the representation of this myth in Renaissance iconography and mythography. The knight's disguise is virtually identical with a conventional illustration of Actaeon in Renaissance emblem literature[2] and editions of the *Metamorphoses*.[3] Moreover, the moral significance of Falstaff's ordeal — the punishment the "unclean knight" receives for his "corrupted heart" and "lecheries" — closely resembles a familiar Renaissance interpretation of Actaeon's fate.[4]

I

Except for one comic variation — Sir John's obesity — there is a point-by-point correspondence between his disguise as Herne the Hunter and the standard Renaissance picture of Actaeon as a composite figure with stag's head, human body, and hunter's clothing. Despite some pronounced variations from this type,[5] it is thus that the Theban hunter appears in Alciati,[6] Posthius,[7] Whitney,[8] Sambucus,[9] and Anulus,[10] emblem-embroidery associated with Queen Elizabeth, in the emblem-literature of the period — and in various illustrated editions of the *Metamorphoses*.[11] This conception[12] is virtually identical with Falstaff's costume in the final scene of *The Merry Wives of Windsor*. The fact that he is impersonating Herne the Hunter would presumably compel him to wear a huntsman's garb, and according to the First Quarto he has "a Bucks head upon him."[13] Shakespeare's fidelity to the conventional iconography of Actaeon should have heightened the visual impact of Falstaff's disguise, enabling the audience to recognize immediately the parody of the mythical hunter in the burlesque "transformation" of the English knight. Indeed, to intensify this comic awareness of the Falstaff-Actaeon parallel, Shakespeare allows Sir John to comment on his own metamorphosis into "a Windsor Stagge, and the fattest (I thinke) i' the Forrest."[14]

This resemblance to the Actaeon of Renaissance iconography is strengthened by a further similarity in the position of the two figures under attack. When the supposed fairies appear, Falstaff resolves to "winke, and couch" as "No man their workes must eie." The exact position in which he couches is not specified, but Rowe's suggestion that he "lies down upon his face" has been followed by many recent editors.[15] In Alciati's emblem Actaeon is almost prone, but he braces himself with both arms and his right knee and turns his head over his left shoulder to face his attackers. Both Sambucus and Whitney, however, depict him as prostrate, though his head is turned upwards and backwards over his right shoulder. In all three of these emblems the fallen hunter is depicted with stag's head, human body, and hunter's garb, but the position of this figure in Sambucus and Whitney most closely approximates that of the couchant Falstaff.

There is, finally, a significant divergence between the iconographical tradition Shakespeare seems to have imitated and Ovid's account of Actaeon's transformation. In Shakespeare, as in Alciati, Sambucus, and Whitney, the hunter attacked (by hounds or fairies) wears a stag's head, but his body is still that of a man. In Ovid, on the other hand, he is completely transformed into a deer before his hounds attack him:

> This done, she makes no further threates, but by and by doth spread
> A payre of lively olde Harts hornes upon his sprinckled head.
> She sharpes his eares, she makes his necke both slender, long and lanke.
> She turnes his fingers into feete, his armes to spindle shanke.
> She wrappes him in a hairie hyde beset with speckled spottes,
> And planteth in him fearefulnesse. And so away he trottes. . .[16]

II

The moral significance of Falstaff's final ordeal likewise shows close affinities with a Renaissance interpretation of the Actaeon myth. Though this scene does indeed exhibit "poetic justice" in investing Falstaff with the horns[17] he had intended for Ford, it also presents an emblematic expression of lust and its chastisement. Falstaff himself, comparing his own metamorphosis with those of Jove, admits (albeit jestingly) that love can make "man a beast" and bring a god very near "to the complexion of a goose." From these examples he draws the logical inference that it is "a beastly fault," a "foul fault." In the fairies' song, which is of central importance in this scene, lust is again the theme; the verses excoriate "sinful fantasy," "lust and luxury," and "unchaste desire." Sir John himself confesses "the guiltiness of my mind" and observes that his

humiliation is "enough to be the decay of lust and late-walking
through the realm." The ethical concept which receives primary
emphasis in this scene is not so much the poetic justice which
enables Ford to gloat over Falstaff's horns ("Now, sir, who's a
cuckold now?—Master Brook, Falstaff's a knave, a cuckoldly
knave; here are his horns, Master Brook") as the exposure and
humiliation of lechery.

Here again the analogy with the Actaeon myth is highly
significant. Though the hero's fate was often interpreted as a
warning against the costs of hunting, which devour the huntsman
financially,[18] an alternative interpretation was familiar to Shakespeare and his audience through Whitney's *Choice of Emblemes.*
Whitney had applied the myth to the ravages of desire, and this is
essentially the interpretation Shakespeare gives the fable in *Twelfth
Night* [*"That instant was I turn'd into a hart; And my desires, like
fell and cruel hounds, E'er since pursue me"*].[19] Whitney's emblem
bears the motto *"Voluptas aerumnosa"* and is accompanied by the
following verses:

> Actaeon heare, unhappie man behoulde,
> When in the well, hee sawe Diana brighte,
> With greedie lookes, hee waxed over boulde,
> That to a stagge hee was transformed righte,
>   Whereat amasde, hee thought to runne awaie,
>   But straighte his howndes did rente hym, for their praie.
>
> By which is ment, That those whoe do pursue
> Theire fancies fonde, and thinges unlawfull crave,
> Like brutishe beastes appeare unto the viewe,
> And shall at lengthe, Actaeons guerdon have:
>   And as his houndes, soe theire affections base,
>   Shall them devoure, and all their deedes deface.[20]

A similar interpretation of the Actaeon myth in terms of *libido* and
illicitus amor had appeared earlier in Sprengius' verses accompanying Virgil Solis' illustration ("Actaeon à proprijs canibus
discerpitur"):

> Sic homo qui mundi saltus perlustrat opacos,
>   In formam cervi quadrupedantis abit.
> Dum varijs animum noxis involvit & anget,
>   Dum lasciva salax gaudia carnis alit.
> Ambulat & caecus, quò perniciosa voluptas

Allicit: hinc pulsat debita poena fores.
Affectus etenim proprio quos pectore nutrit
   Nequitiosus homo, tristia fata ferunt.
Hunc furor, hunc odij pestis miseranda trucidat,
   Huic parat illicitus funera mortis amor:
Singula quid referam? scelerum sua quosque libido
   Dilaniat, rabidum more furente canum.[21]

Although one writer explicitly denied that Actaeon was motivated by lust ("aestusque, sitisque Causa fuit: sed non ulla inhonesta Venus, Quid si te nudam inspexit"),[22] others explained the myth as an example of the dangers of excess in love, in hunting, or in other pleasures. Thus De Bry's emblem of Actaeon bears the motto "Femina casta viros fugat immoderata petentes," and the accompanying verses ("*Actaeon, sive immodicum venandi, & amandi studium*") warn against excessive attachment to love and to the chase:

Qui nemorum & Veneris nimio capiuntur amore
   Intereunt studio, non aliunde, suo.
Si qua tamen castae mens est sibi conscia Famae,
   Illa pudicitiam quo tueatur habet.[23]

According to Golding's prefatory epistle to the Earl of Leicester, Actaeon's fate should be warning to all who delight in "foule excesse of chamberworke":

All such as doo in flattring freaks, and hawkes, and hounds delyght,
And dyce, and cards, and for too spend the tyme both day and nyght
In foule excesse of chamberworke, or too much meate and drink:
Uppon the piteous storie of Acteon ought too think.
For theis and theyr adherents usde excessive are in deede
The dogs that dayly doo devour theyr follower on with speede.[24]

When love transforms Falstaff into "a Windsor stag," his metamorphosis is, like Actaeon's, a symbol of "affections base" and "illicitus amor," an example of "immodicum . . . amandi studium." The moral significance of his disguise conforms closely to contemporary interpretations of the Actaeon myth, but its propriety is also reinforced by allied traditions. The comparison of the lover to a stag[25] is a commonplace of Renaissance imagery, and Elizabethan love-poetry abounds in allusions to Actaeon's fate.[26]

III

Thus, in at least two respects—in form and in significance—
Falstaff's final disguise bears a closer resemblance to Actaeon as
Renaissance iconography had represented him than to the Actaeon
of Ovid's text. In the *Metamorphoses,* the hunter's transformation
into a stag is complete before his hounds attack him; in many
Renaissance illustrations, however—as in *The Merry Wives of
Windsor*—the only sign of his metamorphosis is the stag's head.
Secondly, in Shakespeare's treatment of this motif, the primary
emphasis falls on the nature and effects of lust. For earlier instances
of this interpretation, one must look not to Ovid's verses, but to
emblem literature and illustrations of the *Metamorphoses*—to
Whitney, Sprengius, and De Bry.

Though these parallels point towards a *general* indebtedness to
Renaissance iconography for the form—and probably the
significance—of Falstaff's disguise, the question of *specific* influences is more complex. As Whitney's emblem of Actaeon
provides a very close parallel not only for Falstaff's costume and
position under attack, but also for the moral significance of his
transformation and punishment, Shakespeare may conceivably
have derived both from *A Choice of Emblemes*. Nevertheless,
though Whitney's emblem seems a highly probable·influence, it can
hardly be regarded as an exclusive source. As Miss Freeman has
observed in another context, "The variety of possibilities makes the
certainty of any one of them very doubtful. . . . It is as likely as not
that Shakespeare was acquainted with the work of Whitney, but to
maintain that there was necessarily always direct influence is to
make peculiar to the emblem writers themes and images which were
the common property of the age."[27]

IV

In Falstaff's final metamorphosis Shakespeare seems to have
deliberately parodied a familiar *exemplum* of lust. What of Sir
John's previous "transformations"? Are they likewise parodies of
conventional symbols of "unchaste desire"? Though somewhat far-
fetched, this possibility should not be ruled out as altogether im-

probable. Significantly, all three ordeals are presented in terms of the metamorphosis-tradition. Falstaff himself (V.v) applies the label "transformation" to the episodes of the buck-basket and his disguise as the woman of Brainford, just as, on a later occasion (V.v) he calls attention to his metamorphosis into a "Windsor stag." As his final ordeal obviously recalls the fate of Actaeon, his two previous "transformations" may conceivably parody, to some extent, the humiliations of other unfortunate lovers. Like Sir John, other lechers and adulterers had been enclosed in baskets[28] or donned female clothing,[29] but the most notable instances of such infatuation had been Virgil and Hercules. As these were the examples which should have occurred most readily to a Renaissance audience, let us consider them in detail.

In punishing the would-be adulterer by compelling him to enter a basket, Mistress Ford achieves (as Professor Bullough has noted) a revenge roughly analogous to that which a woman of Rome had inflicted on the amorous Virgil.[30] According to *The Lyfe of Virgilius,* printed at Antwerp by Jan van Doesborgh around 1518,[31] "Virgilius was enamoured of a fayre lady the fayrest in all rome . . . . at the laste she consented & sayd if he wyll come ad [*sic*] mydnyghte to the castell walle she shulde lette dowe [*sic*] a basket with stronge cordes and there to drawe hym uppe at hyr wyndowe & so to lye by eby [*sic*] hyr and have his pleasur and with this answere was virgilius very glad. . . . " Instead of fulfilling her promise, however, the woman "let hym hange in the basket when he was halfe way up to hyr wyndowe . . . tyll all the men in rome wyst it and also the emperour. . . ."

Is this parallel purely fortuitous, or could it have held any real significance for Shakespeare and his audience? At first glance, there would appear to be only one valid point of resemblance between Virgil and Falstaff—the fact that both would-be adulterers are tricked by their intended mistress into entering a basket and are thus punished for their presumption with discomfort and humiliation. The points of divergence, on the other hand, are manifold. The basket serves to conceal Falstaff, but to expose Virgil. The Roman poet is punished with public scorn, the English knight with ducking in the Thames. Moreover, the circumstances under which they enter the basket are quite different; for Virgil it is a means of access to his mistress, for Falstaff a means of escape from the suspicious husband. Nevertheless, though these differences preclude a point-by-point analogy between Falstaff's plight and Virgil's predicament, there are several additional factors which could have made this parallel a suggestive one for a Renaissance audience. First, Virgil had long since become a conventional example of the power of love and man's vulnerability to woman's wiles. Second, several versions of the basket-story include the motif of the husband's sudden return. Third, certain variants incorporate the motif of punishment by water.

As a result of the basket-episode, Virgil had become a stock example of the unfortunate lover in late mediaeval and early Renaissance literature and art[32] "Frequently mentioned in lists of humiliated or deceived lovers,"[33] he appears in Gower's *Confessio Amantis* among a "great companie" which Elde leads towards Venus and which includes David and Bathsheba, Samson and Delilah, Aristotle and Phyllis, and Solomon and his wives and concubines:

> And eke *Virgile* of acqueintance
> I sigh, where he the maiden praid,
> Whiche was the doughter, as men sayd,
> Of themperour whilom of Rome.[34]

In the fifteenth-century romance *Li livre du cuer d'amours espris*, Virgil's basket appears, along with Delilah's shears and Aristotle's bridle, among "spoils of love gone wrong." Two manuscripts of Petrarch's *Trionfi* depict Virgil in the basket, along with Samson and Aristotle, among illustrious victims of Cupid. A Renaissance saltcellar portrays the basket-episode "along with other scenes symbolical of the besetting weakness of wise men — Adam and Eve, Sisera and Jael, Samson and Delilah, Aristotle and Phyllis. . . ."[35] A Swiss embroidery of 1522 shows Virgil in the basket among other instances of the evil effects of lust — Solomon's idolatry, Samson and Delilah, David and Bathsheba, Judith and Holofernes.[36] A title-page border designed by Ambrosius Holbein around 1516 portrays Virgil in the basket along with other familiar examples of the power of women — Samson and Delilah, Aristotle and Phyllis, and Solomon. Another title-page border, designed by Urs Graf in 1519 and frequently reproduced during the following decades, also treats the basket-episode as an instance of unfortunate love. At upper left

Virgil is depicted as suspended in a basket by a woman, while a Cupid appears to be throwing a stone at him. At upper right appears the companion picture of Virgil's revenge on the woman who had humiliated him. A blind Cupid is represented in the lower margin between illustrations of the Judgment of Paris and the fate of Pyramus and Thisbe. As the border occurs on the title-page of *La Bible des Poetes* in 1531, Virgil's humiliation, like Falstaff's, could be regarded as an instance of the "transformation" effected by love. A similar conception of Virgil can be found in Renaissance pageants; according to Philippe de Vigneulles' *Chronique de Metz* a celebration of 1511 included a procession of "eight or nine wagons in each of which was a wise or famous man of ancient times who had been deceived by a woman." After Solomon, Samson, Holofernes, Hercules, and Sardanapalus, there "came Virgil suspended in a basket, and finally Aristotle ridden by a woman."[37]

For Falstaff the basket is not a means of access to Mistress Ford, but a hiding-place from her jealous husband. Although the latter detail is not a conventional feature of the Virgilius legend, it does occur in several variants of the basket-story. In a fourteenth-century French manuscript Queen Racio punishes her would-be lover (Fausse Amour) through a ruse similar to Mistress Ford's. Before receiving her unwelcome suitor, the queen orders "a large basket to be brought to her"; when her servants "announce in well simulated consternation that the king has returned," Fausse Amour "takes refuge in the basket and is swung out the window, let down a short distance, . . . left there", and finally dumped out.[38] In *The Historie of Frier Rush,* published in London in 1620 and containing a woodcut of the basket-episode taken from *The Lyfe of Virgilius,* the sudden return of the husband's servant compels the unfaithful wife to conceal her lover in a cheese-basket hanging out the window. Thereupon Rush "cut the rope that the basket hung by, and down fell Priest and all into a great pool of water that was under the window."[39] Similarly, in a Continental version of the basket-story, a young monk in love with a married woman hides from the husband in "a cheese-basket hanging out the window. The husband, who already knows the facts, cuts the rope and throws the basket into the Danube . . . . "[40]

In several versions of the basket-story, the adulterer, like Falstaff, is finally dumped out into muddy water or a pool of filth. Besides the tales of the monk or priest in the cheese-basket, the same motif occurs in Hans Sach's *Der jung Gesell fellet durch den Korb,* where a painting of a similar scene provides "an object lesson to those who are not faithful in their love":

> A young lady holds a young man suspended in a basket attached to a pole projecting from her house. . . . Then the basket gives way and the wooer falls into a pool of filth below.[41]

In *The Lyfe of Virgilius,* the poet escapes the ducking other adulterers suffer, but in the accompanying woodcut the basket is suspended above the river Tiber. In Spargo's opinion, the tale was probably influenced by the "germanic punishment basket" *(Scuppestol),* in which adulterers and other malefactors were "pulled up . . . and then dumped out in such a way as to fall into a pool or mud-puddle."[42] If this conjecture is correct, the Germanic *Schupfe* may be the prototype not only for the punishment inflicted on Virgil and the adulterer in *The Historie of Frier Rush,* but also for the character of Falstaff's ordeal.

As the Virgilius-legend was common property, Shakespeare and his audience could have encountered it in a variety of works—in the text and woodcuts in *The Lyfe of Virgilius* and *The Deceytes of Women,* in Stephen Hawes's *The Pastime of Pleasure,*[43] or in John Rolland's *The Court of Venus.*[44] Although we can hardly regard any one of these as the specific source of Shakespeare's episode (indeed, much closer parallels can be found in variant versions of the basket-story), they do provide evidence of the popularity of the Virgilius-legend in sixteenth-century Britain. If (like his Actaeon-disguise) Falstaff's basket-ordeal was intended to suggest any well-known *exemplum* of lust, the most obvious prototype, for a Tudor audience, would have been the humiliation of Virgil.

V

If Falstaff's first "transformation" roughly parallels Virgil's humiliation, his second metamorphosis shows some resemblance both in form and in meaning to another classic instance of *libido*—Hercules in amorous bondage to Omphale.[45] In donning woman's clothing and serving Omphale, Hercules had become (like Sardanapalus) a stock example of the corrupting effects of lust. The same procession which represented "Virgil suspended in a basket" among unfortunate lovers also showed Hercules and Sardanapalus spinning.[46] Guarini's *Il Pastor Fido* treats Hercules as a familiar example of the lover *(amante):*

> Ancor non sai,
> Che per piacer ad Onfale, non pure
> Volle cangiar in feminili spoglie
> Del feroce Leon l' ispido tergo,
> Ma della clava noderosa in vece
> Trattar il fuso, e la conocchia imbelle?
> Così de le fatiche, e degli affani
> Prendea ristoro, e nel bel sen di lei,
> Quasi in porto d'Amor solea ritrarsi . . .   [47]

According to Francesco Anguilla, it was love which constrained Hercules ("figurato da i Mitologici per la fortezza") to dress in woman's clothing.[48] Erasmus alludes to the same myth in discussing the proverb "Hercules in Lydia":

> Hercules in Lydia, proverbialiter dicitur qui cultu corporis effoeminatior incedit, indecoro sibi habitu utens, ut miles in toga talari conspicuus. Multorum scriptis celebratur Hercules, muliebribus indutus apud Omphalem Lydiae reginam. Aristides in oratione adversus eliminatores: . . .
> i. Hercules inter Lydos saltavit. Tertullianus libro de pallio: Qualis ille Hercules serico, Omphales fuerit, iam Omphale in Herculis in scorto designata descripsit. ubi pro serico, Beatus Rhenanus Theristro legit. innuit autem, non minus pudendum fuisse Herculi muliebrem cultum assumere, quam Omphale leonina pelle cingi.[49]

Conti explains the myth in terms of *libido:*

> Hic idem post tot superata pericula, post tot latrones de medio sublatos, post purgatum horrendis monstris orbem terrarum, Omphalae amore captus multa turpia, & primis rebus gestis indigna commisit. cur haec literarum monumentis tradita sunt? aut cur ad posteros transmissa? ut nos commonefacerent antiqui sapientes viro bono semper esse vigilandum, quia si parumper oculos à virtute deflexerit atque conniveat, ab appetentia tanquam à rapidissimo fluvio, ad libidinem, & ad illegitimas voluptates defertur, suapteque natura prolabitur. Hic propter muliebres amores postea in crudelissimum mortis genus incidit, quoniam voluptatum finis est omnium dolor & miseriae.[50]
> Fuit deinde Hercules Omphales Lydorum Regis filiae amore captus,

quare multa viro forti indecora facere coactus est: . . . idem inermi
Omphalae leonis pelle concessa inter pedisquas Omphales foemineo
habitu indutus sedentariam artem exercuit, ut testatur Ovid. in
Deianira . . . [51]

In the following century Burton's *Anatomy of Melancholy*[52] and the
emblem books of Peacham,[53] Vaenius,[54] and Solorzano[55] provide
further evidence of the popularity of the Hercules and Omphale
myth as an *exemplum* of the pejorative effects of lust. Although
Shakespeare and his audience probably encountered this story in
Ovid's *Heroides* and Turbervile's translation, it was a familiar motif
in Renaissance literature and iconography,[56] and it seems preferable
to emphasize its importance as part of the general mythological
background of the age rather than try to pinpoint the exact sources
through which the tradition of Hercules in woman's clothing may
have reached the author of *The Merry Wives*.

VI

What inferences may we legitimately draw from these parallels?
Has Shakespeare deliberately constructed his main plot around
three stock examples of lust? Are all three of Sir John's "transformations" symbolic and emblematic — conscious parodies of myth
and legend? Though the elements of parody and conventional
symbolism in Falstaff's final ordeal seem unmistakable, it is
questionable whether they play so significant a part in the two
previous episodes. The analogy with the Actaeon myth is in-
escapable; the parallels with Virgil and Hercules are less obvious
and consequently more doubtful. Whereas Actaeon is the only
widely-known instance of a stag-headed hunter conventionally
allegorized in terms of *libido*, Virgil and Hercules are merely the two
most prominent examples among numerous lovers punished by con-
finement in a basket or shamed by female clothing.[57] In the final
analysis, therefore, the answer must hinge on the issue of dramatic
consistency. If Falstaff's last metamorphosis is an emblematic
parody of lust, it is not illogical to look for a similar employment of
dramatic symbolism in his previous transformations. Unless the
dramatic technique underlying the scenes of the buck-basket and
the impersonation of the old woman of Brainford is radically

different from the method Shakespeare uses in the episode of Herne the Hunter, it seems fairly likely that these too may involve deliberate parody of stock examples of *libido* — especially as all three of Falstaff's "transformations" clearly expose him to ridicule for his lust. If his stag's head and hunter's guise make him a comic counterpart of Actaeon, the basket and female clothing in his two previous misadventures may, not improbably, suggest a similar burlesque of the plight of Virgil and Hercules.

The emblematic value of all three disguises would, of course, have depended largely on their visual impact and the audience's facility at interpreting them correctly. As Professor Merchant has pointed out in his recent study of "Shakespeare's concern with the visual" and "the visual expectations of the audience," the dramatist shared with his age a common background of symbolism and a common taste for the "emblematic" and "significant."[58] If *The Merry Wives* was indeed composed (or perhaps rewritten) for a court performance,[59] then Shakespeare could expect an audience easily capable of interpreting the relatively simple visual symbolism of Falstaff's disguises. If, moreover, the play was specifically "designed for performance at a Garter Feast,"[60] the indirect allusions to Virgil and Hercules as humiliated lovers shamed for their lust would be all the more appropriate. In all three of the knight's amorous misadventures one could recognize a dramatic *exemplum* of the Garter motto, *Hony soit qui mal y pense;* each rendezvous is cunningly designed both to display his lechery — the "corrupted heart" of one who thinks evil ("qui mal y pense") — and to afflict him with shame ("Hony soit"). In this context the moral symbolism of the basket and female clothing is as meaningful — though hardly as obvious — as that of the stag's head.

We should not allow the label "realistic comedy" to obscure the importance of other dramatic modes in *The Merry Wives of Windsor.* The final scene draws on mythological and iconological tradition for its ethical symbolism; both the form and significance of Falstaff's disguise as Herne are, as we have seen, very similar to Whitney's emblem of Actaeon. His two previous "transformations" contain elements which are reminiscent of other legendary examples of *libido;* Falstaff's basket and "woman's apparell" may, therefore, like his "Bucks head," be symbolic and emblematic. If the predominant mode of the drama is bourgeois realism, the

technique underlying one — and perhaps all three — of its major
episodes is the method of mythological symbolism and parody.
Whether or not Shakespeare actually received a royal command "to
write a play of Sir John Falstaff in love"[61] he may (it appears) have
consciously constructed his main-plot around three stock examples
of *libido,* three familiar symbols of "unchaste desire."

CHAPTER IX

The Faerie Queene: Una and the Clergy.

THE SIGNIFICANCE of the "lowly asse" upon which Una rides (I. i. 4) and which the "salvage nation" ignorantly attempts to worship (I. vi. 19) has usually been explained as a reference to ancient superstition or medieval ritual. In Todd's opinion, the latter episode referred to the "objection made against the ancient Christians, that they worshipped an ass."[1] Percival, on the other hand, interpreted it as an allusion to the medieval Feast of the Ass or to Mid-Lenten ceremonies still observed in Spenser's own days—the "popular custom of drawing in pageant a wooden ass to the door of the church, on Palm Sunday . . . ,"[2] to commemorate Christ's entry into Jerusalem. Neither of these suggestions, however, appears completely convincing. Moreover, both of them fail to explain why Spenser should have introduced the ass at all in his portrait of Una. A possible explanation is that this detail symbolizes the ministry—the vehicle of the orthodox doctrine and one of the signs or *notae* of the True Church.

The ecclesiastical associations of Babrius' fable No. 6 ("De Asino gestante simulacrum"),[3] which was popularized by various Renaissance emblem books,[4] would appear to support this interpretation. Alciati's Emblem No. 7, which bore the motto "Non tibi, sed religioni," depicted a throng of worshippers kneeling before a statue of Isis borne on an ass's back. The accompanying verses explained that the ass foolishly imagined himself the object of this devotion, until warned that he was merely the vehicle of the God:

> Isidis effigiem tardus gestabat asellus,
>   Pando verenda dorso habens mysteria,
> Obvius ergo Deam quisquis reverenter adorat,
>   Piasque genibus concipit flexis preces.
> Ast asinus tantum praestari credit honorem
>   Sibi, & intumescit, admodum superbiens:
> Donec eum flagris compescens, dixit agaso,
>   Non es Deus tu, aselle, sed Deum vehis.[5]

Claudius Minoes[6] interpreted this fable as a warning to bishops and priests:[7]

> Sacerdotes, Episcopi, & qui rebus sacris praesunt, in honore sunt habendi, ob id maximè, quòd sacris praesint, quorum sunt administri, licet interdum aut vitiis plusquàm vulgaribus implicati, aut ignari & stupidi habeantur. Hi verò ut suum munus & officium curare vel maximè debent, sic quantum dignitatem sustineant, ipsos subindi animo secum reputare par est. Meminerint tamen se homines esse, nec sibi arrogent impensiùs, quòd tantum ministerium gerant, & rerum divinarum curam, quasi humeris impositam habeant, ne, ut asinus audivit, Non es Deus, sed Deum fers, illi audiant: Non vobis haec, sed Deo soli omnis est tribuenda gloria.[8]

Minoes further explained that the ancient Egyptians had regarded the ass as a symbol of wisdom, fortitude, tireless labour, and frugality—"totius humanae commoditatis assiduus minister."[9]

Geoffrey Whitney's *A Choice of Emblemes* reproduced Alciati's emblem with the same motto. Like Minoes, he applied the fable directly to the clergy:

> The pastors good, that doe gladd tidings preache,
> The godlie sorte, with reverence doe imbrace:
> Though they be men, yet since Godds worde they teache,
> We honor them, and give them higheste place,

Imbassadors of princes of the earthe,
Have royall States, thoughe base they are by birthe.

Yet, if throwghe pride they doe themselves forgett,
And make accompte that honor, to be theires:
And do not marke with in whose place they sett,
Let them behowlde the asse, that ISIS beares,
Whoe thowghte the men to honor him, did kneele,
And staied therefore, till he the staffe did feele.[10]

Though Spenser borrowed the symbolism of the ass and the clergy, he treated the fable with considerable freedom. In Canto VI there is no suggestion that the ass shows undue pride or mistakenly regards himself as a proper object of worship.

The episode apparently refers to the exaggerated reverence which "ignorant Christians"[11] bestowed on their pastors. Since it is Una—the true church—whom they foster, it seems reasonable to infer that they are Protestants. The incident occurs, moreover, at a time when Una's protector, the Redcrosse Knight, has abandoned her—i.e., when England has forsaken the orthodox faith. The sylvan folk who rescue her from Sansloy would seem, accordingly, to represent the rustic population of the countryside, who cherish the Biblical doctrine and its ministry during its persecution, but are none the less too illiterate to understand either. Their attitude both to God's word and to those who preach it tends, therefore, to be superstitious and idolatrous.[12]

As Reformation theologians placed heavy emphasis on the duties of the preaching ministry, Spenser's inclusion of the *asinus portans mysteria*[13] in his first description of the true church was both logical and apposite. The "lowly asse more white then snow" apparently symbolizes that "pura verbi praedicatio,"[14] which Calvin regarded as one of the two signs of the visible church:

Enimverò de Ecclesia visibili, & quae sub cognitionem nostram cadit, quale iudicium facere conveniat, ex superioribus iam liquere existimo . . . Ubicunque enim Dei verbum syncerè praedicari atque audiri, ubi sacramenta[15] ex Christi instituto administrari videmus, illic aliquam esse Dei Ecclesiam nullo modo ambigendum est:[16]

Since the true preaching of the *verbum Dei* was an essential element in the definition and identification of the orthodox church, Spenser appropriately represented both in the same allegorical portrait.

Una — the orthodox doctrine — is carried by her proper vehicle, the ministry of the word.

Spenser may have intended an additional reference to the "white asses" of Judges v. 10.[17] Rupertus Tuitiensis[18] had explained them as the *doctores* of the tribes of Israel, on whose doctrine the Hebrew people reposed. An allusion to this parallel would be especially appropriate in Spenser's symbolic portrait of the Christian church and its ministry.

The parallel between Alciati's emblem of the *asinus portans mysteria* and Spenser's "verbal icon" of Una on the "lowly asse" may, finally, have involved a further analogy; Isis, like Una, was a symbol for veiled Truth.[19] In Plutarch's[20] opinion, she represented the knowledge of divine reality; in addition to revealing the sacred mysteries, she was the guardian of the holy Scriptures. Goropius Becanus[21] regarded her as the *verbum Dei,* the word of God. Una's significance in Spenser's poem is similar — the divine truth expressed in Scripture, with its central mystery of the crucified Christ.

In describing truth as veiled, Spenser was reflecting Christian, as well as Platonic, doctrine. In Book V of *Stromata* Clement of Alexandria had devoted an entire chapter to "Reasons for Veiling the Truth in Symbols" and another to "The Opinions of the Apostles on Veiling the Mysteries of the Faith."[22] In discussing the veiled truths and mysteries of the Christian faith, Clement quoted extensively from the Pauline epistles — Ephesians iii. 3-5, Colossians i. 25-27 and ii. 2-3, Romans xv. 25-26, and I Corinthians ii. 6-7.

Spenser's representation of the ass as the vehicle of revealed truth should not have seemed strange to an audience familiar with Agrippa's *De Vanitate Scientiarum* or Bruno's *Cabala del Cavallo Pegaseo.* Both of these writers, expatiating partly in jest, but essentially in earnest, on "the mysteries of the Asse," had conceived it as the symbol of a "holy ignorance" poor in worldly erudition, but rich in wisdom of the spirit.[23] Cornelius Agrippa composed "A Digression in praise of the Asse," declaring that lest he be falsely accused "because I have called the Apostles Asses, we will discourse in fewe woordes the mysteries of the Asse . . . " Both Christ and Abraham rode on this lowly beast, declared Agrippa, " . . . so that this olde Proverbe emonge the people is not spoken in vaine, which saithe: that the Asse carieth mysteries, wherefore I wil now advertise you famous professours of sciences, . . . that if the unprofitable burdens of humane knowledges be not set aparte . . . yee be utterly and altogether unprofitable to carrie the mysteries of divine wisdome: neither had that *Apuleius* of *Megara,* ever bene admitted to the holy mysteries of *Isis,* if first he had not of a Philosopher ben tourned into an Asse" (Agrippa, 184). The example of Balaam's ass indicated that "the simple and rude idiote doth oftentimes see those things which a Schole Doctoure corrupted with the traditions of men cannot perceive" (*ibid.,* 185). Indeed, there was "no beaste so able to receive divinitie as the Asse, into whome if yee shall not be tourned, yee shall not be able to carrie the divine misteries. In time past emonge the Romaines the proper name of the Christians was that they shoulde be called *Asinarij,* and they were wonte to paint the Image of Christe with the eares of an Asse: a witnes hereof is *Tertullian:* wherefore let not Bishops and Ministers disdeigne nor repute it to theire shame if amonge these Giauntlike Elephantes of Sciences they be Asses and are so called . . . " (*Ibid.,* 185).

For Agrippa the ass was, accordingly, a highly suitable emblem for the Christian clergy, the bearers of the Gospel truth. Christ himself had chosen "his Apostles, not *Rabbines,* not Scribes, not Maisters, not Priestes, but unlearned parsons of the rude people, voyde well neare of al knowledge, unskilful, and Asses" (*Ibid.,* 183). The successors of the Apostles must likewise regard themselves as "asses," unschooled in the wisdom of the world: "Wherefore O yee Asses, which are now . . . under the commaundement of Christ by his Apostles the messengers and readers of true wisdome in his holy Gospel, be you lewsed.from the darkenes of the flesh and bloude, if ye desire to attaine to this divine and true wisdome not of the tree of the knowledge of good and ill, but of the tree of life, the traditions of men set aparte, and every search & discourse of the flesh and bloud . . . " (*Ibid.,* 186, "The Conclusion of the worke").

In Bruno's opinion, the Scriptures symbolized the righteous man by the ass, and both Christians and Jews gloried in this title (Bruno, *op. cit.,* "Declamatione al . . . lettore": "considerate il principio della causa per cui gli Christiani et Giudei non s'adirano, ma piu tosto con glorioso trionfo si congratulano insieme, quando con le metaphoriche allusioni nella santa scrittura son figurati per titoli et definitioni Asini . . . : di sorte che dovumque si tratta di quel benedetto animale, per moralità di lettera, allegoria di senso, et anagogia di proposito s'intende l'huomo giusto, l'huomo santo, l'huomo de Dio"). While the Egyptians had regarded this beast as a hieroglyph of ignorance, certain Talmudists had interpreted it as a symbol of wisdom, "perche à colui che vuol penetrare entro gli secreti et occolti ricetti di quella, sia necessariamente de mistiero d'esser sobrio, et paciente, havendo mustaccio testa, et schena d'asino. Deve haver l'animo humile, ripremuto, et basso; et il senso che non faccia differenza tra gli cardi et le lattuche" (*Ibid.*, "Dialogo Primo"). It was, accordingly, by a species of ignorance — by "asininity" — that man achieved knowledge of the Truth: "Hor se la Sophia scorge la verità per l'ignoranza, la scorge per la stoltitia consequentemente, et consequentemente per l'asinità" ("Dialogo Primo." In this dialogue Bruno utilizes the symbol of the ass to designate three different species of ignorance which unite the human intellect to its intelligible object, Truth. Relying respectively on (1) denial, (2) doubt, and (3) certain "principii . . . conosciuti, approvati, et con certo argomento manifesti, senza ogni demostratione et apparenza," the first is represented by "l'asino pullo fugace et errabondo", the second by a donkey unable to decide between two roads, and the third by the ass and her foal upon which Christ entered Jerusalem. Guided by the light of faith and "cattivando l'intelletto à colui, che gli monta sopra, et à sua bella posta l'addirizza et guida," these cannot err, "perche non caminano col proprio fallace intendimento; ma con infallibil lume di superna intelligenza." These are truly predestined to arrive at the Jerusalem of beatitude and the open vision of divine Truth, "perche gli sopramonta quello, senza il qual sopramontante non è chi condurvesi vagla").

Unlike the worldly-wise, who trusted in his own itellect, the Christian depended solely on revelation: "Cossi [sic] li nostri divi asini privi del proprio sentimento, et affetto, vegnono ad intendere non altrimente che come gli vien soffiato à l'orecchie dalle revelationi o de gli dei o de' vicarij loro: et per consequenza à governarsi non secondo altra legge che de que medesimi" ("Dialogo Primo"). For Pseudo-Dionysius such "holy ignorance" had represented the most perfect knowledge: "O santa ignoranza, ó divina pazzia, ó sopra humana Asinità. Quel rapto, profondo, et contemplativo Areopagita . . . afferma che la ignoranza e una perfittissima scienza . . . " ("Dialogo Primo").[24]

Both Agrippa and Bruno were acquainted with a conventional interpretation of the Biblical "jawbone of an ass" (Judges xv. 16) as the preaching of the Gospel. Stemming from Gregory's *Moralia* (Migne, P.L., LXXV, Paris, 1849, 1023), this exegetical tradition also found expression in the writings of Rabanus Maurus (P.L., CVIII, Paris, 1864, 1194), Paterius (P.L., LXXIX, Paris, 1849, 789), Rupertus (P.L., CLXVII, Paris, 1854, 1048-9), and in the *Glossa Ordinaria* (P.L., CXIII, Paris, 1852-532). It was, in all probability, the primary source of the Renaissance conception of the ass as a symbol of the clergy. "Is it not true," Agrippa demanded, "that *Sampson* with the checke bone of an Asse, strake and slew the *Philistians:* and beinge thirstie, he prayed to the Lorde, who losened a tothe in the jawe of the Asse, and cleane water ranne out, which when he had droncken, his spirites and strength were refreshed? Did not Christe, in the mouthe of his simple Asses and rude idiotes his Apostles and Disciples, overcome and strike all the Philosophers of the Gentiles, and Lawiers of the Jewes, and overthrewe, & caste under foote all mannes wisdome, drinckinge to us out of that checke bone of his Asses, the water of wisdome and everlasting life" (Agrippa, 185).[25]

For Bruno the "anagogico senso" of this text was virtually identical: " . . . dicono gli santi interpreti, che nella mascella de l'asina, cioè de gli predicatori de la legge et ministri della sinagoga: et nella mascella del pulledro de gl'asini, cioè de predicatori della nova legge, et ministri de l'ecclesia militante, delevit eos, cioè scancellò, spinse qué mille, quel numero compito, qué tutti. . . . Et è chiamato il luogho Ramath lechi cioè exaltation de la mascella; della quale per frutto di predicatione non solo è seguita la ruina delle adversarie et odiose potestadi: ma anco la salute de regenerati, perche dalla medesima mascella, cioè per virtù di medesima predicatione son uscite et comparse quelle acque, che promulgando la divina sapienza, diffondeno la gratia celeste, et fanno gli suoi abbeverati capaci de vita eterna" (Bruno, "Declamatione al Lettore").

CHAPTER X

The Faerie Queene: The House of Care.

IN THE FOURTH book of *The Faerie Queene,* Scudamour passes a restless night in the house of Care,

> . . . a blacksmith by his trade,
> That neither day nor night from working spared,
> But to small purpose yron wedges made:
> Those be unquiet thoughts, that carefull minds invade.

The smith is assisted by "sixe strong groomes" who keep the visitor awake most of the evening with the din of their

> . . . huge great hammers, that did never rest
> From heaping stroakes . . .

When the knight finally falls asleep, Care awakens him with a pair of red-hot tongs.

That this episode "symbolizes Scudamour's jealous wretchedness"[1] is as Lemmi observed, perfectly obvious. Indeed Spenser has made the meaning of his "darke conceit" extremely clear. Ate, "that

stryfull hag," has filled the knight's heart "with gealous discontent."
Her slander pierces "His gealous hart" like thorns. After his almost
sleepless night "one mote plainely read" the "signes of anguish" in
his face and "ghesse the man to be dismayed with gealous dread."
Further news of Britomart, whom he erroneously regards as a rival
for Amoret's favor, makes him

> . . . swell in every inner part,
> For fell despight, and gnaw his gealous hart.

Nevertheless, the sources of this episode and the exact significance
of some of its details have remained obscure. In Lemmi's opinion,
Care and his servants owed much to Boccaccio's account of Acheron
and his six children.[2] This interpretation, however, throws
no light on the symbolism of the hammers and anvil or on the personification of Care as a blacksmith. A more probable explanation is
that Spenser has given poetic expression to a contemporary Italian
idiom which described jealousy metaphorically as "martello" or
"martello d'amore."

Florio's Italian-English dictionary, *A Worlde of Wordes,* defines
martello as "a hammer, a sledge, a carpenters mallet. Also iealousie
or suspition in love: panting or throbbing of the hart."[3] *Ammartellare* means "to hammer, to forge, to beate, to stampe, to ap-
passionate with iealousie," and *ammartellato* denotes "one that is
passioned with love or ielousie[.] Also forged or hammered."[4] The
first edition of the *Vocabolario degli Accademici della Crusca* also
notes this meaning of the word:

> . . . E. *Martello* lo diciamo per una certa passione amorosa, che è
> quando si dubita, che la cosa amata non ti sia tolta da altri. Lat.
> *suspicio,* disse Terenzio, onde AMMARTELLATO. Ber. Orl. Perche fu
> l'uno, e l'altro ammartelato, D'altro che d'amoroso struggimento.[5]

Filippo Venuti's *Dittionario volgare, & Latino*—one of the sources
of Florio's book—alludes briefly to this idiom:

> Dar martello, martellare, & Appassionare alcuno] male urere ali-
> quem. Terent.[6]

Lasca's poem "In nome del Bernio," which appears at the beginning of a popular collection of burlesque verse, describes the phrase
"martello d'amore" as synonymous with jealousy:

> Chi Brama di fuggir maninconia,
> Fastidio, affanno, dispeto e dolore:

> Chi vuol cacciar da se la Gelosia,
> O come diciam noi, martel d'Amore:
> Legga di grazia quest' Opera mia . . . [7]

Giovanni della Casa'a "Capitolo del martello" regards insomnia as one of the worst torments of jealousy:

> Tutte le infermita de un hospitale
> Contandogli il francioso & la moria,
> Quanto il martel d'Amore non fano male . . .
>
> In summa questa e una cosa pazza,
>   Et io per me l'ho gia piu volte detto
> Che chi non ha martello in vero sguazza:
> Quando altri per dormir e ito al letto,
>   Comincia i suoi sospiri à ritrovare,
> E beccasi il cervello a bel diletto.
> Non lo farebb' el sonno addormentare,
>   Et chi contasse al' hora i suoi pensieri
> Putrebbe annoverar l'onde del mare.
> Va racconciando insieme i falsi e i veri,
>   La ragiono col tal, la ando la stette:
> Quest'è ch'io non la vidi hoggi ne hieri.

After enumerating a whole catalogue of ills, the poet concludes, "Ma il peggior mal di tutti fu il martello."[8]

The same idiom recurs in Firenzuola's "In lode del legno santo":

> Hor nuovamente vi dico che cava
>   Di fastidio un che crepi di martello
> Guarda se questa è un' opera brava
> Et se pazzi volessin provar quello
>   Et conoscessin la loro malattia
> Tutti ritornerebbono in cervello
> Ch'altro non e 'l martel ch'una pazzia . . . [9]

Berni, in *Orlando innamorato*, speaks of "La gelosia, il furore, e'l martello"[10] and describes Agrican as devoured "di rabbia . . . E di martello, e di furia, e di stizza."[11]

Vernacular translations of Terence employed the same term to express suspicion and jealous despair. Giovanni Fabrini renders a conversation between Gnatho and Thraso in *The Eunuch* as follows:

> G. Nihil minus .i. facias] non far cosa nessuna manco di questa, guardatene, per niente no lo fare [imo] anzi [auge] accrescigli

[magis] piu [suspitionem] il sospetto. T. Cur? perche? G. Rogas?]
dimandimi tu perche? quasi dicendo puo far che tu no lo sappia?
[Scin'?] sai tu perche? [si quando] se qualche volta [illa facit men-
tionem] ella fa mentione [Phaedriae] di Fedria [aut] overamente [si
laudat] se ella lo loda [ut te male urat] per darti martello, per farti
disperare [.][12]

Spenser's description of Scudamour's ordeal seems, then, to be a
detailed elaboration of a conventional Italian metaphor.[13]
Tormented by his jealous suspicion of Britomart and Amoret, the
knight is an *ammartellato,* a man "passionated with love or
ielousie." The hammers which are forging "unquiet thoughts" or
striking his own helmet represent his passionate jealousy, that
"Gelosia," or "Pena, Affanno, Furore, cagionato da gelosia, o da
altra veemente passione, specialmente amorosa," conventionally
symbolized as "Martello di gelosia, o di amore."[14]

The poet may also have recalled the adage "Inter malleum & incudem" ("between the hammer and the anvil"), a proverb describing the state of anxiety:

Μεταξυ του ακμονας και σφυρας id est, Inter incudem & malleum.
Huic non dissimile refertur ab Origene Theolog, quadam in
Hieremiam homilia, his quidem verbis (nam Graeca desideramus)
Iam quoddam est apud nationes tritum vulgi sermone proverbium,
ut de iis qui anxietatibus & ingentibus malis premuntur, dicant, In-
ter malleum sunt & Incudem.[15]

Pierius' *Hieroglyphica* gives a similar interpretation of 'hammer' as
"malorum irritamento":

Videtur verò Malleus pro malorum irritamento accipi: arma si-
quidem, pugiones, cuspides, & cultros malleus excudit, unde mala tot
immortales oboriuntur. Eo etiam fiunt tubae ductiles, per quarum
clangorem animemur in bellum. Eo franguntur opera, & quae solida
sunt conteruntur. Quare nonnulli divinarum literarum interpretes
Zabulum per mallei figuram intelligunt, à quo malae omnes procedunt
cogitationes, pravaque consilia, & bonorum operum perturbationes.[16]

A rather striking analogue to Care and his hammers appears in
Ripa's *Iconologia,* first published in Rome in 1593,[17] three years
before the publication of the fourth book of *The Faerie Queene.*
"Tribulatione" is described as a dishevelled female holding three
hammers and a heart; the hammers (Ripa explains) are like dark
thoughts which continually harass the soul:

> Donna vestita di nero, sarà scapigliata, nella destra mano terrà tre martelli, & nella sinistra un cuore.

> E vestita di nero, perche porta neri, & oscuri i pensieri, i quali continuamente macerano l'anima, & il cuore, non altrimente, che fussero martelli, i quali con percosse continue, lo tormentassero.[18]

Both the concept of care and the percussion-metaphor occur, moreover, in Renaissance etymologies of *jealousy:*

> Zelotypus . . . Zelator, seu aemulator formae dicitur. nam ζηλος, aemulatio est: τυπος, forma. Qui igitur amat ut solicitus sit nequis amore suo perfruatur, zelotypus ext.[19]

> Gelous . . . L. Zelosus . . . Zelotypus. Gr. ζηλοτυπος, ex ζηλος, i. aemulatio, & τυπος i. percutio, tundo, *strucken with emulation;* quia zelotypia *percutit & tundit hominen illum in quo habitat.*[20]

Cicero had referred metaphorically to "his assiduis uno opere eandem incudem diemque noctemque tundentibus,"[21] and Elyot had interpreted this idiom as meaning incessant repetition of the same thing:

> *Eandem incudem tundere,* to labour alway about one thing, to repete one thing continually, to harpe alwaie upon one strynge.[22]

Spenser's exploitation of the hammer-metaphor to express the idea of jealous solicitude was, then, well grounded in Renaissance convention. The hammer[23] was a fairly common symbol for jealous anxiety and could represent either the cause of such "malae cogitationes" or the "pensieri oscuri" themselves.

Giordano Bruno, in turn, makes frequent use of the hammer-anvil image as a symbol of the lover's passion. In his summary of the "Argument" of his comedy *Il Candelaio* (published in 1582) he relates how the courtesan Vittoria "builds fine castles in the air, thinking that this flame of love will melt and precipitate precious metals, and that Cupid's hammer working it on the anvil of Bonifacio's heart, will produce at least enough coin to enable her, when her own trade fails, to adopt that of (a bawd)." In the center of a lover's heart, according to the "Proprologue" of the same play the audience will behold "arrows, bolts, darts, fires, flames, yearning, jealousy, suspicion, despair, intolerance, hatred and rage, cuts, wounds, laments, bellows, pincers, anvils and hammers . . . ."[24]

His dialogue *De gli eroici furori* (published in London in 1585) contains an emblem of hammer and anvil with the motto *Ab Aetna*. In the accompanying verses, Vulcan declares that he has found "a better forger of Aetna, a better smith, anvil and hammer" in the lover's breast, "which exhales sighs and whose bellows vivify the furnace, where the soul lies prostrate from so many assaults of such long tortures . . . and brings a concert which divulges so bitter and cruel a torment." The poem, Bruno explains, depicts "the pains and afflictions inherent in love, especially in vulgar love, which is nothing else than the smith's shop of Vulcan who forges the thunderbolts of Jove to torment delinquent souls. For disordered love bears within itself the germ of its own pain. . . . " Vulcan himself symbolizes "the vindicator the intelligence, which with a certain remorse of conscience (*synteresis*) strikes the transgressive soul as with a heavy hammer." As divine metallurgist he refines and purifies the lover's soul; for "there is no love without fear, zeal, jealousy, rancor," and other passions. Seeking to purge itself and "recover its natural beauty," the "soul uses fire, for like gold mixed with earth and shapeless, it wishes by a vigorous trial to liberate itself from impurities, and this end is achieved when the intellect, the true smith of Jove, sets to work actively exercising the intellectual powers."

Love is "always afflicted and tortured," Bruno continues (in the *persona* of Tansillo), "so that it cannot avoid becoming material for the furnace of Vulcan . . . And no matter how much it may fix itself upon the beloved object, the soul cannot avoid being sometimes agitated and shaken by hopeful sighs, by fears, doubts, zeal, troubles of conscience, remorse, wilfulness, contrition and other tormentors represented by the bellows, coals, anvils, hammers, pincers and the other tools found in the work shop of this sordid and squalid spouse of Venus."[25]

Elsewhere in the same work Bruno (through Tansillo) describes jealousy as "the daughter of love, its companion and its sigh," an "infernal Tisiphone" and "minister of torment" (pp. 90-91). In a later dialogue (through the interlocutors Severino and Minutolo) he symbolizes a lover as a blind man who has been "bitten by the serpent of jealousy" torn from the tresses of Alecto. Though the jealousy belonging to "vulgar love" has no place in "heroic love," nevertheless "heroic jealousy" is "manifest among lovers of the true and the good . . . "[26]

I

Scudamour's sleeplessness and jealousy are conventional characteristics of lover's melancholy (*ilishi* or *heroes*), and the blacksmith Care is himself a personification of the lover's solicitude.[27] As Robert Burton observed, Avicenna had defined heroical love (*ilishi*) as "solicitudo melancholica, in qua homo applicat sibi continuam cogitationem super pulchritudine ipsius quam amat, gestuum, morum." According to Giovanni Michele Savonarola, "Ilischi est sollicitudo melancholica qua quis ob amorem fortem & intensum sollicitat habere rem quam nimia aviditate concupiscit. Et ilishi . . . apud nos vero interpretatur amor." Similarly, for Bernardus de Gordonio, "Amor qui hereos dicitur est sollicitudo melancolica propter mulieris amoren."[28]

Care's dwelling ("beside a little brooke . . . Of muddie water") recalls the setting of Hyginus' fable of the creation of mankind by Cura and Jupiter. According to Burton's account, "Dame Cura by chance went over a brooke, and, taking up some of the dirty slime, made an image of it. Jupiter, eftsoons coming by, put life to it; but Cura and Jupiter could not agree what name to gave him, or who should own him." Saturn resolved the dispute by deciding that "his name shall be *Homo ab humo: Cura eum possideat quamdiu vivat* . . ."[29] The notion of a "house of *Care*," in turn, was familiar from Langland's "castel of care"[30] and Virgil's reference to the lairs (*cubilia*) of Grief and Cares at the entrance of Hell.[31] Neither of the latter passages, however, seems to have exerted much influence on Spenser's account of the smithy and its master. Many of Care's personal characteristics, however, reflect conventional conceptions of care or jealousy current both in classical literature and in Renaissance dictionaries.[32]

The word *care* (or *cura*) possessed several distinct meanings, and Spenser's portrait acquires much of its effectiveness from his exploitation of this ambiguity. In addition to the usual meaning (1) anxiety, grief, or solicitude, it could also denote, more specifically, (2) "the care, pain, or anxiety of love" and (3) the art and labor of the craftsman.[33] Calepine gives all three senses:

> *Cura*, [Cura, pensiero, travaglio . . .] solicitudo, quòd cor edat, & excruciet . . . Pro opere, quod adhibita cura fit . . . Pro amore. [Amore] Virg. 4. At regina gravi iandudum saucia cura.

In personifying Scudamour's jealous anxiety as Care and representing this figure symbolically as an artisan, Spenser combined all three meanings in a single allegorical person. This fusion was all the more apposite since Stephanus had defined jealousy as amorous solicitude and Italian idiom employed *martello* as a synonym for this concept.

In addition to elaborating the idea of care as labor as a vehicle for the concept of care as the lover's solicitude, Spenser invested his master smith with attributes by no means unusual in Renaissance definitions and descriptions of *cura*.

1. Care is a "blacke and griesly" figure. Cooper cites Horace's "atrae curae," and Stephanus quotes the same poet's "atras eximere curas." Florio's translation of Montaigne's *Essays* mentions "Care, looking grim and blacke."[34] Ripa's "Tribulazione" is dressed in black.[35]

2. Spenser conveys the idea of "careworn" by emphasizing the wasted appearance of Care and his dwelling place. This

> wretched wearish elfe,
> With hollow eyes and rawbone cheekes forspent

lives "where the mouldred earth had cav'd the banke," near a stagnant brook. Both Stephanus and Calepine derive the etymology of *cura* from the fact that it corrodes or consumes the heart:

> . . . solicitudo, quod cor edat, & excruciet . . . [36] *Cura* . . . Vehemens & anxia animi solicitudo, dicta (ut ait Festus) quòd cor edat, vel quòd urat.[37]

Cooper quotes Ovid's line "Vitiatum corpus curis amaris", and Spenser himself refers to Scudamour's ordeal as "hart-fretting payne."[38] The derivation of *cura* from *corura* was still a "common etymology" for Robert Burton.[39]

3. Scudamour's jealous suspicion "Gauld, and griev'd him night and day," and Spenser's blacksmith "neither day nor night from working spared." Cooper and Stephanus list several examples of this conventional conception of care as the vigilant enemy of sleep:

Vigilantes curae.
Vigiles incumbunt curae.
Vigili perspexerat omnia cura.
Mens invigilat curis.
Removens soporem cura.
Pervigil, cura.[40]

> Invigilat quieti cura. Stat.
> Insomnes curae. Claud. Watchefulle care, keeping men from sleepe.
> Somnos abrumpit cura. Virgil. Sorrow breaketh sleepe.[41]

Stephanus, Cooper, and Calepine all cite what is probably the classic instance of this concept, Virgil's description of the love-sick Dido, kept sleepless by the thought of Aeneas:

> At regina gravi iamdudum saucia cura
> volnus alit venis et caeco carpitur igni.
> . . . nec placidam membris dat cura quietem.[42]

4. Though Scudamour's jealousy vexes him night and day, he is especially vulnerable at night.[43] Significantly, it is at nightfall that he reaches the house of Care, and he departs at dawn. Stephanus refers to the same idea in Virgil's "Recursat sub noctem cura" and Ovid's "Nox curarum nutrix."

5. Care's labor is devoted to making "yron wedges" ("unquiet thoughts, that carefull minds invade"). Though in classical descriptions of Vulcan's forge the blacksmith is usually preoccupied with framing thunderbolts for Zeus or arms for some hero or god, Lyly's *Sapho and Phao* shows him making six arrowheads for Venus. Among these is jealousy:

> This arrow is feathered with the wings of Aegitus, which never sleepeth for feare of his hen: the heade toucht with the stone Perillus, which causeth mistruste and ielousie. Shoote this, Cupid, at men that have faire wives, which will make them rubbe the browes, when they swell in the braines.[44]

6. Care's incessant labors are merely "to small purpose," and Scudamour seeks "in vaine" their end and cause. This idea of the vanity or purposelessness of care is also conventional, and Cooper cites Lucretius' description of cares as "empty" ("inanes").

7. The symbolism in stanza 44, where the "maister Smith" nips the knight "under his side" with "redwhot yron tongs," closely resembles that of *Griefe* in the "maske of Cupid":

> A paire of Pincers in his hand he had,
> With which he pinched people to the heart,
> That from thenceforth a wretched life they lad,
> In wilfull languor and consuming smart,
> Dying each day with inward wounds of dolours dart.[45]

The imagery in both passages is based on a conventional use of "pinch" to signify the pressure of misfortune or distress,[46] and in both instances the poet has resorted to allegory to represent this "pinch of grief or care." An interesting analogue occurs in Cooper's *Thesaurus:* "Remordet te cura. Virg. Care nippeth thee againe." Stephanus quotes Virgil's "Premere curam sub corde."

8. Care's hands are blistered by the hot coals, and it is "out of the burning cinders" that he snatches the tongs which break Scudamour's slumber. Spenser may have had in mind the comparison of jealousy to coals of fire in *The Song of Solomon* viii. 6, "ielousie is cruel as the grave: the coles thereof are fyrie coles, & a vehement flame."[47] That Scudamour's "soundest sleepe" should be disturbed by "his dayly feare" is also a conventional concept. Stephanus cites Cicero's "Curae plurimae metusque ex somno nascuntur."

9. It is also highly appropriate that Care's bellows should move *Pensifenesse.* Calepine defines *cura* as "pensiero," and both Cooper and Elyot list "thought" among its synonyms.

10. Both Spenser and Lyly stress the analogy between the blacksmith's bellows and the lover's sighs. In Spenser's allegory, however, they are identical, whereas in *Sapho and Phao* they are antithetical:

> It is no lesse unwholsom for Venus, who is most honoured in Princes courtes, to soiourne with Vulcan in a smithes forge, where bellowes blow in steede of sighes, dark smokes for sweet perfumes, & for the panting of loving hearts, is only heard the beating of steeled hammers.[48]

11. In describing the smith's wakefulness, his begrimed and wasted appearance, and the incessant din of his hammers, Spenser may also have recalled a passage in *Ecclesiasticus:*

> So is it of everie carpenter, and workemaster that laboreth night and daye: . . . The smithe in like maner abideth by his anvil, and doeth his diligence to labour the yron: the vapour of the fyre dryeth his flesh, and he muste fight with the heat of the fornace: the noyce of the hammer is ever in his eares . . . : he setteth his minde to make up his workes: therefore he watcheth to polish it perfitely.[49]

12. To Care's assistants Spenser attributes immense strength and size and incessant labor. These too are conventional—but by no means distinctive—aspects of care:

> Incentes curae.
> Maximae & gravissimae curae.

Ipse tibi tua maxima cura.
Exercere vires omni cura.
Fortior obstat curis ducis.
Urgentibus curis.
Urgeri moltis curis.
Exercere vitam curas.[50]

Each stronger than his predecessor, the "sixe strong groomes" who "by degrees . . . were disagreed" represent the increasing intensity of Scudamour's jealous anxiety. The "monstrous Gyant" who strikes last and hardest symbolizes the highest pitch of his anguish, his "maxima cura."

II

Thus the central image of the episode—the figure of the smithy— was a singularly appropriate symbol for the torments of jealous wrath. In the first place, it served as a vehicle for both the conventional meaning of *martello* and the contemporary etymologies of *zelotypus*. In the second place, the forges of Vulcan and Tubalcain —the two most significant classical and Biblical parallels—lent themselves readily to the theme of jealousy. The blacksmith god had long been notorious as the mythological prototype of the jealous husband,[51] and the "sons of Cain" inherited the stigma of their ancestor's murderous jealousy. According to Hebrew and Christian tradition, Cain's crime was inspired not only by envy of Abel's sacrifice, but also by jealousy of the latter's beautiful wife, Leboda or Lubia.[52]

Thirdly, the image of the forge may have served to emphasize the groundless character of Scudamour's suspicions of Britomart and Amoret. Like Oberon's charges against Titania, these are mere "forgeries of jealousy."[53] As in the case of *martello*, Spenser's description of the smithy apparently exploits two conventional meanings of the verb *forge*: (1) "to fabricate . . . (a false or imaginary story, lie, etc.)" and (2) "to shape by heating in a forge and hammering."[54]

Fourthly, forge and bellows had already appeared in medieval literature as symbols of wrath and envy. Dante's *Purgatorio* (xv, 51) had compared to bellows the sighs of the envious ("invidia move il mantaco ai sospiri"). In Chaucer's "Persones Tale" (553-555) ire is described as "the develes fourneys, that is eschaufed with the fyr of helle."

> In this forseyde develes fourneys ther forgen three shrewes: Pryde, that ay bloweth and encreseth the fyr by chydinge and wikked wordes. / Thanne stant Envye, and *holdeth the hote iren upon the herte of man with a peire of longe tonges*[55] of long rancour./ And thanne stant the sinne of contumelie or stryf and cheeste, and batereth and forgeth by vileyns reprevinges.

III

Spenser's personification of jealousy as Care may have been influenced by Benedetto Varchi's *Lezzione sopra la gelosia,* a commentary on Giovanni della Casa's sonnet on jealousy ("Cura, che di timor ti nutri, & cresci"). Of Casa's first line, Varchi observes that the poet expresses the concept of jealousy periphrastically, describing it not as *gelosia* but as *cura:*

> . . . favella il Poeta alla Gelosia, & artificiosamente non la chiama per lo suo dritto nome; ma la circonscrive, dicendo, *Cura, che di timor . . .*[56]

In the same way, Baldassare Stampa had referred to jealousy as "Cura, che sempre vigilante e desta."[57]

In *The Faerie Queene,* Spenser suggests the increasing intensity of jealousy through the symbol of the "sixe strong groomes," each stronger than his predecessor. In the *Lezzione* Varchi singles out Casa's *cresci* for particular emphasis:

> . . . he addeth besides, (*Cresci,* thou growest or increasest) which word no doubt is set downe by him, with great and excellent iudgement, by reason that IEALOUSIE may (as other like Qualities) encrease or diminish . . . [58]

Spenser's description of jealousy stresses its nature, name, origin, development, and effects. All of these points had been singled out for emphasis in Varchi's commentary on Casa's sonnet:

> . . . what thing *Iealousie* is, whence it springeth, how it is nourished, and what a wicked and hurtfull plague it is. And this hee sheweth, by the Effects, and Accidents of the same . . .

> Considering that in these foure Verses here defineth, or rather describeth what IEALOUSIE is; and there being two manner of

Distinctions, the one, which declareth her name, the other, which sheweth her nature: pleaseth it you first to understand that this Greeke word Ζαλοτιπια [sic], compounded of two words, (from whence *Gelosia*, that is IEALOUSIE, commeth in our language) signifieth no other thing, than a certain Emulation, or any Envy, a Forme, or Beautie . . . [59]

Like Spenser, Varchi emphasizes the close relationship of jealousy to love, envy, and fear.[60] All of the "disdainful Disgraces, . . . burning Martyrings, . . . insupportable Punishments, and . . . unspeakable bloudy Passions in Love . . . are nothing . . . in respect of that one damned Plague, and deadly Poyson, cleped IEALOUSIE." No true love can exist without jealousy.

Love (truly) we cannot, unlesse there be some spice of IEALOUSIE therein . . . wheresoever true Love is, there indeed some IEALOUSIE must necessarily be, and where no IEALOUSIE is, there of necessitie can be no true Love indeed . . .

It is, moreover, a form of dread and a species of envy:

. . . IEALOUSIE is a certaine Feare or Doubt, least any one whom we would not, should enjoy a Beautie that wee make account of . . . Now there is no doubt but that IEALOUSIE is a Spice or Species of Envy . . . wheresoever IEALOUSIE is the Precursor, there Envy must be the Follower alwayes . . .

Accordingly, "this our Poet hath done excellent well, to call and as it were define IEALOUSIE to be CARE, that is, a Thought or Passion which proceedeth and leadeth on Feare, which is as much to say, as if it came of Dread and suspect. And by this phrase of speech hee giveth us to understand from whence it springeth . . . "[61]

Like Spenser's episode, Casa's sonnet represents insomnia as an inseparable attribute of jealous Care:

Ivi senza riposo, i giorni mena,
Senza sonno le notti, ivi ti duoli
Non men di dubbia che di certa pena.

In this part [explains Varchi] he goeth on, describing and setting downe that Nature and Life of such as be Iealous, under the description of IEALOUSIE herselfe, who (always) living as it were, in a continual Hell, take no rest in the day; neither can they sleepe at all in the nights, but (ever) grieve and lament, taking on as well for that which is false, as for what they stand in doubt of to be true; imagining many times, and conceiting divers things that are altogether impossible, for this strange Maladie engendreth a continuall and a perpetuall discontentment and disquietnesse in the minde, so that hee is not able, nor hath any power to give over from vexing himselfe, standing (alwayes) watchfull . . .[62]

Unlike Spenser, however, Varchi makes no use of the percussion-metaphor inherent in contemporary etymologies of *zelotypia* or of the symbolism of the hammer and forge.

IV

Scudamour suffers not only from the din of hammers and bellows, but also from the cries of various animals—dogs, the cock, and the owl. These are conventional nocturnal sounds, such as might annoy any victim of insomnia, and, unlike the seven blacksmiths and their forge, they can be taken literally, without an allegorical explanation. Nonetheless, inasmuch as all three of these creatures are noted for their vigilance, they obviously reinforce Spenser's symbolic description of care-ridden wakefulness. Lemmi has emphasized the fact that "the cock is the bird into which Gallus was turned for unwittingly betraying the amours of Mars and Venus, the owl is that into which Ascalaphus was transformed for tattling on Proserpine, and the howling of dogs was associated with Hecate whom . . . Spenser might well have thought of as symbolical of misfortune and sorrow."[63] None of these allusions, however, seems entirely relevant to Scudamour's situation. Gallus was punished specifically for falling asleep:

> at Gallus fertur in somnum versus fuisse: quare nemine praesciente Sol rem conspexit superveniens, Vulcanoque indicavit.[64]

Similarly, the fact that Proserpina ate several pomegranate seeds ("tria grana mali punici, vel novem, ut alii maluerunt')[65] seems to have little bearing on the knight's unwilling vigil. Surely the simpler explanation is, in this instance, also the more appropriate—that Spenser selected these particular animals primarily for their well-known nocturnal vigilance.

The cock was, moreover, a fairly conventional symbol of jealous wakefulness. Ripa's *Gelosia* is represented "con un gallo nel braccio sinistro".

> Dipingesi la Gelosia col gallo in braccio perche quest' animale è gelosissimo, vigilante desto, & accorto.[66]

For approximately the same reason this fowl is also shown with *Sospitione:*

> Il Gallo nel cimiero, Dimostra la vigilanza de sospettosi, essendo il Gallo, come dice Appiano, animale egualmente vigilante, & sospettoso.[67]

The cock also appears in two descriptions of *Sollecitudine.* In one it signifies diligence,[68] in the other, solicitude:

> Si dipinge il Gallo come animale sollecito, il quale all' hore sue determinate, si desta cantando, perche non lascia la sollecitudine finire li sonni intieri . . .[69]

Vigilanza is portrayed

> con un Gallo . . ., perche il gallo si desta nell' hore della notte, all' essercito del suo **canto**, nè tralascia mai di obedire alli occulti ammaestramenti della natura, cosi **insegna à** gl'huomini la vigilanza.[70]

The cock's characteristic jealousy and vigilance also make it an appropriate symbol for self-interest (*Interesse proprio*):

> . . . perche l'interesse tiene altrui in gelosia del proprio commodo, & in continua vigilanza, cosi d'animo, come de' sensi se gli accompagna seco il gallo . . .[71]

On the other hand, Ripa usually represents the owl simply as a nocturnal bird[72] ("uccello proprio della notte") or, more specifically, as a bird of ill omen.[73] Scorn, for instance, is depicted with an owl on his head:

> Lo scorno . . .si dipinge col Gufo, ilquale è uccello di cattivo augurio, secondo l'opinione sciocca de Gentili, & notturno, perche fà impiegar gli animi facilmente a cattivi pensieri.[74]

It was, therefore, highly appropriate that the owl—a nocturnal bird inspiring "cattivi pensieri"—and the cock—a conventional symbol of vigilance and jealousy—should contribute to Scudamour's torment[75] Spenser's allusion to them is, however, perfectly intelligible on the literal level, without resort to allegory.

V

The "sixe strong groomes" whose hammers disturb Scudamour's rest in the House of Care still require explanation. Though Spenser's account of the seven blacksmiths was (as Upton observed)[76] influenced by classical descriptions of Vulcan's forge, the poet's numerical symbolism has remained obscure. Why are Care's assistants specifically *six* in number? Spenser could easily have strengthened his allusion to the Cyclopes by limiting their number to the usual three.

Lemmi pointed out that their number is identical with that of Acheron's offspring. But of Acheron's six children only one was male.[77] In Upton's opinion, Care and "his six servants point out the seven days of the week, revolving round in perpetual labour and trouble: they have no ears to hear, . . . and rest not night nor day."[78] Other interpretations, however, are also plausible. The seven smiths could, with equal propriety, symbolize the seven parts of the night — *vesper, crepusculum, conticinium, intempestum, gallicinium, matutinum, diluculum*.[79] Nor should we overlook Strabo's declaration that the Cyclopes were "seven in number":

> . . . δια Κυκλωπων, ους επτα μεν
> ειναι, χαλεισθαι οε γαστεροχειρας . . .[80]

Nevertheless neither the parts of the night nor the days of the week constitute a completely satisfactory explanation; stanzas 36 and 37 clearly point to a sequence of *six* rather than *seven* units. Spenser does not depict the master-smith as personally wielding one of the "huge great hammers, that did never rest" and that "Like belles in greatnesse orderly succeed." Of the "sixe strong groomes," moreover, he singles out only the last and mightiest for special emphasis:

> He like a monstrous Gyant seem'd in sight,
> Farre passing *Bronteus,* or *Pyracmon* great.

Could Spenser's conception of the six assistants have been influenced by the same homily from which Erasmus and Pierius[81] drew, in part, their own interpretations of the hammer-symbol? Wielders of the hammer (*malleatores*) are (Origen explains) metaphorically sons of Cain, the author of the first fratricide and the direct ancestor of Tubalcain, "qui fuit malleator et faber in cuncta opera aeris et ferri":

> Cain generavit filios, et de Cain ortus est faber aeris et ferri. Ergo ut Zabulus qui omnium tentationum operator est, malleus dicitur, *ita qui ministrat, malleator est filius Cain.* Quotiescunque enim in tentationem incideris, scito malleum diabolem esse, et malleatorem

eum per quem te Zabulus insequitur . . . Quot quot enim in actu suo Zabulum suscipiunt et ministrant ei ad probandum justum, et injustum coarguendum, omnes malleatores sunt. Idcirco si heri malleator eras, et in manu malleum continebas, nunc discens *quia a Cain fratricida oriuntur malleatores,* projice malleum de manu tua . . . Verumtamen finis confractio est atque contritio.[82]

Philo Judaeus, in *De posteritate Caini,* also interprets the figure of Tubalcain as a moral allegory of the soul harassed by its own desires:

Accurately characterizing each one of these he [Moses] goes on to say: 'This man was a wielder of the hammer, a smith in brass and iron work' (Gen. iv. 22). For the soul that is vehemently concerned about bodily pleasures or the materials of outward things, is being ever hammered on an anvil, beaten out by the blows of his desires with their long swoop and reach.[83]

Origen's allegorical interpretation of the sons of Cain as *malleatores* and Philo's conception of Tubalcain as striking the blows of desire could conceivably have suggested to Spenser the propriety of symbolizing the six generations from Enoch to Tubalcain by six *malleatores,* each stronger than his predecessor. Such an allusion to the progeny of the first murderer[84] is by no means inappropriate in a description of the torments of jealousy.

The allusion to Brontes and Pyracmon and the description of the sixth *malleator* as "like a monstrous Gyant" (a phrase which Upton regarded as an echo of Homer's description of Vulcan[85] are especially apt if the sixth groom does indeed represent Tubalcain. Christian apologists sometimes identified the mythological Vulcan with the smith of Genesis iv. 22,[86] and both of these figures vied with the Cyclopes for the credit of having invented the arts of metalwork.[87]

The possibility that Spenser may be evoking the image of Tubalcain's smithy and the generations of the "sons of Cain" is consistent with allegorical interpretations of the Biblical blacksmith and with the Renaissance etymology of *zelotypia.* It provides only a tenuous basis for the poem's numerical symbolism, however, except for the conventional association of Tubalcain's forge with Jubal's discovery of music. William Nelson[88] has recently called attention to the parallel between the imagery of this stanza and Pythagoras' legendary experiments with bells and hammers in ascertaining the principles of harmony. In this tradition the number of smiths rarely exceeds five, and Spenser appears to have followed a relatively late variation on the legend of Pythagoras' (of Jubal's) discovery of music. The salient details of this scene in *The Faerie Queene* the six blacksmiths standing about the anvil, the graduated scale of their hammers, and the comparison with bells of varying "greatnesse" — all have close parallels in Franchino Gafuri's *Theorica Musicae.*

The legend that Pythagoras first discovered the principles of harmony by investigations at a blacksmith's forge and subsequent experiments with bells, strings, pipes, and other media was widely circulated during the late classical period through such writers as Nicomachus, Iamblichus, Gaudentius, Macrobius, Boethius, and Martianus Capella and echoed in countless mediaeval and Renaissance accounts of the origin of music.[89] Hammers, anvils, and bells became closely associated with the iconography of "Musica," and Pythagoras' experiments at the forge and with *Glockenspiel* recur frequently in representations of the liberal arts.[90] When Spenser stresses the "degrees" of his smiths and compares the graduated order of their hammers to that of a series of bells (iv.- v.36), he is drawing on an analogy long traditional in musical theory and iconography.

The six smiths, however, were emphatically *not* conventional in the Pythagoras legend. Some theorists, like Macrobius, had remained silent as to their number. Some had suggested four, while others agreed with Boethius in specifying five (one of whom was subsequently discarded). The first allusion to precisely six blacksmiths occurs, apparently, in Gafuri's *Theoricum opus musice discipline,* published at Naples in 1480 and republished as *Theorica Musicae* in 1492 at Milan. Up to a certain point Gafuri follows Boethius' account of how Pythagoras overheard five smiths at their labors, noticed the musical tones they produced, weighed their hammers, and rejected the fifth hammer as dissonant.[91]

> While Pythagoras was pondering the great variation in musical tones, he chanced to pass by a smithy and overheard the noise of hammers [beating on the anvil] . . . Upon ordering the men to exchange hammers, he learned that the quality of the sound depended not on the strength of the men but on the relative weight of the hammers themselves. After weighing the five hammers, he rejected the fifth as discordant. Of the four remaining, the heaviest

was exactly twice the weight of the lightest, and together they produced the octave . . . Then he redisposed the hammers in the following order, according to weight: 6 pounds, 8 pounds, 9 pounds, and 12 pounds.

Thus far, Gafuri's version differs little from those of his predecessors, but at this point he introduces a significant innovation. In order to include *all* the tones of the octave, he suggests that Pythagoras must have added two additional hammers, to make a total of six.

During this daily investigation of the secrets of harmony, Pythagoras also explored (I am persuaded) not only the combinations of these four tones, but also the other chords by which the art of music is perfected and nurtured. Primarily there are six combinations of tones . . . Hence we believe that Pythagoras exchanged the fifth, inharmonious hammer for another, and then added a sixth . . . Now the order of the six hammers according to weight would have been as follows—4, 6, 8, 9, 12, 16.

Both editions contain woodcuts illustrating the musical smithy. In the 1480 edition a full-page illustration depicts the six blacksmiths standing about an anvil and wielding hammers numbered iiij, vi, viij, viiij, xij, and xvj respectively.[92] In the 1492 edition the woodcut includes the Biblical musician Jubal and several Pythagorean experiments with bells, glasses, strings, and pipes.[93] Jubal is shown observing six blacksmiths whose hammers are numbered 4, 6, 8, 9, 12, and 16; and Pythagoras is represented in the act of striking a series of bells bearing the same sequence of numbers.

Here, portrayed graphically, are the significant details which will recur in Spenser's forge—the "sixe strong groomes" whose hammers "Like belles in greatnesse orderly succeed." Though the poet could have encountered the analogy between the graduated "degrees" of the hammers and the "orderly" succession of bells in virtually any extended version of the Pythagoras legend—from Boethius on down to the Renaissance—the addition of the sixth blacksmith was Gafuri's own innovation, and Spenser must have derived it, either directly or indirectly, from his source.

At a relatively early date, Pythagoras' experiments with hammers had been transferred to Jubal, the "father of all such as handle the harp and organ." Regarding the Pythagoras legend as a fabulous corruption of Scriptural truth, Christian historians not only credited Jubal with the discovery of harmony but also identified the musical smithy as that of his half-brother Tubalcain, "an instructor of every artificer in brass and iron." Mediaeval and Renaissance accounts of the origin of music frequently cited this tradition as an alternative to the Pythagoras story,[94] and, like the Greek philosopher, Tubalcain and his forge became standard figures in graphic representations of the musical art.

Tubalcain's special importance for Spenser's poem, however, lay in his relation to the theme of jealousy. According to Robertus Stephanus, his very name denoted *Aemulatio*,[95] and the fact that he was often identified with Vulcan made him an even more appropriate prototype of "gealous dread." In George Sandys' opinion,[96] "*Vulcan* was truely that *Tuball-Caine* recorded by *Moses.*" Vulcan himself, moreover, had long been a stock example of jealousy. Gower's *Confessio Amantis* has represented his "suspicionem inter [Venerem] et Martem" as an "exemplum contra istos maritos quos Jalousia maculavit."[97] The classical and Biblical blacksmiths thus embodied the same moral concept as Spenser's Care. In the language of Renaissance mythography and etymology, Vulcan = Tubalcain = *aemulatio* = *cura*. Like Tubalcain's smithy, Care's forge is literally a forge of Jealousy.

But for Spenser the tradition of the musical smithy serves a dual purpose. Besides evoking the image of Tubalcain's forge — the forge of *aemulatio* — it also reinforces the principal moral antithesis of Book IV, the contrast between Concord and Discord. In this context the Pythagoras legend suffers a sea change. Though the hammers succeed in "orderly" progression, the poet places his primary emphasis not on their order or harmony, but on the exact opposite: "For by degrees they all were *disagreed*." Instead of music, they produce noise. Whereas Pythagoras and Jubal had been delighted by harmony, Scudamour is tormented by a discordant din:

> And evermore, when he to sleepe did thinke,
> The hammers sound his senses did molest;
> And evermore, when he began to winke,
> The bellowes noyse disturb'd his quiet rest,
> Ne suffred sleepe to settle in his brest (iv.v.41)

In this way an image traditionally associated with concord becomes an *exemplum* of discord.

Care's smithy is, in fact, a compound image. Behind it lie two distinct traditions and two antithetical conceptions of the forge — as a symbol of jealousy (*zelotypia* or *martello*) and as a figure of harmony. In the context of Spenser's allegory of "Friendship" it is precisely this tension of contraries which gives the symbol its force and point. The potentiality for harmony also contains the seeds of dissonance. Just as the same musical instrument can produce either concord or discord, *amicitia* can become *inimicitia*. The "matter" of friendship and jealous hostility, like that of harmony and dissonance, is one and the same.

Like the structure of Book IV[98] the imagery of the smithy episode centers upon the antithesis between concord and discord. As music had long been a conventional symbol for the larger significance of harmony[99] friendship, internal peace, and political order — Spenser could effectively exploit this symbolism both for his image of *amicitia* in Canto ii (IV .ii. 1-2) and for his emblem of jealousy in the House of Care. Transformed into a figure of discord, the Pythagorean forge becomes an image of Scudamour's alienation from Amoret and Britomart through Ate's slanders. It is a broken harmony, the emblem of a broken friendship.[100]

CHAPTER XI

The Faerie Queene: "Errour" and the Renaissance

Truth and error are logical contraries,[1] and (as Spenser's readers were well aware) truth is one like the Phoenix, *unica et semper eadem,* while error is manifold and multiform. In the first canto of *The Faerie Queene* the two antithetical concepts are brought together symbolically in the episode of the Wandering Wood. On the one hand, true Holiness, figured in the Redcross Knight, is appropriately accompanied by Una, a personification of Truth. On the other hand, to convey the idea of Error, Spenser combined two conventional, but different mythological elements — the forest-labyrinth and the serpent-woman. Though both had a long literary history, stemming from classical prototypes, tradition had, on the whole, treated them as two separate and independent symbols. Spenser's originality consisted in introducing them in a single episode and investing them with the same allegorical referent.

This was a happy innovation, for there is an obvious, but significant link between the two symbols in the analogy between the serpent's winding train and the mazes of the labyrinthine wood. By combining them, Spenser gave additional emphasis to their natural bent for suggesting the idea of deviation from the straight or orthodox faith. Nevertheless, he was not content with a purely implicit suggestion of their common meaning, and in Una's explanation that "This is the wandring wood, this *Errours den,*" he gave explicit statement to the identical significance of the two symbols.

The forest-labyrinth is itself a composite symbol, long associated with the idea of error,[2] and Spenser's adjective "wandering" simply renders the Latin root in native English. On the other hand, the association of this concept with the mythological serpent-woman is less conventional, and its immediate background in Renaissance allegory requires further investigation. As a personification of *learned* error, Spenser's monster may have been influenced by Renaissance interpretations of similar serpentine hybrids as symbols of human erudition and rhetorical subtlety.

I

Though scholarship has recognized Hesiod's[3] influence on Spenser's Errour, it has hitherto placed exclusive emphasis on similarities of form. The question of a further parallel—a possible analogy in meaning—has been largely ignored. There is, however, a distinct resemblance between the allegorical significance of Spenser's monster and the meaning which Renaissance commentators found in Hesiod's serpent-woman.[4] In their conception of Echidna as "variam multiformemque mentis vim, & multiplicibus implicitam spiris artem" Spenser could have found a suggestion for representing in "Errours endless traine" the subtle but specious arguments which (except for faith) would enmesh the Christian wayfarer in fallacy and falsehood.

This interpretation usually occurs in the context of a traditional explanation of the Chimaera in terms of the threefold divisions of rhetoric—judicial, demonstrative, and deliberative. As the arguments employed in persuasion were longer, more various, and more involved, deliberative rhetoric had been appropriately symbolized by the dragon, and Chimaera herself had been alleged to be the daughter of Echidna. According to Richerius' *Lectionum Antiquarum,*

> Symbuleuticum genus draconis esse aiunt, quod varium inprimis sit, ac πολυστροφον, id est multarum conversionum, & longiore ad persuadendum orationis tractu utatur.
>
> Monstri vero mater, ab Hesiodo dicitur Echidna, quam non esse aliud volunt, qum ποικιλον νουν και πολυειδη, id est variam multiformemque mentis vim, aut longiorem, & πολυελικτον, id est multiplicibus implicitam spiris artem, Chimaerae instar ignis evomentem globos.[5]

In his *Symbolicarum Quaestionum,* Bocchius applied this interpretation to his emblem (Symbol No. 135) of Bellerophon and the Chimaera, where the monster possesses a lion's head, goat's forefeet, and a serpent's body from the waist down:

> Sunt qui indicari treis velint partes, quibus
> Dives facultas constat omnis Rhetorum . . .
> At quod consulit, draconis est
> Persimile varij, ac flexuosi anfractibus.
> Matrem Poetae monstri Echidnam huius ferunt,
> ΠΟΙΚΙΛΛΟΝ ΕΙΝΑΙ ΝΟΥΝΤΕ ΠΟΝΥΕΙΔΗΑΤΕ,
> id est Variam admodum, atque multiformem vividae
> Vim mentis esse: qua nihil potentius.
> Inde orta fertur artifex audacia
> Mortalium in vetitum negas ruentium, &
> Vomentium ore fulgura, & tonitrua
> Imitantium Iovis supremi, & Daedalae
> Rerum creatricis voluptates simul.[6]

Valeriano's *Hieroglyphica* explained Chimaera's serpentine coils as variety of arguments and emphasized Echidna's manifold and various erudition:

> Deliberativam demum per draconem, ob varietatem argumentorum, longioresque circunductus, & spiras quibus in persuadendo opus est: unde etiam monstri mater, fingitur ab Hesiodo, Echidna nomine, per quam ποικιλον νουν και πολωειδη, intelligi contendunt, quippe mentem multis & variis praeditam disciplinis.[7]

In his commentary of Alciati's Emblem No. 14, Francisco Sanchez of Salamanca echoed Richerius' analysis of Echidna and the Chimaera:

> Draco denique obtineat Symbuleuticum genus, quod varium sit in primis, & longiori ad persuadendum utatur orationis tractu. Monstri

> mater ab Hesiodo dicitur Echidna, quam nihil aliud esse volunt quàm variam multiformemque mentis vim, & multiplicibus implicitam spiris artem, Chimerae instar ignis evomentem globos.[8]

This interpretation had reached the Renaissance through Demetrius Triclinius' scholia[9] on Hesiod's *Theogony,* but the current taste for emblems and hieroglyphics helped to disseminate the conception of Echidna as multiform erudition and the association of the serpent's coils with rhetorical persuasion.

Though Spenser's monster vomits books and papers,[10] instead of fireballs, this variation on her classical prototype is especially appropriate in a personification of learned error. As this detail has been interpreted both as a reference to "the pamphlet publications in the latter years of Henry's reign" and as a symbol of "sophistical and polemical divinity; cabalistical and scholastical learning"[11] it is all the more interesting to find one of the Reformed theologians condemning a libellous opponent as "Echidna Illyrica." In an epistle to "Johanni Matthesio," dated January 8, 1550, Beza writes (apparently of Flacius'[12] attacks on Melanchthon, Beza and other Reformers) in the following terms:

> Has res magnas illustrare, quae invocationem ostendunt, utilius est, quam cum *Echidna Illyrica* certare, cuius venena viros honestos existimo detestari: Non enim pugnat de ullo doctrinae capite, sed narrationes scribit calumniarum et mendaciorum plenas, quibus utrumque agit, ut me populo invisum faciat, et accendat contra me illos ipsos, qui ninc praebent hospitium. Sed Deus . . . defendet me contra hunc Calumniatorem.[13]

II

In the emblem books Spenser would have found yet another serpentine hybrid allegorized as a symbol of wisdom and subtlety. Alciati's Emblem No. 5 had depicted "Sapientia humana" as a "monstrum Biforme," half-man and half-serpent:

> Sed sine vir pedibus, summis sine partibus anguis
>   Vir anguipes dici, & homiceps anguis potest . . .
> Haec vafrum species, sed relligione carentem,
>   Terrena tantùm quique curet, indicat.[14]

Claude Mignault had applied this emblem to the earthly learning of the philosophers:

Hoc informi monstro, quod nec omninò formam humanam, nec omninò serpentinam figuram habeat, natura quidem duplici, quodque necdum certam appellationem sortiri possit, ij notantur, qui anima rationis participe à Deo informati, terrena tantùm sapiunt: & neglecta conditione sui meliore, humi repunt, in naturamque belluinam degenerant. Monstrum enim, ut hîc exprimitur, in hominem non desinit, nec est ferae principium: non enim finem spectant Epicurei homines, propter quam homini sit concessa ratio, qua miserè abutuntur, eamque spontanea quadam & exitiosa ignoratione inficiunt. Tales fuerunt rigidi illi Philosophiae satellites, qui cùm perpetuò dogmatis sapientiae veteris, & sibi parùm constantis adhaeserint, nihil aliud spirarunt quàm quae terrae sunt, tametsi unum illis videretur esse studium caelestia divinaque contemplandi: quos ideò exagitat vir sanctissimus Augustin. libris De civit. Dei, Lactantius, Eusebius, & alij multi.[15]

For Mignault, as for Spenser, the half-human serpent symbolized a form of religious error—that specious and mundane wisdom which is folly in the sight of God. Alciati's emblem, he explained, represented Cecrops, who had first introduced idolatry into Greece:

Opinor autem hîc Alciatum exempli causa Cecropem apposuisse, nec quidem ab re. Ille enim primus idolorum cultu totam Graeciam imbuit, primus Iovem invocavit, simulacrorum usum induxit . . . Hincque colligere licet mundi sapientiam, quam technis & praestigiis satanicis invexere priores illi Principes, meram fuisse stultitiam, cùm perspicuum sit eam longè descivisse ab institutis illis priscorum patrum, qui leges divinas à Noëo, & eius meliori posteritate hauserant. Hos itaque vafros, & religionis expertes, quibus tantùm curae terrena sunt, & quorum Deus venter est, ex hominum albo reiicimus.[16]

III

Spenser's allegory of error thus combines two independent, but not altogether dissimilar, conventions—the forest-labyrinth and the woman-serpent. The propriety of linking them in a single episode derived not only from their common suggestion of involuted complexity, but also from the fairly similar interpretations which literary tradition had ascribed to them. Like the serpentine hybrid, the labyrinth had been interpreted *inter alia,* as a figure of philosophy. According to Boethius' *Consolation,* Philosophy had "so woven me with thy resouns the hous of Dedalus, so entrelaced that it is unable to be unlaced . . ."[17] In his *Aurora,* Peter Riga declared that he had "entered a little way, looked into, but not penetrated far into the Labyrinth of Aristotle, with the aid not of the clue ('filo') of Daedalus, but of the Son ('Filio') of God"[18] A marginal gloss in Calvin's *Institutes* refers to "Philosophorum labyrinthi,"[19] and elsewhere in the same work Calvin applies this figure to philosophy, as well as to oversubtle theological speculation. Condemning the polytheism of the Gentiles and the conflicting opinions of the philosophers concerning God as "immensa illa errorum colluvies," he observes that "suum enim cuique ingenium instar labyrinthi est."[20] Again, in insisting on strict adherence to the Scriptures in discussing such mysteries as the Trinity, he adds:

> Quod si quae subest in una divinitate Patris, Filij, & Spiritus distinctio (ut est cognitu difficilis) ingeniis quibusdam plus facessit negotij & molestiae quam expediat, meminerint labyrinthum ingredi hominis mentes dum suae curiositati indulgent . . .[21]

Similarly, in his *Discourse of Justification* Hooker refers to the "maze the Church of Rome doth cause her followers to tread, when they ask her the way of justification."[22]

Both symbols had been applied to philosophical speculation, but they were also linked by the idea of multiplicity. The adjectives "multiplex" and "multiformis" had been applied to Hesiod's Echidna, and Vellutello had interpreted Dante's "selva erronea" as a symbol of multitude:

> Ma è da notare, che si come selva è propriamente domandata ogni spessa moltitudine darbori, Cosi è dal poeta per selva intesa ogni spessa moltitudine di qual si voglia cose . . .[23]

Like the "many pathes" and "many turnings" of Stanza 10, Spenser's extensive catalogue of trees in the two preceding stanzas serves to emphasize the idea of multiplicity, and the same concept underlies the monster's "many boughtes" and "knots" and "thousand yong ones." These details not only stress the manifold nature of error, but also heighten the contrast with the unity of truth. Error is "multiplex," but truth (appropriately personified by *Una*) is one.

IV

The episode of the Wandering Wood also contains details reminiscent of other literary labyrinths. Despite Chaucer's influence[24] on Spenser's catalogue of trees, there is an apparent difference between the two in context. In *The Parlement of Foules* the tree-list serves primarily to describe the forest locale which provides the logical setting for a conclave of birds; the "congregatio volucrum" takes place in a clearing, or "launde," within this wood. Chaucer's forest is not a wandering wood and he does not compare it to a labyrinth. Though Chaucer does not develop this motif as an allegorical symbol of error, it may like Spenser's wood and the dark forests of Dante and Milton's *Comus,* or the garden of Mirth in the *Romance of the Rose,* serve as a figure of the world. For the Middle Ages, as for the Renaissance, *silva* (or *hyle*) could denote variety, multiplicity, or the realm of matter. On the other hand, Francesco Colonna's *Hypnerotomachia Poliphili* includes a brief and elementary tree-catalogue in a context fairly similar to Spenser's — a forest which resembles a labyrinth, where (as in *The Faerie Queene*) the "trees . . . did spred so broad, that heavens light did hide,"[26] and where the hero has lost his way:

> At length my ignorant steppes brought me into a thick wood, wherinto being a pritty way entred, I could not tell how to get out of it . . . and could not finde any track or path, eyther to direct me forward or lead me back againe. But a darke wood of thick bushes, sharpe thornes, tall ashes haled of the Viper, towgh Elmes beloved of the fruitfull vines, hard Ebony, strong Okes, soft Beeche and browne Hasils, who intertuining one anothers branches with a natural goodwill opposed themselves, to resist the entrance of the gratious sunne shine, with the greene coverture of their innumerable leaves . . . In this unaccustomed labour . . . I grewe extreamely hoate and faynte, . . . breathing out hollow and deep sighes, desiring helpe of the pittifull *Cretensian Ariadne,* who for the destroying of her monstrous brother the *Mynotaur:* gave unto the deceitfull *Theseus* a clew of thred to conduct him foorth of the intricate laborinth, that I also by some such meanes might be delivered out of this obscure wood.[27]

Though Errour resembles the Minotaur as a half-human, half-bestial monster in the center of a labyrinth, her serpentine form sets her apart from her Cretan prototype. Nevertheless, Horologgi's

"Annotationi" on Anguillara's version of the *Metamorphoses* anticipates Spenser in placing a serpentine figure of prudence in the midst of a wood of error. In allegorizing the Cadmus myth, the annotator refers to "prudentia figurata per il serpente, laqual' habita come esso, in una grotta nel mezzo di una foltissima selva di errori." Unlike Spenser's monster, however, Horologgi's serpent is not a half-human hybrid, and she symbolizes true prudence rather than learned error ("ella sola sa trovare la via di uscirne quando vuole").[28]

Redcrosse is by no means the first traveller to encounter a personification of error in a forest. In Lydgate's *Pilgrimage of the Life of Man,* the pilgrim meets Heresy — a concept frequently defined as "error of the intellect"[29] — soon after entering "a woode ful savage":

> I knew nat what was best to done,
> ffor, in a woode, a man may soone
> Lese his weye, and gon amys,
> Or he be war . . . [30]

Heresy, personified as an old hag with a pair of shears, threatens to reshape his scrip, but he refuses until he knows her authority:

> ffor I am callyd "Heresye,"
> The whiche do alwey my labour
> To brynge ffolke in greet errour,
> That ffolwe my condissiouns;
> Make hir hertis to decline
> ffor the trouthe of Iuste doctryne,
> And cause hem ffor to don ther cure,
> And amys to expowne hooly scripture.[31]

Although the primary significance of Spenser's episode is the victory of truth over intellectual error, he also draws on a conventional interpretation of the labyrinth in terms of the worldly pleasures which distract the human soul from its true and proper end. Twice he alludes to the fact that his travellers have been misled by pleasure: "And foorth they passe, with pleasure forward led"; "Led with delight, they thus beguile the way." Moreover, the wanderers are "Furthest from the end then, when they neerest weene." A fairly similar interpretation of the labyrinth occurs in Horologgi's notes on the tale of the Minotaur:

. . . nel laberinto, che è pieno di strade tortuose, che non conducono giamai al desiderato fine; cosi i piaceri, e le delitie intricano, & aviluppano l'huomo in questo mondo . . . , che non può giungner giamai al suo vero fine.[32]

Though the labyrinth had been subjected to a variety of interpretations,[33] it was usually explained as a symbol of the world and human life. Dante's *Convito* had referred to "the wandering wood [*selva erronea*] of this life,"[34] and Olimpio Marcucci regarded the forest of Valvasone's *La Caccia* as an imitation of Dante's *selva oscura:* "La selva è la vita humana piena di intoppi, che ci fanno traviar della vera strada, & smarrirci nelle vanità del mondo, & in ciò ha imitato Dante nel principio della sua comedia."[35] Berchorius explained the labyrinth as a symbol of the world and sin.[36] Reusner interpreted it as "fallacia mundi,"[37] and Paradin conceived it as "the dangerous wandrings, and fearful by wayes of this world."[38] The *Hypnerotomachia* contains a labyrinth highly suggestive of the seven ages of man,[39] and when (at another point in the same tale) the hero finds himself in a "darke place" full of "divers crooked torments, ambagious passages," a marginal gloss explains that this signifies "ignorance, and the wisedome of this world which is no thing els but mere folly."[40]

As the forest-labyrinth had been conventionally allegorized as a symbol of the world, this was a logical setting for Redcrosse to encounter a symbol of worldly wisdom. This concept is obviously embodied in the monster Errour, but it may also be inherent in the wood itself. Though the Wandering Wood may be interpreted broadly as the world, it may, with equal or greater propriety, be given a narrower reference, as a symbol of secular erudition. Though the variety which delights the travellers may conceivably refer to the pleasures of sense, it seems preferable (in view of the intellectual symbolism of Errour) to interpret it specifically in terms of the pleasures of worldly learning. The numerous paths, the failure to lead to an end, the multiplicity and variety of trees may appropriately denote the confusion of the secular philosophers concerning the end and final good of man. In *The City of God,* St. Augustine had contrasted the Christian's "assured hope" in the "true blessedness which [God] will give us" with the "empty dreams" of those "who intend to make for themselves a beatitude extant even in the continual misfortunes of man's temporal mortality":

> About that question of the final good the philosophers have kept a
> wonderful coil amongst themselves, seeking in every cranny and
> cavern thereof for the true beatitude; for that is the final good,
> which is desired only for itself . . . This was the daily endeavour of
> the worldly philosophers, who . . . sought no further than either the
> body, the mind, or both, wherein to place this *summum bonum* of
> theirs. From this tripartite foundation has M. Varro . . . observed
> two hundred and eighty-eight possible though not actual sects, for so
> many different results may be drawn from those three fountains.[41]

Nevertheless, as "the supreme good" is "eternal life," "fondly and
vainly are these men persuaded to find true happiness here."[42]

The tempest which compels the travellers to seek shelter is a fairly
conventional symbol of adversity,[43] and their attempt to seek
"promist ayde" in the wood possibly represents the vain effort to
find true happiness in the world through secular wisdom—to
achieve "beatitude extant even in the continual misfortunes of
man's temporal mortality," through the consolations of a false and
secular philosophy or of a fallacious and worldly church.

V*

Spenser's Errour embodies two distinct traditions concerning the
viper[44]—one drawn from classical mythology, the other derived from
natural history. In her hybrid form—half-woman, half-serpent—
the monster resembles Hesiod's Echidna. On the other hand, her
mortal sting, her method of sheltering her young in her own body,
and the unnatural behaviour of her offspring reflect contemporary
superstitions about vipers. The propriety of combining these
particular traits resides in the fact that the name of the
mythological serpent-woman and the generic term for the female
female viper are identical. "The *Greeks* call the male peculiarly and
properly *Echis*," declared Topsell, "and the Female Echidna . . ."[45]

Since the same term $(\epsilon\chi\iota\delta\nu\alpha)$ could be used to denote either the
female viper or the mythical hybrid, it is not surprising that
Echidna and other classical serpent-women should have appeared

*This section was first published in the *Modern Language Review*, Vol. LVI (1961), pp. 62-
66, and is here reprinted by permission of the editors and of the Modern Humanities Research
Association.

in Renaissance discussions of the viper. Calepine, for instance, in defining the common noun *echidna,* found it advisable to mention the monster Echidna.[46] Pierius introduced both Hesiod's Echidna and Dio Chrysostom's Libyan beast into his treatise *De Vipera;* the latter story, he explained, was a legend about vipers ("Fabula de Vipera ex D. Chrys.").[47] Edward Topsell included Dio's narrative in his chapter "Of the Lamia,"[48] but discussed the Scythian queen of Herodotus and Diodorus Siculus in a separate chapter 'Of the Viper'.[49] He apparently identified Herodotus' monster with Echidna, the paramour of Typhaon and mother of the Chimaera and other monsters:

> . . . and the same *Echidna* to be also the Mother of *Chimaera:* which from the Navel upward was like a Virgin, and downward like a Viper, of which also *Diodorus Siculus,* and *Herodotus* telleth this story . . .[50]

This identification of the mythological serpent-women with the female viper also derived support from classical authors, who had described these hybrid monsters as "viperish." Nonnos's Campe was "viperish Enyo" (εχιδνηεσσα Εννω) with 'viperish feet' (εχιδναι-ων ταρσων).[51] Herodotus had described the Scythian queen as half-viper (εχιδναν), and Diodorus had employed the same term (ἔχιδνης).[53]

Thus, by investing the legendary woman-serpent with characteristics of the female viper — by merging Echidna with *echidna* — Spenser was exploiting an identification implicit in both traditions. Though his portrait represented a distinct innovation on the classical Echidna, it developed a parallel familiar to Pierius and other scholars.

A similar fusion of the same two traditions occurs in *Paradise Lost,* in Milton's account of Sin. As a woman-serpent she resembles the classical Echidna. On the other hand, she carries the viper's mortal sting, and, like the traditional viper's brood, her offspring return to her body for protection, "gnaw My Bowels, their repast" and break violently forth from her womb. Like Spenser, Milton consciously combined details characteristic of two different referents for the same term. In so doing, however, he displayed a greater degree of independence from Spenser than his critics have recognized.

In both poems the behaviour of the monster's offspring reflects two divergent and contradictory beliefs about vipers: (1) that at birth young vipers "eat through the womb and belly of the female" and thus unnaturally destroy the mother,[54] and (2) that, when frightened, they seek refuge in her body.[55] Milton and Spenser both modify these superstitions in such a way that their original incompatibility is no longer apparent. Instead of slaying their mother at birth, like true vipers, Errour's brood unfilially gorge themselves on her blood. Sin's offspring resemble young vipers in gnawing their mother's bowels from within and in their violent eruption from her womb, but their birth, though painful, is not lethal and is hourly renewed. Spenser retains intact the superstition that the young re-enter the parent's mouth, "which way the fright being past, they will return again, which is a peculiar way of refuge."[56] Milton, on the other hand, alters this convention and makes the womb the place of sanctuary.

In several respects Milton's account of Sin's offspring is considerably closer to orthodox viper lore than Spenser's version, and these details he assuredly derived directly from pseudo-scientific tradition rather than from *The Faerie Queene.* Unfortunately, recent scholarship has overstressed Spenser's influence[57] and underemphasized Milton's direct indebtedness to the very traditions which had moulded the Errour episode — Echidna the woman-serpent and *echidna,* the female viper.

A parallel to Milton's exploitation of viper lore has been noted in Prudentius's *Hamartigenia,* which employs an "allegorized instance from natural history of the viper that perishes by the teeth of her progeny," to illustrate how "the soul that mates with the son of Belial brings forth a deadly brood of sins which are conceived from the seed of the serpent . . ."[58] Unlike Milton and Spenser, however, Prudentius did not combine these data from natural history with the figure of the classical woman-serpent.

Such a fusion of mythological and scientific traditions occurred, however, in several Renaissance authors, including Topsell and Pierius. Indeed, it can be traced as far back as Albertus Magnus's *De Animalibus.* After rejecting the belief that the female viper decapitates the male, only to be destroyed by her own brood ("& illi viscera matris corrodunt"), Albertus also dismissed as false or fabulous the opinion that the viper displays a human resemblance:

Quod ergo quidam dicunt viperam in priori parte corporis esse

similem homini & posteriorem deficere in serpentem falsum est
omnino: nisi fabulose a poetis per integumenta metaphorarum
intelligatur.[59]

Like a true viper's brood, Sin's offspring gnaw her bowels and
burst violently forth from her womb. For this detail Milton drew on
one of the most venerable superstitions about young vipers. In
Herodotus's opinion "the young . . . eat their mother while they are
within her; nor are they dropped from her till they have devoured
her womb."[60] According to the pseudo-Aristotelian treatise, *On
Marvellous Things Heard,* "the young ones . . . bite through their
mother's belly."[61] Pliny believed that the female viper bore her
young "at the rate of one a day, to the number of about twenty; the
consequence is that the remaining ones get so tired of the delay that
they burst open their mother's sides, so committing matricide."[62]
The same superstition recurs in the works of Aelian and Nicander:

> Non autem ova parit, sed animantes partus edit, jamjam idoneos ad
> perniciem inferendum; in ipso enim partu matris alvum distrahunt
> et lacerant, perque disruptum ventrem erumpunt, ulciscentes
> patrem in hunc modum.[63]
>
> Ast ubi post vegetam ceperunt pignora vitam,
> Jam propinqua adsunt maturi tempora partus,
> Indignam chari mortem ulciscentia patris,
> Erosa miserae nascuntur matris ab alvo.[64]

The etymology of *vipera* and *echidna* was sometimes traced to
this superstition. According to Isidore of Seville, the viper derived
its name from *vi pariat*:

> Nam cum venter ejus ad partum ingemuerit, catuli non exspectantes
> naturae maturam solutionem, corrosis ejus lateribus, vi erumpunt
> cum matris interitu.[65]

Topsell noted the same tradition:

> The *Grecians* say, that the Viper is called *Echidna, para to echein in
> eaute ten gonen hacri thanaton:* because to her own death she
> beareth her young ones in her belly; and therefore the *Latines* do
> also call it *Vipera, quasi Vi pariat:* because it dyeth by violence of
> her birth or young . . .[65A]

Milton's selection of this particular detail to characterize his
Echidna-like monster was, therefore, semantically apt. Moreover,
his phraseology recalls conventional accounts of the viper's brood.
The phrase "bursting forth" is reminiscent of the terms *erumpere,
perrumpere,* etc., used by Isidore, Aelian, and others. Similarly,

the word "gnaw" apparently echoes the verbs *erodere* and *corrodere* employed by Calepine, Nicander, and Isidore.

Although Milton attributes to Sin the characteristic dogs of Scylla,[66] her strongest affinities are with the mythological serpent-woman Echidna. The behaviour of her litter of hell-hounds, moreover, has been primarily modelled on that of young vipers.[67] There remain, however, several further parallels with Hesiod's monster.[68]

Both Sin and Echidna are infernal guardians. Echidna "kept guard" in Arima, where the rebellious giant, Typhaon, was also confined.[69] Sin guards the gates of Hell, where Satan and his cohorts are imprisoned. The analogy is all the more apt, since the myths of the giants and Titans were traditionally regarded as fabulous corruptions of the revolt of the angels. It is, moreover, further enhanced by Milton's allusion to Hell as "this gloom of *Tartarus*"[70] and his explicit comparison of Satan to *"Briarios* or *Typhon."*[71]

Typhaon and Echidna were 'joined in love' and produced a brood of hell-hounds — Orthus, Cerberus, etc. Similarly, Satan's dalliance with Sin engendered the hell-hound Death.

Each of these serpent-women bore another litter of monsters through an incestuous union with her son. Echidna "was subject to the love of Orthus and brought forth the deadly Sphinx . . . and the Nemean lion . . ." Death begat on Sin the litter of hell-dogs "hourly conceiv'd and hourly born."

With his post as infernal guardian and his ravenous appetite, Death resembles the "flesh-devouring" Cerberus, frequently allegorized as a symbol of the grave. Carolus Stephanus, for example, gave the following interpretation of the monster:

> Mythologici terram interpretantur: dictum qui volunt Cerberum, quasi χρεοβορον, hoc est, carnivorum. Terrae proprium est, cadaver consumere, & ad primam suam originem revocare, hoc est, in humum convertere.[72]

As the son of Typhaon and Echidna, Cerberus is thus the classical prototype of Death, the offspring of Satan and Sin.

Finally, as a fairly literal symbol of remorse,[73] the dogs who gnaw at Sin's bowels possess essentially the same allegorical significance as the eagle (or vulture) in the Prometheus legend and the "undying worm" of the Gospel Hell.[74] According to Topsell, "the Eagle which by the Poets is feigned to eat the heart of *Prometheus,* is likewise by them said to be begotten betwixt *Typhon* and *Echidna* . . . ."[75]

Thus the relationships between Satan, Sin, and their offspring roughly parallel those between Typhaon, Echidna, and their progeny. There is, however, an additional, though remote, analogy with the mating of vipers. Traditionally, the breeding of vipers led inevitably to the death of both parents; the female destroyed the male, and her young slew the mother. Naturalists interpreted this behaviour as "a favourable indulgence and special contrivance of Nature"[76] to restrict the number of these poisonous creatures, as well as an instance of "the justice of Nature."[77] Satan's dalliance with Sin proves spiritually fatal, and the fruit of their unhallowed union is appropriately Death. The propriety of this symbolism, moreover, is heightened by the conventional association of the viper with the devil.[78]

Through their common exploitation of the Echidna-*echidna* parallel and their fusion of details combined from classical myth and fabulous natural history, Spenser and Milton achieved the most memorable Renaissance variants of the woman-serpent motif. Nevertheless, though both figures belong to the same tradition, Milton's Sin is a more complex figure, and the problem of her literary ancestry is more intricate and involved. In emphasizing the direct influence of Spenser's Errour,[79] one should not overlook Milton's conscious evocation of additional analogues in the long dynasty of draconcopedes. In the following chapter I shall consider further aspects of his serpent-woman as variants on a traditional background and as elements in a larger pattern of literary indebtedness.

CHAPTER XII

Paradise Lost: Milton's "Sin."
The Problem of Literary Indebtedness

THE VARIETY of parallels to Milton's "Portress of Hell Gate" has to some extent obscured the pattern of his indebtedness.[1] The problem of evaluating them has been complicated by their very multitude. Since one may easily mistake a striking analogue for a source, it seems advisable to re-examine the relation of these parallels to *Paradise Lost*. Though many of them have long been familiar, others have hitherto escaped observation.

From the outset one must distinguish between two aspects of Milton's literary relationships: 1) his *general* debt to mythological and poetic tradition for the basic conception of his woman-serpent, and 2) his *specific* indebtedness to particular sources for certain details. To confuse these aspects, to stress his affinities with one or two isolated parallels at the expense of his general relationship to a tradition, can easily distort the pattern of his indebtedness.

Moreover, there is a second distinction one cannot afford to ignore. Milton's literary relationships involved several factors besides his sources. The analysis of his indebtedness entails more than consideration of what particular precedents may have given him his "cue." It concerns also the degree to which he imitated or modified these precedents and the extent to which he consciously invited comparison with them. Though the same passage might well have served as source, model, and object of allusion, these three functions are slightly, but significantly, different. The investigation of Milton's literary affinities, accordingly, should include not only the sources which influenced him, but also the models he imitated, and the precedents — both general and specific — which he wished to evoke. For his portrait of Sin the third of these factors was especially important. The basic outlines of his figure were conventional and reflected the image of a distinct tradition.

I

The major tradition behind Milton's infernal portress was much more extensive than scholars have usually realized. Besides the familiar parallels with Spenser[2] and Phineas Fletcher[3] and the less familiar analogy with Hesiod,[4] there were (as Professor John Merton Patrick has recently observed) other precedents in both classical and Renaissance literature. Dio Chrysostom's Libyan beasts,[5] Nonnos' Campe,[6] Apollodorus' Delphyne,[7] the Scythian monster described by Diodorus Siculus[8] and Herodotus,[9] and Comes' Ἀδιχια[10] were all serpent-women. The serpent which tempted Eve was sometimes portrayed as a similar hybrid. Male counterparts to these monsters, moreover, existed in classical and Renaissance conceptions of the giants[12] (especially Typhon),[13] in the devils of Vida's *Christiad*,[14] and in such figures as Cecrops,[15] Erichthonius,[16] Boreas,[17] and Dante's Geryon.[18] In shape Milton's Sin bears a demonstrable resemblance to an entire tradition.

It seems inadequate, therefore, to trace the general conception of Milton's woman-serpent to isolated precedents. Though certain details were probably suggested by Spenser, Fletcher, and Hesiod, he was surely aware of additional parallels for the general shape of his figure. Though he may have intended to suggest an indirect comparison with the hybrid monsters of all three of these poets, the propriety and credibility of his portrait depended, in large part, on its general resemblance to a recognizable tradition.

On the other hand, it would be meaningless to regard as direct sources every remote analogue Milton may have encountered in classical, medieval, or Renaissance literature. Delphyne and Boreas, for instance, obviously had little or no direct influence on Sin. Nonetheless even such minor and relatively insignificant precedents as these contributed indirectly to the strength of a tradition, and it was, in large measure, the tradition in its entirety which he was attempting to evoke.

Thus for the general form of Milton's monster it seems preferable to stress his deliberate exploitation of a distinct convention rather than his specific indebtedness to particular sources. Though he probably sought, and expected, comparison with analogous figures in the *Theogony, The Locusts,* etc., the "probability" of his apparently incredible hybrid was enhanced by the extensive poetic and mythological tradition behind it.

II

Like Spenser and Fletcher before him, Milton endowed the traditional woman-serpent with attributes lacking in many of the classical analogues. Several of these details may be traced with relative accuracy to particular sources among the ancients and moderns. Though he sometimes modified these borrowed elements, he did not entirely obscure their affinities with their originals; in several cases, indeed, he appears to have deliberately invited comparison with particular precedents.

Milton's specific debt to the myth of Scylla for the detail of Sin's hell-hounds is suggested by his reference to the dogs which "Vex'd *Scylla* bathing." The direct influence of the *Metamorphoses* appears in the phrase *"Cerberean* mouths," a literal translation of Ovid's "Cerbereos rictus."[19]

Ovid is not, however, the only possible source for Milton's exploitation of the Scylla legend. *Ciris* also contains a brief account of her transformation.[20] Either or both of these narratives could have inspired the girdle of barking dogs about the waist of Milton's monster.[24] Nevertheless there is a marked difference between these descriptions and Milton's; Sin's dogs are her own offspring, whereas Scylla's are part of her own body. Hyginus, however, adds a detail found neither in *Ciris* nor in the *Metamorphoses;* in his account Scylla, like Sin, is herself the mother of dogs.[22]

Furthermore, there are at least two classical precedents for Milton's fusion of the woman-serpent convention with the myth of Scylla. Nonnos likened Campe to Scylla:[23]

συμφερτῇ δὲ φάλαγγι πολυσκυλάκων κεφαλάων
Σκύλλης ἰστέλεστον ἔην μίμημα προσώπου·

Natalis Comes cited a similar conception of Scylla as a combination of woman, dog and serpent:[24]

Alij dixerunt oculorum tenus Scyllam
pulcherrimam fuisse mulierem, at sex
habuisse canum capita, reliquam corporis
partem guisse serpentum.

There is no known analogue to Sin's metamorphosis in classical or Renaissance accounts of the woman-serpent,[25] and it is possible that for this detail, as for others, Milton was indebted to the myth of Scylla. By thus grafting Scylla's metamorphosis onto the traditional serpentine figure, he strengthened his fusion of the two. Nevertheless the causes of their transformations are distinctly different. Sin's metamorphosis is due to the violent birth of her offspring,[26] whereas Scylla's transformation occurs while bathing in waters poisoned by Circe.

Milton's specific debt to Spenser[27] is evidenced by the exceptional behavior of Sin's progeny, which re-enter their mother's body and unnaturally devour her. Since these details are associated with only one other serpent-woman, it seems probable that Milton got his "cue" from Spenser's description of Errour's brood. Instead of following Spenser's account exactly, however, Milton apparently derived certain details directly from current viper-lore.

Since only two other woman-serpents had been specifically identified as personifications of sin, Milton probably derived this detail from Phineas Fletcher's Hamartia or Sin.[28] Nevertheless there are striking parallels in Comes' Αδικια[29] and in conventional representations of the serpent of Genesis 3.[30] Fletcher may have been influenced by both of these precedents, and Milton may have intended an indirect comparison with them. There is, moreover, a remote analogue in the Libyan beasts, which Dio explained allegorically as symbols of the passions.

In this context Milton's exploitation of the Scylla legend is significant. Gilliam has noted allegorical interpretations of this figure as *libido*[31] and St. John Chrysostom's comparison between Scylla and *hamartia*.[32] Milton appears, therefore, to have combined two mythological figures with similar allegorical referents.

Three woman-serpents besides Milton's had been represented as infernal guardians[33] — Hesiod's Echidna,[34] Nonnos' and Apollodorus' Campe,[35] and Fletcher's Sin. It seems probable that Milton may have had all three in mind, but the close similarity of name and function almost certainly identifies Fletcher as Milton's source for this detail. The link with *The Locusts* is rendered even more explicit by a verbal parallel. Milton's "Portress of Hell Gate" echoes Fletcher's "Porter to th' infernall Gate."[36]

Milton's fusion of Scylla with the serpent-woman again seems appropriate; Virgil had included Scyllae at the gates of the underworld, and Campe, the guardian of Tartarus, combined characteristics of Scylla and the woman-serpent.

In addition to these major parallels, there are several minor analogues. Satan's reference to Sin as "double-formed" suggests classical descriptions of Scylla and the serpent-woman. Herodotus' Scythian queen[37] and Nonnos' Campe[38] were both described as $\delta\iota$-$\varphi\upsilon\eta\varsigma$.[39] The *Aeneid* mentioned "Scyllaeque biformes"[40] at the infernal portals, and *Ciris*[41] described Scylla as "monstro biformi."

The lethal sting characteristic of Hamartia, Errour, and Milton's Sin occurs in none of their classical analogues, except for a remote parallel in Dio's Libyan beasts.[42] Scholars are probably correct, therefore, in tracing this detail to the locusts of Revelations 9: 7-10 and to Dante's Geryon, whose serpentine body culminates in a

> . . . venenosa forca
> che, a guisa di scorpion, la punta armava.[43]

Like Geryon's, Hamartia's serpentine tail is "pointed with a double sting," which she wields like a scorpion. Milton's specific indebtedness to Spenser, however, is indicated by a verbal parallel; Sin's "mortal sting" resembles the "mortall sting" of Errour.[44] Although a "scorpion with icy sting sharp-whetted" accompanies

Nonnos' Campe, this precedent bears little resemblance to analogous details among the moderns.

Sin's quasi-royal status as Satan's vicegerent makes her all but unique among monsters of similar shape. Though Milton probably derived the sovereignty of Sin and Death from Romans 5:14, 21, three significant analogues occur in Greek legend. Although none of them can be regarded as actual sources for Milton's figure, they nevertheless strengthen the propriety of her role. Scythes, son of the Scythian queen by Zeus or Hercules, founded the Scythian royal house.[45] Cecrops, the mythical first king of Attica, was described as συμφυες εχων σωμα ανδρος και δρακοντος.[46] Erichthonius, the son of Hephaestus, was sometimes identified with the Attic king Erechtheus; like Cecrops, he was half-man, half-serpent; "Inferiorem partem draconis habuit."[47]

One should guard against overstressing so tenuous a parallel. Nevertheless, in their affinities with gods and heroes and in their own royal status, each of these figures possesses a special eminence among serpentine hybrids.

There is little evidence that Milton derived any specific details from the serpent-footed giants who strove against Zeus.[48] Nevertheless the analogy is suggestive, as the giants were sometimes identified with the fallen angels, and Satan with Typhon.[49] Vida fashioned his devils in the shape of the giants.[50] Nonnos apparently took Hesiod's Typhoeus as the model for Campe.[51] Comes admittedly modeled his Ἀδικία on the figure of Typhon.[52] Sin's affinities with the rebel hosts are made more explicit by her shape. The nature of her own metamorphosis, moreover, foreshadows their own transformation into serpents in Book X.

Finally, three serpent-women possess the power of sorcery. Milton described Sin as "the Snakie Sorceress" and compared her dogs to those which follow "the Night-Hag" and "*Lapland* Witches." Herodotus' Scythian queen spirited away Hercules' mares while he slept.[53] Topsell associated Dio's Libyan beasts with the Lamia and declared that these monsters drew shipwrecked mariners "into their compass, by a certain natural Magical Witch-craft. . . ."[54] Although these analogues can hardly be regarded as sources for Milton's Sin they strengthen her ties with mythological tradition.

III*

Finally, in her double form — part-woman and part-serpent —
Milton's "Sin" also resembles a traditional conception of the serpent which tempted Eve. This, too,

> . . . seem'd Woman to the waste, and fair,
> But ended foul in many a scaly fould
> Voluminous and vast, a Serpent arm'd
> With mortal sting.

Sir Thomas Browne alludes to this tradition in *Pseudodoxia
Epidemica,* in his chapter "Of the Picture of the Serpent Tempting
Eve".

> In the Picture of Paradise, and delusion of our first Parents, the
> Serpent is often described with humane visage; not unlike unto
> Cadmus or his wife, in the act of their Metamorphosis. Which is not
> a meer pictorial contrivance or invention of the Picturer, but an
> ancient tradition and conceived reality, as it stands delivered by
> Beda and Authors of some antiquity; that is, that Sathan appeared
> not unto Eve in the naked form of a Serpent, but with a Virgin's
> head, that thereby he might become more acceptable, and his
> temptation find the easier entertainment. Which nevertheless is a
> conceit not to be admitted, and the plain and received figure, is with
> better reason embraced.[55]

Like Browne, medieval commentators on Genesis or the *Sentences* of Peter Lombard frequently cite Bede as an authority for
this tradition.[56] They consistently fail, however, to designate a
specific passage in his writings, and the actual source of this belief
remains obscure.[57]

This convention occasionally found its way into natural histories,
and the serpent of Genesis 3 was identified as a *draconcopes.*
Konrad von Megenberg, in his translation of the *Liber de natura
rerum* (ascribed to Thomas Cantimpratensis)[58] describes this
mythical beast as follows:

*First published as "Sin and the Serpent of Genesis 3 (*PL,* II 650-653), *Modern Philology,*
LIV (1957). Copyright 1957 by the University of Chicago.

Draconcopes haizt ain drachenkopp und ist ain slang in Kriechenlant gar grôz und mähtig, sam Adelinus spricht. diu slang hât ainr junkfrawen antlütz geleich ainem menschen, aber daz ander tail irs leibes geleicht ainem drachen. nu sprechent die maister, daz diu slang derlei sei gewesen, diu Evam betrog in dem paradîs, wan Beda spricht, daz diu selb slang ain junkfrawenantlütz hab gehabt, dar umb, daz si mit gleicher gestalt Evam zämt und zuolocket, wan der mensch und ain iegleich tier nimt sein geleichz und ist lustig gegen im. diu selb slang, dô si Evam betrog, zaigt ir neur daz haupt und verparg daz ander tail under der paum pleter und buschen. wie aber der teufel daz gemachen moht, daz diu slang menschleicheu wort sprach, daz ist us verporgen, wir wellen dann sprechen, daz diu selb slang halsâdern and andern gezeug hab gehabt in dem hals und in dem haupt sam ain mensch, dâ mit si geschikt waer zuo mensleichen [sic] worten, reht als wir sehen, daz etleich vogel menschleicheu wort fur pringent, wenn man si des êrsten da mit üebet. iedoch waen ich und ist geläupleich, daz der teufel sich selber verkêrt in ainer slangen weis und auch menschleich sprâch mit Even rett, wan er mag sich verkêren in aller tier form. nu schaw, wie sich der teufel hât gemacht auz menschleichem haupt und auz ains trachen leib, auz dem pesten leiphaftigen dinge und auz dem poesten. der applik was guot und käusch, aber daz end was vergiftig und toetlich.[59]

A marginal gloss to the Chester play on the fall of man, on the other hand, identifies the serpent of Genesis 3 as a sphinx.[60]

Later commentators[61] were often skeptical of this tradition, but, like Browne, they noted its popularity among painters:

Pictores sanè hanc opinionem secuti, historiam huius rei in pictura repraesentantes, muliebri vultu serpentem depingunt.[62]

Pictorial representations of the serpent of Genesis 3 generally fall into three categories: (1) in most cases the tempter is depicted as a bona fide serpent, of considerable length, twined around the tree of knowledge; (2) less frequently the creature has a woman's head but retains its serpentine form from the neck downward;[63] or (3) in other illustrations the serpent is human from the waist up, with a woman's head, arms, and bust. Though rarer than the two preceding types, this version is by no means unusual.[64] A notable example of this third category occurs in Michelangelo's representation of the temptation, on the ceiling of the Sistine Chapel. Milton may well have seen this during his visit to Rome.

Engravings illustrating Andreini's *L'Adamo,* moreover, consistently represent the tempter as a woman from the waist up and a serpent from the waist down.[65]

All three versions, furthermore, occur also in Renaissance literary treatments of Genesis. In the temptation scene in Book IX, Milton follows the first tradition in denying human features to the serpent. Aretino[66] and William Hunnis[67] adhere to the second; Andreini to the third.[68]

Even though Milton, like Browne, rejects the double-formed serpent in favor of the "plain and received figure" in describing the seduction of Eve, "Sin's" close resemblance to a thoroughly conventional conception of the serpent of Genesis 3 is highly appropriate in a poem explicitly devoted to an account of the temptation and fall of man. To the poet's contemporaries this parallel can scarcely have seemed fortuitous. Even though he may be positively indebted to Spenser and Fletcher, it seems probable that the hybrid monsters of all three poets may have been consciously modeled to some extent on the half-human serpent described in medieval and Renaissance interpretations of Genesis.

How far Milton intended his portrait of "Sin" to evoke the image of the biblical serpent is uncertain. Nevertheless, interpreted in terms of this parallel, his figure of the infernal portress seems a particularly striking instance of the principle of decorum—the "grand masterpiece to observe." In the first place, his description stresses comparatively early in the poem the close relationship (the "Fatal consequence" and "secret harmony") which unites Satan and his daughter. They bear a family resemblance. In heaven she has been his "perfect image," "likest to thee in shape and count'nance bright." Now in hell she wears a shape conventionally associated with his execution of the very enterprise he has just undertaken. For the same reason, "Sin's" monstrous transformation anticipates Satan's own metamorphosis in Book X. The punitive deformities of Satan and his daughter are modeled in part on conceptions of the serpent of paradise.

Traditionally associated with the temptation and fall of man, this image indirectly foreshadows the crucial event of the poem and the crisis of Satan's enterprise—the temptation of Book IX. As the symbol of postlapsarian human depravity, "Sin" is appropriately represented in a form reminiscent of the temptation whereby sin first entered the world. It is fitting that Satan's vicegerent on earth should, by her very shape, recall both the diabolical suggestion and the human act which made her so.

IV

"It is therefore as a study in a familiar style, not as a fresh creation, that the picture should be viewed."[69] Though Verity underestimated the originality of Milton's portrait, he correctly emphasized its conventional nature. Its component elements were consciously derivative, and Milton's artistry consisted precisely in combining in a new and striking figure details with which his predecessors had invested the mythological woman-serpent. The primary value of his portrait resided in its formal resemblance to the conventional serpentine hybrid; he enriched it, however, with details suggestive of particular precedents. In this way he could invite comparison with a general tradition and also with specific analogues.[70] He could envoke a chain of literary associations which stretched from Hesiod to Fletcher, a *catena* which linked ancients and moderns alike to his image of Sin.

His method was consistent both with the literary taste and theory of his period and the practice of his immediate predecessors. Aristotle counselled the poet to make his characters "appropriate" and "like the reality."[71] Horace advised him either to "follow tradition or invent what is self-consistent":

Aut famam sequere aut sibi convenientia finge.[72]

Castelvetro followed both of these authorities in holding that the poet should preserve "la continuatione de costumi."[73]

Io chiamo continuatione lontana, quando nel formare i costumi d'una certa persona seguitiamo quello de costumi suoi, che n'hanno scritto prima altri poeti, & in cio ci conformiamo con loro nella guisa, che Horatio consigliava dover far colui, che si metteva a scriver d'Achille dicendo.

Scriptor, honoratum si forte reponis Achillem,
Impiger, iracundus, inexorabilis esto,
Iura neget sibi nata, nihil arroget armis.[74]

Percioche gli altri prima l'havevano costumato cosi.[75]

Sin is an outstanding example of such "continuatione lontana." By "following fame," by investing his figure with the form of the conventional woman-serpent as well as attributes reminiscent of particular parallels, Milton enhanced the propriety, verisimilitude, and probability of his otherwise incredible monster. The outlandish and fantastic portrait could rely on an entire tradition, as well as the specific precedents of Ovid, Fletcher, and others, to make it convincing. Its poetic value resided not only in its own intrinsic merits, but also in the wealth of associations it evoked. Milton's selective exploitation of details derived from classical, Biblical, medieval, and Renaissance sources served a double function. On the one hand, it emphasized Sin's affinities both with a general tradition and with particular analogues. On the other hand, it invited attention to the propriety and skill of his own innovations.

CHAPTER XIII

Paradise Lost: The Devil and Pharaoh's Chivalry. Etymological and Typological Imagery and Renaissance Chronography

MILTON'S ALLUSION to the destruction of Pharaoh's army (PL, I, 306-311) has endured the question of a host of critics and on a wide variety of grounds. Under minute scrutiny it has lost neither its rhetorical force nor its semantic depth; the multiplicity of scholarly methodologies and critical techniques that have been brought to bear upon it have enriched, rather than obscured, its meaning. As the final member of one of the most complex of Miltonic similes, it is no less interesting for its application of classical epic conventions to Biblical subject matter than for its exploitation of Ramist arguments from *similia* ("likes").[1] As an Old Testament "type" it not only foreshadows patterns of New Testament soteriology and eschatology, but epitomizes concepts of retributive justice and divine economy that Milton believes valid for the entirety of human history;[2] combining the functions of historical example and proleptic symbol, it points forward both to the major revolutions of world history and to the more harmless reversals that will occur within the microcosm of the poetic fable. It is an integral part, therefore, not only of the pattern of cosmic history—the course of God's providential "government" of the world, as Milton saw it—but of the structure of the poem itself. Besides this horizontal dimension, moreover, it also possesses a vertical orientation; if it points forward (and backwards) in time, it also looks toward a higher level on the scale of being, representing (like St. Paul) the mysteries of spiritual beings through analogy with human events.

This image is no less relevant, however, for Milton's revaluation of the heroic tradition. By concentrating in a single phrase ("*Memphian* Chivalry") Biblical allusions to overthrow of "horse and . . . rider," epic associations of charioteer and chevalier—and even (perhaps) his own personal prejudices against King and Cavalier!—Milton introduces near the very beginning of his poem an image that unobtrusively undercuts the secular heroic tradition. Though the immediate object of this allusion to Pharaoh's scattered army is to dramatize the plight of the fallen angels—now "rowling in the Flood/ With scattered Arms and Ensigns"—the simile nevertheless performs a more complex function. Pharaoh's order of battle, as described in Exodus—"six hundred chosen chariots, and all the chariots of Egypt, and captains over every one of them"—belongs to a military context not altogether dissimilar to that of classical epic. These are characteristic trappings of an heroic age. Milton's own term "Chivalry," moreover, possesses additional connotations that broaden the heroic analogy, extending it from the mounted warriors of antiquity to the knights of medieval and Renaissance epic or romance. The fate of Satan's legions, like that of Pharaoh's army, exposes (in terms Milton would employ elsewhere) the "ostentation vain of fleshly arm" and the futility of "carnal reliance." It also underlines a further point of resemblance between the Egyptian debacle and the fall of the angels—that in both instances the victory has been the single-handed achievement of God himself; that (in Moses' phrase) "The Lord is a man of war."

This attitude would subsequently receive fuller expression elsewhere in Milton's poetry. In the battle in Heaven, the combined might of the faithful angels cannot prevail over the rebel powers; the situation must await the intervention of the Messiah himself as *deus ex machina,* or perhaps *in Merkabah.* The opening lines of Book IX of *Paradise Lost* express distaste for "fabl'd Knights, . . .

Caparisons and Steeds," etc. A similar attitude towards "instrument of war" is apparent in Milton's description of the Parthian hosts in *Paradise Regained* and in his condemnation of "the mighty of the Earth, th' oppressour" in *Samson Agonistes.*

Finally, in its reference to Busiris, this passage effectively mingles mythological allusion with Renaissance chronology. In doing so, it makes a positive, original—but mistaken—contribution to historiography.

In the following pages I shall re-examine Milton's imagery from three angles: Biblical typology, Renaissance etymological techniques, Historiographical speculations concerning the identity of Busiris and the Pharaoh who perished in the Red Sea, and (finally) the traditional relationship between Busiris and the city of Memphis. First, let us return to the simile itself with its juxtaposition of vegetative and martial imagery, Tuscan and Egyptian geographical allusions, and natural and Biblical history.

I*

In describing the hapless state of Satan's fallen legions Milton employs three different comparisons to express essentially the same concept. "Autumnal Leaves," "scatterd sedge," the "floating Carkases and broken Chariot Wheels" of Pharaoh's host—all three members of this extended simile have the same ultimate referent, "Cherube and Seraph rowling in the Flood With scatter'd Arms and Ensigns." Leaves, sedge, and the ruined Egyptian army are analogous to Satan's routed host. Corresponding to the "Brooks in *Vallombrosa*" and the Red Sea is the "inflamed Sea," the "burning Lake" of Hell.

Milton's own explicit statement of the "point of resemblance" for all three comparisons is phrased in somewhat different terms from those of Whaler's analysis of this simile:

> . . . so thick bestrown
> Abject and lost lay these, covering the Flood . . .

This statement appears at the end of the comparison and obviously summarizes the common meaning of all three members. Moreover,

*First published as "The Devil and Pharaoh's Chivalry," *Modern Language Notes,* Vol. LXXV (1960), pp. 197-201. Copyright 1960 by The John's Hopkins University Press.

the significant "points of resemblance" are still further emphasized by verbal repetition. "Thick" appears twice, in lines 302 and 311. The concept of dispersion is underlined by a similar reiteration— "strow" (302), "scattered" (304), "bestrown" (311), and, finally, Satan's own reference to "scatter'd Arms and Ensigns" in 325. The verb "oerthrew" (306) anticipates "abject" in 312; and Satan himself echoes "abject" (322) and "lost" (316).

The first of these analogies obliquely alludes to the leaf-similes of other epic poets, retaining the emphasis on multitude, the infernal associations, and even the reference to rivers or brooks characteristic of this tradition; yet it also reinterprets this tradition in the context of Biblical typology. The second comparison depends (as critics have long recognized) on the literal meaning of the Hebrew name for the Red Sea (Yam Suf, or Sea of Sedge), as well as on typological interpretations of the Erythraean or Red Sea as a symbol of Hell. The third involves a complex blend of mythographical, chronographical, and typological allusion.

Fundamental to all three comparisons and their common referent, finally, is the idea of "covering the Flood"—the concept of scattered objects floating on a liquid expanse (the brooks of Tuscany, the Red Sea, the infernal lake). This concept had already received expression in 51-53.

> . . . he with his horrid crew
> Lay vanquisht, rowling in the fiery Gulfe
> Confounded though immortal:

and we encounter it again (324-325) on Satan's own lips:

> Cherube and Seraph rowling in the Flood
> With scatter'd Arms and Ensigns.

Two of these three comparisons are rooted in Christian exegetical tradition. Whaler has called attention to the patristic identification of Pharaoh and Satan.[3] Commentators on Exodus 14 and 15 had likened the destruction of the Egyptian army to the punishment of the rebel angels, the Red Sea to the fiery lake of Hell, and Pharaoh himself to Lucifer. Similarly, Isaiah 34:4 ("And all the host of heaven shall be dissolved . . .: and all their host shall fall down, as the leaf falleth off from the vine, and as a falling fig from the fig tree") had been interpreted as an allusion to the Last Judgment and the final expulsion of the evil spirits from their aerial seats into Hell.

Jerome explained Isaiah 34: 4 as a reference to the fate of the evil angels on Judgment Day; the host of Heaven would wither and fall away like leaves at the approach of cold weather:

> . . . et tabescat omnis militia vel fortitudo coelorum . . . in similitudinem foliorum, quae appropinquante frigore, arentia atque contracta de vinea et ficus defluunt.[4]

According to Herveus, Isaiah's leaf-simile described the devils' hopeless alienation from their pristine state:

> "Et omnis militia eorum defluet sicut folium de ficu," quia sicut arboris folium postquam aruerit et ceciderit, nequaquam virescit, et in arborem revertitur, sed in terra putrescit, ita spiritus illi de coelestibus lapsi nequaquam in pristinum statum reducentur, aut per poenitentiam revirescent, sed in gehennalibus poenis aeternaliter putrescent.[5]

Though Milton's comparison of the defeated angels to fallen leaves derives from Scriptural tradition, the detail of "the Brooks in *Vallombrosa*" is his own addition.[4] It serves to complete the simile by providing an analogue to the fiery flood of /312 and the Red Sea of /306.

Although the immersion of Pharaoh's army in the Red Sea was sometimes interpreted as a symbol of baptism,[5] it was frequently regarded as an allusion to the Day of Judgment. Thus Origen explained Exodus 15: 1 in terms of Christ's second advent and Satan's destruction:

> . . . cum venerit in gloria Patris et sanctorum angelorum, cum venerit in majestate sua judicare terram, quando et verum Pharaonem, id est diabolum interficiet spiritu oris sui . . .

The Red Sea represented the fiery floods into which the rebel angels would be hurled on Judgment Day:

> Isti ergo terni statores sunt angeli nequam de exercitu Pharaonis . . ., quos demergit Dominus in Rubrum mare, et ignitis eos in judicii die fluctibus tradet, ac poenarum pelago teget . . .[8]

A Middle English commentary on "The Song of Moses" (Exodus 15) provides a similar interpretation:

> . . . þe cartis of Farao, þat is, þe boostful pride of the devel, and his oost, þat is, alle unri3twise men þat serven to him as hise trewe kny3tis . . . hem he caste into þe see, þat is, alle siche on domesday schal Crist caste wiþ þe devel, fadir of alle þe children of pride, into þe bittir peyne of helle wiþouten eende.

Thus Pharaoh's "electi principes" ("þe chosone princis of Sathan") shall be "drenchid in þe Reed see of eendeless fier." The "waters of the sea" (Exodus 15: 19) symbolize "þe peynes of helle."[9]

Similarly, Rabanus Maurus identified "the enemy" (Exodus 15: 6) with Lucifer, and "the waters" (Exodus 15: 8) with the sulphurous lake of Hell:

> *Dextera tua, Domine, . . . percussit inimicum . . .* Quae inimicum verum et antiquum hostem per crucis mysterium interfecit, et per mortem destruxit eum qui habebat mortis imperium, id est, diabolum, . . . atque draconem, serpentem videlicet antiquum: qui cauda sua detraxit tertiam partem siderum, et misit in stagnum ignis ardentis, qui paratus est sibi et angelis ejus.[10]

Thus the comparisons between Pharaoh's chivalry and the devil's angels, between the Red Sea and the fiery floods were traditional.[11] The terms of Milton's simile involved a theological commonplace. He presented them, however, in reverse order, taking Hell rather than the Red Sea as his point of departure.

As the name Pharaoh had been traditionally etymologized as meaning *dissipans, dissipator,* or *dissipatio,*[12] there may be a certain degree of irony in Milton's reiterated emphasis on the scattered state of the fallen angels. Primarily, however, his stress on the concept of dispersion is based on Biblical diction, which frequently expressed the action of divine wrath through the term *scattering.*[13] Thus Ezekiel 29: 12, 30: 23, and 30: 26 involve threats to "scatter the Egyptians." Numbers 10: 35 and Psalm 68: 1 pray that God's "enemies be scattered." The Magnificat (Luke 1: 51) rejoices that God has "scattered the proud in the imagination of their hearts."

Though Isaiah's leaf-simile and the passage in Exodus describing the fate of Pharaoh's army were traditionally interpreted in terms of the Last Judgment, Milton exploits both of these allusions to portray the state of the fallen angels after their initial fall from Heaven. His approach has some foundation in Biblical exegesis, inasmuch as expositors of Isaiah 34: 4 and Exodus 14 and 15 had frequently cited texts referring to Satan's original rebellion and lapse.[14] Although Hartman's opinion that the "scenes the poet himself calls up mimick hell's defeat before Satan's voice is fully heard"[15] may derive support from the conventional interpretation of Isaiah 34: 4 and Exodus 15 in terms of Judgment Day, Milton's primary referent in this passage is not the devils' future defeat, but the effect of their original overthrow by Messiah.

Although Milton's allusion to "the Brooks in *Vallombrosa*" may indeed represent a "memory of the Italian forests in autumn," its chief value probably resides in its etymology. Not only does its name ("shadowy vale") evoke the Biblical "valley of the shadow of death" (Psalm 23:4), but Milton himself underlines its literal meaning by referring in the same verse to "*Etrurian* shades." This is obviously an appropriate comparison for the regions of "doleful shades" (65) and "utter darkness."

The allusion to "scatterd sedge" serves primarily as a transitional figure between the leaf-simile and the comparison with Pharaoh's cavalry. Like the former it involves a vegetation-metaphor. Like the latter it contains a reference to the Red Sea. Although it appears, at first glance, to be simply another instance of natural detail enriched by geographical allusion, it really introduces the final simile, which is based neither on nature nor on geography, but on Biblical history.

The central irony in Milton's reiterated stress on scattering depends in part on the etymological interpretation of Pharaoh as *dissipator*. The Lord has miraculously scattered the armed hosts of the Egyptian "scatterer" of armies. The same etymology would fit the name (or title) that Milton assigns to the Pharaoh who perished in the Red Sea: for "Busiris" (as we shall see later) could be etymologized in terms of a Hebrew verb meaning "scatter."

Behind Milton's allusion to Busiris, however, lies more than a polylingual pun and an ironic, though metaphorical, elaboration of an *argumentum a nomine*. His identification of Busiris also represents a contribution, albeit a minor one, to Renaissance historiography. The chronology of Busiris, on the one hand, and the identity of the reigning Pharaoh at the time of the Exodus on the other hand had been long-standing problems for patristic and Renaissance historians. The immediate background of Milton's allusion is (as Professor Don Cameron Allen has shown in an important article) Melanchthon's recension of Carion's *Chronicle,* which provided "the authority for Milton's identification of Busiris with the Red Sea Pharaoh. . . ."[16] Behind this work, however, lay an extensive historiographical tradition which is intrinsically interesting in itself.

II *

It was Richard Bentley who first challenged Milton's reference to Busiris (*Paradise Lost,* I, 307) as the Pharaoh whom the Red Sea waves orethrew at the time of the Israelites' Exodus from Egypt:

> And what Authority for making *Pharaoh* to be *Busiris;* their Times and Characters no ways agreeing?[17]

Later commentators[18] have qualified this condemnation, but have nevertheless continued to regard Milton's allusion as a historical inaccuracy. Thus Thomas Newton, commenting on Bentley's objection, observed:

> As to Milton's making Pharaoh to be *Busiris* (which is another of the Doctor's objections to the passage) there is authority enough to justify a poet in doing so, tho' not an historian.[19]

In Masson's opinion, "*Busiris* is a special name given, on speculation, to the Pharaoh who chased the children of Israel"; Milton (he declared) "follows Raleigh," who, "in his *History of the World,* expressly argues that he was 'the first oppressor of the Israelites'."[20] According to Verity, "no one has ever explained" why Milton identifies Busiris "with the Pharaoh who perished in the Red Sea. . . . Either Milton follows some unknown authority, or he treats *Busiris* as a general title for the rulers of Egypt, like Pharaoh'."[21] Hughes has branded Milton's reference as a downright error; "Busiris . . . Milton incorrectly names as the Pharaoh who persecuted the Hebrew 'sojourners of Goshen'."[22] On the whole, scholars have seen in this passage at best a disregard of historical accuracy, at worst a historical blunder.

It is difficult to reconcile this view with the profound interest which, over his entire lifetime, Milton showed in historical studies. Ancient and modern history occupied an important position in his program of private reading at Hammersmith and at Horton.[23] Moreover, his own *History of Britain* and *Brief History of Moscovia* testified to his devotion to the historian's era.[24] Is it probable that so keen a student of history would identify Pharaoh with Busiris without some valid historical basis?

---

*First published in somewhat different form as "Busiris, the Exodus, and Renaissance Chronography," in *Revue belge de philologie et d'histoire,* Vol. XXXIX (1961).

Actually, in the light of Renaissance chronography, Milton's reference to Busiris seems exceptionally appropriate. Let us consider some of the factors that make it so.

In the first place, it is quite possible that Milton never intended the allusion to Busiris as a historical identification—that he meant it as a poetic statement rather than as a biographical gloss. In this case it is clearly no historical error, but a highly appropriate metaphor, centering around the chief point of comparison between Pharaoh and Busiris—the cruelty which both Egyptian Tyrants showed to strangers.[25] Indeed, Milton further emphasizes this particular point by describing the Hebrews as Sojourners.

If taken figuratively rather than literally, the passage poses no historical problem at all. As a poetic comparison between two different persons—the mythological homicide and the Biblical oppressor—it does not suggest that Pharaoh is actually Busiris, but merely that he is *like* Busiris.

Unfortunately, we can hardly bypass the historical issue so easily. For chronographers—classical, medieval, and Renaissance—Busiris was much more than a mythological figment; he was a historical personage and, as such, belonged to a definite place and time. Several of Milton's predecessors had tried to identify him with specific Egyptian kings. To a seventeenth-century reader acquainted with chronological tradition, Milton's allusion would have seemed little more than another answer to a familiar historical problem, another effort towards a more exact biographical identification.

Scholarship has underestimated the complexity of the chronological tradition concerning Busiris. Overstressing Milton's apparent divergence from Raleigh's *History*,[26] it has overlooked the latter's breach with many earlier historians. Whereas Raleigh placed Busiris' reign considerably *before* the Exodus, many of his predecessors had preferred a date several decades *after* this event. Thus Jerome, in his translation of Eusebius' *Chronicles,* assigned Busiris' tyranny to the twentieth year of Rameses' reign and the eighth year of Joshua's leadership:

> Busiris Neptuni et Lybiae Epaphi filiae filius apud vicina Nilo loca tyrannidem exercet, transeuntes hospites crudeli scelere interficiens.[27]

In *The City of God,* St. Augustine declared that these crimes had occurred during the interval between the departure of Israel out of Egypt and the death of Joshua:[28]

> Illo tempore vel rex, vel potius tyrannus Busiris suis diis suos hospites immolabat, quem filium perhibent fuisse Neptuni, ex matre Libya . . . . [29]

Orosius assigned Busiris' activities to the 775th year before the Roman era, approximately thirty years after the plagues of Egypt and the crossing of the Red Sea:

> Item anno ante Urbem conditam DCCLXXV inter Danai atque Aegypti fratrum filios quinquaginta parricidia una nocte commissa sunt . . . Busiridis in Aegypto cruentissimi tyranni crudelis hospitalitas, et crudelior religio tunc fuit: qui innocentem hospitium sanguinem diis, scelerum suorum participibus, propinabat; quod exsecrabile sine dubio hominibus, viderint, an ipsis etiam diis exsecrabile videretur.[30]

Peter Comestor's *Historia Scholastica* listed Busiris' tyranny among the "Incidentia" of the period of Joshua:

> In diebus Josue . . . Busiris tyrannidem exercuit in hospites.[31]

Lucas de Tuy[32] likewise placed Busiris in the time of Joshua, and Alfonso's *General Estoria* assigned Busiris' reign to the fourth year of Joshua's captaincy:

> Andados quatro annos del cabdellado de Josue, regnaua ell rey Busiris en Egipto en una partida de las tierras de cerca las riberas del Nilo, assi como cuenta Orosio en el dozeno capitulo del primero libro: et diz que Busiris era princep cruel que fazio grandes crueldades, assi como dizen del Eusebio en el griego e Jheronimo en el latin, e Lucas e otras Estorias.[33]

According to Alfonso, Busiris' cruelty to strangers dated from a period of drought, when his councillors advised him to sacrifice aliens to his gods:

> . . . et dizen qui ouo luego lluuia a muy grand abondo, et tomo dalli en uso este rey Busiris, quando luuias le fallescien, de matar los huespedes quel uenien, et assi como cuenta Orosio en el dozeno capitulo del primero libro, tenien gelo todos los omnes del regno a muy grant crueldat e grant mal, e aun diz que aquellos sos dioses lo tenien por cosa descomulgada, segunt el entendimiento de su yent, por assi matar los onbres buenos estrannos e que nunqual uuscaron mal ninguno, nin le yazien en ninguna culpa, et que assi esparcie aquel rey el sangre tan layda mientre e a tan grant tuerto, assi que

ombre ninguno que estranno fuesse non osaua entrar a aquel reyno de Menphis.[34]

In these classical and medieval accounts, Busiris remained an essentially legendary figure, whose affinities were distinctly mythological rather than Biblical. None of these writers attempted to identify him with any particular Pharaoh or with the events of Exodus. It is, apparently, to Renaissance historians that we owe the identification of Busiris with one or more of the Egyptian oppressors of the Hebrews.

In Melanchthon's version of the *Chronicles* of John Carion, Busiris followed Osiris, Orus, and Bocchoris in a "Catalogus Regum Aegyptiorum." Unlike most earlier chronographers, Melanchthon stressed the analogy between Busiris' cruelty to strangers and Pharaoh's persecution of the Israelites. He found, moreover, an additional parallel in the extensive program of construction executed under either of these monarchs:

> Deinde BVSIRIS, id est Munitor, qui maxima opera extruxit. Et Diodorus Siculus scribit, eum condidisse Thebas Aegyptias. Cum autem celebrata sit Busiridis crudelitas, quia dicitur mactasse hospites, consentaneum est, famam crudelitatis ortam esse a saevitia, quam erga Ebraeos exercuit, necatis ipsorum infantibus. Et cum Pyramides aliquas construxerit, labore Ebraeorum constructas esse consentaneum est. Nam prope oppidum Busirin sunt tres Pyramides celebratissimae, quarum Plinius mentionem facit. Apparent autem eodem nomine plures fuisse Reges Busirides.
>
> Postea fuit interregnum, quia deleto Rege in Mari rubro, cum educti sunt Israelitae, diu in Aegypto varias seditiones fuisse credibile est.
>
> Post Busiridem nominatur à Diodoro post longum intervallum Rex MIRIS, id est. acerbus vel crudelis.[35]

Significantly, Busiris was the last king Melanchthon named before the Red Sea debacle. His allusion to the king drowned in the Red Sea ("delecto Rege in Mari rubro") was, moreover, sandwiched between two paragraphs referring explicitly to Busiris. Although the references to Pharaoh's infanticide ("necatis ipsorum infantibus") and the construction of pyramids seem to indicate that the author identified Busiris with the tyrant of Exodus 1:8-22 rather than with the monarch of Exodus 14, his account was sufficiently general to admit the latter interpretation. As Professor Allen has justly observed, the *Chronicon Carionis* thus provided Milton with a textual authority for identifying Busiris with the Pharaoh who perished during the Exodus.

Melanchthon combined Scriptural with classical testimony (Diodorus, Herodotus, Pliny), and to his reduction of the Busiris legend to the Biblical oppressor of the Hebrews several later historians were deeply indebted.

In his *Historia Julia,* Reineccius identified Busiris with Orus II, the Pharaoh who had commanded that Hebrew male infants be slain at birth. It was, moreover, his daughter—Thermutis—who adopted Moses as her own son:

> ORVS, alio nomine BVSIRIS, capessit regnum post AMENOPHIN II,
> Cum potentiae suae ab Israëlitarum metueret incrementis, diversis
> gentem premere vexareque laboribus occipit. Nam Nili eis deriva-
> tiones atque aggere imperavit: condit urbem Busirim, reliquisque
> regni urbibus moenia adijcit, & usque ad vesanas Pyramidum ex-
> tructiones provehitur. Dumque ne sic quidem quicquam proficit, ad
> stirpis masculae caedem miseros cogit. Cui saevitiae divinitus sub-
> tractum Mosem adoptari a filia permittit . . . Regnavit ann. 38. ut
> Manetho 36. mens. 5. Exod. 1. 2. Berosus, Diod. Iosephus, Zonaras.
> A crudelitatis fama, quam in Israëliticos infantes exercuit,
> Graecorum extitit figmentum de mactatis à Busiride hospitibus.
> *Nam ita cum Philippo Mel. sentire malim:* à qua sententia expositio
> Diodori discrepans, causam huius allegat sacrificium, quod veterrimi
> reges ad sepulcrum Osiridis peregerint, & ita peregerint, ut ob
> Typhonis memoriam homines rufos ad id deligerent: cumque
> propterea Aegyptij rufi pauci essent, in externos saevirent. Nec au-
> diendus Strabo, qui vel regem, vel Tyrannum Busiridem fuisse
> negat: CùmDiodorus ipsas adeò Thebas, primam regum sedem, ab
> eo conditas velit: quod ego de instauratione harum & novis extruc-
> tionibus, quibus forte eas exornavit, accipio.[36]

Raleigh concurred with Reineccius in identifying Busiris with Orus II, "the first oppressor of the Israelites," but regarded Sesostris II (rather than Amenophis II) as his immediate predecessor:

> Now that *Orus* the second, or *Busiris* was the king that first op-
> pressed *Israel,* and made the edict of drowning the *Hebrew* children,
> which (saith Cedrenus) lasted ten moneths: it is a common opinion
> of many great and most learned writers, who also thinke that
> hereupon grew the fable of *Busiris* sacrificing strangers. It is also a
> common interpretation of that place, *Exod.* 1 that the King who

knew not *Ioseph,* was a king of a new family. That Busiris was of a new family, *Reineccius* doth shew; who also thinkes him Author of the bloudy edict. Nevertheless, true it is, that *Busiris,* according to all mens computation, began his reigne five yeres, according to *Eusebius:* whom very many iudicious authors herein approve[37]

Genebrardus likewise regarded Busiris as the probable author of the Hebrews' travails, basing this identification on an etymology of Busiris from *bâtsar* ("to fortify"):

> Calamitatis auctorem nostri nominant Amenophim. (Alii Busiridem appellant, quod magis convenit: Nam Busiris à Butser Benoni Kal in verbo Batsar deducitur.[38]

James Ussher maintained that Busiris was the brother and successor of the king drowned in the Red Sea:

> *Busiris the son of Neptunus, and Libya the daughter of Epaphus, exercised a tyranny, in the parts joyning upon the river Nile, barbarously murdering all strangers, which passing that way fell into his hands;* whence is that of Ovid. lib. 3. de Tristi, more cruel thow, than was Busiris art . . . Where observe, that this Ramesses, surnamed Myamun, . . . is by Muthological writers, surnamed Neptunus, and was the man who commanded the new born infants of the Hebrews to be drowned; and that left behind him two sons, Amenophis (*i.e.*) Belus of Egypt . . . that oppugner of the Almighty God, and which with his host, was overwhelmed in the Red-sea; and left Busiris his son, so infamous, for butchering of strangers, (a fitting off-spring of such a father) to succeed him . . . [39]

With the possible exception of Melanchthon, Milton seems to have been virtually alone in equating Busiris with the Pharaoh who perished during the Exodus. Classical and medieval historians usually assigned him a later date, during the period of Joshua's captaincy. Renaissance historians—some of them admittedly influenced by Melanchthon—placed him considerably before the Red Sea debacle. Reineccius and Raleigh identified him with the monarch reigning at the time of Moses' birth. In Ussher's opinion, hwever, Busiris' reign began immediately *after* his predecessor's destruction in the Red Sea.

In the light of Renaissance chronography, the conventional criticism of Milton's historical allusion seems, on the whole, invalid. Bentley was obviously mistaken in asserting that the "Times and Characters" of Pharaoh and Busiris were "no ways agreeing."

Newton erred in denying that there was "authority enough for to justify . . . an historian" in identifying the two figures. Masson wrongly concluded that Milton had followed Raleigh. Verity's suggestion that Milton "treats *Busiris* as a general title for the rulers of Egypt, like 'Pharaoh' " lacks supporting evidence.[40]

Seen against the background of Renaissance historiography, Milton's equation between Busiris and the victim of the Red Sea debacle seems a highly apposite historical judgment, rather than a historical inaccuracy. Both the relative dates of Busiris and the Red Sea disaster, and the precise identity of the Pharaoh at the time of the Exodus had long been subjects of controversy. The sequence of kings of the Eighteenth Dynasty was hopelessly confused. Instead of trying to unravel the Gordian knot — of attempting to untangle the complicated skein of Amosis, Amenophis, Chencheres, etc. — he chose the simpler identification suggested by Melanchthon's *Chronicon Carionis.*

Though unusual, this identification was by no means illogical. Busiris had been traditionally associated with the period immediately before or after the Exodus. Not only had chronographers identified the victim of the Red Sea debacle with one of the Pharaohs of the Eighteenth Dynasty, but several Renaissance historians had equated Busiris with particular kings of this dynasty and with the original oppressor of the Hebrews. Since Diodorus regarded Busiris as the last of his line and Melanchthon held a similar opinion of the Pharaoh drowned in the Red Sea, Milton's equation had ample justification in the chronological thought of his day. Within the frame-of-reference of Renaissance historiography, it rested on a firmer basis than the alternative opinions of such historians as Reineccius, Raleigh, and Ussher.

Interpretations of Wisdom 19:13 also reflect the influence of the chronographical tradition we have examined. As the Vulgate version of this text referred specifically to the "inhospitality" of the Egyptians' towards the Hebrews ("Etenim detestabiliorem inhospitalitatem instituerunt"), it was logical to explain this passage in terms of classical accounts of Busiris' inhospitality. Thus Cornelius a Lapide adduced the example of the "Pharaoh" Busiris as an instance of the Egyptians' customary cruelty towards strangers, but did not equate his victims specifically with the Israelites:

> Porrò quàm Aegypti fuerint in hospites saevi, liquet ex Busiride Pharaone, qui Thasium immolavit ad arcendam Aegypti ster-

ilitatem. Idem faciebat ceteris, hospitibus, teste Eusebio in Chron. &
S. August, libr. 18. de Civit. cap. 12 . . . Unde & Virgil. Georg.
3 . . . Idem patet ex crudelitate, quam Aegyptij exercuerunt in
Moysen & Hebraeos hospites. Exodi 1. & sequent. atque ex ijs, quae
de Aegyptiis narrant Arnobius libr. 8. contra Gentes, Minutius in
Octavio, Diodorus Sicul. lib. 2. cap. 4. & alij.[41]

Similarly, Lorinus refers to "Busiridis inhospitalitas" in explaining
the same text:

> Celebris admodum Busiridis Pharaonis immanis saevissimaque in-
> hospitalitas, qui hospitem Thasium immolavit ad avertandam
> sterilitatem Aegypti, & de aliis praeterea ab eodem immolatis
> hospitibus, necnon ab Aegyptiis aliis proditum est litteris eodem
> referri potest quod narrat liber Genesis, de Pharaone, abstulisse
> Saram Abramo. Philo namque illam appellat Regis libidinem in-
> hospitalem.[42]

These interpretations may also have contributed to Milton's identification of Busiris as the Pharaoh of the Red Sea debacle. Nevertheless, in Book XII of *Paradise Lost,* he applies the word "In-
hospitably" to the actions of an earlier Pharaoh—the *rex novus* of
Exodus 1:8,[43]

> . . . a sequent King, who seeks
> To stop thir overgrowth, as inmate guests
> Too numerous; whence of guests he makes them slaves
> Inhospitably, and kills thir infant Males . . .

In these lines he appears to have drawn not only on Exodus 1, but
also on Wisdom 19:13 ("inhospitalitatem instituerunt . . . alii
autem bonos hospites in servitutem redigebant").

III

While Professor Allen has traced Milton's identification of Busiris
to a passage in Melanchthon's version of Carion's *Chronicon,*
Professor Harold Fisch has explored this simile against the
background of other Egyptian (and Babylonian) images in *Paradise
Lost.* Noting "the centrality given to Egypt and to the matter of the
Exodus," he calls attention to Milton's "transformation of the
metaphysical region of Hell into the historical region of Egypt, the
appropriate location for the serpent-nahash-Leviathan-Devil and of
'the great dragon that lieth in the midst of his rivers' of Ezekiel

29:3." Professor James Sims has likewise emphasized the relationship between the "explicit analogy" in this simile and the Biblical allusions in Book VI which "identify Satan and his rebels with Pharaoh and his troops, and the Son of God and his elect angels with Moses and the Israelites." As Professor John Shawcross observes, "references early in the poem equate Satan and the fallen angels with Pharaoh and the Egyptians, then with the locusts . . . , and with the false gods of Egypt and the idol fashioned by Aaron . . . ."[44]

The identification of Busiris as one of the Biblical oppressors of the Israelites — either the *rex novus* of Exodus i.8 (the "new king over Egypt, which knew not Joseph") or alternatively the Pharaoh alleged to have perished in the Red Sea — appears to have been more an innovation on Renaissance chronography than a legacy from classical and medieval historiography. Though the latter frequently treats him as a historical personage, Busiris usually remains "an essentially legendary figure, whose affinities [are] distinctly mythological rather than Biblical." In part this innovation was based on the tenuous evidence of etymology. Melanchthon translated the name "Busiris" as "Munitor" (i.e. "builder of fortifications"). Though he did not explain this derivation, he apparently had in mind the same Hebrew root from which Genebrardus subsequently derived *Busiris*— the verb *bâtsar*. Buxtorf himself (as we have seen) translated this word as *munivit,* and to Melanchthon and Genebrardus the etymology from *bâtsar*[45] (to fortify) may have seemed additionally attractive in the light of Exodus i. 11, "They built for Pharaoh treasure cities, Pithom and Raamses." Moreover, references in classical histories to Busiris as an Egyptian city and mythological accounts of Busiris as a notorious tyrant would further strengthen this identification with one or more of the Pharaohs cited in Exodus. In Busiris the *Munitor,* Renaissance exegetes might (if they exercised sufficient ingenuity, or even a moderate suspension of disbelief) detect the very name of the anonymous *rex novus* who "knew not Joseph" and perfected his despotic character in architectural extravagance and infanticide[46]— or, alternatively, the traits of his successor, the Pharaoh who denied the people "straw to make brick" (Exodus v.7) and perished miserably in the Red Sea.

An awareness of this etymology[47] on the part of Milton and his seventeenth-century readers, could have heightened the proleptic function of the Busiris allusion, pointing forward to both the rise and fall of Satan's kingdom, foreshadowing the construction of Pandaemonium yet exposing it for what it essentially is—the architecture of despotism. Like Busiris, Satan is a builder, a *Munitor*—and a homicide. Like Busiris, he displays the magnificence of an Oriental tyrant. Nevertheless, the same etymology could emphasize not only the analogy between the architectural schemes of Satan and Pharaoh, but also the circumstances of their ultimate downfall. The root *bâtsar* might mean "cut off" as well as "fortify," and Buxtorf translated it both as *praecidit* and *munivit*. (The two senses are closely related.) Such an etymology would be equally appropriate for the fate of Pharaoh's army and that of Satan's legions.

In the immediate context of this simile,[48] however, another etymology—less conventional but hardly less far-fetched than Genebrardus' derivation—would seem to be even more apposite. Conceivably Milton's allusion to Busiris may involve some learned wordplay on the verb *bâzar* ("scatter"). Such a pun would be all the more apposite since *Pharaoh* had also been etymologized as *dissipator* or "scatterer." Not only does this idea constitute the central theme of these lines but reiterated allusions to "scattering" form an explicit verbal link (as well as an implicit thematic nexus) between the several members of the simile. Only a few lines earlier Milton had alluded to leaves that "strow the Brooks" and to "scatter'd sedge"; only a few verses later he would further stress the image of dispersal by verbal repetition: "thick bestrown," "scatter'd Arms and Ensigns." Etymologically, the name "Busiris" would appear to sum up, to condense and focus in a single word, the various allusions to "scattering" dispersed throughout this passage.[49] Instead of (or rather in addition to) Busiris the builder or *Munitor,* Milton has given us Busiris of the scattered army. Technically, this allusion seems to be another example of a rhetorical figure that he exploits frequently in prose and poetry alike—the *argumentum à nomine* or *notatio.* Perhaps rhetorical factors—the opportunity for subtle word-play on the words for "scatter," "cut off," and "build"—were more significant than purely historiographic considerations in his preference for the name Busiris instead of more conventional alternatives: Cenchres, Amosis, Bocchoris, and others.

IV

In his excellent analysis of the imagery of Book I, Professor Fisch called attention to Milton's awareness of "the Hebraic complexes Leviathan-Serpent-Egypt and Lucifer-Nebuchadnezzar-Babylon." Thematically these image-clusters are connected by common motifs — the image of the tyrant; despotic presumption expressed through defiance of divine commands and persecution of God's people; and finally, Jehovah's sudden intervention, bringing terrible retribution upon His adversaries and miraculous deliverance to His elect. The two sets of images are further associated by links between the Mesopotamian Babylon and the Egyptian Babylon (Cairo)[50] later in the same book, and by allusions throughout the poem to still another generation of Oriental despots — the rulers of Islamic Africa and Asia. Besides comparing Satan with Pharaoh and Nimrod — rulers of Egypt and Babylon — Milton describes him as a "great Sultan," an epithet that associates him specifically with monarchs of the medieval and Renaissance East and complements the more customary analogy with tyrants of Biblical antiquity.[51]

In Milton's Leviathan-image critics have recognized a motif familiar in the bestiaries, where the fable of the whale-mistaken-for-an-island serves as an allegory of diabolical deceit, and in St. Gregory's commentary on Job, which likewise interprets Leviathan as a symbol of the devil.[52] Nevertheless, the term possessed additional associations, both in Hobbes' political treatise and in Renaissance lexicons and Biblican commentaries, and these made it a highly apposite figure for a tyrant. Metaphorically, as Schindler explained, the word *Leviathan* signified *princeps* or *rex*. Though it usually denoted a whale, a sea-serpent, or other species of marine monsters, it could also (in the most literal sense) signify "society."

These etymological explanations of *Leviathan* possibly conditioned Hobbes' choice of title for his book. In his treatise (as the appositive structure of the title itself would suggest) the word literally means "commonwealth." Nevertheless, as he must have known, it may also signify "prince" or "king," and in this sense his title suggests a verbal analogy (possibly intentional) with that of Machiavelli's treatise. Like Machiavelli, Hobbes has entitled his treatise *The Prince,* but he has done so in veiled and allusive language, through a Hebrew metaphor.[53]

Milton's antipathy towards Hobbes' doctrines is well known, and it is possible that among the multiple associations of the Leviathan-image in *Paradise Lost* he may have intended an indirect allusion to the Hobbesian ideal of the absolute monarch as autocratic "Governour" and "Mortall God," an ideal that in Milton's view would represent the very apotheosis of tyranny. The political associations inherent in Renaissance etymologies of "Leviathan," moreover, may be equally relevant to a later episode in Milton's epic, the comic transformation-scene in which Satan and his followers are miraculously metamorphosed into serpents. The commonwealth of Pandaemonium, for all its external glitter and regal magnificence, has now become *literally* a Leviathan, a "société de serpents."[54] Here again Milton may be exploiting Hebrew etymology for a rhetorical *argumentum a nomine*.

In Christian exegetical tradition, moreover, Milton would have encountered numerous allegorical interpretations of the Red Sea debacle; some of these would have made the Pharaonic allusions in his simile singularly applicable to the situation of the fallen angels at the beginning of Book I. Just as Pharaoh typified the devil, the overthrow of the Egyptian hosts symbolized the fall of the evil angels, and the Red Sea itself served as a figure of Hell. In Guillaume Pepin's *Expositio in Exodum* Milton's contemporaries could have encountered a detailed "anagogical" commentary stressing the analogies between Pharaoh's army and the devil's legions, and combining the Pharaonic details of Exodus with the Luciferic imagery of Isaiah and the dragon-allusions of the Apocalypse:

> Anagogice . . . Per Egyptios autem persequentes dictos filios Israel intelliguntur mali angeli quorum rex fuit Lucifer. Hi enim ausi sunt persequi bonos angelos & inire cum eis prelium: iuxta id quod scriptum est Apoc. xij. Michael & angeli eius preliabantur cum dracone & draco pugnabat & angeli eius. Hoc autem prelium totum factum est ante vigiliam matutinam .i. ante claram dei visionem. Ubi autem advenit predicta vigilia matutina .i. cognitio beatifica in bonis angelis perseverantibus in gratia & obedientia ad suum conditorem: tunc respexit dominus oculo suo severe iustitie super castra Egyptiorum .i. super multitudine malorum angelorum qui non retulerunt se & sua in deum factorem suum sed praevaluerunt in vanitate sua: & tunc interfecit eos videlicet spiritualiter sicut &

spirituales creature erant: atque de celo deiecit eos dicens regi eorum .i. supremo inter eos illud Esa. xiiij. Ad inferna detraheris cum superbia tua. Et hoc figurative insinuatur per Egyptios qui submersi in mari rubro ferebantur in profundum nec unus quidem superfuit ex eis. Filij autem Israel .i. boni angeli pervenerunt ad portum salutis eterne: & hoc mediante gratia dei . . . Liberavit ergo dominus in die illo filios Israel de manu Egyptiorum .i. bonos angelos videntes deum de medio malorum angelorum qui nunc recte Egyptij .i. tenebrosi dicuntur eo quod manent in tenebris culpe & pene. Et sicut filij Israel pervenientes ad littus maris rubri viderunt ibi Egyptios mortuos: sic & boni angeli existentes in patria vident demones sicut et ceteros damnatos in inferno sine tamen ulla compassione.[55]

V

Though there was ample justification for Milton's Busiris allusion on rhetorical grounds, its historical basis was more tenuous. Professor Allen's valuable suggestion that "in Melanchthon's recension" of Carion's *Chronicon* "we find the authority for Milton's identification of Busiris with the Red Sea Pharaoh" has brought to light an important analogue and probable source. Nevertheless, it is doubtful whether we can consider the *Chronicle* as *the* single authority for Milton's statement; the latter may, in fact, derive from a combination of several sources including not only Melanchthon, but Raleigh, Pliny, Diodorus Siculus, and other historiographers.

In the first place, Melanchthon's Busiris-identification is admittedly hypothetical. In his own words, it is merely *consentaneum* or "reasonable." In an early German translation this reservation becomes slightly stronger; the identification is *wol gleublich* or "credible." According to the translator's gloss, "Busiris ist *vielleicht* [italics mine] der Tyran Pharao zu Mosis zeiten."[56] A similar note of uncertainty is apparent in Raleigh's identification—already well-known to Milton scholars—which equates Busiris with the author of the decree of infanticide (Exodus i).

In the second place, Melanchthon's statement is slightly ambiguous, though the ambiguity results largely from the *context* of his reference to the later king. The *Chronicon* does not explicitly distinguish the Pharaoh who died in the Red Sea from his

predecessor the *rex novus*. Instead the author passes freely from one
to the other without comment, just as Milton's prophetic arch-angel
would juxtapose without explanation the "sequent King" who "kills
their infant Males" and "the lawless Tyrant" who suffers the ten
plagues of Egypt (PL, XII, 165-214) and perishes during the
Exodus. Both writers were apparently relying on their readers'
familiarity with scripture to prevent confusion between the two
Egyptian kings.

Melanchthon's initial observations on Busiris apparently refer to
the earlier Pharaoh. Even though the allusion to Pharaoh's architectural enterprises might conceivably be applicable to either
tyrant, it would be more appropriate for the *rex novus,* whose
projects are outlined in Exodus in greater detail. Moreover,
Melanchthon's specific reference to infanticide (*necatis ipsorum
infantibus*) surely indicates the earlier king. In Menius' German
translation, the identification of Busiris with the *rex novus* is explicit; the translator alludes to the actual promulgation of the edict
commanding the slaughter of the infant males:

> Weil denn Dieses Königes BVSIRIDIS grausamkeit und Tyranney in
> allen Historien seer berümbt ist/ und man von im schreibt/ das er die
> Frembdlinge/ so zu im komen sein/ habe flegen zu tödten/ ist wol
> gleublich/ das dieses gerücht von seiner grawsamkeit erstlich daher
> komen/ das er die armen Leut die Kinder Israel so grausamlich
> geplagt/ und ire kleine Kindlin befohlen hat su tödten.[57]

In this passage Melanchthon's identification of Busiris has been
based largely on two correlations: first, the analogy between the
notorious cruelty that the classical Busiris had shown to strangers
and the more notorious xenophobia of the *rex novus* of Exodus;
secondly, the analogy between the architectural associations of the
name *Busiris* and the architectural program of the "new king" who
"knew not Joseph." The analogy is strengthened (as we have observed earlier) by the etymological interpretation of *Busiris* as
Munitor; the king is called Busiris, "ein Befestiger/ Munitor"
because "er seer gebawet hat." Moreover, his name was specifically
associated with the site of one of the Seven Wonders of the World,
the great pyramids:

> Und das man sagt/ wie er etliche grosse wundersame PYRAMIDES,
> oder Thürme zu Festungen and anderm brauch/ gebawet habe/ ist

> wol gleublich/ das zu diesem Baw die Kinder Israel solch grosse
> arbeit mit Ziegel strechen und breen haben thun müssen. Denn nicht
> fern von der Stad dieses namens BUSIRIS, sind drey seer berhümbter
> Pyramides gewesen/ deren Plinius in seinem Büchern gedenckt.[58]

As the German translator regards pyramids as a species of fortifications (*Thürme zu Festungen*), he has advanced an additional
(though farfetched) argument in favor of the *Busiris-Munitor* interpretation.

Though recent scholarship has emphasized the disagreement
between Melanchthon, on the one hand, and Raleigh and
Reineccius,[59] on the other, there are nevertheless significant points
of resemblance among all three authors in their identification of
Busiris. Reineccius explicitly endorses Melanchthon's argument
that Pharaoh's infanticide was the historical source of Greek legends
concerning Busiris' cruelty to his guests. In identifying the classical
tyrant with the Biblical author of the bloody edict, both Reineccius
and Raleigh follow an interpretation that is apparent in Melanchthon's Latin account and explicit in the German translation.

As Raleigh's allusion to Busiris has already received attention
from Verity and other Miltonists, we shall note only a few points of
agreement or disagreement with other Renaissance histories. Like
Reineccius (and apparently like Melanchthon), Raleigh identifies
Busiris with the author of the bloody edict. With Reineccius,
moreover, he further equates the latter with Orus II. At this point,
however, the two historians disagree. Whereas Reineccius places
Busiris (Orus II) after Amenophis II,[60] Raleigh regards him as the
immediate successor of an "entirely different Pharaoh—Sesostris II,
the blind king." Moreover (Raleigh argues), as Busiris did not
officially begin his reign until *after* the birth of Moses, the decree of
infanticide must have been issued during Sesostris' reign. Nevertheless, Busiris as regent was probably responsible for the edict, and
the powers he held as viceroy fully justify the Biblican reference to
him as a "new *king*." To the familiar picture of Busiris as archetypal
tyrant Raleigh adds a further sign of his tyranny, the suggestion that
he had illegally usurped royal authority:

> Let us therefore consider [Raleigh continues], besides the blindness
> of Sesostris the second, how great the power of the Regents or
> Viceroyes in Aegypt was . . . Therefore perhaps the king did . . .
> resigne his kingdome to him, though his reigne was not accounted to

have begun, till the death of *Sesostris*. But whether Busiris did
usurpe the kingdome, or protection of the land by violence: or
whether the blind king resigned it, keeping the title; or whether
Busiris were onely Regent, whilst the king lived, and afterwards (as is
acknowledged by all) king himselfe: it might welle be said that
Pharaohs daughter tooke up Moses, and that Pharaoh vexed Israel;
seeing he both at that time was king in effect, and shortly after king
in deed and title both. It were not absurd for us to say that the blind
king Sesostris the second oppressed Israel: but forasmuch as it may
seeme that the wicked Tyrant shewed his evill nature even when he
first arose: I thinke it more likely, that Busiris did it, using at first
the power of a king, and shortly after the stile. Thus of the 122.
yeares which passed betweene the beginning of Sesostris his reigne, &
the departure of Israel out of Egypt, 47. being spent; the 75. which
remaine, are to be accounted to Busiris or Orus the second, and his
children. Busiris himselfe reigned 30. yeeres, according to Eusebius
. . . .[61]

On the whole, the differences between Raleigh and Reineccius,
on the one hand, and Melanchthon, on the other, seem to have
been exaggerated. The latter's allusion to infanticide would appear
to justify the interpretation that Reineccius subsequently placed on
his remarks and that Raleigh (with minor variations) would also
follow. The first part of Melanchthon's discussion of Busiris seems to
identify him unmistakably with the *rex novus,* and it is only the
latter part of this account that could provide "authority for Milton's
identification of Busiris with the Red Sea Pharaoh . . . "[62] In the
paragraph immediately following his account of Busiris the infanticide, Melanchthon declares that an interregnum had occurred
in Egypt after the tyrant's death in the Red Sea:

. . . ist das Königreich ein zeitlang one König gewesen/ Denn nach
der Tyrann im Roten Meer mit aller seiner fürnemsten macht und
Fürsten erseufft worden/ wie die Kinder Israel aus Egypten gezogen
sind/ ists gar gleublich/ das hernach lange zeit auffruhr und unruhe
im Reich gewesen sey.[63]

Finally in the paragraph after this statement Melanchthon observes that Diodorus mentions a successor to Busiris only after "gar
eine lange zeit" (*post longum intervallum*).

Although Melanchthon's middle paragraph could be (and has
been) interpreted as "authority" for Milton's statement that Busiris
perished in the Red Sea, it is questionable whether Melanchthon

himself intended to convey this idea. In the first place, he had already identified Busiris with the Pharaoh of the bloody edict; and (as we have noted) it was partly on this statement that Reineccius admittedly based his own identification of Busiris. Secondly, although Melanchthon (like Milton in Book XII) did not distinguish sharply between the two persecuting Pharaohs mentioned in the Biblical account of Moses, he could hardly have regarded them as being one and the same person without contradicting scripture. Thirdly, Melanchthon's account of the interregnum follows immediately after the statement that there had apparently been *numerous kings named Busiris:* "Es scheinet aber als sein viel Könige gewesen die diesen namen BUSIRIS gehabt haben."[64] Conceivably, the Pharaoh of the Red Sea episode could have been one of these. If Milton had attempted to correlate Melanchthon's statements with those of Diodorus Siculus, he could have found reasons for inferring that *both* persecutors had been named Busiris and that they represented respectively the first and the last monarchs of their line.

According to Diodorus, the last king in Busiris' line "bore the same name as the first . . . "[65] If Milton juxtaposed this statement with Raleigh's belief that the earlier Busiris (the *rex novus* of Exodus) had founded a dynasty and with Melanchthon's assertion that an interregnum had followed Pharaoh's death in the Red Sea, he might plausibly infer that the first and last kings in this succession had *both* been called Busiris. If the "new king" who founded the dynasty had borne this name, then the last member of the line, the Pharaoh who brought the dynasty to its sudden and watery end, must likewise have been named Busiris.

Milton's identification of Busiris does not conflict with the views expressed by Reineccius and Raleigh, inasmuch as both of the latter are alluding to the *first* king in the dynasty, whereas Milton is referring to the *last* of his line. Though this identification is not explicit in Carion's *Chronicle,* it would not be an illogical conclusion if Milton had interpreted Melanchthon's statements in the light of Diodorus' remarks.

Resting primarily on deductive inference from the combined assertions of earlier chronographers rather than on the explicit authority of a single historian, Milton's Busiris-allusion bears even greater witness perhaps to his ingenuity as a logician than to his caution as a historian.

VI

Against the background of Renaissance speculations on chronology, Milton's identification seems to have been virtually an innovation; it is the first clear-cut reference to Busiris as the Pharaoh of the Red Sea debacle (for Melanchthon's remarks are ambiguous). Nevertheless, it was not illogical, and in its historiographic context it was scarcely more far-fetched than the traditional interpretations favored by his predecessors and contemporaries. To untangle the complicated web of Renaissance Egyptology — to unravel its genealogical intricacies and chronographical inconsistencies — was a challenge that could be met only by the patience of Job or by the resolution of Alexander. Milton preferred to emulate the latter, and cut the Gordian knot. In so doing, he enhanced the pleasure of his readers and the perplexities of his commentators.

Though these Renaissance historiographical problems are interesting in their own right, they may also cast indirect light on Milton's intellectual background. We may appreciate the boldness of his Busiris allusion more readily, once we have compared it with the frustrated endeavors of earlier historians.

For the *rex novus* of *Exodus* Milton would probably have known at least five alternative identifications familiar to medieval or Renaissance chronographers. Peter Comestor,[66] Guillaume Pepin,[67] Hector Boetius, and David Chytraeus[68] regarded Amenophis as the ruling monarch at the time of Moses' birth. Genebrardus similarly identified the *rex novus* as Amenophis or Busiris.[69] Variations on this name appear in Drusius,[70] who prefers the forms Menophis or Memnon, and in Lucas, Bishop of Tuy,[71] who prefers the variant Monofo. Funccius likewise regards Amenophis as the original persecutor of the Israelites, and equates him with Memnon.[72] According to Syncellus,[73] on the other hand, Moses was born during the reign of Amosis or Tethmosis. In Archbishop Ussher's opinion,[74] the *rex novus* was Ramesses [Rameses] Myamun, or Neptune; Mercator[75] similarly identified him as Armesesmiamum. Holinshed identified him with Orus, and Reineccius[76] and Raleigh[77] equated him with Orus II or Busiris.

Theories as to the identity of the "new king's" successor, the Pharaoh at the time of the Exodus, showed equal diversity.[78]

Numerous authorities — Eusebius, Jerome, Drusius, Reineccius, Pepin, Funccius, Holinshed, Raleigh, Chytraeus, Sebastian Münster — followed Berosus in identifying him with Cenchres (Chencres). Clement of Alexandria and Sextus Julius Africanus, on the other hand, regarded Amosis as the reigning sovereign. Syncellus shared their opinion, but carefully distinguished between *two* Pharaohs who had borne this name: 1) Amos I (Tethmosis) under whom Moses had been born and 2) Amos II (Misphragmuthosis) in whose time Moses had led the Israelites forth from Egypt.

Other historians regarded Amenophis as the ruler of Egypt at the period of the Exodus. This view could be traced back to Manetho and Chaeremon (who represented this event as a victory for Amenophis and his son Ramesses rather than as a defeat). Although Josephus explicitly rejected this identification, several Renaissance historians preferred to follow Manetho in dating the Exodus during Amenophis' reign. According to Mercator, Josephus had confused this event with the expulsion of the shepherd-kings some 350 years earlier by Themosis (Tethmosis). Bunting likewise followed Manetho's chronology, but regarded Amenophis and Rameses (Raëmses) as the same monarch, rather than as father and son. Archbishop Ussher similarly acknowledged Amenophis as the Pharaoh of the Exodus, but equated him with Belus, brother of Busiris.

A fourth tradition can be traced to the historian Lysimachus, who identified Bocchoris as the Egyptian monarch at this time. Though refuted by Josephus, this view was approved by Tacitus and followed by Hector Boetius and other Renaissance historians.

According to Cedrenus, the Pharaoh whose magicians Jannes and Jambres had contended with Moses and Aaron was named Petissonius. Scaliger maintained that the Exodus had taken place under Acherres, the tenth king of the Eighteenth Dynasty. Josephus, on the other hand, dated the Exodus much earlier, during the reign of Themosis (Tethmosis), who had expelled the shepherd-kings.

Historiographers themselves were painfully aware of these conflicting interpretations and of the difficulty of reconciling them. In *Contra Apionem*[79] Josephus argued, in fact, that the very disagreement among Greco-Egyptian historians — Manetho, Lysimachus, Chaeremon, Molon, Apion — undermined their authority. Reineccius[80] called attention to four alternative opinions as to the name of the Pharaoh of Exodus xiv: Chencres (Cenchres), Amosis, Bocchoris, and Petissonius. Genebrardus[81] was aware of at least five alternatives: Tethmosis, Amasis (Amosis), Cenchres, Bachoris (Bocchoris), and Amenophis.

How seriously Renaissance historians took these conjectures is apparent in the changes that Hector Boethius' *History of Scotland* underwent at the hands of later historians. In describing the adventures of Gathelus, eponymous ancestor of the Gaels or Goidelic Celts, Boetius conducted his Grecian hero to the Egypt of Amonophis (Amenophis)—"Pharao Israelitarum flagellum"— father of the Bochoris (Bocchoris) who subsequently perished in the Red Sea. After defending Egypt against the Ethiopians and espousing Pharaoh's daughter Scota (who bequeathed her name to the Scots), Gathelus prudently took cognizance of the plagues of Egypt and left the country before worse calamities should ensue.[82]

Though the Scottish translator, John Bellenden,[83] followed Boetius' account, Holinshed[84] (or his associates) distrusted the references to Amenophis and Bocchoris and accordingly substituted the names Orus and Chencres respectively. Thus Orus, rather than Amenophis, became the *rex novus* who "knew not Joseph," and Chencres replaced Bocchoris as the tyrant who perished in the Red Sea.

Against this background of historiographical controversy, Milton's minor contribution to Renaissance Egyptology may seem relatively sane. Diodorus' statement that Busiris was the last of his line, along with Melanchthon's belief in an interregnum, gave the poet limited authority for identifying the classical tyrant with the Pharaoh of the Exodus. Moreover (as we have noted) the etymological significance of this name reinforced the dominant idea—"scattering" or dispersal—underlying the entire simile. Since modern scholarship is still divided on the chronology[85] of the Exodus and the identity of the reigning monarch (or monarchs), we can surely grant Milton's historiographical innovation the indulgence we usually accord his puns.

VII

Finally, let us return to the epithet "*Memphian.*" Though it has been regarded as a substitute for "Egyptian"[86] (and hence a form of synecdoche), it seems equally likely that Milton may have had in mind the conventional association of the city Memphis with Busiris. According to Eusebius,[87] Memphis had been founded by Epaphus (commonly regarded as grandfather to Busiris), and this opinion had been shared by many subsequent chronographers: Syncellus,[88] Lucas (Bishop of Tuy),[89] Alfonso el Sabio,[90] and Sir Walter Raleigh.[91] Genebrardus[92] had not only endorsed this view, but specifically identified Memphis with Cairo (the Egyptian Babylon). According to Alfonso's[93] *General Estoria,* Memphis was the actual seat of Busiris' reign, and Pliny[94] had associated the two words as place-names.

On the relative dates of the Exodus and the founding of Memphis chronographers were divided. Whereas Eusebius, Syncellus, Funccius, and Raleigh[95] regarded the Exodus as anterior to the founding of the city, other historians held the contrary view. Cedrenus[96] relates that, shortly before the Exodus, the Pharaoh Petissonius consulted the oracle at Memphis. And according to Lucas, Bishop of Tuy,[97] to Hector Boetius, and to Bellenden and Holinshed,[98] the Ethiopians had invaded Egypt during Moses' youth, advancing as far as Memphis.

Milton had adequate authority, not only for regarding Memphis as existing prior to the Exodus, but also for believing it to be the royal seat of Busiris.

CHAPTER XIV

A Mask at Ludlow:
Comus and Dionysiac Revel

RECENT CRITICISM of *Comus* has shown something of a matriarchal bias, stressing the distaff side of the god's genealogy at the expense of his paternal ancestry. Miss Tuve has correctly emphasized the central position of the Circe myth in Milton's masque — the "hinge" on which the invention turns. But Comus is also the son of Bacchus. Milton describes him as "Much like his Father, but his Mother more . . . " In stressing his affinities with the goddess whose "charmed Cup" transformed the taster "into a groveling Swine," we should not overlook his resemblance to the god who "first from out the purple Grape, / Crush't the sweet poyson of mis-used Wine . . . " Bacchus himself was also a magician ot sorts, and the "*Tuscan* Mariners transform'd" (Fig. IV) were not the only victims of his power to foster illusions, perform miracles, and transform shapes. The royal houses of Thebes and Orchomenus could have offered compelling evidence to the contrary.*

* I am indebted to the Northwestern University Press for permission to reprint the revised version of this paper from *Research Opportunities in Renaissance Drama*, Vol. XIII-XIV (1970-71), edited by Professor Samuel Schoenbaum.

Iconographical studies of *Comus*—by Professor Collins Baker, Professor Arthos and Professor Orgel—have called attention to two highly important illustrations of the god of revelry—in Cartari's *Images of the Gods of the Ancients* and in Blaise de Vigenere's French translation of Philostratus's *Images*.[1] The former (Fig. V) is a rather simple picture of the deity as Philostratus[2] had described him:

> The spirit Comus (Revelry), to whom men owe their revelling, is stationed at the doors of a chamber—golden doors, I think they are; but . . . the time is supposed to be at night . . . ; and the splendid entrance indicates that it is a very wealthy pair just married . . . And Comus has come, a youth to join the youths, delicate and not yet full grown, flushed with wine and, though erect, he is asleep under the influence of drink. As he sleeps the face falls forward on the breast . . .; the torch seems to be falling from his right hand as sleep relaxes it. And for fear lest the flames of the torch come too near his leg, Comus bends his lower left leg over towards the right and holds the torch out on his left side, keeping his right hand at a distance by means of the projecting knee in order that he may avoid the breath of the torch.

These details recur in the French translation of Philostratus, but there the illustration (Fig. VI) is far more elaborate. The doorway has swung open, to expose not a *thalamos* or bridal-chamber, but a banqueting-hall equipped with all the paraphernalia of a sumptuous feast—a crowded table, a balcony filled with musicians, a throng of guests, and a ring of dancers. Comus himself has been pushed to the extreme right; leaning against the arch, he faces the spectators rather than the revellers. These additional details apparently represent a rather free adaptation of the last paragraph of Philostratus's description:

> And what else is there of the revel? Well, what but the revellers? Do you not hear the castanets and the flute's shrill note and the disorderly singing? The torches give a faint light . . . Peals of laughter rise, and women rush along with men, [wearing men's] sandals and garments girt in strange fashion; for the **revel** permits women to masquerade as men, and men to 'put on women's garb' and to ape the walk of women.[3]

The textual authority for Comus's spear is somewhat dubious: scholars have not decided whether Philostratus wrote *prolobíoi* or *probolíoi*. At least one modern Hellenist interprets this word as meaning that Comus "holds his left hand up to his ear."[4]

Renaissance translators and mythographers, however, normally read this term as referring to a spear (*venabulum* or *hasta*).

The resemblances between these pictures and Milton's account of Comus are not impressive. In the masque the deity's chief attributes are "a Charming Rod in one hand" and a "Glass in the other." The torches belong to his followers, not to the god himself. He does not carry a spear, and he is far from being overcome with sleep. Since he is described as "ripe and frolick of his full grown age," he may perhaps be older than the youthful divinity Philostratus portrays as *oúpo éphebos*, "not yet full grown." Whether or not he wears the "crown of roses" described by Philostratus and delineated in both pictures we do not know. His nocturnal revels, moreover, are no wedding feast. There is no bridal chamber—unless we wish to regard as such the "stately Palace" where (presumably) he intends to make the Lady his Queen. The chief points of similarity are the "light fantastick round" performed by the revellers in Vigenere's volume and in Milton's masque; the "rosie Twine" wherewith they "Braid [their] Locks"; the banquet-table in the French illustration and the "Tables spred with all dainties" according to Milton's stage direction. For the enchanter's principal attributes—his "wand" and "banefull cup"—we must look elsewhere.

Both, of course, belonged traditionally to Circe and were commonly depicted in Renaissance emblems of the sorceress and in illustrations (Figs. VII and VIII) of Ovid's *Metamorphoses*.[5] But both also pertained to Bacchus and his attendants. Indeed art historians are still debating the problem of the restored hand and cup in Michelangelo's statue of Bacchus; and modern translators of Ovid and Euripides sometimes translate the Dionysian thyrsus as "wand." Though we are probably most familiar with the Bacchic thyrsus as depicted in classical reliefs—a short javelin wound with ivy and tipped with a pine-cone—this version was by no means standard in the Renaissance. In Cartari's picture (Fig. IX) of the "*Tuscan* Mariners transform'd" the thyrsus is simply an ordinary wand entwined with ivy.[6] In other Renaissance illustrations (Figs. X and XI) Bacchus or his followers carry other sorts of ferules—reeds, stalks of fennel, or staffs.[7] The Bacchic *ferula* was, in fact, proverbial; and Renaissance mythographers offered a variety of explanations ranging from discipline to indiscipline, temperance to intemperance. The staffs were intended to steady the reeling devotees. The reeds were substitutes for clubs, which might wreak greater havoc in a drunken brawl. Alternatively, they were scourges, admonitory of the after-effects of actions committed in drunkenness. Like the cup (Figs. XII and XIII), the wand was characteristic of Bacchus.

Iconographically, Milton's tempter displays attributes associated with *both* of his parents; and this dual association — Bacchic as well as Circean — both qualifies and defines the primary symbols of his masque. Revelry or Riot (*cōmos* or *luxus*) is the offspring of drunkenness and sensual pleasure. Either alone had power to brutalize the rational soul, "unmoulding reasons mintage"; but the fruit of their union is doubly powerful, for he possesses the spells of both. It is significant that Milton couples Bacchus's power to transform men into beasts with Circe's and that the victims of Comus's enchantments include "brutish form(s)" — "Woolf, or Bear, / Or Ounce, or Tiger, Hog, or bearded Goat . . . " — associated not only with the goddess of pleasure but also with the god of wine. Extensive though it was, Circe's menagerie did not contain *all* of these beasts; several of them belonged traditionally in Bacchus's entourage.

Before leaving the subject of Comus, let us briefly consider some of the metamorphoses he underwent during the century preceding the Ludlow masque. On the surface, Milton's elegant enchanter seems far removed from the belly-gods of Jonson[8] and Puteanus. Yet it may be significant that Milton, like Jonson, introduces Comus in the anti-masque of a work that does, in the end, offer a higher reconciliation between virtue and pleasure — a theme that receives still greater emphasis in the lines on the Garden of Adonis added in the 1637 version.[9] The belches of Puteanus's divinity seem inconsistent with the Doric delicacy of Milton's master of the revels, and the latter is far less blunt in extolling the kingdom of the stomach, "Ventris regnum." Nevertheless both first appear in a forest setting. Each is, in a sense, "conviviorum . . . Genius" and "laetitiae Praeses." Both describe their revels as religious rites or solemnities ("sacra"); and both make their appeal to pleasure. "Jam Sacra mea, *Phagesia,* sive *Phagesiposia* sunt," declares the divinity of Puteanus's dream-vision, "Scriptoribus memorata, & Luxu Lasciviaque peraguntur. Paucis: totum Voluptatis regnum meum est; nec felix quisquam, nisi qui meus."[10]

In Milton's masque the motif of "swinish gluttony" (as the Lady calls it) is merely one among several facets of "sensual Folly, and Intemperance"; it survives chiefly in the richly spread tables and the "cordial Julep" that the tempter offers the Lady. Nevertheless, as it was a dominant theme in Renaissance discussions of Comus, we should consider how it evolved from Philostratus's account. Philostratus, and Cornutus after him, had described Comus as the daemon "to whom men owe their revelling" (*tò komázein*)—a term often translated as *comessari*. Though this Latin equivalent also bears a variety of senses, one of its primary meanings is to celebrate a nocturnal feast—to hold a banquet after normal dinner-hours. Thus Robert Estienne explains both the Greek and Latin terms as signifying "Post coenam epulari. . . . Pro eo convivio accipit, quod ad multam noctem agitatur post coenam."[11] In this way Comus became associated specifically with the drinking-party and banquet. Henry Estienne defines the common noun *cōmos* as a "compotatio convivialis, ex qua aliquis tandem incidit in Κωμα, id est somnum profundum." Some authorities (he continues) expound this word as "Festivitas in convivio," but "Hilaritas" would be a more accurate reading. Others define it as "Convivium luxuriosum" or "Convivium lascivum," but Estienne himself prefers the term "Comessatio," admitting (however) that *cōmos* has a wider meaning. For *cōmos* comprehends "omne amatoriae lasciviae ac proterviae genus." Sometimes it is applied generally to those who engage in amorous, lascivious, impudent, and wicked (*nequitia*) acts. Sometimes, however, it is restricted more narrowly to men in amorous frolic or riot ("hominibus amatoriè lascivientibus"), whether they are more or less under the influence of Bacchus. The latter, in fact, is the proper signification of the word. *Comessari* means *Bacchari*.

On the basis of this analysis Estienne distinguishes several further senses of this word. *Cōmos* denotes the band of banqueters or revellers, "Comessantium agmen." It also denotes their lascivious acts, "Lascivia & protervia, qualis est comessabundorum, & magis etiam propriè amatorum iuvenum comessabundorum." It may also signify a hilarious feast, "Festum quod magna cum hilaritate peragitur tanquam à comessabundis."

Significantly, *cōmos* is also closely associated with music and the dance. This term denotes a certain dance performed at banquets or drinking-parties, "Saltatio quaedam in comessationibus usitata" — particularly the type of dance known as *hēdýcōmos* ("Iucunda comessatio" or dance of joy). The same word has also been interpreted as signifying a flute; "Exponitur & Tibia comessationibus adhiberi solita ad ebrietatem."

Finally, Estienne turns to Philostratus's personification of *comos.* Comus is "Deus praeses huiusmodi comessationum, seu lasciviae proterviaeque comessabundorum hominum. . . ."[12]

Though certain of these definitions have close parallels in Philostratus's description, Henry Estienne's entry is valuable primarily for its range and for its reliance on numerous classical sources besides the *Images.* Indirectly it enriched the later Comus tradition by adding shades of meaning not readily apparent in Philostratus's text. The conception of *cōmos* as dance ("saltatio") contributed to the god's association with the masked ball. Several of these definitions — the luxurious or lascivious feast, amorous and impudent acts, hilarity, the rout of revellers — recur as *topoi* in Milton's *Comus.* The term *nequitia* ("worthlessness") may suggest a parallel with the etymology of Belial. It may be significant that Milton subsequently planned a drama on the Benjaminites ("Sons of Belial") with the title *Comazontes* (or *The Rioters*) and that there seem to be pronounced affinities between the Comus of the Ludlow masque and the Belial of *Paradise Lost.*

From Henry Estienne's definitions of *cōmos* let us return to the dictionaries of his kinsmen, Charles and Robert Estienne. According to the latter, Comus was the god of revelry and nocturnal dancing, "commessationum nocturnarumque saltationum praeses, in cuius militia authorabantur iuvenes, qui coronati noctu cum facibus musicisque instrumentis ad amicarum fores saltandi canendique gratia concurrebant, procaciterque lasciviebant, ut fores nonnunquam effringerent . . . " After citing Philostratus's image of the god, Estienne calls attention to Varro's derivation of *comessari* and *comessatio* from *cōmos* and observes that in Aristophanes's *Frogs* the term *Crepalocomus* denotes a hymn sung by drunkards, "vinolentorum hymnus." Charles Estienne's entry offers the same account.[13] In these details Comus is again closely associated with song, dance, and drunken feasting. The allusion to these youthful revellers who battered at the doors of houses offers yet another parallel to the "sons of Belial" whom Milton would regard as unruly rioters — *cōmazontes.*

Comessatio (or *cōmos*) in Robert Estienne's definition may denote a late meal, a feast, or a village banquet: "Cibus qui post coenam sumitur. Festus, Comessatio à vicis, quos Graeci κωμος dicunt, appellatur: in his enim habitant prius quàm oppida conderentur: quibus in locis alij alios convictus causa invitabant."[14] The etymological link with "village" is suggestive; when Milton's Comus proposes to appear as "som harmles Villager" he may be making a pun on his own name.

Besides the labors of the lexicographers and Philostratus's description of the god, Renaissance conceptions of Comus were also molded by brief allusions in Philostratus's images "Bosporus" and "Andrii." The former describes Comus as the god of drunkenness and associates him with flute-players and singers: "Comus ipse, id est, ebrietatis deus, pulchri, corollisque insignes. & hic quidem tibia canit, hic vero plaudit, inquit: hic cantat, puto . . . " The latter image associates him with Dionysus' miraculous wine-flow on the island of Andros and describes him as the companion of Laughter: "Navigat & Dionysus ad Andri bacchanalia . . . ," his entourage including satyrs and Sileni and Lenaei, "nec non & Risum & Comum hilarissimos ac bibaccissimos daemones, ut quam suavissime fluvio fruatur."[15] Like laughter, Comus is a "merry devil" — one of the gayest and most bibulous of daemons.

Among the leading Cinquecento mythographers Comus is closely associated with banquets and drinking parties — frequently on the authority of Philostratus, who generally served as the principal authority both for the god's image and for his allegorical significance. According to Lilio Giraldi, Comus is "deus . . . conviviorum & comessationum." Certain Greek writers (Giraldi observes) link him with Dionysus.[16] Cartari specifically stresses his resemblance to Bacchus, who is also frequently depicted as "giovine senza barba, allegro, e giocondo." Comus is "il Dio de i convivij," and in Philostratus's image he stands at the door of a chamber "ove era stato celebrato lieto e bel convivio per due sposi. . . ."[17] In the French translation of Cartari's *Images* by du Verdier, Comus is described as "Dieu des banquets."[18] In Lorenzo Pignoria's edition of Cartari's treatise Comus is still described as "Dio de Convivij, secondo Filostrato," but the author introduces a distinction between temperate and intemperate feasting which offers a thematic parallel to Milton's masque. According to Pignoria, the image of Comus signifies "che li Conviti modesti allegrano li huomini & svegliando li spiriti li fanno divenir arditi, & che all'incontro l'immoderato cibo fa l'humo sonnolento, inetto, ottuso d'ingegno, & debole di corpo." In addition to the conventional representation of Comus with spear and inverted torch, the illustration in this edition also includes an inset supposedly taken from an antique cameo. The god holds an inverted torch—but not a spear—and an amphora stands on a nearby pedestal.[19]

Cesare Ripa's emblem "Convito" (banquet)—unillustrated in the 1630 edition—is admittedly based on Philostratus's image. "Banquet" is described as a laughing youth crowned with a garland of flowers, dressed in green, and holding a burning torch in his right hand and a spear in his left. He is portrayed as young, because this age is more given to feasts and amusements. Since banquets are given for the sake of "commune allegrezza trà gl'amici," he is depicted as "ridente, & bello." The garland of flowers denotes the relaxation of the mind in "delicature, per cagione di conversare, & accrescere l'amicitie, che suole il convito generare." The kindled torch is associated with Hymen, god of weddings, "perche tiene gl'animi, & gl'ingegni svegliati, & allegri il convito, & ci rende splendidi, & magnanimi in sapere egualmente fare, & ricevere con gl'amici offitij di gratitudine."

Ripa's emblems of "Allegrezza" and "Ubriachezza" show little indebtedness to Philostratus's Comus, but they are significant both for their Bacchic imagery and for symbols that recur in Milton's masque. The first emblem of "Allegrezza" (Fig. XIV) portrays a young woman wearing a garland of diverse flowers and holding in her right hand "un vaso di cristallo pieno di vino rubicondo," in her left a golden cup, "una gran tazza d'oro." Her aspect is gracious and beautiful, and she is about to dance in a flowery meadow. The flowers are themselves symbols of Allegrezza. The crystal vase filled with wine and the golden cup signify that Allegrezza does not hide herself, but communicates herself freely and willingly. "La dispositione del corpo, e la dimostratione del ballo è manifesto inditio dell' Allegrezza."

Another emblem on the same theme depicts a young girl crowned with flowers and holding in her right hand a crowned thyrsus wound about with fronds and garlands of diverse flowers. A third emblem of Allegrezza depicts a girl wearing a garland of roses and holding other flowers in her hand. In antiquity these were "inditio di festa, e di allegrezza, perciochè gl'Antichi celebrando i conviti costumorono adornar si di corone di rose, & altri fiori. . . ." Ubriachezza (drunkenness) is symbolized by an old woman, red and laughing, dressed in the color of dry roses. In her hand she holds "un vaso da bevere pieno di vino," and there is a panther beside her. The panther signifies "che gli ubriachi sono furiosi, di costumi crudeli, & feroci, come sono le Pantere. . . ."[20]

A more elaborate emblem of Comus (Fig. XV) occurs in Louis de Caseneuve's *Hieroglyphics and Medical Emblems* (1626) in a group illustrating the four complexions or temperaments. Comus represents the sanguine man, and the author invests him with a variety of attributes and accessories—flowers, indicative of spring; bud, symbolic of youth; flute, a sign of music; myrtle, denoting Venus and the lover; a broken measuring stick ("Radius fractus"), signifying liberality; steps, symbolic of dignity; gold, indicating blood. The commentary cites Philostratus, who had depicted Comus as "commessationum, festivitatumque Deum," and quotes a Latin translation of Cornutus's version of Philostratus. As Caseneuve conceives him, Comus is the god of joy, banquets, songs, and dances—all of which pertain to the sanguine man: "gaudij, comessationum, cantionum, chorearum Deus, quae cùm in homine sanguineo sint, non impropriè illo Dero repraesentantur." The name may signify "festi hilaritas," "saltatio," "vinitorum Hymnus." It may also denote—more specifically—the stately feasts ("solemnes epulas") celebrated for Dionysus. Indeed in this sense (Caseneuve continues) it may apply to the jocular mode of living in which the youth even today are accustomed to frolic "in hilaribus," for the French retain the very name of Comus in their mummings. "Vocamus enim idiomate Gallico *momoum,* cui larvatus, & ludibundus cum talis Bacchanalia peragit." Simply by altering *C* to *M*, Comus becomes Momus; the god of revelry is, *a fortiori,* the tutelary genius of the masque.

In associating Comus, god of revels, with Momus and mummings Caseneuve makes him virtually the patron divinity of the masque—an association that recurs in Blaise de Vigenere and that is ironically significant in Milton's Ludlow masque.

For Comus's association with music and dance Caseneuve cites a variety of classical sources. Anacreon's verse *comon meteísi chaíron* not only represented *cōmos* as dance but also introduced associations with Cupid, Bacchus, and Venus. Pindar had conceived *cōmos* as song, *andrì kṓmou despóta*. Athenaeus had included *cōmos, tetracōmos,* and *hēdycōmos* among flute-songs, "inter tibiales cantiones." On the authority of Philostratus and Cornutus ("Phornutus"), Caseneuve maintains that Comus should be depicted with a *flute* ("Tibia") in his left hand. (Most Renaissance scholars, as we have noted, interpreted the Greek text as indicating a *spear*; and a modern scholar has suggested that he is actually touching his *ear*.) This detail suggests to Caseneuve the fact that the sanguine man delights in music. "Cùm enim sint temperatiore temperamento, quia sanguis temperatus est. . . ." Moreover, music itself is a tempering of voices, "vocum . . . temperamentum." These observations reinforce some of the underlying motifs of Milton's masque—the Platonic conception of the soul as harmony and the symbolic association of music with temperance. They also recall musicological speculation (such as Gafuri's) on the nature of *musica humana*.

The broken measuring-rod is a sign of liberality, which Caseneuve regards as characteristic of sanguine men; they are "benefici & perliberales, propter humoris benignitatem," and hence bestow without measure, "sine mensura dant." This detail derives both from Plautus and from Coelius Rhodigianus: "Radius enim inter alia significat hostorium, sive instrumentum, quo raduntur mensurae. Unde etiam proverbium, ait Coelius Rhodig . . . Sine Radio cumulare, seu absque hostorio, quod est affluenter & ultra mensuram congerere." Similarly, according to Plautus,

> Dij deaeque omnes, tantam nobis laetitiam
> Tot gaudia sine radio cumuletis.

Philostratus and Cornutus had described Comus as standing before golden doors. From this detail Caseneuve argues that sanguine men are worthy of princes' courts, "dignıssimos aulis principum"—a reference that may remind us of the "stately Palace" in Milton's masque. (Comus's palace belongs, on the whole, however, to the tradition of the Circean enchantresses of Renaissance romance.)

Though Comus's association with the sanguine man would ap-

pear to derive in part from Philostratus's description of him as
"flushed with wine" (*erythròs hypò oínou*). Caseneuve has
developed this hint into an allegorical character-sketch of a *persona*
that offers suggestive parallels with Milton's characterization of the
jocund man, "L'Allegro." (Despite ethical differences equally
profound, there remain several striking parallels between the
personae of "L'Allegro" and "Il Penseroso" and the characterization
of Comus and the Lady—but we must consider them elsewhere.)
The general tenor of Caseneuve's portrait can best be summarized
in his own words: "Omnes Comi hactenus recensiti conveniunt cum
sanguineis, qui sunt festivitatum, comessationum, & saltationum
antesignani. In hilaritate nihil sanguineis iucundius, in conviviis
nihil salsius, in choreis nihil promptius: si gaudendum, toto
exultant pectore, si comessandum, pleno risu adsunt, si can-
tandum, pleno ore iubilant, si saltandum, ipsi choragi primi
tripudiant & pede libero plaudunt choreas. Veri Comi sanguinei,
semper Comi comites, & ubique Comum agunt."[21]

One other detail in this commentary may be significant for the
comparison it draws between the Bacchic *cōmos* in India and
similar orgies in the British Isles. Quoting Dionysius of Alexander's
Di situ orbis, Caseneuve cites Eustathius's commentary on the line
Indoì cōmon ágousin aribremétē [eribremétē] Dionýsōi.[22] This
occurs in a passage describing the Bacchic rites of Amnite women in
the British Isles (apparently the Orcades) and drawing an analogy
with Bacchic carousals in India and Thrace:

> Nisiadum spatio non distant littore longo,
> In quibus uxores Amnitum Bacchia sacra
> Concelebrant, hederae foliis, tectaeque corymbis . . .
> Non sic praerupto, qua currit gurgite Ganges,
> Eoi strepero peragunt Comum Dionyso
> Oceani tranans hic navibus aequor apertum.[23]

In one seventeenth-century edition (1697 of Eustathius's commentary and "veterum scholiis" the word *cōmon* is glossed as
eortēn,[24] *i.e.,* festive hilarity. According to Eustathius, this passage
bears the following sense: "mulieres illustrium Amnitarum ex
ulteriori ripa venientes, persolvunt sacra Baccho iuxta ritum,
nocturnae, coronatae hederae nigrifoliae baccis: saltationis autem
dulcicrepus excitatur sonitus . . . Praeterea Rhetorico more
comparans sacra illa alijs, inquit: Non sic Absynthij Thraces,

neque India atrivorticem circa Gangem, bacchanalia peragunt strepero Dionysio: sicut illius insulae mulieres Euge congeminant, id est decantant Evium Dionysium, Evi Evan clamantes: quae quidem sunt voces Dionysium invocantium. Aiunt enim, Amnitarum mulieres per totam noctem choreas ducere, ita ut in hoc Thraces & Indi illis cedant." Eustathius also describes the occurence of the Dionysian *sparagmos* in the British Isles: the Amnite woman who falls with her burden is torn apart.[25]

Milton's setting is, of course, the Welsh border, not the Orcades. In Caseneuve's commentary and the sources cited therein he could, however, have found authority for placing a Dionysian *cōmos* in a specifically British locale.

That Comus should eventually become associated with the masque would seem virtually inevitable. Was it not in his very blood? Both Circe and Bacchus possessed the power to alter men's shapes. The former was frequently allegorized as sensual pleasure. The latter was associated not only with song and dance but (more than any other classical deity, as one modern mythographer informs us) with "the symbol of the mask." According to Walter Otto (whose views should, however, be received with caution), Dionysus was "the genuine mask god," and in ancient Greece he was frequently worshipped in this form.[26] Furthermore he was, of course, the patron deity of the drama — tragedy and comedy, the satyr-play, and the rustic revels out of which these dramatic forms had supposedly developed.

Many of the elements of the masque, moreover, were inherent in Philostratus's account of Comus and his revellers — the torches, the castanets and flutes, and the "disorderly singing." There was even the element of disguise; the revel permitted "women to masquerade as men" (*andrízesthai*) and men to don women's clothing (*thélyn endynai stolēn*) — a phrase significantly borrowed from Euripides's *Bacchae*. To these details we must add the observations by Renaissance lexicographers on *cōmos* as song or dance; mythographical interpretations of Comus as god of nocturnal dancing and drunken feasting; and Caseneuve's link between Comus and Momus, revels and mummings. With Vigenere's account of the god, the masque element receives still heavier emphasis. In the verses accompanying Isaac's engraving he takes the masque and the dance for granted — like the torch and the garlands of flowers—and converts them into a moral emblem. The masque symbolizes the disguised soul who hides his design and veils his thought. The dance and the ball symbolize the inconstant man. Like the torch that consumes itself and like the scattered garlands of flowers, the lover of Comus ultimately loses himself in pleasure.

The "Argument" defines Philostratus's term *kōmázein* as signifying "colationner, rire, danser, & boire," and describes the god himself as the patron of young people who pass the night in feasting and devouring sweetmeats, in singing aubades to their mistresses, or in masking ("en masque où il y a des nopces franches, & assemblees de belles dames"). Vigenere's translation of Philostratus introduces readings that explicitly associate Comus with the dance but that were *not* explicit in the Greek. In the first sentence he translates *tò komázein* (properly, "revelling") as "le rire, gaudir, & baller." In the description of Comus's stance he adds his own conception of the deity, "ce gentil Dieu superintendant du bal & des danses . . ." In his notes he describes Plutarch as discussing "les danses & mommeries nocturnes du bon pere Bacchus, où les femmes follastrans iusques à se ietter hors des gonds, s'equippent & couvrent volontiers de lierre, comme symbolisans à la fureur dont il les a esprises." Moreover, he apparently regards the transvestism described by Philostratus "Comus donne liberté à la femme de con-trefaire l'homme, & l'homme de s'habiller en femme") as a form of mumming or masking. In commenting on this passage he again turns to Plutarch. According to the *Roman Questions,* the musicians of Rome ("iouers d'instrumens") had liberty every January 13th to go about the city "desguisez en femmes." This custom originated on an earlier occasion when they had attended a sacrifice "vestu des robbes de femme pour aller mommer. . . ."[27]

These references reinforce Vigenere's conception of Comus as god of the masque. Though Milton does not emphasize this particular kind of "disguising," it nevertheless provides an additional link between Comus and the "Dark vaild *Cotytto,*" the "Goddesse of Nocturnal sport" whom the Reveller-God invokes at his revels. According to *Paulys Real-encyclopädie,* the celebration of her feast—the Cotyttia—involved dances in which "Männer in weiblicher Kleidung unter orgiastischer Musikbegleitung auftraten; daher haftete den Kotys-Verehrern der Vorwurf der *impudicitia* und *mollitia* an . . ."[28] Renaissance lexicographers and mythographers frequently described Cotytto as the goddess of shamelessness ("Dea impudentiae" or "impudicitiae") and of turpitude ("daemon turpitudinis"). Her priests, known as *Baptae* (because the initiates were soaked with hot water) apparently impersonated the goddess. According to Charles Estienne, Probus believed her to have been a dancer ("saltatricem"), "unde etiam sacerdotes ejus lascivis saltationibus mores ejus referebant." Estienne describes them as conducting "nocturna sacra . . . . saltationibus, & omni voluptatum generi indulgentes."[29] Lilio Giraldi identifies her with Proserpina, citing references to her rites in Horace, Virgil, and Juvenal, and observing that Porphyrion regarded them as "sacra. . . inferorum," sacrifices to the daemons of the underworld.[30] Thomas Farnaby interprets Juvenal's allusion to Cotytto and her priests as an allusion to the latter's dancing ("Ad lassitudinem saltare, *vel* fictam deae personam delassare"), adding that the goddess herself had been a female musician or dancer ("E psaltria seu saltatrice deam impudentiae"). His paraphrase links the Cotyttia and the Bacchanalia together as examples of turpitude and shamelessness.[31]

Many of these scholars allude to Eupolis's comedy *Baptae* ridiculing the Cotyttia and their lascivious priests. Milton had classical precedent, therefore, for portraying (and condemning) the rites of Cotytto on the stage. Primarily, however, his allusion reinforces elements already closely associated with the traditional Comus — disguising, dancing, nocturnal orgies — and such moral concepts as pleasure, lasciviousness, and shamelessness. His references to Hecate and Cotytto place his convivial reveller in a more sinister light.

Iconographically Milton's Comus betrays his Dionysian as well as his Circean ancestry; his wand and cup link him rather with Bacchus and Circe than with the Comus whom Philostratus had described. Thematically, on the other hand, his affinities with the Comus of Renaissance tradition are more apparent. Though his magical powers derive from Circe and Dionysus rather than from the Comus of the mythographers, they are exercised in a context that belongs to the traditional Comus. If the palace in the forest recalls Circe and her medieval and Renaissance successors, the nocturnal revelry — the feasting, music, and dancing — are reminiscent of current interpretations of *cŏmos* and *comessatio*.

They are characteristic not only of the god of wine, but also of his *son,* the Bacchic *revel.* Milton's enchanter is a composite figure combining aspects of the traditional Comus with those of the traditional Bacchus and Circe. If the parents represent intemperance — excess in wine and in sensual pleasure — the son embodies not only these vices but others derivative from them: excess in revelling and feasting — and perhaps in masquing.

Deriving not only from Philostratus by way of the mythographers but also from the lexicographers with their minute distinctions among the various senses of *cōmos,* the Renaissance tradition concerning the daemon of revelry was variegated and at times inconsistent. Interpretations could vary in complexity between the extremes represented by Cartari and Caseneuve. In moral stance they might range from Ripa's approbation to van Putten's invective. Some might oversimplify Philostratus's account, progressively narrowing *cōmos* to *comessatio* and thence to *banquet*; others might elaborate Philostratus's description by introducing additional senses derived from the lexicographer or from a variety of classical sources. Nevertheless the very complexity of this tradition might serve as an aid to poetic invention; it left the writer at liberty (albeit a restricted liberty) to select, reorder, and elaborate his cardinal symbols and motifs while remaining more or less faithful to mythological convention. Though retaining traditional materials, he was nonetheless free to recombine them — to *innovate* on tradition. Thus Milton retains the conventional *cōmos* — in the sense of song, dance, and banquet. He retains its association with nocturnal revelry and with sensual and erotic pleasure. He retains its association with the band of revellers, the *cōmos* who in Philostratus's account accompany the god. In the Trinity manuscript the anti-masquers enter with revelry ("Intrant κωμαζονιες), "com[ing] on in a wild & humorous antick fashion."

Nevertheless Milton rather skilfully undercuts the Comus tradition, subtly altering some of its conventional values. Ironically the *peripeteia* of his masque expels the patron divinity of masquing; paradoxically he transforms the "revels" — the formal dance at the conclusion of the performance — into a "victorious dance" of triumph over the defeated daemon of revelry. Comus himself is thus reduced to an emblem of "sensual Folly, and Intemperance." The early published versions of the poem further heighten the antithesis between temperate and intemperate pleasure by adding lines describing the heavenly delights that await the virtuous. In alluding to the "revels" of the "jocund Spring" in his celestial abode, the Attendant Spirit provides the final answer to Comus's summons to "Midnight shout and revelry . . ."

Fig. V.   Vincenzo Cartari, *Le imagini de i dei de gli antichi* (Venetia, 1571), p. 416. HEH
375693. *Reproduced by permission of The Huntington Library, San Marino,
California.*

Fig. VI.   Philostratus, *Les Images,* tr. Blaise de Vigenere (Paris, 1629), p. 9 HEH 10212.
Reproduced by permission of The Huntington Library, San Marino, California.

Compagni d'Vlyſſe mutati in
Porci.   172

Fig. VII.   Gabriele Simeoni, *La Vita et Metamorfoseo d'Ovidio* (Lyons, 1584), p. 184,
Emblem 172, HEH 136144. *Reproduced by permission of The Huntington
Library, San Marino, California.*

Fig. VIII. George Sandys, *Ovids Metamorphoses* (Oxford, 1632), title-page (detail), HEH 62871. *Reproduced by permission of The Huntington Library, San Marino, California.*

Fig. IX.   Vincenzo Cartari, *Le imagini de i dei de gli antichi* (Venetia, 1571), p. 433. HEH
375693. *Reproduced by permission of The Huntington Library, San Marino,
California.*

CVM VIRTVTE ALMA CONSENTIT VERA VOLVPTAS.

SYMB. X

Fig. XI.   Achille Bocchi, *Symbolicarum Quaestionum . . .Libri Quinque* (Bononiae, 1555), p. xx, Emblem X. HEH 113013. *Reproduced by permission of The Huntington Library, San Marino, California.*

Vini, vis. 96

Fig. XII. Henry Peacham, *Minerva Britanna* (London, 1612), p. 96. HEH 69059. *Reproduced by permission of The Huntington Library, San Marino, California.*

Vini natura.

Fig. XIII.   Henry Peacham, *Minerva Britanna* (London, 1612), p. 191, HEH 69059.
Reproduced by permission of The Huntington Library, San Marino, California.

Della nouiffima Iconologia
A L L E G R E Z Z A.

Fig. XIV.   Cesare Ripa, *Iconologia* (Padua, 1630), p. 28. HEH 144263. *Reproduced by permission of The Huntington Library, San Marino, California.*

SANGVINEVS.

E M ·B L E M A   III.

Comus hic hortorum, & speciosus flore iuuenta,
  Tibia cui, myrthus, fractus & est radius.
Effert se gradibus, quibus itur ad aurea tecta,
  Hac iuuenis sunto symbola sanguinei.

Fig. XV.   Ludovicus Casanova, *Hieroglyphicorum et Medicorum Emblematum . . .* (Lugduni, 1626), p. 31, in Joannes Pierius Valerianus, *Hieroglyphica* (Lugduni, 1626). HEH 246285. *Reproduced by permission of The Huntington Library, San Marino, California.*

Epilogue

FOR THE MOST PART, the motifs we have examined share a common background of myth and natural history, modified by similar rather than identical exegetical assumptions. As conventions of a traditional, but often fabulous, natural history, they have been subjected by successive generations of interpreters to an equally traditional tropological approach to nature, analogous to moral or spiritual interpretations of Scripture and classical myth. Incorporated into encyclopedias and lexicons and iconographies as well as poetic fiction, they once formed part of a kind of cosmic dictionary, a universal repertory of symbols; and as such they provided a convenient source of imagery and correlative commonplaces for artists and poets alike.

In both of these aspects—the exploitation of pseudo-zoological fables and a moralistic approach to natural history—this tradition possessed extraordinary longevity; and it is easier to demonstrate its continuity than to explain its origins and its decline. Animal fables, metaphors and proverbs based on the real or imaginary characters and habits of beasts, tendencies to draw moral inferences from natural phenomena or to exploit them as correlative images for psychological phenomena are common to many cultures, however primitive or sophisticated; moreover, they recur in both oral and written traditions. Vestiges of the animal symbols exploited by ancient artists survive in popular speech today. A man may still be as hungry as a wolf or as greedy as a pig, as brave as a lion, as crafty as a fox, as timid as a hare, as rude as a bear; as blind as a bat, as lecherous as a sparrow, as proud as a peacock, as mean as a snake. Call him an ape, and he will justly resent the aspersion on his originality; a shark, and he will correctly recognize the slander against his business ethics.

Many of these animal epithets, however, are unstable; and their meaning and connotations vary in different contexts. An insensitive man may be as thick-skinned as an elephant; a hypersensitive person as mindful of former injuries as the same beast. The dog may be proverbial for his fidelity; the Ulster hero Cu Chulainn could willingly assume the epithet "Hound"; but, for the most part, canine metaphors have remained as pejorative as they appear to have been in the heroic age of Greece. "Thou heavy with wine, thou with the front of a dog but the heart of a deer," Achilles cries to Agamemnon. [1]

In emblem literature the cat is a conventional symbol of liberty; when applied to a man or woman in current usage, the metaphor carries altogether different connotations: the man is a philanderer, the woman a backbiter. In India a name like "Gander," or in Tibet "Diamond Sow," may denote exceptional sanctity, but such honorifics have been conditioned by specific religious contexts; elsewhere they would be terms of invective.

The animal imagery of heroic poetry forms a special category. Like images drawn from other aspects of nature or from art, they may lend variety or contrast to a conventional description of battle or heighten its dramatic values and its tragic impact without evoking specific ethical concepts. In comparing an army to a threatening stormcloud, the din of battle to the roar of mountain torrents; a single hero to a baleful star, a river in spate, a whirlwind, a consuming flame, or a deadly serpent; a wounded warrior to a severed flower, a falling tree, a hooked fish, the poet is emphasizing the destructive force of battle, the lethal power of the hero, the conscious evocation of admiration, pity, or fear. (The serpent-simile may also recall superstitions concerning the hero's posthumous existence in this form, and fire-images may likewise suggest the preternatural light and heat associated with certain heroes.)[2] On the other hand, animal images may exemplify martial fortitude, courage as well as strength in battle — or its contrary vice. Agamemnon taunts his troops by comparing them to deer: "Why is it that ye stand thus dazed, like fawns that, when they have grown weary with running over a wide plain, stand still, and in their hearts is no valour found at all?"[3] Sarpedon complains that the Trojan princes "cower as dogs about a lion . . . ."[4] Idomeneus stands "amid the foremost fighters like a wild boar in valour . . . ."[5] Ajax and Hector fight "like ravening lions or wild boars, whose is no weakling strength."[6] In the midst of battle the Trojans surround Odysseus, "even as hounds and lusty youths press upon a boar on this side and on that . . . ."[7] In the battle before the ships Hector fights like "a wild boar or a lion" among hounds and huntsmen, "exulting in his strength, and these array them in ranks . . . , and stand against him . . . ; yet his valiant heart feareth not nor anywise quaileth, though his valour is his bane; and often he wheeleth him about and maketh trial of the ranks of men, and wheresoever he chargeth, there the ranks of men give way . . . ."[8] Diomedes attacks the sons of Priam as "a lion leapeth among the kine and breaketh the neck of a heifer or a cow . . . ."[9] The Greek champions felled by Aeneas are like two lions, raiders of cattle and farmsteads, finally slain at the hands of men.[10] Aeneas himself strides "like a lion confident in his strength . . . ."[11] Subsequently Agamemnon attacks the fleeing Trojans, "driven in rout . . . like kine that a lion hath scattered . . . ."[12] On a later occasion a double simile likens the retreating Ajax not only to the lordly lion — a lion "driven from the fold of the kine by dogs and country folk" — but also to an humbler beast: "a lazy ass about whose ribs many a cudgel is broken, and he goeth in and wasteth the deep grain, and the boys beat him with cudgels, though their might is but puny, and hardly do they drive him forth when he hath had his fill of fodder . . . ."[13]

Agamemnon slays two sons of Priam "as a lion easily crusheth the little ones of a swift hind . . . ."[14] Later in the battle, when the Trojans beset Odysseus but scatter in flight at the approach of Ajax,

Homer evokes the image of a wounded stag torn by jackals until "God bringeth against them a murderous lion, and the jackals scatter in flight, and he rendeth the prey . . . ."[15]

Though the comparison with deer often serves as a term of abuse, it carries no pejorative connotations on this occasion, nor does it imply timidity or cowardice. In like manner the canine simile, usually unfavorable, may serve as a term of praise; in the Doloneia it accentuates the speed with which the Greek scouts pursue the Trojan spy: "And as when two sharp-fanged hounds, skilled in the hunt, press hard on a doe or a hare . . . , and it ever runneth screaming before them; even so did the son of Tydeus, and Odysseus . . . cut Dolon off from the host and ever pursue hard after him."[16] On another occasion the armies rage like wolves, wreaking havoc without thought of flight and gladdening the heart of Strife.[17]

Conversely, the analogy between a warrior and a spirited horse acquires ironic overtones when applied to the idle and uxorious Paris: "Even as when a stalled horse that has fed his fill at the manger breaketh his halter, . . . and as he glorieth in his splendour, his knees nimbly bear him to the haunts and pastures of mares . . . ."[18]

In a much earlier epic, Gilgamesh and Enkidu are compared to wild oxen in strength. In other heroic societies legendary or historic warriors bear names or titles reflecting the ferocity, strength and fury of various beasts: war-elephants and stallions, wild boars and wolves, bears and lions, predatory birds like the eagle and the hawk. In later emblematic and bestiary literature many of these would become conventional symbols of vice; but in oral and literary epic alike the heroic tradition is essentially imitative and conservative, and many of these images survive in Renaissance epic and romance without pejorative connotations or as ambiguous symbols that could be applied at will to virtues or vices.

Like the animal imagery of heroic poetry, that of parables and prophecies, omens and proverbs appears in the earliest written literature and can be traced back to the frontiers of prehistory. In comparison with the later tradition we have examined, such imagery may seem unsystematic, but such an impression may be unwarranted. To apply the standards of a highly developed exegetical tradition to preliterate or early literate cultures may be misleading. As anthropologists have demonstrated in studies of surviving primitive societies, a complex symbolic system may be fully operative even though it has not been fully rationalized. The beast imagery of remote antiquity is lost to us, and we can only guess at its nature on the basis of very limited evidence. Though it could not be subjected to the kind of systematic codification and classification that encyclopedists and commentators bestowed on the animal imagery of the Middle Ages and Renaissance, we cannot assume that it did not form a coherent, integrated — and perhaps highly complex — system.

The decline of this medieval and Renaissance tradition presents additional problems. That it *has* declined is evident. Though some of the conventional associations still survive — the courage of the lion, the timidity of the hare — the majority are obsolete; and one must rely on historical scholarship to explicate allusions to the imaginary habits of bears and beavers, vipers and basilisks, or the worm ichneumon. Similarly, though authors continue to draw ethical inferences from nature, these are usually less conventional, less systematic, and less comprehensive. One must turn primarily to science fiction to encounter an unabashed exploitation of imaginary zoological marvels often in conjunction with moral, spiritual, or political allegory.

This decline cannot be attributed entirely to altered structures of belief; otherwise it should have occurred long before. Renaissance naturalists frequently questioned the conventional marvels, even though they faithfully reported them, and one doubts that the poets who exploited them in fables and allegories were much more credulous. The majority of Milton's monsters are indigenous to hell. (Though this detail may recall Tasso's argument that monstrous births were the result of sin, it serves primarily to emphasize the perversity of evil and to accentuate the element of illusion.) Incredulity operated in a more oblique fashion to banish the figments of the older pseudo-biology. As they vanished gradually from scientific treatises, they became increasingly unfamiliar to the average layman, forfeiting their value as commonplaces for poetic or rhetorical persuasion. For poets who elected to stoop to truth, or for rational theologians, in turn, there would be little point in basing their arguments on discredited and obsolescent superstitions.

The pursuit of a rational religion and the preference for a literal rather than allegorical approach to Scripture also undercut tropological, typological, and spiritual interpretations of the book of nature. Finally, neoclassical critical emphasis on probability and verisimilitude and hostility to the allegorical mode tended to discourage the symbolic approach to nature and the exploitation of a fabulous natural history as a source for allegories and exempla.

How far an earlier generation of poets actually credited these marvels is a question that must remain unanswered. C. S. Lewis raised this point in *The Discarded Image*[19] but concluded that one could "only guess at the answer." He suggested, however, "that an absence of vocal and clearly held disbelief was commoner than a firm positive conviction." Moreover, the Platonism of the Middle Ages and the Renaissance provided a further "source of credulity": if "the visible world is made after an invisible pattern, . . . the expectation that an anagogical or moral sense will have been built into the nature and behaviour of the creatures would not be . . . unreasonable."

Similar points have been raised apropos of metaphysical imagery and its relation to the theory of universal analogy and cosmic correspondences.[20] Patristic allusions to the poetic, architectural, rhetorical or musical skills displayed by the Creator in fashioning the world have evoked further questions concerning cosmic symbolism in medieval and Renaissance arts.

Fiction creates its own world, however, and one should be cautious in exploring its relation to theories of the "real" world, whether this is the world of Hermetic physics or that of the medieval bestiary. (Indeed, for several of the authors we have examined, the "real" world is most significant in its fabulous or largely imaginary aspects; the traditional view of nature most valuable as it approaches the boundaries of fiction. For other writers the reverse may be true.) As every Renaissance musician was aware, harmony is common to *musica mundana* and to *musica instrumentalis*, but one should not regard every motet or fantasia as an image or epitome of the cosmos. Correspondences are the staple of Hermetic physics and of rhetorical treatises on wit; but it would be rash to conclude that every metaphysical conceit reflects a confirmed belief in universal analogies.

On the other hand, the theory of correspondences could conceivably be relevant not only for conceits based on what the poet accepted as valid cosmic analogies, but even for correspondences that he regarded as purely imaginary. The notion of the world as metaphor could cast a reflected glory on more fortuitous metaphors. The theory of universal analogies could lend apparent probability to his most outrageous conceits, serving (like his parodic exploitation of scholastic logic) both as an instrument of persuasion and as a kind of plaything, to be bandied about in a game of ironic wit.

In criticizing the bestiary imagery of late medieval and early Renaissance poets we should not underestimate the extent to which their rhetoric and poetics not only shaped their presentation of natural history but also affected their attitudes towards its literal truth. For writers accustomed, by theory and practice, to seeking ethical and metaphysical doctrines in pagan myth and a variety of allegorical senses in Scripture, the factual basis of these zoological marvels might well seem secondary in importance to the moral or spiritual inferences that might be extracted from them. A myth or a parable could exemplify the teachings of moral philosophy as vividly as historical fact; even though the latter might possess greater evidential value in influencing the judgment and winning assent, the former might strike the imagination more forcibly. Unlike the fables of mythology, however, those of natural history might conceivably be valid on the literal as well as the allegorical level. If the events of the Old Testament prefigured those of the New, if the divine Author of the Scriptures had concealed moral, allegorical, and spiritual senses under the coded symbols of the letter, it was at least probable that He had followed the same method in composing the book of nature, and that its sundry creatures might indeed be types and shadows of the invisible spiritual world. Like the Scriptures themselves, the book of creatures possessed divine authority. The standard natural histories, in turn, depended largely on venerated human authority: the testimony of Aristotle and Theophrastus, Aelian and Pliny, Solinus, Bede, St. Albertus Magnus, and names equally revered.

A later generation would show less reverence for the testimony of authors. Bacon and his disciples would regard it as a formidable obstacle to the advancement of learning. Yet even in directly challenging "the Goliah and Giant of Authority," Thomas Browne could still link it with sense and reason as one of the "three deter-

minators of truth . . . ."[21] If one recalls the reluctance with which
Renaissance anatomists and illustrators reconciled themselves to the
inaccuracies of Galen, in spite of the clear evidence they beheld at
the dissecting table, one can understand the unwillingness of many
Renaissance naturalists to discard the figments of the older pseudo-
zoology, and one can better appreciate the generally conservative
attitude of medieval encyclopedists toward this tradition. Moreover,
scholastic and humanist curricula usually centered on standard
texts, and medieval and Renaissance rhetoric alike regarded the
testimony of authors as an acceptable form of inartificial proof.
(Even in contemporary classrooms a student is all too likely to
accept a standard text more or less at face value, without
challenging its authority or attempting to sift the credible from the
doubtful.)

The pains taken by various poets in both periods to maintain the
pretense of following a real or imaginary authority[22] (Chaucer's
Lollius, Ariosto's Turpin) may have been an ironic distortion of this
principle; nevertheless the pretense served, like the sophisms of
certain metaphysical poets, to foster the illusion of probability. The
same poets could also exploit the *mirabilia* of nature in much the
same way. Incredible though these might seem, they had
nonetheless been vouched for by writers of high renown. They
possessed undeniable *auctoritas,* even though they remained un-
substantiated by experience or reason; and a poet might exploit
them, seriously or in jest, to lend apparent probability to his own
fictions.

NOTES

INTRODUCTION

1. Torquato Tasso, *Il Mondo Creato,* ed. Giorgio Petrocchi (Firenze, 1951), pp. xxxvii, xli-xlv, 157-274.

2. C.S. Lewis, *The Discarded Image: An Introduction to Medieval and Renaissance Literature* (London and New York, 1974), p. 150.

3. For the moral and spiritual interpretation of nature in Rabanus Maurus' *De universo,* Alexander Neckam's *De naturis rerum,* Robert Holcot's commentary on the Book of Wisdom, and the encyclopedias of Thomas of Cantimpré and Berchorius, see D.W. Robertson, Jr., *A Preface to Chaucer: Studies in Medieval Perspectives* (Princeton, N.J., 1969), pp. 296, 305-307. For Berchorius's "moralization of the encyclopedia of Bartholomew Anglicanus," see Robertson, pp. 232, 310. For the continued popularity of Bartholomew during the Renaissance, see A.R. Hall, *The Scientific Revolution 1500-1800: The Formation of the Modern Scientific Attitude,* Second Edition (Boston, 1962), p. 72. For discussion of the bestiary tradition, see Florence McCulloch, *Mediaeval Latin and French Bestiaries,* rev. ed. (Chapel Hill, N.C., 1962); Margaret W. Robinson, *Fictitious Beasts: A Bibliography* (London, 1961); Beryl Rowland, *Animals with Human Faces: A Guide to Animal Symbolism* (Knoxville, Tenn., 1973); idem, *Chaucer's Animal World* (Kent State Univ., Ohio, 1971); *Le bestiaire divin de Guillaume, clerc de Normandie . . . avec une introduction sur les bestiaires,*

volucraires et lapidaires du moyen âge, considérés dans leurs rapports avec la symbolique chrétienne par C. Hippeau (Geneva, 1970; reprint of the editions of 1852-1877).

4. In citing the works of Berchorius I have followed the nomenclature of the edition (Venice, 1583) that I originally consulted in writing several of the essays in this volume: *Reductorium morale* (the moralized encyclopedia based on Bartholomew Anglicus), *Dictionarium seu Repertorium morale* (the moralized dictionary, cited hereafter as *Repertorium morale*), and *Reductorium morale super totam bibliam*. Although Berchorius's commentary on the *Metamorphoses* once formed part of the *Reductorium morale,* it circulated independently in manuscript and first appeared in print as the work of Thomas Waleys (*Metamorphosis Ovidiana moraliter . . . explanata*); I shall cite this work hereafter as *Ovidius moralizatus*. The student will, however, encounter alternative titles for several of these works in recent scholarship. Robertson describes (p. 232) the *Repertorium* as containing "a moralization of the Bible, a scriptural dictionary, a moralization of the *De proprietatibus rerum* of Bartholomew Anglicanus, and a commentary on Ovid's *Metamorphoses.*" In *Meaning in the Visual Arts* (p. 157) Panofsky refers to the Ovidian commentary as Book XV of the *Repertorium morale;* in his *Renaissance and Renascences in Western Art* (p. 79n), however, he corrects this assertion, observing that the earlier version of Berchorius's Ovidian treatise had been "destined to form the Fifteenth Book of his *Reductorium morale* (as opposed to his better-known *Repertorium morale*). . . ." Berchorius's Ovidian commentary appeared in print as early as 1509, "whereas the first printed edition of the *Reductorium,* comprising only the first fourteen books, did not appear until 1521." The student will also recall the long-standing confusion between Bartholomew Anglicus, the thirteenth-century author of *De proprietatibus rerum,* and the fourteenth-century Bartholomew de Glanville.

5. See Erwin Panofsky, *Meaning in the Visual Arts: Papers in and on Art History* (Garden City, N.Y., 1955) and idem, *Renaissance and Renascences in Western Art* (New York, Evanston, San Francisco, London, 1972), passim.

6. In spite of doubts raised by Renaissance naturalists, much of the fabulous natural history inherited from ancient and medieval sources survives not only in popular literature like Topsell's *Historie of Foure-Footed Beastes and Serpents* but also in learned treatises by Gesner and other scholars. See Hall, pp. 31, 284; Marie Boas, *The Scientific Renaissance 1450-1630* (New York, 1966), p. 58.

7. *The Prose of Sir Thomas Browne,* ed. Norman J. Endicott (Garden City, N.Y., 1967), p. 634. For discussion of the *Hieroglyphica* and its influence, and an account of the controversies concerning its origin, authorship, and authority, see Pauly-Wissowa, *Real-Encyclopädie der classischen Altertumswissenschaft,* s.v. "Horapollon"; *Nouvelle biographie générale,* s.v. "Horapollon."

8. Panofsky, *Meaning in the Visual Arts,* pp. 158-160.

9. Endicott, p. 18. 10. Endicott, p. 21. 11. Endicott, p. 42. 12. Endicott, pp. 184-185. 13. Endicott, p. 133. 14. Endicott, p. 196. 15. Endicott, pp. 215-216. 16. Endicott, pp. 142-145. 17. Endicott, p. 80. 18. Endicott, pp. 17-18.

19. For medieval poets and artists (Panofsky suggests, *Meaning in the Visual Arts,* pp. 45-46) the primary sources of mythographical information were the

encyclopedias compiled by such writers as Bede, Isidore of Seville, Rabanus Maurus, Vincent of Beauvais, and Bartholomew Anglicus; medieval commentaries on classical texts; and special treatises on mythology.

20. Panofsky, *Renaissance and Renascences in Western Art,* p. 78n; idem, *Meaning in the Visual Arts,* p. 46.

21. See St. Augustine, *The City of God,* Books VI, VII, VIII, for a discussion of natural theology as distinct from civil theology and fabulous theology.

CHAPTER I

1. Erwin Panofsky, *Meaning in the Visual Arts* (Garden City, N.Y., 1955), pp. 26, 29, 41.

2. E.H. Gombrich, *Art and Illusion: A Study in the Psychology of Pictorial Representation* (2d. ed., rev; Princeton, 1969), p. 9.

3. Ashley H. Thorndike, *Shakespeare's Theater* (New York, 1960), p. 146.

4. Geffrey Whitney, *A Choice of Emblemes* (Leyden, 1586). HEH #79714. Aphoristic and emblematic materials were frequently classified according to the topics of invention—an order of arrangement which could lend itself readily to logical or rhetorical exploitation and which was frequently observed either in the text or in the index but sometimes in both. Thus an edition of Erasmus's *Adages* published at Frankfurt-am-Main in 1599 (HEH 219509) refers in its title to its disposition according to commonplaces: ". . . *Adagiarum Chiliades iuxta locos communes digestae."* The same volume also contains an "Index Proverbiorum iuxta locos." In several editions of Alciati's *Emblemata,* the emblems are arranged according to *topoi.* Thus in an edition published at Lyons in 1550 ("apud Mathiam Bonhomme"), the illustrations fall under the following headings and in the following order: 1) "Deus, sive Religio"; 2) "Fides"; 3) "Prudentia"; 4) "Iustitia"; 5) "Fortitudo"; 6) "Concordia"; 7) "Spes"; 8) "Pudicitia," etc.

5. Signature Bvi, at end of Book I. HEH #87539.

6. See Chapter Ten.

7. Whitney, p. 8; *Centum Fabulae . . . a Gabriele Faerno* (Antwerp, 1573), p. 161, HEH #123437. See my "Una and the Clergy: The Ass Symbol in *The Faerie Queene," JWCI,* XXI (1958), 134-137, and Chapter Nine.

8. Eugene M. Waith, *The Herculean Hero in Marlowe, Chapman, Shakespeare, and Dryden* (New York, 1962), pp. 39-59; Douglas Bush, *Mythology and the Renaissance Tradition in Poetry* (new rev. ed.; New York, 1963).

9. Joannes Pierius Valerianus, *Hieroglyphica* (Lugduni, 1626), pp. 147, 576 (HEH #246285); this work had been first published (posthumously) in 1566. Cesare Ripa, *Iconologia* (Padova, 1630), pp. 178-180 (HEH #144263); this book had been first published in 1593. Henry Peacham, *Minerva Britanna* (London, 1612), p. 36 (HEH #69059). *Achillis Bocchii Bonon. Symbolicarum Quaestionum . . . Libri Quinque* (Bononiae, 1555), p. cxiii (HEH #113013). See also Kathleen Williams, *Spenser's World of Glass: A Reading of The Faerie Queene* (Berkeley and Los Angeles, 1966), p. 60n., on Bocchi and Ripa; Barbara Kiefer Lewalski, *Milton's Brief Epic: The Genre, Meaning, and Art of Paradise Regained* (Providence and London, 1966), p. 404, for parallels in George Sandys, Georg Pictor, Jean

Baudouin, and Alexander Ross. Frances A. Yates, *Giordano Bruno and the Hermetic Tradition* (New York, 1969), pp. 206-211, suggests that Greene's account of Vandermast's defeat by an Oxford friar may have been partly influenced by recollections of Bruno's discomfiture in a disputation with Oxford scholars during Prince Albert Alasco's visit. In the *Pneumatica* of Hero of Alexandria, theorem 41 ("On Hercules and the Snake") describes an automaton depicting Hercules attacking the dragon of the Hesperides. "When an apple is lifted, Hercules shoots a dragon which then hisses." For an account of this device and a Renaissance illustration, see John Webster Spargo, *Virgil the Necromancer* (Cambridge, Mass., 1934), pp. 127-128.

10. Whitney, p. 15; see Part III, Chapter 8. I am indebted to Professor William S. Heckscher for valuable criticism of my Actaeon study.

11. Edmond Faral, (ed.), *Les Arts Poétiques du XIIe et du XIIIe Siècle* (Paris, 1958), pp. 129-130. Cf. the Latin *ebenus* (ebony) and *ebur* and *eburneus* (ivory); and the Italian *ebano* (ebony) and *eburneo* (ivory).

12. See Donald L. Guss, "Donne's 'The Anagram': Sources and Analogues," *HLQ,* Vol. XXVIII (1964), pp. 79-82, for a discussion of Tasso's "Sopra la Bellezza" and Berni's sonnet "Chiome d'argento fine, irte e attorte."

13. *Twelfth Night,* Act I, Scene 5.

14. Panofsky, *Meaning in the Visual Arts,* pp. 28-34, 40-41.

CHAPTER II

1. *The Poems of John Marston,* ed. Arnold Davenport (Liverpool: Liverpool Univ. Press, 1961), pp. 72-73. Cf. Alvin Kernan, *The Cankered Muse: Satire of the English Renaissance* (New Haven: Yale Univ. Press), pp. 60-61, on Marston's attitude to obscurity in satire; see also Arnold Davenport ed., *The Collected Poems of Joseph Hall* (Liverpool: Liverpool Univ. Press, 1949), pp. xxv-xxxiv, on obscurity in Roman and Renaissance satire and on Hall's "quarrel" with Marston.

2. Jean Seznec, *The Survival of the Pagan Gods: The Mythological Tradition and Its Place in Renaissance Humanism and Art,* trans. Barbara F. Sessions (New York: Harper & Row, 1961), p. 314; DeWitt T. Starnes and Ernest William Talbert, *Classical Myth and Legend in Renaissance Dictionaries* (Chapel Hill: Univ. of North Carolina Press, 1955), p. 341. Douglas Bush, *Mythology and the Renaissance Tradition in English Poetry,* new revised edition (New York: W.W. Norton, 1963), p. 29, correctly describes the passage as a "satirical hint."

3. Seznec, p. 314.

4. Davenport, *Marston,* p. 230, observes that "there is no evidence . . . that Hall was indebted to any of these books in his satires; but M[arston] himself is certainly indebted to Comes for much of the mythology he uses." For Marston's attack on Hall, see pp. 30, 37, 81-82, 164-65, 229-30, 244-45, 355-56, et passim.

5. Davenport, *Hall,* p. 33.

6. Cf. Davenport, *Hall,* pp. 49, 192. Hall is referring to J.C. Scaliger's *Teretismata.*

7. Seznec, p. 314.

8. For the authorship of these works, see Seznec, pp. 170-79, 246-47. For

Renaissance editions of the *Liber* and *Libellus,* see ibid., pp. 225-26.

9. Robert Burton, *The Anatomy of Melancholy,* 2 vols (London, 1837), 2:191, 272, 525.

10. Burton, 2:190-91, 217, 229, 282, 290, 525.

11. See i.a., the following studies: Don Cameron Allen, "Ben Jonson and the Hieroglyphics," *PQ* 18 (1939): 290-300; Rosemary Freeman, *English Emblem Books* (London: Chatto & Windus, 1948); Arthur Henkel and Albrecht Schöne, eds., *Emblemata: Handbuch der Sinnbildkunst des 16. und 17. Jahrhunderts* (Stuttgart: J.B. Metzler, 1967).

12. Seznec, p. 280; Starnes and Talbert, p. 139.

13. Seznec, p. 280; Starnes and Talbert, pp. 44-45.

14. Several recent scholars have justly emphasized the role of the mythographies, dictionaries, and similar reference works in Renaissance education as aids to "imitation" of the ancients. See T.W. Baldwin, *William Shakespeare's Small Latine and Lesse Greeke* (Urbana: Univ. of Illinois Press, 1944) on the influence of Giraldi, Conti, and Textor and the florilegia of Farnaby, Mirandula, and Palmer; Donald Lemen Clark, *John Milton at St. Paul's School* (New York: Columbia Univ. Press, 1948), pp. 205-7, on handbooks recommended by schoolmasters such as Brinsley and Hoole for "principal places for imitation," variety and copy of Poetical phrases," or "store of Epithetes"; and Davis P. Harding, *Milton and the Renaissance Ovid* (Urbana: Univ. of Illinois Press, 1946), pp. 30-33, 43-44, 50-53, on reference works recommended by Hoole and Brinsley as aids to "imitation," on Milton's observations on the "rules of imitation" recommended by schoolmasters, and on his synthesis of classical and post-classical sources. See also Starnes and Talbert, p. 341.

15. See Harding, pp. 31-32. Hoole's allusion to Smetius is a reference to Henrich Smet; Harding renders this name as Smith.

16. Cf. Starnes and Talbert, p. 101.

17. Cf. DeWitt T. Starnes and Gertrude E. Noyes, *The English Dictionary from Cawdrey to Johnson, 1604-1755* (Chapel Hill: Univ. of North Carolina Press, 1946); Starnes, *Renaissance Dictionaries, English-Latin and Latin-English* (Austin: Univ. of Texas Press, 1954); id. *Robert Estienne's Influence on Lexicography* (Univ. of Texas Press, 1963).

18. Starnes and Talbert, pp. 60-61, 73, 109, 117, 126-28, 228.

19. Ibid., p. 228. Many of the more dubious parallels included in this book originated in claims made by earlier source-hunters — usually on the basis of analogues that were little more than commonplaces.

20. Seznec, pp. 288-90.

CHAPTER III

1. Wilbur Owen Sypherd, *Studies in Chaucer's Hous of Fame* (Chaucer Society, London, 1907), p. 14; see A.C. Garrett, "Studies on Chaucer's House of Fame," *Harvard Studies and Notes in Philology and Literature,* v (1896), 151-175.

2. Adolf Rambeau, "Chaucer's Hous of Fame in seinem Verhältnis zur Divina Commedia," *Englische Studien,* III (1880), 235.

3. T.R. Lounsbury, *Studies in Chaucer,* II (1892), 246; Sypherd, p. 89n.

4. Rambeau, passim; Sypherd, p. 89 n.; Cino Chiarini, *Di una imitazione inglese della Divina Commedia: La Casa della Fama di Chaucer* (Bari, 1902), pp. 95-97. Cf. F.N. Robinson (ed.), *The Works of Geoffrey Chaucer,* 2nd ed. (Boston, 1957), pp. 781-782. Cf. Charles Muscatine, *Chaucer and the French Tradition* (Berkeley and Los Angeles, 1957), p. 110.

5. Robinson, p. 778; F. Cumont, "Le mysticisme astral dans l'antiquité," *Bulletin,* Académie Royale de Belgique, 4th Ser. (1909), pp. 258 ff., 278 ff.; see also the unpubl. diss. by Rob Roy Purdy, *The Platonic Tradition in Middle English Literature,* summarized in *Bull. of Vanderbilt Univ., Abstracts of Theses,* XLVII (1947), 15-16.

6. Papias, *Vocabularium* (Venice, 1485), "Aquila ab acumine oculorum, dicta quia irreverberato visu solem aspiciat." Cf. Rabanus Maurus (*P.L.,* cviii, col. 974); Hugo of St. Victor (*P.L.,* CLXXVII, col. 53); Bartholomeus Anglicus, *De Rerum Proprietatibus* (Nuremberg, 1519), Book XII, Chap. 1, *De Aquila*"; Petrus Berchorius, *Dictionarium seu Repertorium Morale* (Venetiis, 1583), *s.v.* "Aquila": "Aquila dicitur quasi habens acutos oculos."

7. See *C. Plinii Secundi Naturalis Historia,* ed. D. Detlefsen (Berlin, 1867), II, 126-127, on the keen eyesight of the sea-eagle or osprey.

8. W.M. Lindsay (ed.), *Isidori Hispalensis episcopi Etymologiarum sive Originum Libri XX,* Vol. II (Oxonii, 1911) Book XII, Chap. 7; cf. *P.L.,* LXXXII, col. 460.

9. Gregorius Magnus, *Moralia in Job,* Book IX, Chap. 32 (*P.L.,* LXXV, cols. 884-885).

10. **Moralia,** Book IX, Chap. 33 (P.L., LXXV, col. 886).

11. *Moralia,* Book XIX, Chap. 27 (*P.L.,* LXXVI, col. 131).

12. St. Gregory the Great, *Morals on the Book of Job* (Oxford, 1850, pp. 495-496.

13. *Moralia,* Book XXXI, Chap. 47 (*P.L.,* LXXVI, cols. 625-626). Cf. Rabanus Maurus, *De Universo,* Book VIII, Chap. 16 *(P.L.,* cxi, cols. 243-244); idem, *Expositio super Jeremiam,* Book xx *(P.L.,* cxi, cols. 1258-59); Hugo de S. Victore, *De Bestiis et Aliis Rebus,* Book I, Chap. 56 (*P.L.,* clxxvii, cols., 53-54); Bartholomeus, Book xii, Chap. 1; Berchorius, *Reductorium Morale* (Venetiis, 1583), p. 184.

14. *Sententiarum,* Book III, Chap. 15 (*P.L.,* LXXXIII, col. 691).

15. *Allegoriae in Sacram Scripturam* (*P.L.,* CXII, col. 862).

16. Hugo de S. Victore, *De Bestiis,* Book I, Chap. 56 (*P.L.,* CLXXVII, col. 54).

17. Idem, *Expositio Moralis in Abdiam* (*P.L.,* CLXXV, cols. 377-378).

18. Alexander Neckam, *De Naturis Rerum Libri Duo,* ed. Thomas Wright (London, 1863), pp. 71-72.

19. Venetiis, 1583, p. 186.

20. Berchorius, *Reductorium Morale,* pp. 183-184. This work (which consists essentially in a moral interpretation of Bartholomeus Anglicus' *De Proprietatibus Rerum*) should not be confused with Berchorius' *Reductorium Morale super Totam Bibliam* (see fn. 19, supra). See Ernest H. Wilkins, "Descriptions of Pagan Divinities from Petrarch to Chaucer," *Speculum,* XXXII (1957), 513.

21. Berchorius, *Repertorium Morale,* s.v. "Aquila," pp. 198-200: "Sic verè . . . praelatus & praedicator, & quilibet vir perfectus debet habere visum clarissimae discretionis, intantum quod solem . . . i. claritatem bonorum aeternorum debet . . . speculari. . . ." Like the eagle, the prelate should provoke his subordinates "ad volandum sursum, & ad videndum, & respiciendum, advertendum, & cogitandum Dei speculationem, & bonorum aeternorum contemplationem. . . ." Job XXXIX. 27 ("elevabitur Aquila") signifies "quod nos debemus habere . . . Luminosam speculationem. . . ."

22. See also *Glossa Ordinaria* (*P.L.,* CXIV, col. 726), "Aquila omnes praedicatores, qui mente longinqua conspiciunt. . . ."

23. *Comedia di Dante degli Allagherii col Commento di Jacopo della Lana Bolognese,* ed. Luciano Scarabelli, II (Bologna, 1866), 103.

24. *Petri Allegherii super Dantis ipsius Genitoris Comoediam,* ed. G.J. Vernon and Vincentio Nannucci (Florençe, 1845), pp. 60-61.

25. Sypherd, pp. 55-56; Rambeau, pp. 233-234; See also Bruno Sandkuehler, *Die frühen Dante-Kommentare und ihr Verhältnis zur mittelalterlichen Kommentartradition* (München, 1964).

26. *L'Ottimo Commento della Divina Commedia,* ed. Accademici della Crusca, III (Pisa, 1829), 427; cf. *Commento alla Divina Commedia d'Anonimo Fiorentino del Secolo XIV,* ed. Pietro Fanfani, III (Bologna, 1874), 352.

27. *L'Ottimo Commento,* p. 427.

28. [Petrus Berchorius], *Metamorphosis Ovidiana Moraliter a Magistro Thoma Waleys Anglico . . . Explanata* (Paris, 1515), fol. LXXXII.

29. Ibid., fol. v. Cf. the analogous passage in the Copenhagen commentary on the *Ovide Moralisé* (Jeannette Theodora Maria Van 't Sant, *Le Commentaire de Copenhague de l'Ovide Moralisé* [Amsterdam, 1929], p. 28); Miss Van 't Sant (pp. 17-18) regards the Copenhagen commentary as a translation of the Latin commentary preceding Berchorius' *Ovidius Moralizatus.*

30. Odo died in 1415. See Johannes Osternacher, "Die Ueberlieferung der Ecloga Theoduli," *Neues Archiv der Gesellschaft für ältere deutsche Geschichtskunde,* XL (1915), 333n.

31. *Theodolus cum Commento* [*"magistri Odonis natione picardi"*] (s.l., 1487). For Chaucer's knowledge of the *Ecloga Theoduli* see Ferdinand Holthausen, "Chaucer and Theodulus," *Anglia,* XVI (1893-94), 264-266, and George L. Hamilton, "Theodulus: A Mediaeval Textbook," *MP,* VII (1909), 169-185. Odo is commenting on the line "Splendorem tanti non passus Juppiter auri."

32. Cf. the following variants: 1) *Actores* [*sic*] *cum Glosa Octo Libros . . . Continentes* (Lugduni, 1489), "impletudinem sapientie": 2) Ecloga Theodoli (Impensis Iudoci pelgrim & Henrici Jacobi, 1508), "plenitudinem sapientie"; 3) *Theodoli cum Commento* (Londoniis, 1515), "plenitudinem sapientie"; 4) *Authores cum Commento* (Lugduni, 1519), "plenitudinem sapientie."

33. *Theodolus cum Commento* (s.l., 1487). Odo is commenting on the quatrain beginning "Idaeos lepores puer exagitat Ganimedes."

34. Cf. *Conradi Hirsaugiensis Dialogus super Auctores sive Didascalon,* ed. Georg Schepss (Wurzburg, 1889), pp. 77-78.

35. See Robert J. Allen, "A Recurring Motif in Chaucer's 'House of Fame',"

JEGP, LV (1956), 393-405, on Chaucer's "contrast between the learned eagle and the 'lewed' poet."

36. Robinson, p. 784. Cf. Chaucer's translation of Boethius: "and I schal fycchen fetheris in thi thought, by whiche it mai arisen in heighte. . . . I have, forthi, swifte fetheris that surmounten the heighte of the hevene. Whanne the swifte thoght hath clothid itself in tho fetheris, it despiseth the hateful erthes, and surmounteth the rowndnesse of the grey ayr; and it seth the clowdes byhynde his bak, and passeth the heighte of the regioun of the fir . . . til that he areyseth hym into the houses that beren the sterres. . . ." For parallels between Boethius and Chaucer's *Hous of Fame,* see Bernard L. Jefferson, *Chaucer and the Consolation of Philosophy of Boethius* (Princeton, 1917), pp. 140-142.

37. *Saeculi Noni Auctoris in Boetii Consolationem Philosophiae Commentarius,* ed. Edmund Taite Silk (Rome, 1935), p. 222.

CHAPTER IV

1. Kenneth Sisam (ed.) *The Nun's Priest's Tale* (Oxford 1927) vii-viii; see also Kate Petersen *On the Sources of the Nonne Prestes Tale* (Boston 1898); and E.P. Dargan 'Cock and Fox: A Critical Study of the History and Sources of the Mediaeval Fable' *MP* IV (1906) 38-65.

2. See Sisam, ed. cit. vii-xxvi; J.R. Hulbert 'The Nun's Priest's Tale' in *Sources and Analogues of Chaucer's Canterbury Tales,* ed. W.F. Bryan and Germaine Dempster (Chicago 1941), 657, 662; Albert Leitzmann (ed.) *Die Fabeln Gerhards von Minden* (Halle a. S., 1898) 166.

3. Dominicus Bassi (ed.) *Phaedri Fabulae* (Torino 1936) 10.

4. Léopold Hervieux *Les fabulistes latins* II (Paris 1894) 168. In Adhemar's *Fabula antiqua ex Phaedro* (ibid. 136), the fable concludes: 'Qui se laudari verbis subdolis gaudent, ferunt pennas [*sic pro* poenas] turpi poenitentia indiscretas.'

5. Ibid. 201.

6. Ibid. 236.

7. Ibid. 265.

8. Ibid. 480.

9. Ibid. 423.

10. Ibid. 323. In *Gualterianae fabulae* also (ibid. 387) the fable ends with these lines.

11. Ibid. 355.

12. Ibid. 236. See *Speculum Historiale* IV 3.

13. Hervieux, IV (Paris 1896), 242. Odo entitles the fable 'De Caseo et Corvo. Contra vanam gloriam.'

14. Ibid. 419.

15. Hervieux, II 559. In *Romuli vulgaris breviatae fabulae* (ibid. 250) the fable is entitled 'Quod qui adulatorum verbis credunt, bonum quod habent amittunt'. In *Romuli Anglici cunctis exortae fabulae* (ibid. 575), it concludes with a similar *moralitas.*

16. Ibid. 521. The *moralitas* in *Ex Romulo Nilantii ortae fabulae rhythmicae* (ibid. 724) stresses the same point. The opening and concluding verses of the

analogous fable in *Ex romulo Nilantii ortae fabulae metricae* (ibid. 664-5) emphasize the danger of believing falsehood, but do not mention flattery.

17. The same moral appears in Neckam's *Novus Aesopus* (ibid. 407):

> Hec reticere monent stultum, ne forte loquendo
> Secretum prodat quod reticens tacuit.

Cf. 'La sentence de la fable' in the *Isopet de Chartres* (Julia Bastin *Recueil General des Isopets* I Paris 1929 147-8).

18. Alexander Neckam *De naturis rerum* ed. T. Wright (London 1863), 206. Cf. the marginal gloss, 'De adulatione'. Neckam's acknowledged source for the fable is Apuleius, who (in Book IV of *Florida*) admits his debt to Aesop. See *Apulei Opera Omnia* II, ed. F. Oudendorpius and Ioannes Bosscha (Leyden 1823), 108 ff. John de Bromyard's *Summa Praedicantium . . . Prima Pars* (Venice, 1586) 322 also interprets the fable as a warning against flattery without and vainglory within: 'Sic multi, dum adulationibus extra, vel vana gloria intus, pulsantur & commendantur, os inaniter gloriando aperiunt, & fructum humilitatis, quem habent apud Deum, amittunt. Et pro laude, quam apud homines quaerunt, deridentur . . .'

19. Bastin I 84.

20. Ibid. II (Paris 1930), 110-1. *Isopet I* (ibid. 226-7) and *Isopet III de Paris* (ibid. 394) contain substantially the same 'moralité.'

21. Karl Warnke (ed.) *Die Fabeln der Marie de France* (Halle 1898) 49.

22. Gerhard von Minden finds essentially the same moral—a warning against false praise ('valsch lof')—in the fables of fox and crow (18) and cock and fox (167).

23. Hervieux II 142.

24. Ibid. 274-5.

25. Ibid. 308.

26. Ibid. 299.

27. Hervieux IV 372.

28. Warnke 200.

29. Hulbert, 657, 662, Cf. John de Bromyard, 431, 'finaliter de insidijs ad litigium ventum est, in quo sibi mutuo maledicebant; Gallus enim dixit, . . . maledictus, qui suadet alteri oculos claudere, quando pericula imminentia videre deberet, vulpes econverso dicere potuit. Maledictus, qui suadet alicui loqui, quando tacere deberet. Sic mali mutuo se decipiunt, multaque loqui, & fieri suadent, & rogant, quae ad animarum pertinent deceptionem, dum enim falsus homo falsa suggestione, vel malitiosa defensione, ut quando se veritate defendere non potest, ad malitias convertitur . . .' A curious feature of Bromyard's version of the story is that the two protagonists curse each other instead of their own folly ('Maledictus qui *suadet*'). He interprets the story as an exmple of how the crafty are sometimes deceived by reciprocal tricks: 'Quomodo vero per insidias proprias, & reciprocas quandoque capiuntur. & decipiuntur, fabulae exemplum ostendit de vulpe, & gallo.'

30. For discussions of this and similar interpretations, see Francesco Novati "Li Dis du Koc"; de Jean de Condé e il gallo del campanile nella poesia medievale' *Studi Medievali* I (1904-5), 465-512; Charles Dahlberg 'Chaucer's Cock and Fox' *JEGP* LIII (1954) 277-90; Mortimer J. Donovan 'The *Moralite* of the Nun's Priest's

Sermon' *JEGP* LII (1953) 498-508.

31. Jacob Grimm and Andreas Schmeller (eds.) *Lateinische Gedichte des X. und XI. Jh.* (Gottingen 1838) 352.

32. Allusions to flattery or vainglory sometimes occur in the course of the narrative — though rarely in the moralitas — of the fable of cock and fox. In 'De Vulpe et Gallo' in *Monachii Romuleae et extravagantes fabulae* (Hervieux II 278), the cock sings 'cum elacione'. 'Vulpes et Gallus' in *Bernae Romuleae et diversae fabulae* (ibid. 308) tells how 'Gallus, elevatus et elatus, audita adulatione,' closes his eyes and is taken by the fox. 'De Gallo et Vulpe' in *Romuli Anglici cunctis exortae fabulae* (ibid. 599) describes the cock as 'amator laudis'.

Explicit allusions to vainglory and flattery occur, moreover, not only in the 'moralitas' of the tale of fox and crow, but also in the fable itself. In *Gualterianae fabulae* (ibid. 387) 'Credit Corvus adulatori, dumque cantat'. Neckam's *Novus AEsopus* (ibid., 407) describes the crow as 'adulanti credens'. *Romuli Anglici nonnullis exortae fabulae* (ibid., 559) refers to the crow as 'laudis gloriam cupiens ampliorem'. In *Romuli Anglici cunctis exortae fabulae* (ibid., 575), 'Hiis . . . laudibus Corvus deceptus, ut Vulpi placere possit et ampliores laudes promereri, cantare cepit.' John de Bromyard (322) describes the crow as 'inaniter gloriando'. The Latin poem *Gallus et vulpes* (Grimm and Schmeller, 345-6) mentions the fox's flattery and the cock's desire for glory:

Dolo parat insidias,
Et primum blandis mitibus
His adulatur vocibus.

Et avidus gloriolae
Verbis cedit vulpeculae.

Flattery also plays a major role in a fable in *Johannis de Capua directorium humanae vitae* (Hervieux V 201) where the cock ('confidens blanditiis vulpis') descends from his tree and is devoured.

33. Hervieux II 355 ('stulti'), 599 ('imprudenter'), 575 ('levibus et minus providis hominibus'), 724 ('fatuos'); Bastin, I, 84 ('musart et sot') and II 226 ('fols'). In John of Capua's fable (Hervieux V 201) the fox devours the cock and comments on his folly: 'Ecce inveni sapientem absque omni prudentia.' To this moral the narrator adds, 'Hanc parabolam tibi dixi, quod gallus merito precogitasset inveteratum odium inter ipsum et vulpem; sic gallus factus est cibus vulpis.'

34. See Hervieux II and IV, *passim;* Bastin I and II, *passim.* The statement of the moral varies in length. Though it is normally short and succinct, it may sometimes be fairly long and elaborate, as in *Gallus et vulpes.*

35. Hervieux II (*Gualteri Anglici fabulae, Gualterianae fabulae,* Neckam's *Novus AEsopus*). In *Isopet de Chartres* (Bastin I) the French verses explaining the moral of the fable are followed by a Latin couplet also stating the moral. In *Isopet III de Paris* (Bastin II) the prose interpretation of the 'moralite' is concluded by a French couplet.

36. Bastin, I and II (*Le 'Romulus' de Walter l'Anglais, Isopet I, Avionnet, Isopet III de Paris*); Hervieux II (*Gualteri Anglici fabularum subditiciae moralitates, Romuli Anglici cunctis exortae fabulae, Ex Romulo Nilantii ortae*

fabulae rhythmicae). The *Isopet de Chartres* (Bastin I) labels these concluding sections 'L'essemple de la fable,' 'La sentence de la fable,' or 'L'exposition de la fable.' In *Odonis de Ceritona fabulis addita, collectio prima* (Hervieux IV) they are headed 'Conclusio,' 'Constructio,' 'Expositio,' or (as in the *Collectio Secunda*) 'Mistice.'

37. Donovan, 498, 507; see also J. Burke Severs 'Chaucer's Originality in the *Nun's Priest's Tale' SP* XLIII (1946) 22-41.

38. *Johannis de Schepeya Fabulae,* in Hervieux IV 446-8. Fable No. 65 bears the heading 'De hoste non armando'; the three other fables are entitled 'De hosti non credendo'.

39. For discussions of this tale in relation to *Le Roman de Renart* and 'The Nonne Preestes Tale' see Dahlberg, 283-4, and Léopold Sudre *Les Sources du Roman de Renart* (Paris 1893), 311-2.

40. W.W. Skeat (ed.) *Notes to the Canterbury Tales* (Oxford 1894) p. 257; F.N. Robinson (ed.) *The Works of Geoffrey Chaucer,* 2d. ed. (London 1957) p. 754.

41. Sisam, 53. Neither Ecclus. 27, 26 nor Prov. 29, 5 is mentioned in any of John de Sheppey's fables. Nevertheless, Fable No. 59 ('Vulpes et lupus in puteo') concludes with the following moral (Hervieux IV 442) from Prov. 26, 26, 'Ecce quam malitiose una maliciosa bestia fraudavit aliam; unde convenienter dicitur Proverbiis, xxvi: Qui operit fraudulenter odium, revelabitur malicia sua.' Verses 24-8 concern deceit and flattery. This fable is entitled 'De malicia et fraude dyaboli et hominis.'

42. Sisam (53) observes that *Ecclesiaste* 'may stand for Solomon in any of his works.'

43. Although Skeat denies that Chaucer may be referring to Ecclesiastes, it is significant that this text contains apparently the only reference to *adulation* in the Vulgate Old Testament. Cf. the commentaries on this text in the Glossa Ordinaria (P.L. 113, 1123) and Jerome's *Commentarius in Ecclesiasten* (P.L. 23, 1061-2).

44. Donovan, 498; cf. Dahlberg, 290.

45. *P.L.* 109, 844; Strabus 113, 1196.

46. *P.L.* 109, 848. Rabanus entitles this chapter of his commentary 'De amicis bonis et malis, falsis et veris.' Cf. Strabus 113, 1196: *'Non credas inimico.* Historice de falsis amicis agit, a quibus cavere debemus. Mystice vero haereticos notat . . .' For similar interpretations of Ecclus. 19, 4 and 27, 26, see *P.L.* 109, 890, 966; 113, 1203, 1213.

CHAPTER V

1. For the "three styles" and the "rota Vergilii" see Edmond Faral, *Les Arts poétiques du XIIe et du XIIIe siècle* (Paris, 1924), 86-8, 312; *Poetria magistri Johannis anglici de arte prosayca metrica et rithmica,* ed. Giovanni Mari, *Romanische Forschungen,* 1902, *13:* 888-900, 920.

2. Charles Muscatine, *Chaucer and the French Tradition* (Berkeley and Los Angeles, 1957), 237-243, approaches "The Nonne Preestes Tale" in terms of the "mixed style" and Chaucer's "transition from rhetoric and heroic back to the naturalism of the farm. . . ."

3. Johannes Anglicus (John of Garland), pp. 888, 900.

4. For other aspects of Chaucer's indebtedness to medieval science in this tale, see Walter Clyde Curry, *Chaucer and the Mediaeval Sciences* (New York, 1926), 219-240, "Chauntecleer and Pertelote on Dreams"; Pauline Aiken, "Vincent of Beauvais and Dame Pertelote's Knowledge of Medicine," *Speculum,* 1935, *10:* 281-287; Kenneth Sisam (ed.), *The Nun's Priest's Tale* (Oxford, 1927), *passim;* and the editions by Skeat and Robinson.

5. Sisam (p. 37) regards this line as a reference to Chauntecleer's "coral-red comb and feathers of burnished gold." Although these details may indeed indicate the cock's choleric complexion, Chaucer must surely have had in mind the medieval doctrine that *gallus domesticus* is a choleric bird. Pertelote's words refer to the cock's natural temperament, and we must, accordingly, reject Sisam's view (p. 37) that "Complexion now has the narrow sense 'colour & texture of the skin of the face. . . .' "

6. John of Trevisa (tr.), *Bartholomeus de Proprietatibus Rerum* (London, 1535), p. 170. See *Bartholomei Anglici . . . de rerum proprietatibus* (Nuremberg, 1519), Book XII, Chapter 16, "De gallo": "Gallus itaque est avis calide & sicce complexionis: & ideo multum habet audacie & animositatis propter quod contra suos adversarios pro suis uxoribus audacter pugnat. . . ."

7. Albertus, pp. 201-202, "Sed gallus est animal cholericum, quod attestatur parvitas capitis respectu proportionis corporis sui et siccitas cerebri, quia parvum habet caput et cerebrum siccum."

8. *Ibid.,* p. 202.

9. *Ibid.,* p. 201.

10. Aristotle, *Historia Animalium,* tr. D.W. Thompson (Oxford, 1910), I, p. 1; VI, p. 9.

11. Trevisa, p. 170; cf. Bartholomeus, ". . . zelat & uxores suas: invento cibo voce quadam eas convocat & sibi subtrahit ut eas reficiat atque pascat: pinguiorem & teneriorem quam plus diligit: secum quietis gratia vicinius collocat: & ipsius presentiam circa se plus affectat: de mane cum ad pastum evolaverit latus suum lateri ipsius primo applicat & per quosdam nutus ipsam ad sui copulam allicit & invitat: & pro ipsa tanquam zelotypus specialiter pugnat. . . . Rostro & pedibus victum quaerit: paleam & pulverem sulcat et reversat & invento grano ad gallinas vociferat & eas vocat. . . ."

12. *Speculi Maioris Vincentii Burgundi . . . Tomi Quatuor* (Venice, 1591), I, *Speculum Naturale,* p. 204, "Gallinis mortuis gallus moerore confectus, abstinet de cantu prae dolore"; "levi susurrio gallinas suas vocat ad esum grani. . . . Gallus gallinam advocatam pascit, & tunc eam ad labores impraegnationis, & partus cogit." Cf. *ibid.,* p. 205. Vincent's source, like Conrad's was the *Liber de natura rerum.*

13. Conrad von Megenberg, *Das Buch der Natur,* ed. in Modern High German by Hugo Schulz (Greifswald, 1897), pp. 159-160, "Hat er Korn gefunden, so lockt er die Hennen mit leisem Gackern zum Futter. . . . Sind dem Hahn alle Hennen gestorben, so magert er vor Leid ab und kräht nicht mehr aus grosser Trauer."

14. Alexander Neckam, *De laudibus divinae sapientiae,* ed. Thomas Wright

(London, 1863), p. 392,

> Nobile dum reperit granum, tunc murmure
> Munificus socias convocat ille suas.
> Corripit errantes promptas parere marito,
> Blanditiis mulcet obsequiisque juvat.

15. Pliny, *Natural History,* III, Loeb Classical Library (London and Cambridge, Mass., 1940), pp. 321-323. Cf. Vincent, p. 204. For the possible relation of this passage to Chaucer's "as it were grim leoun," see Sisam, p. 46; Mortimer J. Donovan, "The *Moralite* of the Nun's Priest's Sermon,"*JEGP,* 1953, *52:* 503.

16. Petrus Berchorius, *Reductorium Morale* (Venice, 1583), p. 208, "super caput christam [*sic*] habet rubeam pro corona." Cf. Bartholomeus, "cristam rubeam gestat in capite pro corona."

17. Berchorius, p. 209, "Vel dic etiam secundum Plin. quod gallus potest significare milites."

18. Pliny, p. 323.

19. Neckam, pp. 391-392.

20. Jean de Condé's *Li Dis du Koc* extolls the cock as a model for knights ("li chevaliers"). The "gentil oisiaus, cointes et fiers, nobles et biaus," sheathes his spurs while tending his hens, but bares them to attack any felon who attempts to injure his mates. He carries both banner and shield. If deprived of food for eight days, he nevertheless refrains from eating the first grain given him and bestows it instead on his hens. See Novati, pp. 486-487; Charles Dahlberg, "Chaucer's Cock and Fox," *JEGP,* 1954, *53:* 282.

21. Vincent (p. 204) explains the cock-fight as a duel for supremacy.

22. Though Pliny and Neckam border on panegyric, St. Ambrose's encomium is even more extravagant. (*P.L.,* XIV, cols. 240-241.) Cf. Vincent, p. 204.

23. Neckam, *De Naturis Rerum,* ed. Thomas Wright (London, 1863), p. 120. In Nivard's *Ysengrimus* (ed. Ernst Voigt [Halle a.S., 1884], p. 251), Sprotinus boasts his suzerainty over twelve hens. Jean de Condé (Novati, p. 488) praises the cock's "seigneural" government over his hens.

24. Pliny, p. 321; Vincent, p. 204. Cf. Sisam, p. 33; Donovan, p. 503.

25. Neckam, *De Laudibus,* p. 391,

> Gallus adest cantu distinguens temporis horae
> Instinctu genii nunciat ore diem.

26. Albertus, p. 202.

27. Vincent, p. 204. Cf. St. Gregory, *Moralia in Job* (*P.L.,* LXXVI, col. 529); Hugo of St. Victor, *De Bestiis* (*P.L.,* CLXXVII, col. 33).

28. Neckam, *De Naturis,* p. 121.

29. Though medieval scientists disagreed as to whether the cock crowed every hour or merely every third hour, they accepted essentially the same physiological explanation for his accuracy. Since Chauntecleer crows "whan degrees fiftene were ascended," Chaucer has obviously followed the former tradition. Any medieval reader familiar with natural history should have readily perceived the causal connection between the cock's choleric complexion and his chronometrical accuracy.

30. Neckam, *De Naturis,* p. 121, "Non est autem facile assignare unde palearis rubricata, quae fulgo dicuntur barbae, proveniant."

31. Job 38:36. Cf. Gregory's *Moralia* (P.L. LXXVI* cols. 527-530); Hugo of St. Victor *De Bestiis* (P.L.*CLXXVII, cols. 33-35); Donovan, p. 502.

32. Neckam, *De Naturis*, p. 120. For the traditional comparison of the cock to doctors or preachers, see the studies by Novati, Donovan, and Dahlberg. Cf. the Latin *Gallus et vulpes* (Novati, p. 471), "Per gallum decentissime doctores subintellige"; John of Garland's poem *De mysteriis Ecclesiae* (*ibid.*, p. 472).

33. Trevisa, p. 170.

34. See James R. Hulbert, "The Nun's Priest's Tale," in *Sources and Analogues of Chaucer's Canterbury Tales*, ed. W.F. Bryan and Germaine Dempster (Chicago, Ill., 1941), pp. 645-663; Kate Petersen, *On the Sources of the "Nonne Prestes Tale"* (Boston, 1898).

35. Faral, pp. 119, 135-136; Cicero, *De Inventione*, Loeb Classical Library (London, 1949), p. 70, "Ac personis has rebus attributas putamus: nomen, naturam, victum, fortunam, habitum, affectionem, studia, consilia, facta, casus, orationes." See also Geoffrey de Vinsauf's *Documentum de modo et arte dictandi et versificandi* (Faral, p. 310).

36. Cicero, pp. 70-72.

37. Faral, p. 136.

38. Se Boyar, pp. 177, 185.

39. See Ernest H. Wilkins, "Descriptions of Pagan Divinities from Petrarch to Chaucer," *Speculum,* 1957, 32:511-522. In the *Reductorium* Chaucer could have found a detailed and systematic allegorical exposition of the attributes which Chauntecleer shares with the cock of Bartholomeus' chapter "De gallo."

CHAPTER VI

1. Bartlett J. Whiting, "The Wife of Bath's Prologue," *Sources and Analogues of Chaucer's Canterbury Tales* (Chicago, 1951), pp. 207-222; Robert Dudley French, *A Chaucer Handbook*, 2nd ed. (New York, 1947), p. 277; Francis Lee Utley, *The Crooked Rib* (Columbus, Ohio, 1944).

2. W. A. Clouston, *The Book of Sindibad* (Glasgow, 1884), pp. lv-lvi, cited Jankyn's "book comprising tales of the wickedness of wives" as evidence that "collections of 'proverbs' against women were common in England in the days of Chaucer." He overlooked, however, the analogy between the fate of Jankyn's volume and the destruction of the similar collection in the Oriental story.

3. Dean S. Fansler, *Chaucer and the Roman de la Rose* (New York, 1914), p. 173; F. N. Robinson, ed., *The Works of Geoffrey Chaucer*, 2nd ed. (London, 1957), p. 702.

4. For a bibliography of *Sindibad*, see Victor Chauvin, *Bibliographie des Ouvrages Arabes*, VIII (Liege et Leipzig, 1904), 1-219. For an account of the origin and diffusion of this story-collection, see Alessandro d'Ancona, ed., *Il libro dei Sette Savj* (Paris, 1864) and Hermann Brockhaus' study in the same volume; Domenico Comparetti, *Researches Respecting the Book of Sindibad* (London, 1882); Clouston; Adolfo Bonilla y San Martin, eds., *Libro de los engaños & los asayamientos de las mugeres* (Barcelona y Madrid, 1904); Killis Campbell, *A Study of the Romance of the Seven Sages with Special Reference to the Middle*

English Versions (Baltimore, 1898); Alexander Haggerty Krappe, "Studies on the *Seven Sages of Rome," Archivum Romanicum,* VIII (1924), 386-407; IX (1925), 345-365; XI (1927), 163-176; XVI (1932), 271-282; XIX (1935), 213-226; Angel González Palencia, ed., *Versiones castellanas del "Sendebar"* (Madrid y Granada, 1946); John Esten Keller, ed., *El Libro de. los Engaños, Univ. of North Carolina Studies in the Rom. Langs. and Lits.,* XX (1953); *The Book of the Wiles of Women, Univ. of North Carolina Studies in the Rom. Langs. and Lits.,* XXVII (1956). The following studies are also useful, though largely out of date: A. Loiseleur Deslongchamps, *Essai sur les fables indiennes et sur leur introduction en Europe* (Paris, 1838); Heinrich Adelbert Keller, *Li Romans des Sept Sages nach der Pariser Handschrift* (Tübingen, 1836); *Dyocletianus Leben von Hans von Bühel* (Quedlinburg und Leipsiz, 1841). For an English translation of *The Seven Vazirs,* see Clouston.

5. Hermann Brockhaus, "Zur Geschichte der *Sieben weisen Meister," Blätter für literarische Unterhaltung,* Nos. 242-243 (Aug. 30-31, 1843). Cf. H. A. Keller, *Li Romans,* p. clxxxvi, *Dyocletianus,* pp. 34, 54.

6. Comparetti, pp. 19, 24-26, 29, 31, 34. Clouston (p. 83) entitles this tale "Story of the Man who Compiled a Book on the Wiles of Women." D'Ancona (p. xviii) calls it "La raccolta delle astuzie femminili." E. Tez's translation of Brockhaus's essay, "I Sette Savj nel *Tuti Namah* di Nakhshabi" (d'Ancona, p. ix), entitles it (VIII, 69, 177), "Enxemplo del Mançebo que non queria casar fasta que sopiese las malades de las mugeres" (Gonzalez Palencia, p. 46), "El libro de las astucias de las mujeres" (González Palencia, p. xxv), and *Tas ponerias holas kai ta technasmata ton kakon gynaikon* (Jo. Fr. Boissonade, ed., *Syntipas, De Syntipa et Cyri filio Andreopuli Narratio,* Paris, 1828, 88). Alfons Hilka, ed., *Historia Septem sapientum I* (Heidelberg, 1912), xxiv, refers to this story as "Ingenia."

7. Comparative tables showing the occurrence of this and other tales of the Sindibad group can be found in González Palencia, xxiii-xxvii; Comparetti, p. 25; Paul Cassel, ed, *Mischle Sindbad, Secundus Syntipas* (Berlin, 1888), p. 362, Hilka, pp. xxiv-xxv.

8. Comparetti, p. 5.

9. Two Greek versions of *Syntipas* (each based on three different codices) have been edited by Victor Jernstedt and published with a preface by Peter Nikitin; see *Mich. Andreopuli Liber Syntipas, (Mémoires de l'Académie Impériale des Sciences de St. Pétersbourg,* VIIIe Série), Vol. XI, No. 1 (St. Petersburg, 1912). In Nikitin's opinion, version "II" is the better text, and the version published by Boissonade and Alfred Eberhard is actually a *retractatio* or *metaphrasis* of this *recensio prototypa.* Nevertheless, except for minor differences in phraseology, the account of the book-burning episode is essentially the same in both texts. See Clouston, pp. 258-263, for a partial translation of "The Wiles of Women" into English.

10. Frédéric Macler, tr., *Contes Syriaques, Histoire de Sindban* (Paris, 1903), pp. 60-61). Macler inserted this translation (based on the *retractatio* of *Syntipas*) in his French version of the Syriac text edited by Baethgen; in the latter version, a lacuna occurs at the very beginning of this tale. See Friedrich Baethgen, ed.,

Sindbad oder die sieben weisen Meister (Leipzig, 1879), p. 33, "Es war einmal ein Mann, der hatte hoch und heilig geschworen, keine Frau zu nehmen, bevor er so weit gekommen sei, die ganze Arglist der bosen Weiber kennen zu lernen . . ."

11. Cf. Jernstedt, pp. 70-71.

12. González Palencia, pp. 1-66; J. E. Keller, ed., *El Libro de los Engaños*. For an English translation, see Clouston; J. E. Keller, tr., *The Book of the Wiles of Women*. See also George T. Artola, "Sindibad in Medieval Spanish," MLN, LXXI (1956), 37-42.

13. See J. E. Keller, *Motif-Index of Mediaeval Spanish Exempla* (Knoxville, Tenn.; 1949), K. 1227.

14. González Palencia, p. 48. Comparetti (p. 26) observed that the same ruse appears in *Çukasaptati,* which "puts principally in evidence the cunning behaviour of the woman towards the young man, suppressing almost entirely all that has reference to his studies of female wiles . . ."

15. Brockhaus, No. 243. See also Wilhelm Pertsch, "Über Nachschabi's *Papagaienbuch,*" *Zeitschrift der deutschen morgenländischen Gesellschaft,* XXI (1867), 505-551.

16. Ezio Levi, *Poeti antichi lombardi* (Milan, 1921), p. 119.

17. August Wulff, *Die frauenfeindlichen Dichtungen in den romanischen Literaturen des Mittelalters bis zum Ende des XIII. Jahrhunderts* (Halle a.S., 1914), pp. 146-147.

18. A. Tobler, "Proverbia quae dicuntur super natura feminarum," *Zeitschrift für romanische Philologie,* IX (1885), 302.

19. *Syntipas; Libro de los Engaños;* Nachschebi.

20. The identification of the owner or collector of the book of woman's wiles as a scholar is traditional. The *Sindibadnameh* (composed in 1375 on the basis of a Persian prose narrative translated from the Arabic) describes him as a "wise man" and a "master" (Clouston, pp. 83-86; Comparetti, p. 6). Ibn Arabshah's *Fakihat al-Khulafa* (a work of the fifteenth century) calls him a philosopher: see M. Cardonne, *Mélanges de littérature orientale, ri, 1770],* I (Paris, 1770), 23-25. H. A. Keller (*Dyocletianus,* p. 54) observes that "Das altdeutsche gedicht von Aristoteles erzählt, als demselben das weib den bekannten schimpf angethan, sei er auf eine insel geflohen

. . . heiz Galiciâ:
dâ bleip er, unde machte dâ
ein michel buoch und schreib dar an
waz wunderlicher liste kan
daz schoene ungetriuwe wip,
und wie diu leben unde lîp
manigem hât verseret."

Comparetti, p. 26, calls attention to the fact that both in *Çukasaptati* and in Nachschebi's story "the man who is duped has a sacred character, being in the first a Brahmin, in the other a Dervish." Cf. also Inayat Allah's tale of a Brahmin who, after learning the orthodox Vedas, seeks to acquire the "tiria bede" ("the science or mystery of women"); see *Tales Translated from the Persian of Inatulla of Delhi,* (London, 1786), 226-231.

21. See Robinson, p. 698; there he further observes that "Professor R. A. Pratt has in preparation an edition of an antifeminist compilation under the title of the Jankyn Book." See also Robert A. Pratt, "Jankyn's Book of Wikked Wyves: Medieval Anti-matrimonial Propaganda in the Universities," *Annuale Mediaevale,* 3 (1962), pp. 5-27; idem, "Saint Jerome in Jankyn's Book of Wikked Wyves," *Criticism,* 5 (1963), pp. 316-322.

22. In the Sindibad tradition the most imposing collection of women's ruses appears in the story in the *Sindibad-nameh,* where the scholar's own researches are supplemented by "a treatise on this subject" and "a commentary"—the fruit of forty years of travel; see Clouston, pp. 83-84.

23. In the *Sindibad-nameh,* however, the scholar's own collection is over-shadowed by the compilation he receives from a stranger; see Note 22.

24. This identification of the victim of the book-burning episode as a Roman is unique. It has no parallel in the "Eastern" versions of the Seven Sages. Although a Roman setting occurs in the frame narrative of the "Western" versions, this group does not contain the story of "The Man Who Understood Female Wiles." It is conceivable that the author of *Castigabricon* may have fused details derived from both traditions. For a comparative table of stories in the "Western" versions, see Campbell, p. 35.

25. Although "The Man Who Understood Female Wiles" does not occur in published versions of *Mischle Sendabar* (see Cassel's edition and the medieval Latin translation edited by Hilka), Professor Lillian H. Hornstein has called to my attention an additional "book-burning" analogue in each of two Hebrew manuscripts of the Seven Sages, recently transliterated, translated, and edited by Dr. Morris Epstein, in an unpublished dissertation in the New York University Library. See Adolf Neubauer, *Catalogue of the Hebrew Manuscripts in the Bodleian Library,* I (Oxford, 1886), No. 1466; II (Oxford, 1906), No. 2797.

CHAPTER VII

1. N. S. Bushnell "The Wandering Jew and *The Pardoner's Tale"* SP XXVIII (1931) 450-460; F. N. Robinson (ed.) *The Complete Works of Geoffrey Chaucer* (London 1957) p. 731; Marie Padgett Hamilton 'Death and Old Age in *The Pardoner's Tale,'* SP XXXVI (1939) 571-576; W. J. B. Owen 'The Old Man in *The Pardoner's Tale,'* RES, NS II(1951) 49-55; G. C. Sedgewick 'The Progress of Chaucer's Pardoner, 1880-1940', MLQ I (1940), 431-458; Barbara M. H. Strang, 'Who is the Old Man in The Pardoner's Tale'? N&Q, NS VII (1960) 207-208. The essays by Owen and Sedgewick are reprinted in *Chaucer: Modern Essays in Criticism,* cd. Wagenknecht (New York 1959) pp. 126-165. Also relevant are articles by P. Miller *Speculum* XXX (1955) 180-199, G. R. Coffman *Speculum* IX (1934) 249-277 and A. L. Kellogg *Speculum* XXXVI (1951) 479. See also G. G. Sedgewick, "The Progress of Chaucer's Pardoner, 1880-1940," in *Chaucer: Modern Essays in Criticism,* ed. Edward Wagenknecht (New yori, 1959, pp. 126-158.

2. G.L. Kittredge 'Chaucer and Maximianus' AJP IX (1888) 84-85. Cf. also Boethius (pp. 320-321 of Chaucer's translation, ed. Robinson, op. cit.).

3. *Poetae Latini Minores,* ed. Aemilius Baehrens (Leipzig 1883) p. 326; cf. p. 328, 'incurva senectus'.

4. Nisard, in fact, renders *prona senectus* as *vieillard,* but *ruitura senectus* as *vieillesse* (p. 594).

5. Baehrens, p. 317.

6. See Hamilton, p. 576.

7. Cf. PL CCIX 262; LXXXIII 81-82.

8. Frederick Tupper 'The Pardoner's Tale' in *Sources and Analogues of Chaucer's Canterbury Tales* ed. W. F. Bryan and Germaine Dempster (Chicago 1941) p. 436.

9. Baehrens, p. 576.

10. PL CCXVII 706. For other parallels with Innocent's *De Contemptu Mundi* in *The Canterbury Tales,* see Robinson, pp. 694-696, 729-730. Robinson also notes (p. 731) a resemblance between this passage and Ecclesiasticus VIII. 6.

11. Cf. Rabanus' commentary on this text (PL CIX 686).

12. PL CXIV 832.

13. PL CVIII 460. Miller observes that 'Rabanus' gloss reflects an opposite sense of figurative age than that understood with reference to the *vetus homo.'*

14. Tupper, pp. 415-438.

15. PL XVII 758-759.

16. PL CCXVII 723.

17. In Robinson's opinion (p. 731), the 'cheste' the old man is willing to exchange for a hair-cloth is not a coffin, but a 'clothes-chest'. It may, of course, contain other worldly goods, including whatever money he may possess. His willingness to part with this 'cheste' is a further instance of *contemptus mundi,* analogous to his indifference to the treasure.

If (as several editors think) the 'cheste' is a 'box containing his property, and the 'heyre clout' a 'haircloth for burial,' then the old man appears to be voicing a commonplace of both classical and Biblical tradition, and highly appropriate to the theme of the Pardoner's sermon. The contrast between man's worldly possessions and the native nakedness with which he enters and leaves the world had long been a conventional argument against love of riches.

18. PL CCXVII 717. Cf. Bede (PL XCIII 93).

19. Cf. the behaviour of Life in Passus XX *Piers Plowman* XX (B) 142-50; and cf. Kellogg pp. 473-4 ('The essential contrast . . . is between living in accordance with "goddeswille and living right at our owen wille" ' etc.).

20. In *The Parson's Tale,* the antithesis between "lordes" and "cherles" is discussed under the heading of *Avaricia* and related specifically to the theme of death.

21. *The Parson's Tale* discusses these virtues under the heading *Remedium contra peccatum Ire.*

22. *Pace* Sedgewick (Wagenknecht, p. 127).

CHAPTER VIII

1. See Geoffrey Bullough (ed.), *Narrative and Dramatic Sources of Shakespeare,* II (London and New York, 1958), 16-18.

2. See Henry Green, *Shakespeare and the Emblem Writers* (London, 1870); *idem, Whitney's "Choice of Emblemes"* (London, 1866); Rosemary Freeman, *English Emblem Books* (London, 1948).

3. See Erich Krause, *Die Mythen-Darstellungen in der venezianischen Ovidausgabe von 1497* (Wurzburg, 1926); M. D. Henkel, "Illustrierte Ausgaben von Ovids Metamorphosen im XV., XVI. und XVII. Jahrhundert", *Vorträge der Bibliothek Warburg, 1926-1927,* ed. Fritz Saxl (Leipzig and Berlin, 1930), pp. 58-144.

4. For parallels between the Actaeon of the emblem books and Shakespeare's allusions to the myth in *Titus Andronicus, Twelfth Night,* and *The Merry Wives of Windsor* (II.i.), see Green's *Shakespeare and the Emblem Writers,* pp. 275-279, 515.

5. Illustrations of the Actaeon myth sometimes represent him in entirely human form (immediately before his metamorphosis) or in the form of a deer (immediately after his transformation). Under the heading "Acteon mutato in cervo", *Ovidio methamorphoseos vulgare hystoriado* (Venice, 1508, fol. xxi) shows him both as a hunter surprising the bathing nymphs and also as a stag attacked by dogs. Similarly, in an edition of Nicolo de' Agostini's translation of Ovid (*Di Ovidio le Metamorphosi . . . tradotte dal latino,* Venice, 1547, fol. 25), the still-human huntsman is depicted (at left) in the act of surprising the nymphs and (at right) as a stag attacked by hounds. Cf. Krause, p. 22. In the emblems of De Bry and Oraeus, Actaeon wears stag's horns, yet retains not only his human body but also his human head and countenance. See *Emblemata Nobilitati et vulgo scito digna singulis historijs symbola adscripta . . . Omnia recens collecta, inventa, & . . . in aes incisa a Theodoro de Bry Leodiense* (Francoforti ad Moenum, 1593), Plate No. 7; *Viridarium Hieroglyphicorum Morale . . . Per Henricum Oraeum Assenheim* (Francofurti, 1619), No. 47, p. 94.

6. *Omnia Andreae Alciati V. C. Emblemata* (Antwerp, 1581), p. 214 (Emblem No. 52). In this plate Actaeon (with stag's head, human body, hunter's attire) has fallen to the ground and is being attacked by his hounds.

7. *Johan. Posthii Germershemü Tetrasticha in Ovidii Metam. Lib. XV. quibus accesserunt Vergilij Solis figurae* (Frankfurt, 1569), p. 40. Plate No. 4 of Book III ("Actaeon in cervum") depicts him (with stag's head, human body, hunter's garb) in the act of surprising the nymphs at their bath. Plate No. 5 ("Actaeon à canibus dilaceratur") shows him as a stag attacked by hounds (p. 41).

8. Green, *Whitney's "Choice of Emblemes",* p. 15; cf. pp. 321-322 for Actaeon's fate as portrayed by Alciati, Aneau, and Sambucus; see also Plates 20 and 25.

9. Green, *Whitney,* Plate 25. Except for the border, Sambucus' Actaeon emblem is identical with Whitney's. Green has observed (p. 322) that "Sambucus . . . supplies the motto which Whitney follows", and Whitney appears to have derived his emblem from the same source. See *Emblemata . . . Ioan. Sambuci Timaviensis Pannonii, Quarta Edito* (Lug. Batav., 1599), p. 118.

10. Cf. Bartholomaeus Anulus, *Picta Poesis* (Lugduni, 1564), p. 44; Anulus' emblem of Actaeon ("Ex Domino Servus") portrays the hunter in the act of surprising Diana and her nymphs at their bath. Standing erect, clad in hunting costume, and carrying a javelin in his left hand, Actaeon retains his human shape, except for his stag's head.

11. Cf. *Les XV. livres de la metamorphose d'Ovid . . . contenans l'olympe des histoires poétiques* (Paris, 1539), fol. 42; *Metamorphosis Ovidii . . . expositae . . . per M. Johan. Sprengium Augustan. Unà cum . . . iconibus a Vergilio Solis . . . delineatis (s.l.,* 1563), p. 40; *La metamorphose d'Ovide figurée* (Lyons, 1583), "Actaeon mué en cerf"; *Le metamorphosi d'Ovidio ridotte da Gio. Andrea dell' Anguillara in ottava rima* (Venice, 1584, p. 66; *P. Ovidii Nasonis metamorphoseon plerarumque historica naturalis moralis* εχψρασις (Frankfurt, 1619, pp. 55-57; *Ovidio istorico, politico, morale brevemente spiegato, e delineato* (Venice, 11680), p. 25; see also Henkel, Abb. 16; Krause, pp. 21-23. *La Vita et* **Metamorfoseo d'Ovidio, Figurato & abbreviato in forma d'Epigrammi da M.** *Gabriello Symeoni* [*Lione, 1583*], *No. 42* [*"Ateone mutato in Cerbio da Diana"*], *p. 54; Picta Poesis Ovidiana . . . :, Fausti Sabaci Brixiani, Aliorumque clarorum virorum . . . Epigrammatis expositarum . . . Ex recensione Nicolai Reusneri* (Francoforti ad Moenum, 1580), "De Diana et Actaeone", fol. 34. Reusner's edition contains two illustrations of Actaeon; in his encounter with Diana the hunter wears a stag's head but retains his human shape (fol. 34^r), while in the scene of his slaughter by his hounds (fol. 34^v) he has been completely transformed into a stag.

12. Cf. the representation of "Acteon devoured by his hounds" on a "jacket or tunic of 'black work' " which is "said to have belonged to Queen Elizabeth" and is now in the Victoria and Albert Museum. In this surviving example of Renaissance "emblem-embroidery" the prostrate Actaeon wears a stag's head, but retains his human torso and clutches a hunting horn in his right hand. Two of the emblematic embroideries on the jacket are "faithful copies of plates in Whitney; and the device of Actaeon is presumably derived from the same source, although there is some modification of the design." See Freeman, pp. 94-95; M. Jourdain, *The History of English Secular Embroidery* (London, 1910), pp. 143-154. Later instances of this convention can be found in Henry Peacham, *Minerva Britanna* (London, 1612), p. 175; and in *D.* **Ioannis de Solorzano Pereira** *. . . Emblemata centum* (Matriti, 1653), p. 246. Peacham's emblem ("Laboris effecta") shows Actaeon prostrate and attacked by his hounds. He retains his human form and hunter's clothing, but wears a stag's head (turned over his left shoulder) and clutches a hunting horn in his left hand The figure of Diana appears in the background, and Peacham's anagram equates the goddess with "Anna Dudleia"("e l'nuda DIANA"), to whom the emblem is dedicated ("to the no lesse vertuous then faire Mrs. Anne Dudleie"). See Freeman, p. 76. Solorzano's emblem No. 33 ("In Nimis deditos Venationi") depicts Actaeon in the act of running away from his hounds. He wears a stag's head, but retains his human body and hunter's garb.

13. W. W. Greg (ed), Shakespeare's Merry Wives of Windsor 1602, Tudor and Stuart Library (Oxford, 1910), *"Enter sir John with a Bucks head upon him."* Again, according to a later stage direction in the Quarto, *"Falstaffe pulles of his bucks head, and rises up."* Moreover, the dialogue of the Quarto explicitly invests the fat knight with a stag's head:

Sir Hu. See I have spied one by good luck,
    His bodie man, his head a buck.

14. In the Quarto, Falstaff similarly observes that *"love transformed himselfe*

into a bull,/ And I am here a Stag, and I thinke the fattest/ In all *Windsor* forrest"; the Queen of the Fairies also alludes to the metamorphosis-motif ("About it then, and know the truth,/ Of this same metamorphised youth").

15. John Munro (ed.), The London Shakespeare (London, 1958), II, 857; H. C. Hart (ed.), *The Merry Wives of Windsor* (The Arden Shakespeare, Second Edition, London, 1932), p. 211; Sir Arthur Quiller-Couch and John Dover Wilson (eds.), *The Merry Wives of Windsor* (Cambridge, 1921), p. 100; George Van Santvoord (ed.), *The Merry Wives of Windsor* (The Yale Shakespeare, New Haven, 1922), p. 86.

16. Bullough, p. 53. We should note, however, an additional link between Actaeon's fate and Falstaff's punishment, in Golding's use of the word "pinch" in the line, "First Slo did pinch him by the haunch, and next came Kildeere in"; see Bullough, p. 54.

17. For an "emblem of the stag" to signify cuckoldry, see Miss Freeman's discussion of Webster's *The White Devil* (p. 100).

18. Cf. Agostini (1547), fol. 26; Ovidio (1508), fol. xxi.

19. Green, *Shakespeare and the Emblem Writers,* pp. 275-279. The comparison of the lover to a stag and the hound-desire simile are both traditional and sometimes appear independently of each other. Thus Petrarch's sonnet "I dolci colli ov' io lasciai me stesso" compares himself to a "cervo ferito di saetta", but does not introduce the hound-desire image; see Francesco Petrarca, *Il Canzoniere,* ed. Dino Provenzal (Milan, 1954), p. 248. On the other hand, in "the *Cerva Bianca* of Antonio Fregoso — an allegorical poem published in 1510 and frequently reprinted in the sixteenth century — a nymph whom Diana has changed into a white hind, pursued by the hounds of desire and thought, leads the hunter through various perils and adventures into the City of Love and to Love's eternal throne." See Edmund G. Gardner, *The Arthurian Legend in Italian Literature* (London, 1930), p. 324. A woodcut in the 1525 edition published at Venice illustrates the pursuit of the deer by the two hounds "Desio" and "Pensier"; see Raimond van Marle, *Iconographie de l'Art Profane au Moyen-Age et à la Renaissance . . . II. Allégories et symboles* (La Haye, 1932), pp. 105, 108. For the stag as a symbol of desire, see the exegetical tradition associated with Psalm xliii.I ("Quemadmodum desiderat cervus ad fontes aquarum", etc.); cf. the interpretations of St. Augustine (P.L., XXXVI, col. 464 ff.), the *Glossa Ordinaria* (P.L., CXIII, col. 905), and Rabanus Maurus (P.L., CXII, col. 893).

20. Whitney, p. 15. Sambucus' emblem of Actaeon (*Emblemata,* p. 118) also bears the motto "*Voluptas aerumnosa*", but the explanatory verses interpret the myth in terms of the expenses of hunting; see Footnote 13.

21. *Metamorphoses Ovidii* (1563), p. 41. This plate (Book III, No. 5) is preceded by No. 4 ("Actaeon in Cervum"), p. 40. Green overlooks the similarity between Whitney's interpretation and that of Sprengius.

22. Bullough, p. 8. See the verses by Faustus Sabaeus in *Picta Poesis Ovidiana,* fol. 34[r].

23. Van Marle, pp. 448-496. De Bry, p. 24; cf. the German verses on this emblem ("*Actaeon, Von unmassiger Wollust in Lieb und Jagwerck*"), p. 25,
   Wer seine Tag Zubringen thut/
   Mit Frawen und mit Jägers muth/

Der wirt von den die er ernehrt/
  Gleich wie von Hunden auffgezehrt/
Ein ehrlich Weib vor solchem Mann/
  Mit gutem fug sich huten kan/
Wenn sie in fleucht/ und jn verjagt/
  Dass er fon jr kein Unehr sagt.

24. Arthur Golding, *The .XV. Bookes of P. Ovidius Naso, entituled Metamorphosis, translated oute of Latin into English meeter* (London, 1575).

25. In Renaissance emblem books, the wounded stag is a conventional symbol of the lover. Cf. *Les Devises ou emblèmes heroiques et morales, inventées par le S. Gabriel Symeon* (Lyon, 1559), pp. 33-34; Claude Paradin, *Les Devises Heroiques* (Paris, 1571), pp. 300-301; P.S. (tr.), *The Heroicall Devises of M. Claudius Paradin . . . Whereunto are added the Lord Gabriel Symeons and others* (London, 1591), pp. 354-355; *Hadriani Junii Emblemata* (Lugduni Batavorum, 1596), pp. 53, 129; Otho Vaenius, *Amorum Emblemata* (Antwerpiae, 1608), pp. 154-155, 240-241. For Shakespeare's possible knowledge of the work of P.S., see Freeman, pp. 62-63.

26. Cf. Hyder Edward Rollins (ed.), *The Paradise of Dainty Devices* (1576-1606) (Cambridge, Mass., 1927), pp. 54, 218; Sidney Lee, ed., *Elizabethan Sonnets* (Westminster, 1904), I, 159, 240, 301; II, 160. For the lover's metamorphosis into "a wounded hart" and the comparison of the lover to a hunter devoured by his own hounds, see II, 17, 20-21. In the "Argument" to *Il Candelaio,* Bruno transfers the imagery of the Actaeon myth to the courtesan Vittoria and her foolish lover Bonifacio: "Consider then: it was his infatuation with Vittoria that first put him in the way of being deceived, and when he tried to enjoy her, he became deceived indeed; prefigured, in fact, by Actaeon, who went hunting for horned beasts and when he thought of enjoying Diana, was turned into a stag himself. So it is not surprising that this man was ripped and torn in pieces by these ruffianly hounds." (*The Candle Bearer,* tr. J.R. Hale, in **The Genius of the Italian Theater,** ed. Eric Bentley, New York, 1964, p. 203.)

For Bruno, as for many of his contemporaries, the Actaeon myth was equivocal; it could apply not only to "vulgar love" at its vulgarest, but also to "heroic" or Platonic love. In *De gli heroici furori* (Giordano Bruno, THE HEROIC FREN-ZIES, tr. Paul Eugene Memmo, Jr., Chapel Hill 1966, pp. 216-227) Diana becomes the "splendor of the intelligible species" and Actaeon a Platonic lover. "I say very few are the Actaeons to whom destiny gives the power to contemplate Diana naked, and the power to become so enamoured of the beautiful harmony of the body of nature . . ., that they are transformed into deer, inasmuch as they are no longer the hunters but the hunted . . . The result is that the dogs, as thoughts bent upon divine things, devour this Actaeon and make him dead to the vulgar, to the multitude . . .

27. Freeman, p. 63n.

28. For Hippocrates, Ovid, and other victims of the basket-episode, see John Webster Spargo, *Virgil the Necromancer: Studies in Virgilian Legends* (Harvard Studies in Comparative Literature, X, Cambridge, Mass., 1934), Chapter 5, "Virgil in the Basket", pp. 136-197.

29. For Sardanapalus in woman's clothing as a symbol of "intemperantia & libydo", see Erasmus, *s.v.* "Sardanapalus", col. 1045. Cf. *Emblemata Florentii Schoonhovii* (Goudae, 1618), pp. 25-27; Solorzano, pp. 267-268.

30. Bullough, p. 8.

31. Spargo, pp. 237-240. Cf. William J. Thoms (ed.), *Early English Prose Romances, New Edition* (London, 1907), pp. 219-220. See also H. Kjellin, "Vergilius i korgen och som trollkarl", *Festschrift Roosval* (Stockholm, 1929), pp. 142ff., and G. F. Koch, "Virgil im Korbe", *Fetschrift Erich Meyer* (Hamburg, 1959), pp. 105-121.

32. Spargo observes (p. 254) that as "the story of Virgil in the basket was the most popular of all these tales, it follows that it was most frequently represented in art."

33. Spargo, p. 382.

34. *Jo. Gower de confessione Amantis* (London, 1554), fol. clxxxix^r. Cf. fol. cxxvii^v. See also Reinhold Pauli, ed., *Confessio Amantis of John Gower* (London, 1857), III, 4, 366.

35. Spargo, pp. 168, 255-258.

36. Van Marle, p. 463.

37. Spargo, pp. 259-266, 179. For illustrations of these title-borders, see pp. 264, 266.

38. Spargo, p. 158.

39. Thoms, p. 437; cf. Spargo, pp. 189, 258.

40. Spargo, p. 189.

41. Spargo, p. 185.

42. Spargo, pp. 147-155.

43. Stephen Hawes, *The Pastime of Pleasure,* ed. William Edward Mead, EETS, o.s., CLXXIII (London, 1928), lines 3626-3729, pp. 138-141.

44. Spargo, p. 192.

45. Cf. Ovid's *Heroides,* ed. Henri Bornecque (P;aris, 1928), "Deianira Herculi", lines 53-110; George Turberville (tr.), *The Heroycall Epistles of the Learned Poet Publius Ovidius Naso,* ed. Frederick Boas (London, 1928), pp. 117-118. Hercules in female clothing is "scuticae tremefactus habenis"; Falstaff in "womans apparell" is soundly cudgelled.

46. Spargo, p. 179.

47. Battista Guarini, *Il Pastor Fido* (Parigi, 1731), p. 21.

48. *Discorso di Francesco Anguilla, Sopra Quell' Oda di Safo, che comincia, "Parmi quell" huomo eguale esser à i Dei",* (Venice, 1572), p. 4.

49. Erasmus, col. 1189.

50. Conti, p. 709.

51. Conti, p. 699.

52. Robert Burton, *The Anatomy of Melancholy* (London, 1845), pp. 567-568; arguing that lovers are "commonly slaves, captives, voluntary servants, *Amator amicae mancipium",* Burton relates how "Hercules served Omphale, put on an apron, took a distaff and spun . . . "

53. Peacham's emblem of Hercules with the distaff (p. 95) bears the motto *"Vis Amoris".* The accompanying verses elaborate this theme.

54. Cf. Vaenius' emblem of Hercules with the distaff (pp. 82-83), "Amor addocet artes".

55. Cf. Solorzano, pp. 262-268.

56. For Renaissance and later examples, see A. Pigler, *Barockthemen: Eine Auswahl von Verzeichnissen zur Ikonographic des. 17. und 18. Jahrhunderts* (Budapest, 1956). II, 111-116. Cf. Ernest Diez, "Der Hofmaler Bartholomäus Spranger", *Jahrbuch der Kunsthistorischen Sammlungen des allerhöchsten Kaiserhauses,* XXVIII (No. 3), 114.

57. For analogues of the basket episode, see Bullough, pp. 3-44.

58. See W. Moelwyn Merchant, *Shakespeare and the Artist* (London, 1959), pp. 3, 7, 9. For other examples of Shakespeare's debt to contemporary iconography, see Green's *Shakespeare and the Emblem Writers.* Prof. William S. Heckscher has kindly called my attention to the emblematic character of the cushion with which Falstaff mocks the royal crown in *I Henry IV.* For the pillow or cushion as a symbol of idleness and lechery and for its connection with the proverbial *pluma Sardanapali,* see Erwin Panofsky, *Albrecht Dürer* (Princeton, 1943), I, 71; II, 27, fig. 98 and 103; *idem, Studies in Iconology* (New York, 1939), p. 88, fig. 65; *idem, Hercules am Scheidewege* (Leipzig, 1930), p. 97. Prof. Heckscher also calls attention to the parallel between Falstaff's prone position on the ground and the iconographical motif which represents physical contact with the earth as a symbol of fleshly lust; cf. *Reallexikon zur deutschen Kunstgeschichte,* s.v. "Dornauszieher".

59. Bullough, pp. 3-4; Quiller-Couch and Wilson, pp. xii-xiii, xxii.

60. Munro, pp. 775-776.

61. Bullough, p. 3.

CHAPTER IX

1. *The Faerie Queene, Book One,* A Variorum Edition, ed. F.M. Padelford, Baltimore, 1932, p. 243.

2. *Ibid.,* 243.

3. *Gabriae Graeci fabellae XXXXIIII,* Lyons, 1551, pp. 282-3:
   Humeris Asinus gestabat simulacrum argenteum,
   Quod unusquisque occurrens adorabat.
   Superbia verò elatus, nolens manere Asinùs,
   Audivit, Non es tu Deus, sed fers Deum.
Babrius' *affabulatio,* or moral, applied the fable specifically to men in positions of authority and dignity: "Quòd oporteat eos qui in dignitatibus constituti sunt, cognoscere se esse homines."

4. For Spenser's relation to the emblem books, see Henry Green, *Shakespeare and the Emblem Writers,* London, 1870, *passim;* James G. McManaway, " 'Occasion' (*F.Q.* II, iv, 4-5)," *MLN,* XLIX, 1934, pp. 391-3; Rosemary Freeman, *English Emblem Books,* London, 1948, *passim.*

5. *Omnia Andreae Alciati V.C. Emblemata: Cum commentariis . . . per Claudium Minoem Diuionensem,* Antwerp, 1581, 48. Minoes (49-50) quoted Babrius' tetrastich and a Latin version by Gabriel Faernus of Cremona. See

Fabulae Centum ex Antiquis Auctoribus Delectae et a Gabriele Faerno Cremonensi Carminibus Explicatae, Rome, 1563, 94-5. Plate No. 95 ("Asinus simulacrum gestans") depicts an ass bearing an image of Isis, preceded by kneeling worshippers and followed by a man with a club. The verses are as follows:

Simulacrum asellus baiulans argenteum,
Cum id transeuntes flexo adorarent genu,
Sui hoc honoris gratia est fieri ratus.
Iamque insolenti elatus arrogantia,
Nolebat asinus esse, donec aspero
Probe dolatus fuste clunes, audijt,
O stulte, non es tu deus, sed fers deum."

Faernus, like Babrius, applied the fable to men in authority: "Se norit hominem, qui magistratum gerit."

6. Claude Mignault of Dijon.

7. Minoes (49) also regarded the story as a moral for "praefectis Imperatorum aliorumque principum."

8. *Alciati Emblemata,* 48-9.

9. *Ibid.,* 50. Minoes' acknowledged source is Pierius' discussion of the ass in Book XII of the *Hieroglyphica.* See Ioannes Pierius Valerianus, *Hieroglyphica,* Venice, 1604, 120-1. Regarding the ass as the symbol of "Labor indefessus atque servilis," Pierius explained that "apud Hebraeos, praecipue Cabalisticos, asinus est sapientiae symbolum. . . . " Minoes ignored Pierius' discussion of other, less favourable, interpretations of the ass; see *ibid.,* 115-18.

10. *Whitney's "Choice of Emblemes,"* A Fac-simile Reprint, ed. Henry Green, London, 1866, 8. See also pp. 245-6.

11. See *The Faerie Queene, Book One,* p. 240.

12. Cf. Acts xiv. 11-18, where the people of Lystra attempt to worship Paul and Barnabas as gods.

13. See Erasmus, Adagiorum Chiliades, Basle, 1536, 398-9. No. 1204 concerns "Ονος αγων μυστηρια, id est. Asinus portans mysteria." Franciscus Sanctius, *Comment. in And. Alciati Emblemata,* Lyons, 1573, 39-40, quoted Babrius' fable, Erasmus' adage, and a passage from Aristophanes' *Frogs:*

Ita per Iovem sum asinus vehens mysteria
Verum ita non iam sustinebo diutius.

Though Percival cited Aristophanes' *Frogs* ("ass leading the mysteries") and "Phaedrus's *[sic]* fable based on this," he overlooked the Renaissance application of this symbol to the clergy (see *The Faerie Queene, Book One,* 243).

14. John Calvin, *Institutionis Christianae Religionis Libri Quatuor,* Geneva, 1617, 208.

15. Una's "milke white lambe" probably represents "Christ crucified" — the object of the church's preaching (cf. 1 Corinthians i. 23). Nevertheless it may also symbolize the *Coena domini* — one of the two sacraments acknowledged by the Reformed Church. Stanza 4 thus invests Una with both of the signs, or *notae,* of the true church: (1) the ministry of the word (represented by the ass) and (2) the administration of the sacraments (symbolized by the lamb).

16. Calvin, 208.

17. "Speak, ye that ride on white asses, ye that sit in judgment, and walk by the way."

18. Migne, *Patrologia Latina*, CLXVII, Paris 1854, 1028.

19. In *Emblematum Liber* (1531) Alciati depicted the statue of the goddess as veiled. (See Freeman, Plate 4.) Cf. Plutarch, "De Iside et Osiride;" in *Plutarch's Moralia*, V, tr. Frank Cole Babbitt, Loeb Classical Library, London, 1936, 23, 25.

20. Plutarch, 9.

21. *Opera Ioan. Goropii Becani*, "Hermathena," Antwerp, 1580, 106.

22. See *The Writings of Clement of Alexandria*, tr. William Wilson (Edinburgh, 1869), Vol. II, p. 254-261.

23. See Dorothea Waley Singer, *Giordano Bruno: His Life and Thought*, New York, 1950), pp. 120-125; V. Spampanato, *Vita di Giordano Bruno* (Messina, 1921), pp. 185-186, 379; *idem, Giordano Bruno e la letteratura dell'asino* (Portici, 1904); Henrie Cornelius Agrippa, *Of the Vanitie and Uncertaintie of Artes and Sciences*, tr. James Sanford (London, 1569, "A Digression in praise of the Asse," p. 183; Giordano Bruno, *Cabala del Cavallo Pegaso*, Paris (really London), 1585; Frances A. Yates, *Giordano Bruno and the Hermetic Tradition* (New York, 1969), pp. 259-261.

24. Cf. Bruno's "Sonetto in lode de l'Asino" in his *Cabala del Cavallo Pegaso:*
O Santa asinità, sant' ignoranza,
Santa stolticia, et pia divotione;
Qual sola puoi far l'anima si buone,
Ch' human ingegno et studio non l'avanza . . . .

25. Frances Yates (pp. 259-261) observes that by the ass Bruno is symbolizing the "mystical Nothing beyond the Cabalist Sephiroth." He "proclaims his admiration of Apuleius the magician, and of the full magic of the *Asclepius* by taking the Apuleian Ass as his hero." In her opinion, the symbol of "the Apuleian Ass as a natural philosopher was almost certainly suggested to Bruno by his great hero, Cornelius Agrippa of Nettesheim, the magician."

CHAPTER X

1. C.W. Lemmi, 'The Symbolism of the Classical Episodes in *The Faerie Queene*', PQ viii (1929), 271.

2. *Ibid.*, pp. 271-272; Ray Heffner, ed, *The Faerie Queens, Book Four* (Baltimore, 1935, Variorum Edition), pp. 196-199. Cf. Giovanni Boccaccio, *Genealogiae deorum gentilium libri*, ed. Vincenzo Romano, I (Bari, 1951), 124-134.

3. John Florio, *A Worlde of Wordes, Or, Most copious, and exact Dictionarie in Italian and English* (London, 1598), *s.v. Martello*.

4. *Ibid., s.v. Ammartellare, Ammartellato*.

5. *Vocabolario degli Accademici della Crusca* (Venezia, 1612), *s.v. Martello*.

6. Filippo Venuti da Cortona, Dittionario volgare, & Latino (Bolonia, 1578), p. 539.

7. *Il primo libro dell'opere burlesche. Di M. Francesco Berni, di M. Gio. della Casa, del Varchi, del Mauro* . . . (Firenze, 1548).

8. *Le terze rime di Messer Giovanni dalla Casa di Messer Bino e d'altri* (1542), in *Tutte le opere del Bernia in terza rima* (1545), 142-143. Lasca's poem 'Sopra la gelosia' (*Rime di Anton Francesco Grazzini*, II, Florence, 1742, pp. 146-151) also includes insomnia as a characteristic of jealousy.

9. *Le rime de M. Agnolo Firenzuola Fiorentino* (Fiorenza, 1549), p. 119.

10. Book I, V, 5. 11. Book I, XVIII, 58.

12. Giovanni Fabrini da Fighine Fiorentino, *Il Terentio Latino, comentato in lingua Toscana* (Vinegia, 1558), p. 125. Cf. *Le Comedie di Terentio volgari* (Vinegia, 1546), p. 39, 's'ella lo lodara per farti martello, sai tu?' See Terence's *Eunuchus* III. i.

13. For additional examples of *martello* in Italian literature, see *Vocabolario degli Accademici della Crusca*, quinta impressione, *s.v. Ammartellare, Ammartellato, Martello.*

14. *Ibid., s.v. Martello.*

15. *Adagiorum Des. Erasmi Roterodami chiliades quatuor* . . . *quibus adiectae sunt Henrici Stephani Animadversiones* (Parisiis, 1579), col. 27, Proverb No. 1116. See Morris Palmer Tilley, *A Dictionary of the Proverbs in England in the Sixteenth and Seventeenth Centuries* (Ann Arbor, 1950), H62, 'Between the Hammer and the anvil.'

16. *Hieroglyphica, sive de sacris Aegyptiorum, aliarumque gentium literis commentarij Ioannis Pierii Valeriani* (Basileae, 1575), p. 353 ('De malleo'). An illustration entitled 'Malorum Irritamentum' depicts a man beating out two swords on an anvil with a hammer.

17. Rosemary Freeman, *English Emblem Books* (London, 1948), p. 79.

18. Cesare Ripa, *Iconologia overo descrittione d'imagini delle virtù, vitij, affetti, passioni humane* (Padova, 1611), p. 521.

19. Robertus Stephanus, *Dictionarium seu thesaurus Latinae linguae* (Venice, 1551), *s.v. Zelotypus.* Cf. *Ambrosii Calepini Dictionarium* (Venetiis, 1571), *s.v. Zelotypus:* 'Zelotypus, . . . suspiciosus in amore, quenque id solicitum habet, ne quis eo perfruatur, quod ipse amat: quasi dicas formae aemulatorem. Nam ζηλος, aemulationem, & τυπος, formam significat.' The same combination of words (*zelos* and *typos*) could also be interpreted as 'blow of jealousy', for *typos* meant not merely *form*, but also 'a blow' or 'the effect or product of a blow'.

20. John Minsheu, *Ductor in Linguas, The Guide into Tongues* (London, 1617), *s.v. Gelous.*

21. *De oratore*, II, XXXIX.

22. *Bibliotheca Eliotae. Eliotes Dictionarie the second tyme enriched* . . . *by Thomas Cooper* (Londini, 1552), *s.v. Incus.* Cf. Stephanus, *s.v. Incus.*

23. Interpretations of 1 Kings VI. 7 sometimes associated the din of hammers with the blows of adversity.

24. Giordano Bruno, *The Candle Bearer*, tr. J.R. Hale, in *The Genius of the Italian Theater*, ed. Eric Bentley (New York, 1964), pp. 200, 207.

25. Giordano Bruno, *The Heroic Frenzies*, tr. Paul Eugene Memmo, Jr. (Chapel Hill, 1966), pp. 165-167.

26. Memmo, pp. 242-243, 250-251.

27. Cf. Robert Burton, *The Anatomy of Melancholy* (London, 1837), Vol. II,

pp. 299-399, 422-429, for solicitude and jealousy as symptoms of love.

28. Burton, II, p. 207n; Giovanni Michele Savonarola, *Practica medicinae* (Venice, 1497), HEH#95857, "De egritudinibus capitis"; Bernardus *de Gordonio, Practica sive Lilium Medicinae* (Venice, 1498), HEH #100359, "De egritudinibus capitis," on *ilisci* as "sollicitudo melancolica." Cf. D.W. Robertson, Jr., *A Preface to Chaucer* (Princeton, 1969), pp. 458-460, on Bernard of Gordon and his conception of *heroes* as a "melancholy solicitude arising from the love of a woman." Cf. *ibid.*, p. 111, on January's "Height fantasye and curious bisynesse" in the Merchant's Tale. Since *cura* is frequently translated as *business* (cf. Chaucer's translation of Boethius' *Consolation of Philosophy*), Spenser's allusion to Care as "Full busily unto his worke ybent" — ceaselessly laboring at manufacturing his "yron wedges" or "unquiet thoughts, that carefull minds invade" — and the reference to Scudamour's "dayly feare' that "busily" molests his idle brain in sleep would appear to contain literal as well as symbolic expressions of the lover's *cura* and *solicitudo melancholica*. In this connection Professor Harry Berger's suggestion ("Busirane and the War Between the Sexes," *ELR,* Vol. I [1971], pp. 99-121) that the name of the enchanter Busyrane in Book III signifies "busy-reign" (besides the usual interpretation of this figure as a symbol of tyrannic love, through the more obvious allusion to the Egyptian tyrant Busiris) acquires additional significance. Both Busyrane and the blacksmith Care would appear to function as personifications of the lover's "melancholy solicitude" (*ilishi* or *hereos*). It is significant that in Canto 11 of Book III (which treats the house of Busyrane and Love's spoils) the poet apostrophizes "Fowle Gealosie, that turnest love divine/ To ioyless dread, and mak'st the loving hart . . . feed it selfe with selfe-consuming smart." The conception of *hereos* or "heroic love" as melancholy solicitude is further emphasized by the fact that Scudamour leaves the house of Care "Full of melancholie and sad misfare. . . ." Cf. Burton, Vol. II, pp. 199-200 on the "tyrant love."

29. Cf. Burton, I, pp. 276-277, on Hyginus' Fable No. 220: and Hyginus' *Fabulae* in *Mythologici Latini,* ed. Hieronymus Commelinus (Heidelberg, 1599), p. 124, "Cura cum quendam fluvium transiret, vidit cretosum lutum; sustulit cogitabunda, & coepit fingere hominem."

30. See the B-text of *Piers Plowman,* Passus I, line 61.

31. *Aeneid,* VI, 274.

32. We need not, of course, infer that Spenser derived his conception of Care specifically from *this* source. Nevertheless the dictionaries provide a valuable compilation of classical references to *care*. Except where otherwise specified, all quotations from Cooper, Stephanus, or Calepine have been taken from their definitions of *cura*. The classical sources of these quotations are specified in the Renaissance dictionaries themselves, as well as in modern lexicons. For Spenser's relation to Renaissance dictionaries, see D.T. Starnes and E.W. Talbert, *Classical Myth and Learning in Renaissance Dictionaries* (Chapel Hill, N.C., 1955), pp. 44-110.

33. Lewis and Short, *A Latin Dictionary* (Oxford, 1933), *s.v. cura; Thesurus linguae Latinae* (Lipsiae, 1909), *s.v. cura; Totius latinitatis lexicon,* ed. Aegidius Forcellinus and Josephus Furlanettus (Prati, 1861), *s.v. cura.*

34. Burton Stevenson, *Stevenson's Book of Proverbs, Maxims and Familiar Phrases* (London, 1949), p. 288.

35. Ripa, p. 521.

36. Calepine.

37. Stephanus.

38. Cf. *N.E.D.*, *s.v. care*, 'care-pined hearts'.

39. Cf. Burton, Anatomy (London, 1837), Vol. I, p. 276.

40. Stephanus, Cf. *ibid.*, *s.v. vigil:* '**Curae** vigiles', 'Dolores mei vigilant sine fine', 'Curis vigilantibus excita', etc.; Calepine, *s.v. vigil*, 'Et renuant vigiles corpus miserabile curae'.

41. Cooper, *Thesaurus* (1573).

42. *Aeneid*, IV, 1-5.

43. Cf. the expression 'Carebedd', *N.E.D.*, *s.v. care*.

44. *The Complete Works of John Lyly*, ed. R. Warwick Bond (Oxford, 1902), II, 410.

45. Book III, XII, 16.

46. *N.E.D.*, *s.v. pinch*.

47. *The Bible* (Geneva, 1560). Cf. *N.E.D.*, *s.v. care*, 'carescorcht'.

48. Bond, II, 373.

49. *The Bible* (Geneva, 1560), Ecclesiasticus XXXVIII. 27-28. The Authorized Version substitutes 'will waste his flesh' for 'dryeth his flesh'. The idea of wakefulness emerges more strongly in the Vulgate ('vigilia sua') and in the Authorized Version ('And he will be wakeful').

50. Stephanus.

51. Thus Desportes refers to 'le mari jaloux de la belle Cypris Qui forge a Jupiter le tonnerre et l'orage'. (See *Oeuvres de Philippes Desportes*, ed. Alfred Michiels, Paris, 1858, p. 73). Cf. Robert Burton, *The Anatomy of Melancholy* (London, 1845), p. 634, 'Abraham was jealous of his wife because she was fair: so was Vulcan of his Venus, when he made her creaking shoes, saith Philostratus, *ne moecharetur, sandalio scilicet deferente,* that he might hear by them when she stirred.'

52. See *The Jewish Encyclopedia* (New York and London, 1902), *s.v. Cain; Encyclopaedia Judaica* (Berlin, 1932), *s.v. Kain; Testamentum patris nostri Adam,* ed. Michael Kmosko, *Patrologia Syriaca,* Pt. I, Vol. II (Paris, 1907), cols. 1313-1314, 1344, 1349.

53. *A Midsummer-Night's Dream*, II, ii.

54. *N.E.D.*, *s.v. Forgery*.

55. Italics mine.

56. *Due lezzioni di M. Benedetto Varchi* (Lione, 1560), p. 25. Varchi observes (pp. 25-26) that Ariosto employs a similar device in describing jealously (*Orlando Furioso*, Canto 31, Stanza I): 'Il che fece ancora l'Ariosto nella prima stanza; il quale innanzi, che le dicesse il nome propio, la dinoto con cinque vocaboli peggior l'uno, che l'altro; che furono questi, sospetto, timore, martire, frenesia, & rabbia.' Varchi's lecture on Casa's sonnet was subsequently translated into English by Robert Tofte, as *The Blazon of Iealousie: a Subject not written of by any heretofore* (London, 1615). In Varchi's opinion (Tofte, p. 7), no poet had

discussed the subject of jealousy 'so much' or 'so learnedly' as Ariosto and Casa.

57. See Appendix II, 'Rime di Baldassare Stampa', in Gaspara Stampa's *Rime*, ed. Abdelkader Salza (Bari, 1913), p. 204. Tofte translates this poem in the notes to *The Blazon of Jealousie* (p. 23) 'because it is annext unto this Worke of *Benedetto Varchies'*.

58. Tofte, p. 22.

59. *Ibid.*, pp. 9, 11.

60. A detailed discussion of the relationship of jealousy to envy, fear, and love also appears in an appendix entitled 'Se la Gelosia può esser senza biasimo' (Varchi, pp. 71-104). Jealousy is identified as a species of envy (p. 83), but (p. 88) 'il genere vero, & propio, & prossimo della gelosia non è invidia, ma paura, o sospetto, o dolore.' Moreover (pp. 98, 100), 'l'amore dilettevole non può essere senza gelosia, & . . . dove non è gelosia, o tanto o quanto, non è amore. . . . Anzi dico più, che quanto sarà maggior l'amore, tanto sarà maggior la gelosia, & all'encontro. . . . ' Cf. also 'Quistione Settima' of Varchi's *Lezzione d'Amore* ('Se Amore può essere senza gelosia'), in *Lezzioni di M. Benedetto Varchi* (Fiorenza, 1590), p. 375. See also Burton's discussion of jealousy, pp. 626-660.

61. Tofte, pp. 5-6, 12, 22, 55.

62. *Ibid.*, pp. 44-45.

63. Lemmi, pp. 271-272.

64. *Natalis Comitis Mythologiae* (Francofurti, 1584), p. 154.

65. *Ibid.*, p. 250.

66. Ripa, p. 194.

67. *Ibid.*, p. 495. 68. *Ibid.*, p. 488. 69. *Ibid.*, p. 487.

70. *Ibid.*, p. 533. The cock also represents solicitude and vigilance in Ripa's description of *Studio* (pp. 505-506), 'Il Gallo si pone da diversi per la sollecitudine, & per la vigilanza'.

71. *Ibid.*, p. 265.

72. See the descriptions of *Buio*, *Carro della Notte*, and *Hora Nona*, *ibid.*, pp. 54, 67, 229.

73. See *Genio Cattivo*, *ibid.*, p. 196.

74. *Ibid.*, p. 473.

75. Though the dog's conventional vigilance hardly requires comment, Spenser's reference to 'the dogs' which 'did barke and howle' all night is particularly appropriate, in view of Petronius' description of care as *latrans*. See *Thesaurus linguae Latinae*, *s.v. cura*.

76. John Upton, ed., *Spenser's Faerie Queene*, II (London, 1768), p. 592; Variorum Spenser IV, 197.

77. Boccaccio, pp. 129-134. Acheron's only son was Ascalaphus; his five daughters included the three furies (Alecto, Tisiphone, and Megaera), Victoria, and Styx.

78. Upton, II, 592.

79. Isidore of Seville, *Etymologiarum libri XX*, Book v. Chapter 31, 'De nocte' (*P.L.* LXXXII, Paris, 1850, col. 218). Cf. Rabanus Maurus, *De universo*, Book X, Chapter 7, 'De septem partibus noctis' (*P.L.* CXI, Paris, 1864, col. 292-293). See also Honorius Augustodunensis, *De imagine mundi*, Book II, Chapter 32, 'De

septem temporibus noctis' (*P.L.* CLXXII, Paris, 1854, col. 150-151).

80. *The Geography of Strabo* (London, 1927, Loeb Classical Library), IV, 168.

81. Pierius, p. 353, 'Sed super hoc plura legas homilia tertia in Hieremiam apud Adamantium'. See S. *Eusebii Hieronymi translatio homiliarum Origenis in Jeremiam,* 'Homilia tertia', in P.L. xxv (Paris, 1845), col. 606-615; 'Origenis in Jeremiam homilia XX, De eo quod scriptum est: *Quomodo confractus et contritus est malleus universae terrae',* in P.G. XIII (Paris, 1862), col. 525-534; cf. Jeremiah I, 23. For the source of Erasmus' proverb and Pierius' hammer symbolism, see P.G. XIII, col. 526: 'Jam quoddam est et apud nationes tritum vulgi sermone proverbium, ut de his qui anxietatibus et ingentibus malis premuntur, dicant, inter malleum sunt et incudem. Tu autem hoc refers ad Zabulum et draconem, qui istiusmodi semper in Scripturis pro varietate causarum nominibus insigniuntur.'

82. *Ibid.,* p. 527. Italics mine.

83. *Philo,* tr. F.H. Colson and G.H. Whitaker (London and New York, 1929), II, 393.

84. Origen's homily may have suggested another detail in stanza 37. The massive hammer of the sixth servant 'seem'd a rocke of Diamond it could rive.' Though the diamond's strength was proverbial, it is significant that Origen develops at length (col. 526-527) the comparison between the saint tried by temptations and the adamant tested by hammer and anvil.

85. **Upton, p. 592; cf. *Iliad,* XVIII, 410, πελωρ αιητον.**

86. *P.L.* VI (Paris, 1844), col. 213n.

87. Flavius Josephus, *The Antiquities of the Jews,* tr. William Whiston (London and New York, n.d.), p. 4; Isidore of Seville, *Etymologiarum* (*P.L.* LXXXII, Paris, 1850, col. 314, 318); Stephanus, *s.v. Cyclops.*

88. See William Nelson, *The Poetry of Edmund Spenser* (New York and London, 1963), p. 250, on Pythagoras' experiments with hammers and bells and on the *discordia concors* in Scudamour's heart.

89. For a detailed survey of this tradition, see Hans Oppermann, "Eine Pythagoraslegende," *Bonner Jahrbücher,* CXXX (Bonn, 1925), 284-301.

90. See Raimond van Marle, *Iconographie de l'art profane au moyen-âge et à la renaissance: allégories et symboles* (La Haye, 1932), pp. 216-225, 232, 258.

91. *Theorica Musice Franchini Gafuri Laudensis* (Milan, 1492), foll. 16*b*-17*b*. For a comparison of the two editions, see Gaetano Cesari's preface in the facsimile reproduction of the 1492 edition (Rome, 1934), 36-91.

92. Cf. the reproduction in Cesari, p. 50.

93. *Theorica Musice,* fol. 18*a*. For reproductions see Oppermann, 299; *Catalogue of Manuscripts and Early Printed Books . . . of the Library of J. Pierpont Morgan: Early Printed Books,* II (London, 1907), 116; Nan Cooke Carpenter, *Music in the Medieval and Renaissance Universities* (Norman, Okla., 1958), 179.

94. One of the most detailed accounts of Jubal's discovery occurs in Pedro Cerone's *El Melopeo* (Napoles, 1613), pp. 228-229. Though this work was published too late to influence Spenser, it provides a valuable example of how completely the Pythagoras legend could be retailored to fit Jubal and his blacksmith brother.

95. *Interpretatio Nomin. Hebr. Chald. Graec. & Lat.* (Paris, 1532), fol. 36.

96. *Ovid's Metamorphosis. Englished, Mythologiz'd and Represented in Figures* (Oxford, 1632), 157.

97. G.C. Macaulay (ed.), *The Complete Works of John Gower. The English Works,* II (Oxford, 1901), 419-422.

98. See Calvin Huckabay, "The Structure of Book IV of the *Faerie Queens,"* *Studia Neophilologica,* XXVII (1955), 53-64.

99. Cf. John Hollander, *The Untuning of the Sky* (Princeton, 1961), passim.

100. Spenser's poetic exploitation of the Pythagoras legend should not obscure the probability that, like most of his contemporaries, he accepted it as fact rather than fiction. The tradition of the musical smithy went virtually unchallenged until Dr. Charles Burney delivered the deathblow in 1789. See Charles Burney, *A General History of Music,* ed. Frank Mercer, I (London, 1935), 342-347.

CHAPTER XI

1. Benjamin Whichcote, *Select Sermons* (Edinburgh, 1742), p. 78, *"Truth clears itself, and discloses its contrary, Error."*

2. Ovid employs the terms *error* and *fallacy* to describe Daedalus' maze (*Metamorphoses,* Book VIII).

3. *The Faerie Queene,* Book One (A Variorum Edition, Baltimore, 1932), p. 182. Cf. Hesiod's *Theogony,* lines 295-305, and Spenser's Echidna (FQ, VI, vi 9-12).

4. Though Echidna was commonly interpreted in terms of natural phenomena, this conception was irrelevant to Spenser's Errour. See Ioannes Pierius Valerianus, *Hieroglyphica* (Basle, 1575), p. 103. Cf. Hans Flach (ed.), *Glossen und Scholien zur Hesiodischen Theogonie* (Leipzig, 1876), *passim.*

5. Ludovicus Caelius (Richerius) Rhodiginus, *Lectionum Antiquarum Libri XXX* (Basle, 1566), p. 478.

· 6. Achilles Bocchius, *Symbolicarum Quaestionum de Universo Genere* . . . *Libri Quinque* (Bononiac, 1555), pp. 304-6.

7. Pierius Valerianus, p. 16.

8. Franciscus Sanctius Brocensis, *Comment in And. Alciati Emblemata* (Lugduni,· 1573), p. 69. See Alciati's Emblem No. 14.

9. See Flach, p. 246. Cf. Sanctius, p. 69, "Haec Scholiastes Hesiodi tamen interpretes in Theogonia, Chimaeram sensu allegorico tres exponunt Rhetoricae partes, Dicanium seu iudicialem, Panegyricam, seu demonstrativam, Symbuleuticam, seu deliberativam." This allegorical explanation of the Chimaera in terms of rhetoric was also ascribed to St. Gregory Nazianzen. Cf. Pierius Valerianus, p. 16.

10. For the parallel with Philologia in Martianus Capella's *De Nuptiis Philologiae et Mercurii,* see F.J.E. Raby, *A History of Secular Latin Poetry in the Middle Ages* (Oxford, 6934), I, p. 103; Ernst Robert Curtius, *European Literature and the Latin Middle Ages,* tr. Willard R. Trask (London, 1953), p. 38; C.S. Lewis, *The Allegory of Love* (London, 1953), p. 80.

11. FQ, I (Variorum), pp. 184, 458.

12. *Corpus Reformatorum,* ed. C.G. Bretschneider, VII (Halle a.S., 1840), col. 53ln.

13. *Ibid.,* col. 531.

14. *Omnia Andreae Alciati V.C. Emblemata: Cum Commentariis . . . per Claudium Minoem Divionensem* (Antwerp, 1581), p. 39. The motto of Emblem No. 5 is Sapientia humana stultitia est apud Deum. For a study of Renaissance anti-intellectualism, see Howard Schultz, *Milton and Forbidden Knowledge* (New York, 1955).

15. Alciati, p. 40.

16. *Ibid.,* pp. 40-1.

17. Book III, Prose 12; *The Works of Geoffrey Chaucer,* ed. F.N. Robinson, Second Edition (London, 1957) p. 357.

18. Raby, II, p. 36.

19. *Johannis Calvini . . . Institutionis Christianae Religionis Libri Quatuor* (Genevae, 1617), fol. 46.

20. *Ibid.,* fol. 6. 21. *Ibid.,* p. 23.

22. Richard Hooker, *Of the Laws of Ecclesiastical Polity,* I (Everyman's Library, London, n.d.), p. 20.

23. Vellutello, *op. cit.,* on *Inferno,* Canto I.

24. For other tree-lists, see Robinson, pp. 793-4; Robert A. Pratt, "Chaucer's Claudian," *Speculum,* XXII (1947), p. 423.

25. Although there is a reference to Chaucer's "errour" in line 156, this has no bearing on the tree-list of lines 176 ff.

26. FQ, I, j, 7.

27. R.D. (Robert Dallyngton?), tr., *The Strife of Love in a Dream* ed. Andrew Lang (London, 1890), pp. 5-6. This English translation of Colonna's work was printed at London in 1592 (*ibid.,* p. v)

28. Anguillara, fol. 37.

29. Cf. Ripa, p. 243. "L'Heresia, secondo San Tomaso sopra il libro quarto delle sentenze, & altri Dottori, é errore dell'Intelletto, al quale la volontà ostinatamente adherisce intorno à quello, che si deve credere, secondo la Santa Chiesa Cattolica Romana."

30. John Lydgate, *The Pilgrimage of the Life of Man, EETS, es,* LXXXIII, Part II (London, 1901), p. 459.

31. *Ibid.,* p. 506. For another parallel with *The Pilgrimage of the Life of Man,* see FQ, I (Variorum), p. 414, where F.M. Padelford compares the Redcross Knight's encounter with Errour and the pilgrim's meeting with Rude Entendement.

32. Anguillara, fol. 113.

33. For the labyrinth as a symbol of "carnale amore," see Giovanni Boccaccio, *Il Corbaccio o il Laberinto d'Amore,* ed. Nicola Bruscoli (Bari, 1940), p. 195.

34. *The Convivio of Dante Alighieri* (London, 1940), p. 351.

35. Erasmo di Valvasone, *La Caccia* (Venice, 1602), fol. 155.

36. (Petrus Berchorius,) *Metamorphosis Ovidiana Moraliter a Magistro Thoma Waleys Anglico . . . Explanata* (Paris, 1515), fol. lxix, "Dic quod dedalus est peccator quem minos idem diabolus in labyrintho viciorum et bonorum huius

mundi inclusit; et ipsum tot criminibus circunvoluit: quod viam in terram exeundi non invenit: immo sepe fit quod ubi exire de labyrintho mundi vel pote crediderit ibidem fortius se immittit. ps. Viam civitatis habitaculi non invenerunt. Quare quicunque in labyrinthum mundi vel peccati se immiscuerit vel implicaverit per malas consuetudines exinde amplius vix exibit. Mat. v. Amen dico tibi non exibis inde."

37. *Emblemata Nicolai Reusneri* (Frankfurt, 1581), pp. 151-2, "irremediabilis error. / Sic mundus latebris caecis, flexuque doloso / Corruptos animos hominum frustratur: & implet / Innumeras errore vias: vis unde reverti / Saepe datur: tanta est miseri fallacia mundi."

38. *The Heroicall Devices of M. Claudius Paradin,* tr. P.S. (London, 1591), pp. 118-9 "This simbole of the Labirinth, which the Lord of Boisdaulphin, Archbishop of Ambrune useth, may perchance signifie, that we are lead by the grace of God to finde the way that leadeth to eternall life, the same giving the thread as it were of his holy precepts into our hands, which when we have once taken hold of, and do follow, we turne away from the dangerous wandrings, and feareful by wayes of this world."

39. Lang, p. 154. An anonymous poem in the same volume ("Anonymi Elegia ad Lectorem") likewise refers to the labyrinth as a symbol of human life ("expressaque tota / in Laberintheis vita hominem tenebris"). Cf. Conti (p. 743), "Nihil aliud significare voluerunt per illum labyrinthum, nisi perplexam esse, multisque difficultatibus implicatam vitam hominum, cum ex aliis aliae semper graviores oriantur: e quibus nemo se, nisi per singularem prudentiam & fortitudinem, explicare potest." The title-page of Arnold Freitag's *Mythologia Ethica* (Antwerp, 1579) refers to the same symbol ("In quo humanae vitae labyrintho demonstrato, virtutis semita pulcherrimis praeceptis, veluti Thesei filo docetur"); see Henry Green (ed.), *Whitney's "Choice of Emblemes"* (London, 1866), Plate 38.

40. Lang, p. 66.

41. St. Augustine, *The City of God,* tr. John Healey, ed. R.V.G. Tasker, I (London, 1950), p. 231.

42. *Ibid.,* p. 237.

43. Cf. Alciati, p. 347.

44. Roland H. Botting, 'Spenser's Errour', P.Q. XVI (1937), 73-8; *The Faerie Queene, Book One,* A Variorum Edition (Baltimore, 1932), pp. 182-3: Hesiod, *Theogony,* ll. 295 ff.

45. Edward Topsell, *The History of Four-Footed Beasts and Serpents* (1608), 1658 ed., p. 800.

46. *Ambrosii Calepini Dictionarium* (Lyons, 1647), *s.v.* 'Echidna'.

47. *Ioannis Pierii Valeriani Bellunensis, Hieroglyphica, Seu de Sacris Aegyptorum aliarumque Gentium Literis Commentarii* (Venice, 1604), pp. 138-45.

48. Topsell, p. 354. Cf. *Dio Chrysostom,* I, Loeb Classical Library (1932), pp. 236-47, 'The Fifth Discourse: a Libyan Myth'.

49. Cf. *Herodotus,* II, Loeb Classical Library (1921), pp. 206-9; *Diodorus of Sicily,* II, Loeb Classical Library (1935), pp. 26-7.

50. Topsell, p. 800.

51. Nonnos, *Dionysiaca,* II, Loeb Classical Library (1940), p. 81.

52. *Herodotus,* p. 206.

53. *Diodorus of Sicily,* p. 26.

54. Sir Thomas Browne, *Works,* ed. Geoffrey Keynes, II (1928), p. 237; Botting, pp. 75-6.

55. Browne, p. 238; Botting, p. 76. Cf. Thomas Bewick, *A Natural History of Reptiles, Serpents, and Insects* (Alnwick, 1809), pp. 11-12.

56. Browne, p. 238. In *Pseudodoxia epidemica* (Book III, chap. xvi, "Of the Viper") Browne specifically rejects the tradition that young vipers gnaw their way through their mother's body; on the contrary, "the young one (*sic*) supposed to break through the belly of the Dam, will upon any fright for protection run into it; for then the old one receives them in at her mouth, which way the fright being past, they will return again, which is a peculiar way of refuge." Though the two superstitions are mutually contradictory, Milton and Spenser appear to have incorporated (with some slight modifications) elements of both. The fact that in both instances the litter exhibits behavior characteristic of a "generation of vipers" is a striking example of literary decorum.

57. Grant McColley, *'Paradise Lost',* H.T.R. xxxii (1939), 195; John M. Patrick, 'Milton, Phineas Fletcher, Spenser, and Ovid—Sin at Hell's Gates', *N. & Q.,* n.s. III (1956), 384-6.

58. Ann Gossman, 'Milton, Prudentius, and the Brood of Sin', *N.&Q.,* n.s. IV (1957), 439-40. See *Hamartigenia,* ll. 562-636.

59. Albertus Magnus, *De Animalibus* (Venice, 1519), p. 203. Cf. ibid. p. 202, on *dracopopodes:* 'Dracopopodes dicunt greci serpentem de ordine tertio & genere draconum quem dicunt vultum virgineum imberbis hominis habere: & talem serpentem a fide dignis audivi interfectum esse in insula Germanie: & diu monstratum nostris temporibus omnibus volentibus cum videre donec computruit: & morsus eius est sicut aliorum draconum.'

60. *Herodotus,* pp. 136-7. 61. Aristotle, Minor Works, Loeb Classical Library (1936), p. 321.

62. Pliny, *Natural History,* III. Loeb Classical Library (1940), p. 401.

63. Aeliani, *de Natura Animalium,* ed. Friderieus Jacobs, I (Jena, 1832), p. 10.

64. Nicander, quoted by Topsell, p. 802.

65. Migne, *Patrologia Latina,* LXXXII (Paris, 1850), col. 443.

65a. Topsell, p. 800. Calepine (s.v. 'Vipera' and 'Echidna') cites the same etymologies.

66. J.F. Gilliam, 'Scylla and Sin', *P.Q.* XXIX (1950), 345-7.

67. Milton's substitution of Scylla's dogs for the viper's brood may involve a Latin pun. In describing the behaviour of vipers, Isidore and other commentators had referred to the young serpents as *catuli.* In its broadest sense, this term could comprehend the young of any animal, but it normally referred specifically to young dogs.

68. See Hesiod's *Theogony,* in *The Homeric Hymns and Homerica,* Loeb Classical Library (1936), pp. 100-3.

69. Carolus Stephanus, *Dictionarium Historicum, Geographicum, Poeticum,* 1596 (s.v. 'Typhoeus') declared that after rebelling against Zeus. Typhoeus had been blasted by lightning '& sub Inarimen insulam detrusus, ut placet Homer. in

Catalogo Virg. 1. Aeneid . . . Lucan. lib.4'.

70. Campe (whom Nonnos had described as 'a woman to the middle of her body') was likewise a 'gaoloress' of the giants and Cyclopes in Tartarus. See Apollodorus, *The Library,* I. Loeb Classical Library (1921), p. 11.

71. For the parallel between Satan and Typhon, see Davis P. Harding, *Milton and the Renaissance Ovid,* Illinois Studies in Language and Literature, XXX (Urbana, 1946), 85.

72. Stephanus, s.v. 'Cerberus'. Cf. Calepine, s.v. 'Cerberus'.

73. I.e. *re-mordere.*

74. Mark ix. 44, 46, 48.

75. Topsell, p. 800.

76. Browne, p. 239.

77. *Ibid.,* p. 240.

78. Pierius, p. 146. 'Quid vero malum daemonem per Viperinam figuram iudicamus, multorum consensus accedit. Nam & apud D. Hieronymum Draco inter Diaboli cognomenta numerantur. . . .' Jerome, commenting on Job xx. 16, explained the viper as 'aperta diaboli tentatio' (Migne, *Patrologia Latina,* XXIII (Paris, 1845), col. 1134).

79. For the influence of Ovid, Fletcher, and Spenser on Milton's Sin, see A.W. Verity's edition of *Paradise Lost* (Cambridge, 1936), II, 418-19.

CHAPTER XII

1. The most thorough discussion of classical, medieval, and Renaissance analogues to Milton's serpent-woman is to be found in John M. Patrick's Milton's Conception of Sin as Developed in Paradise Lost (Logan, Utah, 1960), Patrick calls attention to the frequently-neglected parallels with Nonnos' Campe, the serpent-footed giants of classical mythology, and other examples of the human-serpent symmelus. Emphasizing the link between the theriomorphic shape of Sin and the metamorphosis tradition, he argues that the "dominant idea in all these closely related pictures of sin is that of *man somehow becoming beast."* See also John M. Patrick, "Milton, Phineas Fletcher, Spenser and Ovid—Sin at Hell's Gates," *N & Q,* n.s., III (1956), 384-386 (cited henceforth as Patrick); A.W. Verity (ed., *Paradise Lost,* II (Cambridge, 1936), 418-419; J.F. Gilliam, "Scylla and Sin," *PQ,* XXIX (1950), 345-347; Davis P. Harding, *Milton and the Renaissance Ovid,* Illinois Studies in Language and Literature, XXX (Urbana, 1946), 95-98; Thomas Newton (ed.), *Paradise Lost,* I (London, 1778), 141-144, 150-151; John S.P. Tatlock, "Milton's *Sin and Death,"* *MLN,* XXI (1906), 239-240; Grant McColley, "Paradise Lost," *Harvard Theological Review,* XXXII (1939), 181-235; Richard Meadowcourt, *An Essay upon Milton's Imitations of the Ancients* (London, 1741), pp. 17-19; Douglas Bush, *Mythology and the Renaissance Tradition* (Minneapolis, 1932), pp. 284-285 n.

2. Cf. Errour (*FQ,* I, i, 13-26) and Echidna (*FQ,* V,x,10; V,xi,23; VI,vi,10-12). See Merritt Y. Hughes (ed.), *Paradise Lost* (New York, 1935), pp. 62 n., 67 n.; Newton, I, 143 n.

3. *The Locusts, or Apollyonists,* I, 10-12; *The Purple Island,* XII, 27-31. See

Verity, p. 418; Tatlock, p. 239.

4. *Theogony,* lines 294 ff. See Verity, p. 419; Newton, p. 143 n.

5. John Upton (ed.), *Spenser's Faerie Queene,* II (London, 1758), 341, has been virtually the only critic to note this parallel. See *Dio Chrysostom,* I (Loeb Classical Library: London, 1932), 237-247; "The Fifth Discourse: A Libyan Myth": "The face was that of a woman, a beautiful woman. The breasts and bosom, and the neck, too, were extremely beautiful. The rest of the body was hard and protected by scales, and all the lower part was snake, ending in the snake's baleful head. . . . And while they overcame other creatures by force, they used guile with man, giving them a glimpse of their bosom and breasts and at the same time they infatuated their victims by fixing their eyes upon them. . . . But as soon as a man came within reach they seized him in their grasp; for they had clawlike hands too, which they had kept concealed at first. Then the serpent would promptly sting and kill him with its poison; and the dead body was devoured by the serpent and the rest of the beast together." In Dio's view, this legend reveals "the character of the passions, that they are irrational and brutish and that, by holding out the enticement of some pleasure, they win over the foolish by guile and witchery and bring them to a most sad and pitiable end. These things we should always keep before our eyes to deter us . . . whenever we are in love with luxury, or money, or sensual indulgence, or fame, or any other pleasure, lest, coming too near to these unscrupulous passions, we be seized by them for the most shameful destruction and ruin conceivable."

6. Nonnos, *Dionysiaca,* II (Loeb Classical Library: London, 1940), 79-81: "A thousand crawlers from her viperish feet . . . were fanning Enyo to a flame, a mass of misshapen coils. Round her neck flowered fifty various heads of wild beasts: some roared with lion's heads . . . ; others were spluttering foam from the tusks of wild boars; her countenance was the very image of Scylla with a marshalled regiment of thronging dogs' heads. Doubleshaped, she appeared a woman to the middle. of her body, with clusters of poison-spitting serpents for hair. Her giant form, from the chest to the parting-point of the thighs, was covered all over with a bastard shape of hard sea-monsters' scales. The claws of her wide scattered hands were curved like a crooktalon sickle. From her neck over her terrible shoulders, with tail raised high over her throat, a scorpion with icy sting sharp-whetted crawled and coiled upon itself. . . . Such was manifold shaped Campe . . . , that blackwinged nympth of Tartaros . . . ."

7. Apollodorus, *The Library,* I (Loeb Classical Library: London, 1921), 49. Typhon set Delphyne to guard the crippled Zeus and his severed sinews in the Corycian cave: ". . . and he set to guard them the she-dragon Delphyne, who was a half-bestial maiden."

8. *Diodorus of Sicily,* II (Loeb Classical Library: London, 1935), 27: "At a later time, as the Scythians recount the myth, there was born among them a maiden sprung from the earth; the upper parts of her body as far as her waist were those of a woman, but the lower parts were those of a snake. With her Zeus lay and begat a son whose name was Scythes. This son became more famous than any who had preceded him and called the folk Scythians after his own name."

9. *Herodotus,* II (Loeb Classical Library: London, 1921), 207-209. While

searching for his mares, which had been spirited away during his sleep, Hercules came "to the land called the Woodland, and there he found in a cave a creature of double form that was half damsel and half serpent; above the buttocks she was a woman, below them a snake. When he saw her he was astonished, and asked her if she had anywhere seen his mares straying; she said that she had them, and would not restore them to him before he had intercourse with her; which Heracles did in hope of this reward." The monster was queen of the country, and from Scythes — the third of three sons whom she bore to Hercules — descended the whole line of Scythian kings.

10. *Natalis Comitis Mythologiae* (Frankfurt, 1584), pp. 657-660; "atque nos aliquando his Graecis carminibus universam vim iniustitiae aut iniuriarum attigimus ludentes." In Laurentius Gottius' translation Comes' figure of Unrighteousness (αδιχια) became *Improbitas:*

> Improbitate magis non est mortalibus ulla
> > Res gravis: humanum destruit illa genus. . . .
> Tempora lambebant densi pro crinibus angues,
> > Atque ungues curvi, pesque draconis erat.
> Affectare ausa est coelestia regna tonantis,
> > Tentavitque volans deiicere inde Deos.

11. See my article, "Sin and the Serpent of Genesis 3," *MP*, LIV (1957), 217-220.

12. Patrick, 385-386, has cited classical references to the serpent-footed giants in Apollodorus, Ovid., Claudian, and Horace. Cf. *Aetna*, in *Minor Latin Poets* (Loeb Classical Library: London, 1934), 362-363, and the note on this subject in Apollodorus, I, 43 n. Comes (648) quoted Ovid's reference to their serpentine feet in the *Fasti*. Pierius cited Aetna, the *Fasti*, and other works on this point (*Ioannis Pierii Valeriani Bellunensis, Hieroglyphica* [Venice, 1604], 160).

13. Patrick, 386 n. Cf. Frazer's note in Apollodorus, I, 47 n; Comes 654, 656; Vincenzo Cartari, *Le Imagini dei Dei degli Antichi* (Padua, 1602), 401; "Il di sopra era in forma di huomo tutto coperto di penne . . . . Le gambe erano serpenti, che ne havevano de gli altri attorno. . . . " Cartari (400) and the edition of Comes' *Mythologiae* published at Patavia in 1637 (345) included illustrations of this figure as human from the waist up, with serpentine legs. Cf. Milton's reference to "*Typhon* huge ending in snaky twine" in "On the Morning of Christ's Nativity."

14. Upton, II, 341. See *Marci Hieronymi Vidae Christiados Libri Sex* (Oxford, 1725), p. 9:

> ". . . adsunt
> Lucifugi coetus varia atque bicorpora monstra,
> Pube tenus hominum facies, verum hispida in anguem
> Desinit ingenti sinuata volumine cauda."

15. Apollodorus, II, 77: "Cecrops, a son of the soil, with a body compounded of man and serpent, was the first king of Attica. . . . "

16. *Hygini Fabulae,* ed. Mauricius Schmidt (Jena, 1872), p. 20: "ex semini eius [Vulcani] . . . natus est puer, qui inferiorem partem draconis habuit; quem Erichthonium ideo nominarunt. . . . " Pierius (166) also referred to "Erichthonium, quem alij pedes Anguineos habuisse . . . scribunt. . . . "

17. See Pierius (161): "Boream quoque ventum aiunt hieroglyphice Viperinis caudis, pedum loco, praeditum figurari . . ."

18. *Inferno,* Canto 17. See Tatlock, p. 239.

19. Harding, p. 98; Meadowcourt, p. 18; Newton, p. 144 n.

20. Virgil, II (Loeb Classical Library: London, 1946), 408-411.

21. *Ciris,* line 56, "candida succinctam latrantibus inguina monstris." *Metamorphoses,* XIII, lines 732-3, "illa feris atram canibus succingitus alvum, virginis ora gerens. . . ." Line 75 of Virgil's *Sixth Eclogue,* is identical with the verse from *Ciris.* See Newton, p. 143 n. Cf. *Metamorphoses,* VII, line 65; XIV, lines 59 ff.

22. Hyginus, 25: "Ex Typhone gigante et Echidna Gorgon, . . . Scylla quae superiorem partem mulieris inferiorem canis et canes sex ex se natos habebat. . . ." Both of Scylla's parents were half-serpentine.

23. Nonnos, II, 80.

24. Comes, 876.

25. Dante (*Inferno,* Canto 25) and Ovid (*Metamorphoses,* IV, lines 563 ff.) provide obvious parallels for the transformation of man into serpent; both passages have sometimes been regarded as Milton's "sources" for Satan's similar transformation in Book X.

26. The account of Death's violent birth, as well as the behavior of Sin's litter of dogs in re-entering her body and gnawing her bowels, was probably influenced by contemporary superstitions about vipers. Cf. Ann Gossman, "Milton, Prudentius, and the Brood of Sin," *N&Q,* n.s., IV (1957), 439-440.

27. Hughes, p. 67 n; Patrick, p. 385.

28. Tatlock, p. 239; Patrick, p. 385.

29. Like original sin, Improbitas (Ἀδικία) destroys the human race; like Satan, she attempted to seize Heaven and overthrow God.

30. See note 11. There is also a remote parallel in Pierius' interpretation of the giants as a symbol of evil (160): "Diodorus quoque per Serpentum voluminibus implicatum, malum interpretatur, praecipueque Gigantum genus qui terrarum orbem olim oppressere."

31. Gilliam, p. 346.

32. Gilliam, p. 346.

33. Though Apollodorus' Delphyne was a guardian, she was not, strictly speaking, infernal.

34. Echidna "kept guard" in a subterranean cave in Arima.

35. Apollodorus, I, 11, described Campe as the "gaoloress" of the giants in Tartarus.

36. Verity, p. 422.

37. Herodotus, II, 206.

38. Nonnos, II, 80.

39. Diodorus, I, 93, used the same expression (διφυης) to describe Cecrops. The adjective is not uncommon, however; Apollodorus (I, 12) applied it to Chiron.

40. *Aeneid,* Book VI, line 286.

41. Line 67. See note 47 for a similar description of Erichthonius.

42. The Libyan monster had a snake's head, rather than a sting, at the end of its

tail (Dio Chrysostom, I, 241).

43. *Inferno,* Canto 17. See Edmund Spenser, *The Faerie Queene, Book One,* A Variorum Edition (Baltimore, 1932), p. 183.

44. Patrick, p. 385.

45. Herodotus, II, 207-209; Diodorus, II, 27.

46. Apollodorus, II, 76.

47. Hyginus, 20. Cf. Comes, 998-9.

48. Patrick, pp. 385-386.

49. Harding, pp. 85-87.

50. See note 14.

51. Nonnos, II, 79 n.

52. Comes, 657, The verses on   Αδιχια **appear** in the chapter "De Typhone."

53. Herodotus, II, 207.

54. Edward Topsell, *The History of Four-Footed Beasts and Serpents* (London, 1658), p. 354.

55. Geoffrey Keynes (ed.,), *The Works of Thomas Browne* (London, 1928), III, 95.

56. See Peter Comestor, *Historia scholastica,* chap. xxi: "Elegit (Lucifer) etiam quoddam genus serpentis, ut ait Beda, virgineum vultum habens, quia similia similibus applaudunt, et movit ad loquendum linguam eius, tamen nescientis, sicut, et per fanaticos, et energumenos loquitur, nescientes" (J.-P. Migne (ed.), *Patrologia Latina,* Vol. CXCVIII, col. 1072). Cf. St. Bonaventura, *Perlustratio in secundum librum sententiarum* (Friburgi, 1493), Question 2 to Distinction 21; "Verum est enim quod si fuisset in effigie humana affabilior fuisset. sed divina providentia non debuit hoc permittere. sed cautelam diaboli debuit temptare. & ideo concessum est sibi corpus serpentis quod tamen habebat faciem virginis. sicut dicit Beda. & religuum corpus erat serpentis. ut sic ex una parte posset latere. ex altera deprehendi." Alexander of Hales, *Liber secundus summae* (Nuremberg, 1481). cites the same tradition, in Question 119: "serpens enim ille sicut dicit beda, vultum **habuit** virgineum. ut per simile facilius deciperet. similitudo enim mater est falsitatis." In discussing this point, Pererius and De Pitigianis both cite the commentary by Dionysius Carthusianus on Book II of the *Sentences,* Distinction 21.

57. See the following treatises ascribed to Bede in the *Patrologia Latina: Hexaemeron, sive libri quatuor in principium Genesis* (Vol. XCI) and *In Pentateuchum commentarii* (Vol. XCI) and the following dubious or spurious works: *De sex dierum creatione liber* (Vol. XCIII) and *Quaestiones super Genesim* (Vol. XCIII). I have discovered in none of these writings any reference to the tradition that the serpent of Genesis 3 had a woman's face.

58. See introduction to Konrad von Megenberg, *Das Buch der Natur,* ed., Franz Pfeiffer (Stuttgart, 1861), p. xxix.

59. Ibid., pp. 27-71. Cf. Vincent of Beauvais, *Speculi maioris tomi quatuor,* Vol. I: *Tota naturalis historia* (Venice, 1951), p. 251: "Ex libro de nat. re. Draconcopedes serpentes magni sunt, & potentes, facies virgineas habentes humanis similes, in draconum corpus desinentes. Credible est huius generis illum fuisse, per quem diabolus Evam decepit, quia (sicut dicit Beda) virgineum vultum

habuit. Huic etiam diabolus se coniungens vel applicans, ut consimili forma mulierem alliceret, faciem ei tantum ostendit, & reliquam parten corporis arborum frondibus occultavit."

60. Hermann Deimling (ed.), *The Chester Plays*, Part I ("Early English Text Society, Extra Series," Vol. LXII (London, 1892)), p. 28. In this play the devil disguises himself as an adder with wings and a maiden's face:

"A manner of Adder is in this place, that wynges
like a byrd she hase, feete as an Adder, a maydens
face ; her kinde I will take" (ibid., p. 28).

61. See Nicolaus de Lyra, *Expositiones librorum Testamenti Veteris ac Novi;* (Rome, 1471) on Genesis 3: "Aliqui tamen dicunt quod ille serpens habebat faciem gratiosam & virgineam. Sed hoc de scriptura nullam habet autoritatem." Franciscus de Pitigianis, *Commentaria scholastica in Genesium* (Venice, 1615), p. 471, repeats verbatim Pererius' criticism: "Verum hanc sententiam merito deridit Lyranus: reperiri enim tale genus serpentis, adhuc inauditum, & a nullo philosophorum, aut cui fides haberi possit, traditum est: quocirca ut plane fabulosum & commentitum explodi debet" (cf. Benedictus Pererius, *Commentarium et disputationum in Genesim, tomi quatuor* (Coloniae Aggrippinae, 1601), p. 280).

62. Pererius, p. 280.

63. Cf. Masolino's painting of the temptation, in the Brancacci Chapel in Florence.

64. Scholastic tradition tends, on the whole, to support the second version rather than the third. The statements that the serpent had the *faciem* or *vultum* of a maiden do not, however, specifically exclude the representation of the tempter as a human from the waist up. At least one commentator, furthermore, seems to authorize the latter interpretation; see Guillermus Vorrillo, *Quatuor librorum sententiarum compendium* (Basel, 1510). Question 2 to Distinction 21 of Book II: " . . . quod haec tentatio incepit a serpente: patet manifeste Genesis. Sed qualis fuit hic serpens? Dicit Beda, quod inferius habebat modum serpentis, superius pulcherrimae virginis."

For a painter the third version offered potentialities denied by the others. Besides being more striking pictorially, it allowed the tempter to offer Eve the fruit with his own hand. The ordinary serpent could, at the most, hold the forbidden apple in its mouth, and the serpent with only a woman's head could merely ebguile with words.

65. Giovanni Battista Andreini, *L'Adamo* (Milan, 1617), pp. 42, 44, 46, 49, 78, 81. In Act II, scene 3, the Serpent describes himself thus:

"Ma perche van le sia
Saver, che quegli son, ch'al gran Fattore
E d'eterno terrore
Fra mille squamme di dipinta serpe
Parte ombrai di me stesso, e 'l resto volli
Humano tutto, e di donzella il volto."

A marginal gloss cites as authorities Bonaventura and Bede: "D. Bonavent. 2 libr. sententiarum dist. 21. q. 2. inquit, quod serpens tam etsi reliquam partem corporis habebat serpentis erat tamen eius facies, Virginis sic testante Beda" (p. 43).

66. Pietro Aretino, *Il Genesi* (Vinegia, 1591), Book I: "Lo scaltrito dello avversario transformato del primo Agnolo nel primo Demonio, invidiando lo stato concesso al Re del mondo dallo Imperadore del Paradiso, celando tra le frondi lo scaglioso del suo busto, e del suo estremo apparito in sembianza di Donzella, si acconcio ne gliocchi (sic), e ne i gesti tutta la mansuetudine, e tutta la piacevolezza, nella quale il sagace della fraude si reca."

67. William Hunnis, *A Hyve Full of Hunnye: Contayning the Firste Booke of Moses, Called Genesis, Turned into English Meetre* (London, 1578), p. 4: "This serpent was Lucyfer which a little before for hys outragious pride was driven out of heaven and as Bede, and the maister of Stories saith, went upryghte, and had the face of a woman: but others doe wryte that God permitted the Devell to speake in the (serpent)."

68. See n. 65.

69. Verity, pp. 418-419.

70. Newton, p. 143 n., and Meadowcourt, p. 19, suggested an additional analogue, in Horace's *Ars Poetica* (lines 3-4).

71. W. Hamilton Fyfe (ed.), *Aristotle's Art of Poetry* (Oxford, 1940), p. 41. Fyfe interprets this passage as meaning that "delineation of character . . . must be *appropriate* to the kind of person represented, and *like* the original in the saga story, e.g., Achilles in any tragedy must have high courage and a hasty temper."

72. Horace, *Ars Poetica*, line 119.

73. Lodovico Castelvetro, *Poetica d'Aristotele Vulgarizzata et Sposta* (Basilea, 1576), p. 326.

74. Cf. *Ars Poetica*, lines 120-122.

75. Castelvetro, pp. 326-327.

CHAPTER XIII

1. Cf. James Whaler, "The Miltonic Simile," *PMLA*, XLVI (1931), 1034-74; idem, "Compounding and Distribution of Similes in *Paradise Lost*," *MP*, XXVIII (1931), 313-27; "Grammatical Nexus of Miltonic Simile," *JEGP*, XXX (1931), 327-34; Christopher Grose, "Some Uses of Sensuous Immediacy in *Paradise Lost*," *HLQ*, XXXI (1968), 211-22; idem, "The Rhetoric of Miltonic Simile" Diss. Washington Univ. 1966; and my "The Devil and Pharaoh's Chivalry," *MLN*, LXXV (1960), 197-201, and " 'From the Safe Shore': Milton and Tremellius," *Neophilologus*, XL (1960), 218-19.

2. For Milton's use of typology, see William G. Madson, *From Shadowy Types to Truth: Studies in Milton's Symbolism* (New Haven, 1968). Among studies of Milton's treatment of history, see C.A. Patrides, *The Phoenix and the Ladder: the Rise and Decline of the Christian View of History* (Berkeley, 1964); C.H. Firth, "Milton as an Historian," *Proceedings of the British Academy, 1907-1908*, pp. 227-57; Balachandra Rajan, "*Paradise Lost:* The Hill of History," *HLQ*, XXXI (1967), 43-63.

3. "The Miltonic Simile," *PMLA*, XLVI (1931), 1047; see Rupertus, *P.L.*, CLXX, col. 73, and CLXVII, col. 569, and S. Bruno Carthusianus, *P.L.*, CLII, col. 1349.

4. *P.L.*, XXIV, cols. 370-71. Cf. *Glossa Ordinaria, P.L.*, CXIII, col. 1277; Haymo of Halberstadt, *P.L.*, CXVI, cols. 890-91.

5. *P.L.*, CLXXXI, col. 323.

6. In his "Pindarique Ode" on "The 34 Chapter of the Prophet *Isaiah*" Cowley describes the leaves of Isaiah XXXIV: 4 as autumnal. The host of Heaven shall fall "Thick as ripe *Fruit*, or yellow *Leaves* in *Autumn* fall." *Poems* (London, 1656), p. 49. Through such details as this the Biblical simile becomes partly assimilated to the leaf-similes of Homer, Virgil, Dante, and Tasso. For the infernal association of several of these similes, see the notes by Merritt Y. Hughes, A.W. Verity, Scott Elledge, and others and the discussion by C.M. Bowra, *From Virgil to Milton* (London and New York, 1965), pp. 240-241. Virgil applies this image to the multitudinous dead beside the river Styx; Dante to the souls of the dead beside the river Acheron; Tasso to the multitude of the devils driven back to Hell. Cf. *Aeneid*, VI, 309-310; *Inferno*, III, 112-114; *Jerusalem Delivered*, IX, stanza 66; *Iliad*, VI, 146 sq. See also James P. Holoka, " 'Thick as Autumnal Leaves'—The Structure and Generic Potentials of an Epic Simile," *Milton Quarterly*, Vol. X (1976), pp. 78-83.

7. P.L., CLII, col. 1348; XXXIX, cols. 1635, 1791-93; CLXXV, col. 655.

8. P.G., XII, cols. 332, 334. Cf. Bede, P. L., XCI, col. 311; Rabanus, P.L., CVIII, cols. 68-9; Strabus, P.L., CXIII, cols. 227-28.

9. Thomas Arnold (ed.), *Select English Works of John Wyclif*, III (Oxford, 1871), 19, 23.

10. P.L., CVIII, cols. 69-70.

11. Cf. Rupertus, P.L., CLXVII, cols. 645-47.

12. P.L., LXXXII, col. 278; CLII, col. 1349.

13. For additional instances, see *Cruden's Complete Concordance* (London, 1930), s.v. *scatter, scattered, scattereth, scattering*.

14. Rupertus, P.L., CLXVII, cols. 645-50; Jerome, P.L., XXIV, col. 371, Cf. Gregory the Great, P.L. LXXIX, col. 187, "Quid ergo Aegypti nomine accipitur nisi a coelorum sedibus angeorum lapsa multitudo?"

15. Geoffrey Hartman, "Milton's Counterplot," ELH. xxv (1928). 7.

16. Don Cameron Allen, "Milton's Busiris," *MLN*, Vol. LXV (1950), pp. 115-116.

17. Richard Bentley (cd.), *Milton's Paradise Lost, a New Edition* (London, 1732), 16.

18. Cf. John Marchant (ed.), Paradise Lost (London, 1751), I, 60; H.J. Todd (ed.), The Poetical Works of John Milton (London, 1826), II, 51: "Pharaoh has been called by some writers Busiris, as Dr. Pearce and Hume have noted."

19. Thomas Newton (ed., Paradise Lost (London, 1778), I, 38-39.

20. David Masson (ed., The Poetical Works of John Milton (London, 1890), III, 392-93.

21. A. W. Verity (ed.), Paradise Lost (Cambridge, 1936), II, 380-81.

22. Merritt Y. Hughes (ed.), Paradise Lost (New York, 1935), 19.

23. See James Holly Hanford, "The Chronology of Milton's Private Studies," PMLA, XXXVI (1921), 251-314.

24. See C. H. Firth, Milton as an Historian," in *Proceedings of the British Academy*, 1907-1908, 227-257; Harris Fletcher, "Milton's *History of Britain*," *JEGP** XXXV (1936), 405 ff.: R. R. Cawley, *Milton's Literary Craftsmanship, A Study of A Brief History of Moscovia* (Princeton, 1941).

25. Masson observed (392-93) that Busiris figures in Greek legends as a king of Egypt noted for this persecution of foreigners. According to Greek mythology, Busiris slaughtered on the altar of Zeus all foreigners who entered Egypt; *The Exford Classical Dictionary* (Oxford, 1949), s.v. Busiris.

26. Cf. Verity, 381, Raleigh expressly states that Busiris was 'the first oppressor of the Israelites' (p. 204) and that after *two* intervening reigns came 'Cenchres drowned in the Red Sea' (p. 187, 1621 ed).

27. *S. Hieronymi Interpretatio Chronicae Eusebii Pamphili, P.L.*, XXVII, cols. 197-200. Cf. *Josephi Scaligeri Animadversiones in Chronologica Eusebii,* in *Thesaurus Temporum Eusebii Pamphili* (Amstelodami, 1658), 36. See also *Georgii Syncelli Chronographia,* ed. P. Iacobus Goar (Parisiis, 1652), 152.

29. St. Augustine, *The City of God,* tr. John Healey (London and New York, 1945), 186.

29. P.L., XLI, col. 570.

30. P.L., XXXI, cols. 719-20. Cf. *ibid.,* col. 920, "Busiris in Aegypto peregrinorum infeliciter incurrentium impiissimus immolator . . .".

31. *P.L.,* CXCVIII, col. 1272.

32. Julio Puyol (ed.), *Crónica de España por Lucas, Obispo de Tuy* (Madrid, 1926), 38; *Lucae Tudensis Chronicon Mundi,* in *Hispaniae Illustratae,* ed. Andreas Schottus (Francofurti, 1608), III, 12.

33. Alfonso el Sabio, *General Estoria, Segunda Parte,* ed. A. G. Solalinde, L. A. Kasten, and V.R.B. Oelschläger (Madrid, 1957), 22.

34. *Ibid.,* 23.

35. *Chronicon Carionis Expositum et Auctum . . . a Philippo Melanthone et Casparo Peucero* (Witebergae, 1580), 34-35. This account of Busiris does not appear in Carion's original version. For an account of the various versions and editions of this work, see *Corpus Reformatorum,* ed. C. G. Bretschneider (Halis Saxonum, 1844) XII, 707-710. Cf. Diodorus Siculus, *The Library of History,* tr. C. H. Oldfather (*Loeb Classical Library,* London and New York, 1933), I, 160, 234, 300; *C. Plinii Secundi Naturalis Historiae,* ed. Joannes Harduinus (Parisiis, 1685), V, 300.

36. *Historia Julia, sive Syntagma Heroicum . . . Pars Prima . . . Auctore Reinero Reineccio Steinhemio* (Helmaestadii, 1594), 259. Italics mine.

37. Sir Walter Raleigh, *The History of the World* (London, 1621), 204.

38. *Gilb. Genebrardi . . . Chronographiae Libri Quatuor* (Parisiis, 1600), 66.

39. James Ussher, *The Annals of the World* (London, 1658), 21.

40. Chronographers regarded Pharaoh — but not Busiris — as a common term for Egyptian Kings. On the other hand, they sometimes declared that more than one Pharaoh had borne this name. Diodorus referred to two different sovereigns named Busiris, and Melanchthon believed that there were several kings called by

this names ("plures fuisse Reges Busirides"). In Contra Secundinum Manichaeum, St. Augustine employed the plural form of this name (P.L., XLII, col. 601): "Denique etiam ipse antiquorum vel fabulae vel historiae pauciores habent Medeas et Phaedras, quam facinorum aliorum flagitiorum que mulieres; pauciores Ochos et Busirides, quam impitatum aliarum et scelerum viros." Vide also D.C. Allen, *Milton's Busiris*, in MLN, LXV (1950), pp. 115-116.

41. *Corn. Cornelii a Lapide . . . in Librum Sapientiae Commentarius* (Parisiis, 1639), 331.

42. *Joannis Lorini Avenionensis . . . Commentarii in Sapientiam* (Lugduni, 1607), 698-99.

43. Neither Hughes nor Verity has noted this parallel.

44. Don Cameron Allen, "Milton's Busiris," *MLN* LXV (1950), 115-116; Harold Fisch, "Hebraic Styles and Motifs in *Paradise Lost,*" in *Language and Style in Milton,* ed. Ronald David Emma and John T. Shawcross (New York, 1967), pp. 45-48; James H. Sims, *The Bible in Milton's Epics* (Gainesville, Fla., 1962), p. 224 (discussed by Fisch; p. 45); John T. Shawcross, "*Paradise Lost* and the Theme of Exodus," *Milton Studies,* II (1970), 3-26.

45. *Johannes Buxtorfi Lexicon Hebraicum et Chaldaicum,* 6th ed. (Londini, 1646), *bâtsar*, p. 79, "Praecidit, Vendemiavit . . .Munivit." Cf. William Gesenius, *A Hebrew and English Lexicon of the Old Testament,* trans. Edward Robinson, ed. Francis Brown et al. (New York, 1928), *bâtsar*, p. 130, "cut off, make inaccessible (esp. by fortifying), enclose." Melanchthon explains the name as follows: "BVSIRIS, id est Munitor, qui maxima opera extruxit"; and Genebrardus offers a similar explanation: "Nam Busiris a Butser Benoni Kal in verbo Batsar deducitur." See Allen and n. 35 and 38 sup.

46. In identifying Busiris as "author of the bloudy edict" of drowning the male infants, Raleigh acknowledged his debt to Reineccius, who in turn had already confessed his own indebtedness to Melanchthon. Both Melanchthon and Reineccius, moreover, had referred to the site of the famous pyramids as Busiris; and Sebastian Munster had described Busiris' construction of Heliopolis. Cf. *Cosmographiae Universalis Lib. VI . . . autore Sebast. Munstero* (Basileae, 1554), p. 1132, "Interpretatur Heliopolis Solis civitas, estque posita in aggere. & habet Solis templum, constructa olim a Busire rege: fuitque tanta ut murus per c. ratum complecteretur. 140. stadia, habens centum portas."

47. Milton's exploitation of Hebrew etymology in his interpretation of Babylon (*confusio*) and for the names of his angels and demons is wellknown. For new light on his use of Hebrew roots in *Comus* see Sacvan Bercovitch. "Milton's 'Haemony': Knowledge and Belief," *HLQ* XXXIII (1970), 351-59.

48. The suggestions of darkness in this simile (the phrase *"Etrurian* shades" echoes the literal meaning of "*Vallombrosa,*" which in its own turn recalls the psalmist's "valley of the shadow of death") and the imagery of multitude provide additional links with Egypt and the underworld. For St. Gregory the Great, Egypt not only represents darkness but also signifies the multitude of angels fallen from Heaven. Cf. *Patrologia Latina,* Vol. LXXIX, col. 187, for his comment on the Egyptian allusion in I Reg. vi. 6 (i.e. I Samuel vi. 6), "Aegyptus quippe tenebrae dicitur. Quid ergo Aegypti nomine accipitur, nisi coelorum sedibus angelorum

lapsa multitudo? Et quid in Pharaone Aegypti rege, nisi ipse tenebrarum auctor diabolus designatur?"

49. Cf. Buxtorf, s.v. *Bázar,* p. 65, "Sparsit, Dispersit, Dissipavit"; Gesenius, s.v. *bázar,* p. 103, "scatter." Allusions to Jehovah's "scattering" His foes recur frequently in the Old Testament and are echoed in the Magnificat (Luke i. 51).

50. Cf. Münster, p. 1133, who describes Cairo as "Babylon Aegypti" and asserts that it was "sedes Sultanorum Aegyptiorum." This makes Milton's description of Satan as a "great Sultan" especially appropriate in the light of his references to Cairo, Memphis, and other Egyptian cities. Since various writers identified Cairo with Memphis, and since Cairo is the Egyptian Babylon, Milton's "Memphian" allusion (which links Busiris with this city) reinforces the association of Satan with Babylonian tyranny, both Egyptian and Mesopotamian.

51. Cf. Merritt Y. Hughes, "Satan and the 'Myth' of the Tyrant," in *Ten Perspectives on Milton* (New Haven, 1965), pp. 165-95.

52. For Leviathan as devil, see St. Gregory the Great, *Moralia, sive Expositio in Librum B. Job, Patrologia Latina,* Vols. LXXV, cols. 644-646, 824; Vol. LXXVI, cols. 682-718.

53. See my "Leviathan and Renaissance Etymology," *JHI,* XXVIII (1967), 575-76.

54. See n. 53, sup; cf. Giovanni Diodati, *La sainte Bible* (Amsterdam, 1669), index of proper names.

55. *Expositio in Exodum iuxta quadruplicem sacre scripture sensum: literalem scilicet, moralem, allegoricum, & anagogicum: authore fratere Guillelmo Pepino* (Parisijs, 1534), fol. ccliv. Cf. fols. ccxlviii-ccliv, for moral and allegorical interpretations of Pharaoh. Cf. Dante's "Epistle to Can Grande" for allegorical, tropological, and anagogical interpretations of the Exodus.

56. *Chronica Carionis ganz new latine geschriben von . . . Philippo Melanthone,* tr. Eusebius Menius (Witteberg, 1560), fols. 60-61. For Melanchthon's Latin text, see Allen, p. 116.

57. Menius, fols. 60-61. 58. Menius, fols. 60-61.

59. Both Raleigh and Reineccius have been described as "tilting against Melanchthon's interpretation"; see Allen, p. 116.

60. See Note 36 sup.

61. Sir Walter Raleigh, *The History of the World* (London, 1621), p. 204.

62. Cf. Allen, p. 116.

63. Menius, fols. 60-61.

64. Menius, fols. 60-61.

65. *Diodorus of Sicily,* trans. C. H. Oldfather (New York : Loeb Classical Library, 1933), I, 161. Cf. ibid., pp. 235, 301, on "the impiety of Busiris" and his "slaying of foreigners."

66. *Petri Comestoris Historia Scholastica, Patrologia Latina,* Vol. CXCVIII, col. 1141.

67. Pepin, fol. viii.

68. *In Exodum Enarratio Tradita a Davide Chytraeo* (Vitebergae, 1570), pp. 86-87.

69. *Gilb. Genebrardi Chronographiae Libri Quatuor* (Parisiis, 1600), p. 66,

"Calamitatis auctorem nostri nominant Amenophim. (Alii Busiridem appellant, quod magis convenit . . .)"

70. *Sulpicii Severi Aquitani Historia Sacra,* ed. I. Drusius (Franekerae, 1607), p.82.

71. Julio Puyol, *Crónica de España por Lucas, Obispo de Tuy* (Madrid, 1926), pp. 31-32.

72. *Chronologia . . . autore Johanne Funccio Norimbergense* (Witebergae, 1570), p. 29.

73. *Georgii Syncelli Chronographia,* ed. P. Jacobus Goar (Parisiis, 1632), p. 68.

74. James Ussher, *The Annals of the World* (London, 1658), pp. 12, 21.

75. *Chronologia . . . auctore Gerardo Mercatore* (Coloniae Agrippinae, 1569), p. 23.

76. See n. 36 sup.

77. See n. 37 sup.

78. See Appendix A, *Univ. Rev.—Kansas City,* 37 (1971), pp. 228-231.

79. *Flavii Josephi Hebraei . . . Contra Apionem Libri II* (Coloniae, 1534), p.318.

80. *Historia Julia, sive Syntagma Heroicum . . . Pars Prima . . . auctore Reinero Reineccio Steinhemio* (Helmaestadii, 1594), p. 261.

81. Genebrardus, p. 68. "Qui eos expulit Pharo mari obrutus Tethmosis nominabatur. Ibid. *Joseph e. Manethone Aegyptio. vel Amasis, Euseb. Iustin Martyr ex Appione & Pelomone* [sic], vel Cenchris duodecimus Pharo. *Turon, lib. 1. hist.* Quem & Bachorim vocatum dicunt, de quo mira *Tacitus Annal, lib. 21.* Amenophis aliis."

82. Hector Boethius, *Scotorum historiae a prima gentis origine* (Parisiis, 1527), fol. I.

83. John Bellenden, trans., *. . . the history and Croniklis of Scotland . . . Compilit be . . . Hector Boece* (Edinburgh, [1542?]), fol. I.

84. Raphael Holinshed, *The Historie of Scotlande* (London, 1577), p. 1.

85. Cf. *The Interpreter's Dictionary of the Bible* (New York, 1962), s.v. *Exodus,* pp. 190-91, on speculations concerning the chronology of the Exodus.

86. A. W. Verity, ed., *Paradise Lost* (Cambridge, 1936), II, 381.

87. *J. J. Scaliger, ed., Thesaurus Temporum, Eusebii Pamphili . . . Chronicorum Canonum . . . interprete Hieronymo* (Amsterdam, 1658), p. 15fi Patrologia Latina, Vol. XXVII, col. 190.

88. Syncellus, p. 152.

89. Puyol, p. 38; cf. *Lucae Tudensis Chronicon Mundi,* in *Hispaniae Illustratae,* ed. Andreas Schottus (Francofurti, 1608), Vol. III, p. 12.

90. Alfonso el Sabio. *General Estoria, Segunda Parte,* ed. A. G. Solalinde, L.A. Kasten, and V. R. B. Oelschlager (Madrid, 1957), p. 22.

91. Raleigh, p. 205.

92. Genebrardus, p. 69.

93. Alfonso, p. 23, " . . . et cuenta Ovidio en la glosa de la epistola de Deyanira que enviava ella a Hercules, que en aquel reyno Menphis, o regnava Busiris, que non llovie si no por ventura . . . " "Ombre ninguno que estranno fuesse non osava entrar a aquel reyno de Menphis."

94. *C. Plinii Secundi Naturalis Historiae,* ed. Joannes Harduinus (Parisiis, 1685), V, 300.

95. Syncellus, p. 152; Raleigh, p. 205; Jerome, *P.L.*,* Vol. XXVII, col. 190; Scaliger, p. 78. Scaliger's edition of Eusebius dates the Exodus in the 505th year after Abraham, but places the founding of Memphis nineteen years later in the 524th year after Abraham. Funccius, p. 33, follows Eusebius in placing the foundation of Memphis *after* the Exodus. Dating the latter event in the 2454th year of the world, he assigns the foundation of Memphis to the 2473rd year of the world and the twelfth year of Cherres' reign in Egypt: "MEMPHIS in Aegypto condita, ab Epapho. Euse."

96. *P.L.*, Vol. CXXI, col. 114.

97. Puyol, p. 34.

98. Hector Boethius, fol. I; Bellenden, fol. I; Holinshed, p. 1.

Chapter XIV

1. For the iconography of *Comus,* see Orgel, *infra,* n. 2, John Arthos, *On "A Mask Presented at Ludlow-Castle"* (Ann Arbor, 1954). For Renaissance paintings of Comus, see Edgar Wind, *Bellini's Feast of the Gods* (Cambridge, Mass., 1948), pp. 45-55, on Bellini's picture of the god of revelry, and *idem, Pagan Mysteries in the Renaissance* (rev. and enlarged ed.; New York, 1968), p. 140, on Mantegna's painting of the "Realm of Comus." Though Mantegna left this work (executed for Isabella d'Este) unfinished, it was completed by Lorenzo Costa; Erwin Panofsky, *Studies in Iconology* (New York, 1962), p. 153. For the Renaissance Bacchus and Comus, see Jean Seznec, *The Survival of the Pagan Gods,* tr. Barbara F. Sessions (New York, 1961); and Wind, *Pagan Mysteries.* For the Circe tradition, see Douglas Bush, *Mythology and the Renaissance Tradition in English Poetry* (new rev. ed.; New York, 1963); Merritt Y. Hughes, "Spenser's Acrasia and the Circe of the Renaissance," *JHI,* IV (1943), 381-399.

2. The "first engravings" for Cartari's *Images* (in 1571) were designed by Bolognino Zaltieri. Seznec observes (p. 255n.) that Philostratus's *Imagines* "provided Zaltieri with elements of several of the illustrations" including that of Comus. Cartari's book was first printed without illustrations in 1556. The illustration of Comus in the 1581 (Lyons) edition of Cartari's *Imagini* has been reproduced by Stephen Orgel in *The Jonsonian Masque* (Cambridge, Mass., 1965). The details of this illustration closely resemble those of Zaltieri's illustration of Comus in the 1571 quarto printed at Venice by G. Zilletti (Fig. V, *supra*).

3. Philostratus, *Imagines,* ed. and tr. Arthur Fairbanks, Loeb Classical Library (London and New York, 1931), pp. 8-13. Vincenzo Cartari, *Le Imagini de i dei de gli antichi* (Venetia, 1571), p. 416, HEH #375693; *Les Images ou Tableaux de platte peinture des deux Philostrates sophistes Grecs . . . Mis en François par Blaise de Vigenere Bourbonnois* (Paris, 1629), pp. 9-17, HEH #10212. The plates were executed by Iaspar Isac (Jaspar Isaac). The Isaac engraving of Comus has been reproduced by Arthos from the 1615 edition and by Orgel from the 1614 edition. The illustration shown above (Fig. VI) has been reproduced from the 1629 edition (printed at Paris "Chez Claude Sonnius"), formerly in the Bridgewater Library.

Precisely when it entered that collection is unknown, but the little evidence available seems to argue against its having been in the possession of the Egerton family at the time when Milton was composing his masque.

4. Philostratus, Loeb, p. 8n. Liddell and Scott, *Greek-English Lexicon,* define *probolion* as "a boar-spear" on the authority of Xenophon. W. Pape, *Griechisch-Deutsches Handwörterbuch,* defines *prolobion* as earlobe, "das aüsserste, hangende Ohrläppchen."

5. Renaissance illustrators sometimes represented Circe with both wand and cup. *Cf.* Gabriello Symeoni, *La Vita et Metamorfoseo d'Ovidio* (Lyons, 1584), printed "per Giovanni di Tornes," Emblem 172, p. 184, "Compagni d'Ulysse mutati in Porci." (See Fig. VII.) In George Sandy's *Ovids Metamorphosis* (Oxford, 1632) both of these attributes occur in two different illustrations—one on the title-page (Fig. VIII) and the other in an illustration to Book XIV (p. 454). In several illustrations of Alciati's emblem "Cavendum à meretricibus," Circe carries a wand but no cup; *cf.* Rovillio's editions (Lugduni, 1549, 1564, 1566), Bonhomme's editions (Lyons, 1549, 1550), Plantin's edition (Antwerp, 1577), and the de Marnes-Cavellat edition (Paris, 1583), in the Henry E. Huntington Library collections. Whitney's emblem (Leyden, 1586), p. 82, bears the motto "Homines voluptatibus transformantur"; though the accompanying verses echo Horace's reference to Circe's *pocula,* the illustration (like its prototype in Alciati) depicts the wand but does not include the cup.

6. Cartari, p. 433.

7. For the reed or stalk of fennel, as well as the wand-like thyrsus, see Cartari, p. 429. In Peacham, pp. 96, 191, the cup is a Bacchic attribute, but in one illustration (p. 96) the god also carries Mercury's caduceus. In Bocchi's emblem (pp. xx-xxi) Silenus holds both cup (or rather libation-dish) and staff.

8. See Orgel's discussion of Jonson's antimasque.

9. See Diekhoff's appendix to *A Maske at Ludlow,* on "The Text of *Comus,* 1634 to 1645," pp. 251-75, and Tillyard's essay on "The Action of *Comus,*" pp. 43-57.

10. *Eryci Puteani Comus, sive Phagesiposia Cimmeria. Somnium* (Oxonii, 1634), pp. A2r and v, 8-12; for the popularity of this work, see Ralph H. Singleton, "Milton's *Comus* and the *Comus* of Erycius Puteanus," *PMLA,* LVIII (1943), 949-957. In his preface, Puteanus (Hendrik van der Putten) inveighs against the "religion of pleasure" and the rites of *luxus* (luxury and "riot") and lasciviousness: "Voluptatis religio omnium paene aetatum gentiumque scelere constituta est, luxu lasciviaque crevit. Sua ubique vitiis Numina data sunt, ut impius esset, quisquis sapiens, ut malus quisquis virtutem inculcaret. Quia vero non Bacchus, non Venus, non alia potentia insaniam conviviorum & **commessationum implebant, coli apud Graecos COMUS coepit adeoque** diffusum est Ventris regnum, ut nec terrarum finibus clauderetur. Haec sacra profanare ausus sum: descripsi, & quasi aliquam Sapientiae partem colerem, impius in Luxum Lasciviamque sui."

11. Robertus Stephanus, *Thesaurus Linguae Latinae* (1576-1578), *s.v. Comessor.*

12. *Henricus Stephanus, Thesaurus Linguae Graecae* (1572), *s.v.* Κῶμος.

13. Robertus Stephanus, *s.v. Comus;* Carolus Stephanus, *Dictionarium*

Historicum Georgraphicum, Poeticum, . . . *Editio Novissima* (Oxonii, 1670), *s.v.* *Comus.*

14. Robertus Stephanus, *s.v. Comessatio.*

15. *Philostrati Junioris Imagines,* ed. F. Morellus (Parisiis, 1608), pp. 750, 768.

16. *De Düs Gentium* . . . *Historia* . . . *Lilio Gregorio Gyraldo* (Basileae, 1560), p. 46.

17. Cartari (1571), pp. 414-415.

18. Vincent Cartari, *Images des Dieux,* tr. Anth. du Verdier (Lion, 1624), p. 525.

19. *Seconda Novissima Editione delle Imagini de gli dei delli Antichi di Vicenzo Cartari Reggiano, Ridotte da dapo a piedi alle loro reali, & non più per l'adietro osservate simiglianze,* . . . *da Lorenzo Pignoria Padovano* (Padova, 1626), p. 341. Pignoria's revision had been published earlier in 1615.

20. Ripa (1630), Pt. I, pp. 28-29, 147; Pt. III, p. 145.

21. *Hieroglyphicorum et Medicorum Emblematum* ΑΠΑΕΚΑΡΟΥΝΟΣ *Auctore Ludovico Casanova* (Lugduni, 1626), pp. 31-39. This work was published by Paul Frellon along with a collection of hieroglyphic books including Valeriano's treatise and additions by other writers: *Hieroglyphicorum collectanea ex Veteribus, et Neotericis descripta in Sex Libros* . . . *digesta, et nunc primum Ioannis Pierii Valeriani & anonymi cuiusdam sexaginta Hieroglyphicorum Libris aucta.*

22. Henry Estienne translates this line (line 578) as "Indi commessationem agitant valde strepero Dionyso"; *Dionysii Orbis Descriptio* (Oxonii, 1697), p. 53; *cf.* Estienne's edition (1577), p. 82, and p. 156, "Insularum alius tractus. In Orchadum scilicet, quae secundum alios numero triginta sunt. Qui verò è regione Amnitae sint, ingenuè fateor me planè ignorare."

23. Caseneuve credits these verses to Priscian but adds that the latter revised the penultimate line to read "Indi solemnes epulas peragunt Dionyso." On this authority Caseneuve argues that "Hic Comus pro solemnibus epulis ponitur." Milton's Comus, after bidding "welcom" to "Joy, and Feast, / Midnight shout, and revelry, / Tipsie dance, and Jollity," refers to his rites as "Our concealed Solemnity."

24. See note 21 *supra.*

25. *Dionysii Alexandrini de Situ Orbis Liber,* . . . *Unà cum Eustathii Thessalonicensis archiepiscopi Commentarijs* . . . *nunc primùm in Latinum sermonem conversis,* . . . *per Bernardum Bertrandum* (Basileae, 1556), p. 182.

26. Walter F. Otto, *Dionysus: Myth and Cult,* tr. Robert B. Palmer (Bloomington and London, 1965), pp. 86-91; *cf.* E. R. Dodds, *The Greeks and the Irrational* (Berkeley and Los Angeles, 1951), p. 94 on Dionysus as "god of the masquerade."

27. Vigenere, pp. 10-17.

28. *Real-encyclopädie der klassischen Altertumswissenschaft, Neue Bearbeitung,* ed. Georg Wissowa and Wilhelm Kroll (Stuttgart, 1922), *s.v. Kotys.*

29. Carolus Stephanus, *s.v. Baptae, Cotytto.* Cf. Robertus Stephanus, *s.v. Baptae, Cotyto;* Henricus Stephanus, *s.v.* Βαπτρια, Κοτις.

30. Giraldi, p. 201.

31. *Junii Invenalis et Auli Persii Flacci Satyrae: Tertia Editio* (Londini, 1620), p. 13.

EPILOGUE

1. Homer, *The Iliad,* tr. A. T. Murray, Vol. I (Cambridge, Mass. and London, 1960), p. 19.

2. See, for example, Jane Harrison's discussion of the hero's close association with the serpent and Cedric H. Whitman's analysis of the fire imagery in the *Iliad*.

3. *Iliad,* Vol. I, p. 141.

4. *Iliad,* I, p. 229.

5. *Iliad,* I, p. 171.

6. *Iliad,* I, p. 321.

7. *Iliad,* I, p. 511.

8. *Iliad*, I, p. 547.

9. *Iliad,* I, p. 207.

10. *Iliad*, I, p. 235.

11. *Iliad,* I, p. 217.

12. *Iliad,* I, p. 493.

13. *Iliad,* I, pp. 521-523.

14. *Iliad,* I, p. 489.

15. *Iliad,* I, p. 517.

16. *Iliad,* I, p. 463.

17. *Iliad*, I, p. 485.

18. *Iliad,* I, p. 299.

19. C. S. Lewis, *The Discarded Image: An Introduction to Medieval and Renaissance Literature* (London and New York, 1974), pp. 151-152.

20. See J. A. Mazzeo, "Metaphysical Poetry and the Poetic of Correspondences," *Journal of the History of Ideas,* Vol. XIV (1953), pp. 221-234; idem, "A Seventeenth-Century Theory of Metaphysical Poetry," *Romanic Review,* Vol. XLII (1951), pp. 245-255; Marjorie Hope Nicolson, *The Breaking of the Circle* (New York, 1962).

21. Endicott, pp. 99, 190.

22. See the discussion of authority formulae by Alice S. Miskimin, *The Renaissance Chaucer* (New Haven and London, 1975).

INDEX